SOCIAL
INTERPRETATION

AMERICAN GOTHIC
by Grant Wood

SOCIAL INTERPRETATION

Principles and Practices of Community and Public-School Interpretation

By
ARTHUR B. MOEHLMAN
Professor of School Administration and Supervision,
University of Michigan; Editor, *The Nation's Schools*

D. APPLETON-CENTURY COMPANY
Incorporated

NEW YORK   LONDON

COPYRIGHT, 1938, BY
D. APPLETON-CENTURY COMPANY, INC.

All rights reserved. This book, or parts thereof, must not be reproduced in any form without permission of the publisher.

3127

PRINTED IN THE UNITED STATES OF AMERICA

IN MEMORIAM
MAURICE REED KEYWORTH
January 20, 1884—June 22, 1935

AN ABLE AND FAR-SIGHTED EDUCATIONAL LEADER WHO COMBINED A DEEP LOVE FOR DEMOCRACY WITH RARE MORAL COURAGE, AND WHOSE CONTRIBUTIONS TO THE ADVANCE OF PUBLIC EDUCATION IN MICHIGAN STAND AS HIS MOST FITTING MEMORIAL.

PREFACE

During the ten years that have elapsed since *Public School Relations* was published a great change has taken place in both concept and practice of the interpretation activity. In 1927 the public schools were still riding the prosperity wave. Money came easily, and the need for institutional interpretation appeared to be just another academic idea. Whenever a need became urgent, an emotional high-pressure campaign, following both the best and worst practices of the business world, quickly brought the needed authority for much unwise borrowing and for desirable increases in teachers' salaries. Then came the depression, and public education learned to its surprise what happens when a poorly balanced tax system, operating through archaic administrative organization, meets a depression, and a large social activity labors in a heavy sea of popular misunderstanding. The doctrine of expediency and empiricism so comforting to the majority of the teaching profession was reaping its logical harvest. Searching hastily for a remedy, the educational world quickly recognized the need for social interpretation, and the teaching profession tried to make up for lost time.

There has been a progressive evolution of concept, emphasis, and pointing in this area beginning with *Publicity* and traveling through *Public Relations* to the more comprehensive view of *Social Interpretation*. As a result of experience gained in teaching and from research, my own point of view has undergone certain modification since the publication of the pioneering *Public School Relations*. These changes have been toward a more completely functional concept of the interpretative activity as basic and complementary to all institutional planning and progress. The first four chapters are devoted as a unit to a progressive development of a point of view which permeates the balance of the book. Much less emphasis is placed on printed material and conventional publicity and much more on the importance of good institutional practice and efficiency, specialized adult education, and the fundamental value of confidence growing out of personal contacts.

Presentation of the functional philosophy of public-school administration does not deny the existence of other points of view but seeks rather to present in complete form for the first time the program possibilities growing out of a series of unified principles. It is not the purpose of this book to evangelize or to indoctrinate for the acceptance of the functional viewpoint but rather to make that viewpoint easily available for study and consideration. Acceptance or rejection is clearly the prerogative of the mature reader. It is reasonable to assume that the functional point of view will please neither the conservative empiricist or opportunist nor the radical reformer.

Social Interpretation has been written both for the man in the field and as a text for graduate students in education. To meet this dual need all extrinsic material that tends to slow up reading interest in the conventional text has been omitted or relegated to the bibliographical appendix and conventional footnote citations purposely kept at a minimum. Since no single text is completely satisfactory for advanced work, a special teaching outline covering method, practical problems, and specific reference to different points of view has been developed to serve as a guide for classroom use.

It is not expected that any one reading this book will become immediately capable as an interpretative specialist. Such a possibility is beyond the scope of any book. However, if the principles advocated are studied sincerely and activity projected upon them, it may be safely stated that the possibility of increasing social understanding and appreciation of the educational function may be progressively achieved.

In the preparation of this volume and the teaching outline, I am deeply indebted to many graduate students for contributions in the form of field problems. I am also especially grateful to numerous friends and colleagues who read portions of the manuscript and made valuable suggestions for improvement. They include: Doctor M. M. Chambers, American Council on Education; Professor

PREFACE

David D. Henry, Wayne University; Professor Clyde R. Miller, Teachers College, Columbia University; Doctor Eugene B. Elliott, State Superintendent, Doctor Lee M. Thurston, Deputy Superintendent, and John R. Emens, Assistant Superintendent, all of the Michigan State Department of Public Instruction; Arthur H. Rice, Editor of the *Michigan Education Journal;* Dean J. B. Edmonson, Doctor Carl E. Guthe, Director of the University Museums and Chairman of the Social Science Division, Professor Stuart A. Courtis and Associate Professor Edgar G. Johnston, all of the University of Michigan; and Doctor Paul T. Rankin, Detroit Public Schools. To Bernice Hannan Lee I am indebted for technical editing and to Mynette Long for faithful and accurate preparation of the manuscript. The shortcomings are my own.

A. B. M.

CONTENTS

PREFACE . . . . PAGE vii

PART I
A POINT OF VIEW

CHAPTER
1. THE SCHOOL IN SOCIETY 3
2. THE DEMOCRATIC PROCESS 26
3. PROPAGANDA AND THE SCHOOLS 53
4. THE TEACHING PROFESSION 82

PART II
EDUCATIONAL POLICIES

5. PRINCIPLES OF INTERPRETATION 103
6. FUNDAMENTAL POLICIES 117
7. THE COMMUNITY SURVEY 138

PART III
INSTITUTIONAL AGENTS

8. THE BOARD OF EDUCATION 161
9. THE SUPERINTENDENT AND STAFF 187
10. THE BUILDING PRINCIPAL 207
11. THE TEACHING PERSONNEL 228
12. THE NON-TEACHING PERSONNEL 247

PART IV
INSTITUTIONAL AND COMMUNITY AGENCIES

13. THE STATE EDUCATIONAL AUTHORITY 261
14. THE TEACHING PROFESSION: PROGRAM 279
15. THE CHILDREN 295
16. THE PARENT-TEACHER ASSOCIATION 313
17. PARENT COUNCILS AND VARIATIONS 335

CHAPTER	PAGE
18. THE LAY ADVISORY COMMISSION	345
19. COMMUNITY LAY GROUPS	358
20. THE RADIO	376
21. THE NEWSPAPER	388
22. SCHOOL PUBLICATIONS	407
23. THE SCHOOL PLANT	428
24. THE SCHOOL IN ACTION	447
RECOMMENDED READINGS RELATED TO SOCIAL INTERPRETATION	461
UNPUBLISHED RESEARCH ON SOCIAL INTERPRETATION	475
INDEX	479

ILLUSTRATIONS

American Gothic by Grant Wood (Courtesy of the Art Institute of Chicago) . . . . *Frontispiece*

FACING PAGE

An information station and exhibition cases in the modern style attract visitors (Fresno, California, Public Schools) . . . 192

Clear glass partitions allow the public to see how business is conducted (Fresno, California, and Highland Park, Michigan, Public Schools) 193

Pleasant reception and telephone clerks are an asset in conducting the school's business (Hamtramck, Michigan, Public Schools) 224

Homelike reception rooms make the school an attractive place for parents to visit 225

Parents as well as children enjoy such activities as puppet shows and the construction of miniature villages (Detroit, Michigan, Public Schools) 304

In many high schools children discuss and appraise current photoplays (Weequahic High School, Newark, New Jersey) . . 305

Nature aids in softening architectural lines and planting also has acoustical value (Culver Military Academy) 430

The corridor educational exhibit has teaching value for the students and interpretative value for the adult (Detroit and Hamtramck, Michigan, Public Schools) 431

An attractive entrance corridor welcomes both students and parents. A dedication tablet is also used as an interpretative device (Detroit and Hamtramck, Michigan, Public Schools) 442

School sites well screened through the use of shrubs and trees reduce neighborhood conflicts (Cooley High School, Detroit, Michigan, and Columbia High School, South Orange and Maplewood, New Jersey) 443

PART I
A POINT OF VIEW

Chapter 1

THE SCHOOL IN SOCIETY

A DEMOCRATIC institution, reduced to its simplest terms, is merely a means for providing an essential social service through the willing coöperation of the people accompanied by the efforts of specialized personnel. The success of the work is dependent on how efficiently the institution serves the social need and how well the people understand and how highly they appreciate its work. The process by which these two needs are accomplished includes a wide range of activities that may be collectively considered as *social interpretation*.

Social interpretation is in fact an ancient activity that has always formed an integral part of all institutional operation, varying however in purpose and form with the character of the social organization. The institutional aspect of social interpretation in a democratic pattern is quite different from interpretation in an autocracy. Intelligent use of the interpretative activity as related to public education in the United States is contingent upon the degree of understanding of democratic institutions. It is therefore necessary to establish a point of view toward the nature and purpose of social organization, particularly in certain of its institutional aspects, so that consistent and harmonious plans for institutional improvement may be developed. Ignorance of the nature and limitations of institutions leads at times to strange errors in interpretative purposes and questionable practices. On the other hand, worship and glorification of the structure of an institution frequently obscure rational consideration of purpose and also produce strange results.

An example of the effects of lack of understanding is the frequently heard professional demand that school boards be eliminated because they cramp the teachers' efforts toward improvement of the schools. Here we have an expression of professional impatience with the slow processes of democracy and a lack of appreciation of the cooperative nature of American public education. Worship of mere structure and tradition to the halo stage is so obvious in many of our conventional institutions of higher learning that it requires no elaboration.

Institutions are always imperfect in the performance of their duties and may cramp essential social effort. There is always grave danger in substituting form for substance, and institutional constrictions that retard essential social change can be removed only through revolution or gradual evolution. Knowledge of the nature of social organization may permit progressive change of the educational institution through gradual evolution. An attempt will be made to present a brief overview of the nature of the democratic process of education through consideration of: (1) cultural organization, (2) the state, (3) institutional limitations, (4) the educational function, and (5) educational interpretation.

CULTURAL ORGANIZATION

A culture seeks to protect itself from disintegration by developing a social discipline maintained through tradition and custom, and written rules which are called law. This internal group discipline is used as a shield against aggression and environmental dangers that arise from the outside.

Every culture from the simplest to the most complex possesses at least five common elements including material arts, esthetic arts, social arts, cosmology, and means of communication or language. These cultural elements are concerned with the means for making a livelihood, seeking and expressing beauty in all activities, striving toward the good life for all of its members communicating with one another, and providing for the maintenance and perpetuation of individual and group life through social organization.

Institutions

Out of his needs and experience man has evolved means through which cultural needs and values may operate more easily and also be better protected and conserved. These means are called *institu-*

tions and in their major aspects include the family, the church, and the state.

By means of the family biological reproduction was safeguarded. A more or less permanent primary unit during infancy gave children an opportunity to be protected until they were mature enough to meet their environmental problems.

The innate desire of man to solve the riddles of the natural phenomena and his place in the universe led to the growth of reverence, fear, magic, mysticism, symbolism, and finally ritualism. The magic and religion of the less organized society developed into the church in a more organized society.

To maintain internal discipline and to provide against the dangers of foes, the state gradually evolved as the third major institution. Theoretically, the state is a disinterested third party around which the common law of public opinion apparently crystallized.

For discussion purposes a social institution may be considered as an agency or means through which the fulfilment of a desirable social need is made easily possible. From the functional standpoint an institution is only a means and not an end in itself. Permanent value lies within the function, not in the instrument of achievement. The fundamental purpose of social form must be understood to avoid the ever present dangers of the short view which leads to institutionalism or the upholding of the authority and sanctity of established organization as an end in itself.

Since an institution is chiefly an organization device for the facilitation of a social purpose, it is possible to express this organization need in different ways at different times and places. Study of diverse institutional forms indicates that variation of form is frequent. There are many expressions of family organization; the church exists in numerous forms and structures; and there are many variations in the organization of the state.

Social purpose may have ultimate value, but its institutional expression must be considered as purely contemporary, and form should never be placed above substance. Current expressions of institutional forms possess no sanctity except that of tradition, familiarity, and apparent practicability. The approval of existing forms and practice by the group mind may be considered as a form of sanctity. The realistic appraisal of institutions must consider how well they serve the fundamental purpose for which they rose out of man's inventive genius. The final importance of man as opposed to these things can never be lost to view.

Primitive Education

In simple cultures the perpetuation of the group, its achievements and living practices were provided for through biological production and nurture of the immature within the family, progressive adjustment of the young to the cultural patterns of the group, and the maintenance of adult solidarity and conformity through the power of the chief and the magic of the medicine man. The alliance between the state and church, between the chief and the medicine man may be discovered early in the cultural development of man. Within the simpler groups the educational process of social reproduction through the adjustment of the growing individual to his environment was completely integrated in every aspect of the culture. The mother was the first teacher. As the children grew to maturity, there was provision for differentiation of training for boys and girls in terms of their social specialization. Boys and girls served as apprentices to their fathers and mothers respectively. Later the adult community took charge of the adolescent male, and this period of training and discipline terminated in his final acceptance through initiation into full adult community membership.

Within the simple social organization there is no high institutionalization of the adjustive function. It is part of all the child sees and does. Methodology is simple and failure unknown, since time and individual capacity are unconsciously provided for. There are numerous exceptions to this generalization since many societies, including some fairly simple ones, have highly complex puberty ceremonies for both sexes, and in some groups a strong social influence is exerted by the establishment of community houses in which boys and girls are segregated into what may be considered immature men's clubs and women's clubs.

THE STATE

In the process of time the simple social organization of primitive cultures gradually evolved into the present-day state.[1] Form and practices changed, and a great diversity of organization developed. The state was always a means, not an end in itself, in the process of development. The welfare and happiness of the individual and the group determined both its form and limits of authority. Since it was a means of facilitating the individual and social purposes of man, it was bound to reflect the economic activity concerned with man's efforts to make a livelihood. Additions to its powers were made in the course of time. To the maintenance of internal discipline, otherwise expressed as providing for order and justice between individuals and groups, and the defense of the group against outside force or aggression, there were gradually added the promotion of the economic welfare of all groups and participation in the more generalized educational function. Since different cultures have developed diverse types of institutional organization, different types of states have similarly placed varying emphasis on all their normal purposes, particularly in the field of economic welfare and education.

Concepts of the State

The functional concept of the state as a means rather than an end in itself has also been considerably varied in practice. Two basic ideas have gradually evolved. These are the state as master and the state as servant or, expressed in different terms, the totalitarian and pluralistic types. The totalitarian concept, though still admitting the welfare of the people as its fundamental purpose, is considered a sacrosanct institution over and above the people to which has been granted, by some magic or cosmic process, a power inherent in the institution itself. Assumption of this power has naturally led to unusual domination, control, and direction of all other institutional activities including home, church, and the diverse manifesta-

[1] For philosophical discussion of the state see Harold J. Laski, *The State in Theory and Practice* (New York, The Viking Press, 1935), Chap. I.

tions of economic activity. Carried to its logical conclusion such control leaves the individual no existence outside of the state pattern. He bears the same relationship to the state that the ant does to his insect community.

The democratic way of life is reflected in the agency created for its promulgation and maintenance—the democratic state. The democratic state is pluralistic—its sovereignty is inherent in all of the people—and its function is to serve as a social facilitating agency for the individuals and groups of which it is comprised. In it institutional agencies are considered as a means to an end. The pluralistic state has no finality either in name or form; it may and does appear differently in different periods and places. Its essential and fundamental characteristics should be tolerance, freedom, coöperation, and opportunity to strive for the good things in life.

The democratic state is characterized by tremendous diversity in interests and beliefs; even fairly complete uniformity is much more rare than many have brought themselves to believe. "One hundred percentism" is a fairy tale devised by Babbitts. Except for brief intervals in times of great emergency, it is impossible to secure unanimity of views and total support of programs. It is only as the freedom of the individual to differ and to persuade others by lawful means to do likewise is maintained through the exercise of our agitative liberties—freedom of publication, freedom of petition, freedom of assembly, and freedom of worship—that democracy can exist and progress. Exercise of these liberties normally produces much diversity of interest, opinion, and thought. In times of stress or great fear these liberties tend to be restricted by the group. Constant struggle is necessary to maintain them at all times.

The rigid restriction of civil liberties during the World War, with the exception of freedom of worship, illustrates this case. The post-war reaction of economic and social fear and of intolerance carried reprisals against freedom of the individual to a high point. The indictment of Victor L. Berger, Wisconsin socialist; the alien raids of Attorney-General A. Mitchell Palmer; Attorney-General Thomas W. Gregory's popular statements that free expression of opinion was dangerous to democratic institutions; the war of intolerance as indicated by the revival of the Ku Klux Klan and the Guardians of Liberty; and the reprisals against pacifists indicate the extent of this reaction. The organization and aggressive program of the Civil Liberties Union, the gradually increasing protests of liberal and far-sighted individuals have done much to restore these essential liberties. However, twenty years after the World War it cannot be said that they are as secure as before 1917. Each major war in which the United States engages apparently aids in weakening civil liberties and making aggressive popular struggles for their retention more essential.[2]

Individual freedom is limited by the need for protecting the rights of the group and of society. In so far as the individual's actions represent danger to other individuals, society maintains the right to restrict them. Thus many restrictions govern the rights of the individual in the use of automobiles on public highways and numerous statutory enactments to restrict competition and unfair trade practices have been passed by state and Federal legislatures.

The people within a modern democratic state are organized and operate to a considerable extent through voluntary associations called *interest groups*. In their more dynamic and selfish aspects they resolve themselves into pressure groups. These associations include capital, labor, management, the professions, religious, social, political, and cultural groups. They are as diverse and numerous as there are group interests.

The function of the democratic state is to secure group action through the voluntary coöperation of these numerous and diverse individual and group interests. The democratic state is not primarily coercive in character. Except in grave emergencies coercion is applied only in areas where the majority of people believe uniformity essential.

It naturally follows that the democratic state must be an impartial state, a coördinator, a common denominator through which

[2] For a condensed account of post-war reaction, see Dwight L. Dumond, *Roosevelt to Roosevelt* (New York, Henry Holt and Co., 1937), Chap. X.

these numerous interests may express themselves. In practice it is true that certain interests may and do exercise unusual power temporarily. It must also be borne in mind that our current efforts toward the democratic way of life represent merely a developmental phase and that culture groups learn how to establish adequate controls and balances between conflicting forces only through the slow and painful process of experience that grows out of the rise of new problems as a result of changing environmental conditions. However, over a long period of time the combination and pressure of opposed interest groups tend to restore a workable if not always a completely rational alignment.

Democratic Elements

The pluralistic or democratic state possesses certain definite characteristics that are not common to the totalitarian concept. Since sovereign power resides in the people as a whole, the state as an institution operates under a definite delegation of power and authority derived from the people and is subject to periodic popular review and appraisal. True, functional emphasis is placed on the importance of personality.

Although plans approved by the majority may become operative, there are sufficient safeguards to protect minority interests, and a definite deliberative technique whereby minority groups may make themselves felt and through strength of opposition modify majority legislative plans. In fact one of the grave dangers of current democratic government is the possibility that a small, well-organized minority through the use of propaganda and political pressure can maintain or project plans low in group value.

Illustrations are numerous. Four diverse instances may suffice. Loosely organized majority opinion has struggled for several generations to provide adequate protection with respect to hours and minimum wages for women industrially employed. Similar efforts are still in progress to eliminate the exploitation of the child as cheap labor. Both major parties have given lip service both in the nation and in the states to the popular demand for the elimination of the spoils system in government yet make strenuous under-cover effort to prevent its effective practice. Northern industrialists have for generations kept the agrarian South and West at an economic disadvantage by their control of the tariff. The fundamental right to differ is at once the great strength and also a source of weakness in democratic organization.

The right of the individual to differ from accepted patterns of thought and procedure is protected by judicial review except during times of severe crisis. The right not only to differ but also to convert others by peaceable means to the minority viewpoint, an outstanding characteristic of our culture, produces great diversity of viewpoint and program. A certain tolerance toward diversity in point of view has been developed through the operation of the democratic ideal of live and let live.

Professional Administration

In the simple democratic state the leaders were elected directly by the people. As the state grew in size and complexity, the need arose for continuing personnel to carry on the routine and technical executive activities of government.

The earliest types of continuing personnel were friends and henchmen following the political leaders in and out of office. The flexibility of this arrangement was more than offset by the inefficiency of the individuals in accomplishment and the lack of continuity in the work itself. From this partisan beginning there evolved a civil governmental service of clerical and technical specialists who were appointed to their tasks because of special fitness and then protected from the onslaughts of the job-hungry politician. The development of the professional governmental employee resulted in a large efficiency in functioning. However, as government became more technical in character, more executive responsibility and power were delegated to the professional government worker, and bureaucracy developed. Bureaucracy is simply a method of carrying on governmental activity through the professional technical heads of various departments and bureaus.

Much unforeseen power has gradually been acquired by the civil employees of democratic government in all states where this elaboration of executive authority has developed. The bureaucrat interprets the statutes approved by the legislative body. Sometimes the interpretation is more comprehensive than the statute. Although judicial review of administrative rulings is always possible, a large body of administrative rules and procedures has developed and has been accepted in actual practice. Thus the actual power of the democratic civil servant has been expanded far beyond the original concept of this work. In addition the civil employees in their interest-group organization have developed a considerable power of their own through friendship, propaganda, and direct political activity. Even a popular democratic legislature cannot ignore their influence. The grave danger from the civil servant who has control of the technical procedure of government, and is hence capable of dominating an institution, is the use of the institution for his own ends—a reversal of function. This brief review of the development of the democratic civil service is necessary to point out the dangers as well as the possibilities that democratic social organization faces in maintaining institutional alertness to individual and social need.

INSTITUTIONAL LIMITATIONS

A social institution is an essential means or agency for the facilitation of a social purpose. As stated earlier, social purpose may remain reasonably constant except in scope, but actual institutional form may change radically. There is nothing of final value in an institution except as it definitely serves its functional purpose. Democratic institutions exist at the pleasure of the people. The people provide means by statute whereby they may have information of institutional functioning brought to their knowledge. Since the institutional personnel operate upon the will of the people, they are concerned also in presenting the people with the best possible view of the value and importance of work accomplished by them. So long as democratic organization exists, it is essential that the process of keeping the people informed of institutional worth be continued. In simple social organization, oral reports to the electorate and informal community appraisal are sufficient, but as governmental and institutional activity increases in scope and complexity, the means of keeping the people informed also increases in volume, in type, and in methodology.

In addition to the legal and official channels through which information may be promulgated the people have also provided themselves with extralegal means of appraisal by means of individual and group study, the press, and numerous personal and group agencies. The democratic citizen has a responsibility to keep himself informed of the operation of agencies and activities provided for his welfare, and, in like manner, the institution has a moral responsibility toward his employer, the citizen. Unusual demands on time and energy make it difficult for all of the people to participate as actively as they theoretically should; consequently, the stewardship responsibility of the institutional personnel becomes even greater.

The nature and scope of the interpretative activity must be definitely oriented to institutional function. Since the institution exists merely as a facilitating device, it possesses no inherent authority to perpetuate itself in form and size except as expansion of function requires. Institutional personnel has a moral and social responsibility to divorce personal interest from social need and to limit its efforts to attempting to show value, condition, and need. It is extremely questionable whether the institution has any right to force its own enlargement in terms of the desires and ambitions of its personnel. It is logical to assume that when condition and need have been presented, its responsibility is definitely terminated. Aggressive attempts to achieve plans and programs through use of institutional propaganda power and political pressure technique are not within the scope of institutional authority. The power to determine the need for enlargement and change in policy resides definitely in the people and is exercised by their representatives in legislative assembly.

Since governmental personnel is human, it is subject to human weaknesses. It is the normal desire of an individual to project his personality as far as possible. This projection takes the form of increased power. Control of the power motif is one of the serious problems always confronting democracy. The will to power is not confined to the technical personnel of government, but also finds frequent expressions in the political, economic, religious, and social areas of human endeavor. Governmental organization sometimes goes far beyond its normal area in interpretation and through the skilful use of propaganda and institutional spheres of influence seeks to enlarge both authority and support. It is possible to find such examples in the current functioning of many governmental agencies. The perversion of normal informational service into high-powered propaganda is unfair to the people and dangerous to the democratic way of life. Apart from the rather remote expectation that governmental agencies will develop a stronger ethical concept of the responsibilities to the people, the only hope of preventing dynamic democracy from degenerating into a completely controlled bureaucratic or even totalitarian state is through extralegal appraisal agencies set up by the people themselves to safeguard their interests. The institution cannot be permitted to live and grow save as it serves ever more effectively individual and social need.

THE EDUCATION FUNCTION

The fundamental purpose of any plan of education in all cultures is social reproduction. It furnishes means through informal and formal agencies whereby the biological products of the race may be adjusted to the individual and social life of the group.

A democratic plan of education includes more than the mere transmission of the social heritage and an attempt to reproduce existing institutions in static form. The purpose of democratic education is the development of well-integrated individuals who can live successfully in an ever changing dynamic culture. The children must be able to see the problems arising in their own and the social life; they must be able to solve these problems within the limits of their individual capacity and must will to take the steps necessary to achieve solution. The democratic school is also required to indoctrinate individuals with the democratic tradition which in turn is based on the agitative liberties of the individual and the needs of society. The adequate expression of the democratic educational process is the progressive teaching of children and adults, in terms of their maturity, to be open-minded, tolerant, and kindly toward the beliefs of others; to collect evidence and facts; to think logically and reasonably; to make wise individual and social choices; and to develop for living and improvement in living the essential disciplines of self-direction, self-appraisal, and self-control.

As the most important agency of social propaganda in the state, the democratic public school does not hang suspended in space. It is no more free than are any other facilitating agencies provided by the people for the satisfaction of their individual and social needs. It does not operate in a social vacuum responsive only to academic whim. It lives and works at all times within the limits of the social pattern which, in practice, means the adult world. Since the partnership between home and school is expressed administratively by small localities, there will tend to be a considerable variation in the limits of realistic functioning between different states and areas within each state.

The traditional and legal concept of the American public schools is that of an impartial, classless agency where all of the children of all the people, unless their parents will otherwise, may receive instruction.

Legal Structure

In the more primitive cultures the educational function is all inclusive in scope, yet simple in structure. As the social organization becomes more complicated, the educational activity becomes enlarged and expanded; new organization forms appear; and new types of control are essential. The responsibility of the home has been successively supplemented by educational controls established by the church and later by the state. However, neither in the simple nor complex cultures has the educational function ever been completely institutionalized, with the exception of relatively recent efforts in the totalitarian states.

The history of public education in the United States is not dissimilar. As need arose, the families, acting in their community relationship, voted to supplement the educational authority of the home by the addition of common schools maintained at public expense.

State Organization

Public education in the United States is legally a function of the several states through specific delegation of this authority by the people. Their delegation is expressed in state constitutions, amplified by statute and sustained by judicial review and appraisal.

Legal organization of the educational function came into existence gradually in the United States when the people of a state, as a group, willed to have public education. This will arose out of tradition and custom and made itself felt through propaganda and pressure by individuals and lay groups. As a result of these movements, the people in all of the states have expressed their general will in the provisions pertaining to education through the state constitution, which determines the framework, character, and limitations of the delegated powers. The legislature has progressively translated the constitutional mandate into a body of laws which, taken collectively, are known as the public-school code. The school code provides for a mandatory minimum program of education to meet the needs of the entire state for the perpetuation of democratic government, permissive legislation to allow each district to develop education in accordance with its ascertained needs, and generous interpretation by boards of education of what is necessary for "the proper establishment, maintenance, management, and carrying on of the public schools of such district."

In the mandatory laws each state provides for the means by which public education shall be administered locally. School districts are created as state agencies through these laws, each of which is empowered to carry on public education under the statutes and under the appraisal of the state department of public instruction. The legal organization of public education thus provides for centralization (state) of general policy-making, and decentralization (local) of policy execution. It also provides for liberal powers of interpretation by school districts to meet special local conditions.

Local Organization

The people of each legal school district elect according to law a body of representatives through which the general educational plan is to be made effective. Each of these school boards is the supreme educational authority within the district, deriving its powers from the general expression of the will of all the people in the state, expressed in constitution and statute, and acting as the local legislative body in carrying out this collective will within the district limits.

The local board of education, as a board and not individually, has legislative and appraisal power under the law. An individual board member has no authority to promulgate, to change, or to interfere with the operation of the educational plan. The board of education operates only when sitting as a board. Since the actual process of instruction is a highly complicated and technical activity, the state has provided for its legal delegation to individuals specifically trained and legally certificated. Each board of education therefore delegates, in accordance with statutory requirements, the actual executive function of carrying out the broad legal policies to a professional executive including superintendent, staff specialists, principals, and teachers.

Each of these professional executives acts under the laws of the state and under the policies and approved means of procedure of the board of education in carrying out the general will of the people with respect to public education. They have no authority beyond that legally prescribed by state and by their local board of education. Neither superintendent, principal, nor teacher as a private individual has any right to interfere with or to change the legal expression of popular will. The professional executives are merely the legally qualified agents to whom the executive function has been delegated.

The School State

To insure easy means through which to maintain direct control and the partnership concept, the people have developed the educational function parallel to the civil organization. This distinctive separateness of education from general civil government has resulted in the establishment of the school state which operated as a nonpartisan social activity culminating in the state legislature which is responsible for changes and enlargements. The majority of the local administrative districts have fiscal independence in accordance with specific legislative provision. School officers are usually chosen at separate elections, a procedure which enables the people to center their attention directly on the single issue of education without interference or the confusion created by mingling with other issues. As a result the United States now possesses forty-eight independent public-school systems, each responsible to and controlled by the people within the legal area of the state. Rational uniformity is secured through competition, imitation, and the effects of individual and group leadership.

Limitations

However, the complete authority over education has never been delegated to the state. American schools still represent legally a partnership between home and state. The parent's right to control the education of his child, within limits, is an inherent right. On the other hand, the right of the local community to control its schools is a privilege which the state has seen fit to delegate to it, and which the state may and does modify or diminish from time to time with no serious question of its constitutional authority to do so. The delegation of authority whereby the local community controls, to a large measure, the nature and extent of its educational effort is a unique feature of the American public-school system. The people even go further and, by providing special voluntary agencies for the education of their children, retain the right of the family to protest against the manner in which the state operates its schools. The voluntary school is functionally an agency of protest and the means whereby the home may exercise freedom of choice.

Extralegal Organization

The legal structure of the school state is supplemented in functioning by a series of extralegal organizations or interest groups that play a definite part in the operation of the public elementary and secondary schools. These voluntary interest groups are diverse in character and include both lay and professional groups. Starting with the parents, the strongest organization is probably represented by the parent-teacher association. With a membership of over two million, and an organization in every state, this group plays an important part in the determination of educational policy.[3] The schools are naturally the major professional and economic interest of the teachers, and the organized teaching profession is potentially the most influential of all groups in determining institutional operation. Institutions of higher education have dominated the secondary school for generations through control of entrance requirements, their reflected prestige, and their control of coöperative regional accrediting associations. Other interest groups have been important in educational development; the chamber of commerce and organized labor have both played a definite part in the shaping of existing school policy. And in recent years the influence of the private philanthropic organizations or foundations has been in greater evidence. Their ability to subsidize research and to attract educational leaders to the support of their programs makes them no mean power in the future of education.

The foundations subsidized by Rockefeller money have left their permanent imprint on medical research and education, upon public health throughout the world and in preprimary education through their support of experimental nursery schools. Several national surveys of aspects of educational activity that may have a large future influence on the educational program have been financed by these foundations. The American Council on Education, a coöperative extralegal institution, is supported by funds received from several foundations. Grants in aid of research to learned societies within the past two decades have progressively increased. The roster of executives operating these foundations includes many outstanding leaders formerly in public education.

Despite the number, size, and power of these extralegal directive

[3] Paid membership was 2,056,777 in April, 1937. See Chapter 16 for detailed discussion.

groups, it is doubtful whether their direct control is as great as generally assumed. It is doubtful whether even the united opposition of powerful and selfish interests can prevent ultimate institutional adjustment to social need. Public education in the past has developed as a result of social need, regardless of professional opinion and selfish interest-group desire.

The number and diversity of extralegal groups interested in one or more aspects of the educational process is probably the best institutional safeguard. Progressive and courageous leadership from lay interest groups will also stimulate the process of change and reduce the lag between community need and institutional effort. The conservator interest at one end of the scale can be balanced by the ultra-reformist at the other end.

The educational professional interests will probably tend to be somewhere near the safe middle ground of slow and rational change. This expectation is probably due to the fact that the teaching profession as a whole is not much higher in mentality than the rest of the people, sets great store upon security and social recognition, has been strongly conditioned in the traditions of the past, and is itself affected by the autocracy of internal organization. All of these factors combine to produce a group that will tend more strongly toward conservatism than progressivism. It is therefore reasonable to assume that the public-school organization will probably represent a normal resistance to rapid change and will maintain itself in harmony with the underlying community public opinion.

Custom and Tradition

The most potent factor in the functioning of the educational activity is custom and tradition, which represent the mores or slowly changing opinion and beliefs of the people. In one sense the legal structure is only a congealing or crystallization of these beliefs into statutory form as a protective device against sudden possible minority whims. The great majority of extensions of the educational program start as private ventures, are cautiously taken into a few school systems as experimental effort, and then slowly accepted by other progressive centers. Social acceptance is built gradually and is followed by the demand for general legislation. This new legislation is usually permissive in form and applies to particular districts. If universal need for the activity is recognized, the legislation may ultimately become mandatory. Sometimes, as in the famous Kalamazoo case, the first legal sanction is given by judicial review at the insistence of some taxpayer. Thus the public-education program has expanded both downward, in the case of the kindergarten, and upward in the case of the high school and more recently the junior college. Once statutory sanction has been given, the institutional course cannot be changed until that sanction is removed or modified. The time required for modification makes logical defense possible. However, the vital educational function rests directly upon public opinion and is maintained by it. The legal structure is not a means of strait-jacketing the process, but in its mandatory aspects furnishes protection from disturbance and in its permissive aspect indicates popular willingness to allow for desirable regional extension.

Legislation in advance of popular recognition of need is difficult to secure except through minority pressure tactics and is impossible to maintain in the face of popular protest. Statutory enactment in many instances follows after the fact and establishes protection for the activity involved. The nature and value of statutory structure are frequently overlooked by the teaching profession. Since the democratic plan is flexible, permitting experimentation and extension according to need, the enactment of hard and fast statutes should be considered as an organization device to conserve values and to provide a time element during which the institution may develop protection against waves of mass emotion.

The recent depression furnishes an unusually good illustration. During the dark months of 1932 there was much confusion concerning public education. The tax structure had broken down; selfish interest groups, including the United States Chamber of Commerce, realtor groups, taxpayers' associations, and many other groups who were not specifically interested in a program of democratic education, took advantage of the occasion to attempt further reduction in both revenue and program; candidates for state legislatures and local boards of education consequently ran on platforms of economy and restriction. The outlook for public education in December, 1932, was dark.

Parents and teachers became slowly aware of conditions and developed a counter public opinion. This more rational and sober point of view began to make itself felt by the time the state legislatures met early in 1933. Reactionary forces tried to reduce and constrict the educational activity. However, they were immediately confronted by the barrier of statutory enactment which first required removal. Legal amendment takes time. There is also a normal hesitation on the part of the cautious representative to wreck past legislative effort that seems to be working well. In the normal breathing space afforded by existing statutes the parents and the teaching profession were able to bring to bear the aroused pressure of a public opinion that insisted on saving the schools. By March the schools had safely weathered the crisis. Although the total expenditures were not increased, in at least six instances instead of being cut during this trying period state support was actually increased.[4]

Public education finally rests on public opinion, and its existence depends on the maintenance of a public attitude of understanding and confidence. Public opinion develops out of a feeling or conviction toward already accepted beliefs or through the process of education or the impact of propaganda toward the acceptance of new beliefs. Although a large reservoir of static opinion exists in customs and traditions, it is obviously necessary to maintain and improve these attitudes by the process of educating the adult population to current institutional conditions and needs.

EDUCATIONAL INTERPRETATION

The problem of institutional interpretation is complementary to rational operation. The school as a social institution under close popular surveillance and control can operate efficiently only to the extent that community confidence results in wholesome coöperation with its program and in provision for adequate finance. Confidence

[4] North Carolina, South Carolina, Florida, Minnesota, Washington and Wisconsin increased state appropriations in 1933; during 1935 increases in state support were made in Alabama, Georgia, Illinois, Ohio, Michigan, Minnesota, Missouri, Montana, North Carolina, Pennsylvania, Texas, Vermont, West Virginia, and Washington.

can be established only as the people understand and appreciate the significance and value of program. Keeping the people informed of institutional performance and need is the activity of interpretation. No democratic institution can function effectively except on a basis of popular confidence. So long as our democratic form of social organization and institutional pointing prevails, it will be essential to provide within the institutional pattern means for the continual education of the people. The totalitarian state does not require program interpretation in the same sense or to the same extent as the pluralistic state, although it does lean heavily upon the dissemination of biased propaganda.

Social interpretation for the schools may be considered as those institutional activities which keep the institution aware of community opinion and needs and keep the people informed of the purpose, value, conditions, and needs of public education. In its functional aspects there is a minimum of propaganda in the interpretative process. It is an ethical attempt to maintain the institution close to the people through understanding and appreciation. As pointed out earlier in this discussion, the institutional limits on interpretation are definite and precise. The selfish interests of civil and professional personnel must not be permitted to use the methods of pressure politics to produce statutory change whose social value may be doubtful or for which the people are not ready. Institutional responsibility is confined to the collection, interpretation, and promulgation of all of the facts concerning condition and needs and to the attempt to create a legitimate supporting public opinion.

Complexity of current organization and problems will determine the extent and character of the interpretative activity. The problem of community size, the difficulty of numbers, the cultural and racial diversity of population, the levels of intelligence, the complexity of the school program, the competition of other public institutions, the demands of competing group activities, and the relatively small amount of time available to the individual to keep informed—all combine to produce conditions that will be reflected in the interpretative practice.

The requirement of continuity, simplicity, and adjustment to the varying population demands really means that the problem of interpretation is, in the final analysis, one aspect of a continuing program of adult education. Through such a program the people may be kept constantly aware of their socio-civic responsibilities upon whose improved functioning the hopes for the ultimate achievement of a democratic way of life must rest. The public school is only one of a series of public institutions of whose value and needs the people must be kept aware. It is in reality a generalized function presented here only in its public educational aspects.

SUMMARY

Democratic social organization has grown out of the progressive efforts of man to provide a series of social institutions through which his individual and group needs might be more easily carried out. Since man's tendency is to organize, emotionalize, glorify, and finally to deify his past efforts, these means frequently become ends in themselves and are placed in a sacrosanct position that leads to concepts of infallibility. Institutionalism is a danger that must be avoided by dynamic democracy.

Increasing complexity of social activity has led to a larger popular delegation of authority over the educational process to the democratic state. Public education in the United States has evolved as a partnership concept wherein the home and state coöperate in the essential program of child training. The parents have retained their right to differ with their own institutions and to set up agencies of protest—the voluntary schools. Through partnership with the state, the retention of the right to differ, and the planning of the educational activity by states in an organization distinct from but parallel to civil government, the people exercise an unusual degree of direct control over public education in its institutional aspects.

Democratic institutions can function effectively only as the people are kept aware of their purpose, value, conditions, and needs, thus placing upon public institutional personnel the legal and moral obligation of interpreting these popular agencies through continuous informational programs based on fact, simple in form, continuing in type, and reaching all members of the community.

The effectiveness of the democratic school is conditioned therefore by the degree of community confidence. This confidence is built upon understanding, trust, and appreciation. To retain and develop such support the public school must strive to achieve its ideal of equality of opportunity in terms of capacity, to be non-sectarian, non-partisan, and classless. It must itself become democratic.

So long as the democratic school remains an impartial social agency around which all interest groups can rally for the satisfaction of certain common interests, and so long as this institution is sufficiently capable of interpreting itself to society at large, will it be able to function effectively.

Chapter 2
THE DEMOCRATIC PROCESS

INSTITUTIONS and programs in the totalitarian state are maintained by a high emotionalization of ideals, through control and use of all agencies of propaganda, and through the application of *force majeure;* whereas in a democracy they are perpetuated through public opinion. Under the first type of society interpretation is a process of carefully controlled state propaganda through which unity of aim and effort is supported; in the second, it is a process of informal and formal adult education, as a fact-finding and fact-interpreting activity, by which sustaining public opinion is built.

The process of social interpretation whether in education or other aspects of civil government is more laborious and difficult under a democratic state than under any type of totalitarianism. The democratic process will be considered in terms of: (1) democratic organization, (2) the rôle of public opinion, (3) institutional lag, (4) how change occurs, (5) the rôle of education, and (6) difficulties in functioning.

DEMOCRATIC ORGANIZATION

The democratic organization of life may be considered as that form where the individual and the group interests are in relative balance. It rests at the midpoint of a scale between extreme individualization or anarchy on the one hand, and extreme socialization or true communism on the other. The attempt to secure perfect balance between the individual and the group is extremely difficult and represents a constant struggle on current levels and ideals of operation. Perfection in functioning must be considered as an ideal which may be achieved only as mankind advances in wisdom. The struggles between individual and group interests result in a dynamic social organization, in which the golden age is considered to be either in the past or in the future, in which the present is never completely satisfactory.

Personality

The outstanding characteristic of democratic philosophy is the value placed on personality and the importance of the individual as the instrument of the creative and appraisal processes. With its roots deeply imbedded in the Christian tradition, democracy believes that the individual is significantly but not exclusively important in the scheme of cosmic evolution. In practice the democratic state provides definite safeguards for individual protection. In its written agencies of social organization are specific means by which the individual may defend himself from group incursions upon his functions.

The group attempts through various agencies to mold the individual from birth until death to a safe mean conformity or workable unity of thought and conduct. The home, the church, the state, and the community successively and concurrently bring to bear upon the child during the period of immaturity all of the encircling controls that society has developed to interpret group life and to secure solidarity and uniformity. These restrictions are necessary to protect the group from ruthless and predatory individual conduct and, by the same token, to allow individual freedom. As protection against these demands, the individual possesses certain personal liberties which are expressed in law and imbedded even more deeply in the philosophy of the people. The individual may escape to a certain extent from the natural tyranny of the group, although the maintenance of these civil rights requires a constant struggle.

Variation

Progress is possible only as the individual breaks the conventional patterns of thought and action and strikes out boldly in his chosen area of personal achievement. If the achievement has merit, the group generally accepts it without much thought of the possible consequences. Witness the successful history of the automobile and the radio. If the people fail to discern merit, the individual still has the satisfaction of personal expression. Progress is initiated through individual effort and achievement, but becomes socially effective only when the group accepts the new idea or practice and either adds it to the already age-high pile of patterns or substitutes it for one of the old ones. The group acts to constrain and to bend the individual to its patterns. The strong and gifted personality may rebel and start a new trail; the group may accept the new; and so the cultural pattern expands with each generation to become an enriched heritage for those who are to come. Individual variation has no bounds. When it happens in science and industry, it is called *progress* and is often accepted, but when it occurs in social organization—the state—it is called *radicalism* and receives much more searching scrutiny. This differentiation is natural for the people can easily discern advantages and personal benefits in inanimate things, whereas their social conditioning makes it much more difficult to react objectively to structural changes that will quickly affect their immediate and emotional group relationships. So Henry Ford's cheap automobile, and Thomas A. Edison's incandescent light bulb appealed to popular imagination and changed popular practice while the "radicalism," at least to the Republican Party, of William Jennings Bryan, required eight years to become the "progressivism" of Theodore Roosevelt and sixteen years to become in part the "conservatism" of William Howard Taft.

Personal Liberty

The foundation of democratic functioning lies in the concept that all social institutions provide means for the maintenance of the individual's right to differ with organization theory and practice. The right of assembly, freedom of speech, freedom of publication, freedom of religion, and the right of the individual to convert others to his views by peaceful means approved by law form the key-stone of the democratic arch. So long as the individual is safeguarded in the possession of these civil rights, it will be possible to proceed from one stage of development to another with little friction. They furnish at once the protection against social strait-jacketing and the means for orderly change. They also give to democratic society its dynamic character.

Provision for the maintenance of social rights is just as necessary. The group needs definite protection against anarchy and disorganization which threaten the operation of the social function. The individual cannot be allowed freedom to differ for the mere purpose of expressing himself if his actions offer danger or injury to other individuals or to society as a whole. In faith to this democratic tenet, the government of the United States has always enacted legislation to restrict the individual for the benefit of all.

The right to differ from accepted views results in a tremendous amount of diversity in belief and practice. Even if a democratic organization started with a completely homogeneous cultural group, the same differences would rapidly develop. When a social organization like that of the United States starts with a great diversity in cultural groups, an even greater basic diversity is obvious. Add to this cultural diversity the large area of the country and its regional differences, and the difficulty of attaining complete conformity even if it were desirable must be obvious. There is a popular acceptance of certain generalized philosophies and procedure patterns, but outside of this area of basic conformity essential to the welfare and safety of the group there is progressively greater diversity and greater freedom in thought. However, the mass of individuals, with little opportunity to develop their creative talents, are followers of conventional practice and modes of thought. The static conformity characteristic of this group is one reason for institutional lag.

Interest-Group Organization

As the nation has grown in size and in complexity, the individual has evolved secondary organizations for mutual protection and advancement of social interests and for ease in living. These organizations are called *interest groups* and include political, religious, economic, social, professional, and educational units. Many of these groups are so strongly organized that membership is almost a ritual and sacred obligation; others have a loose structure. Some are permanent, others temporary. A unified and continuing program of objectives is carried on by some, whereas others work for the immediate achievement of a single purpose. There is as wide a gap in functioning as in organization, for some groups are highly democratic in form and functioning, and others are highly centralized and autocratic. In certain cases groups of people band together for the advancement of mutual interest, and in others individuals join as contributing members, after an idea has been agreed upon and publicized by a small group of individuals.

Obviously, the interest group has become the protector of some individuals and the exploiter of others. It safeguards and attempts to advance an individual's interest demanding in return a cohesion and loyalty in group activity. Except in the case of a few outstanding and independent leaders, it is correct to state that the individual to-day operates entirely through the technique of interest-group organization.

These interest groups may operate in a perfectly functional manner by developing a program and achieving it through the education of other groups to their point of view, in other words, creating a wide public opinion for their plans. The Garden Club of America is illustrative of this type. Its purpose is to provide greater beauty in living through more effective use of flowers, shrubs, and trees. Its members practice in their own private gardens, attempting through example and through exhibits, "shows," and the dissemination of information to secure a more general acceptance of their ideals and also through the process of adult education to develop a finer conscience toward civic improvement. The spread of the garden movement in recent years is astounding evidence of the possibilities of rational adult education. It is definitely a case of a movement growing through general acceptance of its own intrinsic worth. Its stimulation of the florist and nursery industry is a by-product.

Pressure Groups

Many interest groups are not willing to operate in this manner, but attempt to secure quick realization of their objectives through the use of economic and political pressure. They become pressure groups which represent a specific activity-phase of the interest group. By use of propaganda, political threat, blackmail tactics, and even bribery, they force the legislatures to do their bidding and enact protective and many times discriminatory statutes. The W. C. T. U. is an illustration of the propaganda method; labor and the American Legion of the political threat technique; and the Anti-Saloon League and the Association for the Repeal of the Eighteenth Amendment in their attempts to secure enactment and repeal of the prohibition amendment were both guilty of political threat and political blackmail combined. Certain utility interests, especially the railroads in the nineties, also illustrate the political pressure and bribery technique.

The official records of the Federal Trade Commission (1928-1932) indicate clearly that the power utilities have been conducting pressure propaganda against public ownership in recent years through advertising, the newspapers, subsidizing of textbook authors, the lecture platform, the radio, and the screen. This propaganda has expressed itself positively in maintaining the corporate position and negatively in attempting to silence all opposition by subtle and indirect methods.

There should be a sufficient diversity of strong interest groups for the country as a whole so that over an appreciable period of time it would be difficult for a single group to secure and maintain a selfish objective harmful to the general social interest. The interplay and competition between these groups should be a safeguard for democratic organization. For every propaganda there is normally a counter propaganda, although care must always be taken to prevent the stifling or overwhelming of either minority or majority expression. Analysis at any specific period may show exceptions to this generalization; finance groups may and do exert undue influence and indirect power; heavily intrenched interests are prone to exploit weaker ones, but if the long view is taken, there is much evidence to show that rational if not harmonious balance is gradually restored when necessary by statutory control. The great current weakness is that the source of propaganda is frequently not revealed and that the people as a whole have not been trained to detect hidden propaganda. The public schools have completely neglected this essential need, and the average adult has relatively little opportunity to steer a straight course through this confusing sea. Study of the methods by which the United States was finally drawn into the World War illustrates the power of hidden propaganda. Pressure advertising that in many instances makes an inferior product more eagerly sought than a superior one which provides for only normal promotion is an example of open propaganda.

Individual Diversity

If individuals operated constantly in terms of a specific interest, the problem of forming and maintaining public opinion might be much more simple than it is. However, man is a creature of many interests, and his conduct is not always predictable. The typical individual has a family which includes relatives and forms a primary interest group by itself. In its milder extension the family provides individual members with jobs. Analysis of any industrial corporation in terms of numerous family interests will yield interesting results. In its worst public manifestations it takes the form of nepotism. The typical individual is also a member of a church, is affiliated with a political party, is associated with a specific economic interest group, loosely affiliated with a social group, and a member of some fraternal order, apart from numerous other relations. These narrow and diverse interest groups constantly compete not only for the individual's time but also for his support. His opinions change as his point of emphasis changes, and he may actually have a half dozen different opinions on a subject at various times. He may even be subjected to so many diverse pressures from his different group affiliations that his opinion on a problem from an economic angle may be neutralized by a counter opinion stimulated by a religious or social group. This phenomenon may be frequently observed among professional politicians subjected to numerous pressures. Neutralization in this case is generally a convenient illness, absence from a meeting, hiding, or actually refraining from voting. Therefore, an individual may be simultaneously an economic radical, a political conservative, and a reactionary in education.

One example of this type of person was a national manufacturer who died recently. His industrial philosophy, opposed to everything that was standard practice, was based on the belief that constant improvement was not only possible but actually essential to our economic life. In politics, he supported Theodore Roosevelt and Woodrow Wilson; yet he financed Billy Sunday's emotional evangelism and considered every departure from the classical tradition in the schools as sacrilege. Another is recalled by conversation with a very liberal "new dealer" who felt that the "schools are trying too much experimentation. I have a child of ten who does not know the alphabet yet."

Within the course of a few years an individual may change and find himself a progressive politically, a moderate in economic fields, and a reactionary in religion. Appeal and interest will determine the specific reaction at any time. Though constancy is theoretically possible in terms of unifying purposes and ideals in current practice, it is only in areas where the pressure of conflicts is not great that any degree of constancy may be expected. Because of this diversity it is difficult in a democracy to secure unified opinion even within a single group.

The spread of ideas within an interest group tends to be as great as the variation between groups, and this diversity is a safeguard that makes American democracy possible. If all individuals were always aligned with a special group and a specific opinion, democratic government would be much more difficult. In the United States there are no closed classes and final class opinions. Catholics do not vote as Catholics, but according to a spread of interests; labor has not yet furnished an example of a solid vote; thousands of Americans of German extraction voted for Woodrow Wilson in 1916; thousands of Catholics voted against Al Smith in 1928; liberal Protestants are favorable to parochial schools and liberal Catholics strongly support public schools; teachers support all expressions of political opinion; whereas in the last election economic, even banking interests, were not unanimous in their support of Alfred M. Landon.

Even in the bigotry of the Ku Klux Klan, regional differences of opinion marked this movement in the South, the West, and the prairie states. Lack of political and social group solidarity is a source of strength for the democratic tradition. By and large, there is a broad thread of general tolerance and a sense of fair play that characterizes American life.

Opinion Differences

It might be assumed theoretically that within a dynamic culture differences of opinion would tend to follow a normal distribution with approximately 5 per cent of reactionary and of radical opinion at either end of the scale. Conservative and progressive thought might balance with 15 per cent each allowing a majority of 60 per cent as representative of the so-called middle area of ranging from mild conservatism to mild progressivism. In actual fact if a complete distribution of community opinion in the United States could be made to-day, it would probably show a decided skew toward conservatism in terms of political and educational change and a similar skew toward progressivism in economic and social areas.

The increasing American trend toward conservatism is due to a number of factors among which may be included an apparently large satisfaction with respect to its past economic achievements, a growing spirit of protective nationalism, the shift from a pioneering to a territorially stabilized country, the shift in mean population toward middle age, the efforts of established economic groups to maintain themselves, and the increasing emotional strength of the American individualistic tradition. The political astuteness of Franklin D. Roosevelt during his first administration in sensing this condition may possibly be illustrated by his adroit balancing of a move to the left with a counter move to the right although maintaining a general personal liberal attitude. Even though reëlected by an electoral vote of 523 to 8 in 1936, this election certainly cannot be described as a heavy swing to the left.[1] Within less than six months conservative opinion appeared to be strong enough to prevent his attempt to change the Supreme Court. Even the labor movement as measured by the history and policy of the American Federation of Labor has represented a unique degree of con-

[1] See Dwight L. Dumond, *Roosevelt to Roosevelt,* Chap. XIX. See also David Lawrence, *Who Were The Eleven Million?* (New York, D. Appleton-Century Co., 1937).

servatism. A possible explanation is that the American tends to radicalism only when frightened.

The choice of representatives for school board, city council, state legislature, and the national congress is a direct reflection of this division of thought. The typical board of education is essentially dominated by conservative thought since parents and pressure groups attempting to shape community thought apparently desire their representatives to be sound and stable men fully capable of protecting the educational institution from sudden change and the possible loss of the cumulative cultural ideals of values as interpreted by these groups in terms of their own interests. This apparent inability of the adult to adjust to changing educational needs may also be a reflection of the absence of an intelligent program of interpretative education through which a more rational appreciation of the need for change might be developed.

Value of Extreme Opinion

Democracy operates through the interaction of pole opinions passed through the filter of moderate opinion. The more dynamic the democratic culture the greater the diversity and spread of opinion extremes. Both the Nazi and Fascist cultures may also be considered as highly dynamic, but they allow little safe opportunity to hold different opinions. Extremes of opinion have definite values to the social order that are frequently overlooked. The reactionary is the conservator of group ideals which he identifies with his own interests. He acts as a brake against rapid social change on current levels of functioning. If properly balanced, his function is an important one, but if he is in too definite control, the brake may stop instead of slowing the car and cause trouble through explosive action. The radical is the instrument of social ferment. It is his normal function to point out weaknesses and needs vociferously, to stimulate and to stir to thinking the middle opinion group. His is the voice in the wilderness, viewing with alarm and pointing out the road to social salvation. If he successfully performs his function, part of his program is usually taken over slowly by the progressive segment and more slowly by the central opinion. Thus democratic social action results from the individual and group conflict of extreme left and right opinion resulting in a natural compromise by the middle group.

Though both reactionary and radical have a normal braking and stimulative function in democratic society, it seems undesirable that either extreme be entrusted with full power. They are not functionally capable of its exercise. Control by either extreme may be dangerous to social welfare through excessive retardation or acceleration of social processes. Either extreme would require the use of force to maintain itself successfully. In the final analysis a government must rest on sound majority opinion, and neither extreme of opinion can ever marshal sufficient support save on a coercive basis.

Over an appreciable length of time social organization depends for stability upon the understanding and support of majority opinion. Orderly social progress in a democracy is best made on the basis of compromise between the conservative, progressive, and middle-of-the-road opinion. This generalization does not preclude or exclude the possibility of the ultimate development of a higher level of coöperation and the possible development of intelligent machinery for such improved organization. On the other hand, the current value of both reactionary and radical opinion to democratic society should be recognized, and its proponents need not be condemned out of hand but listened to as valuable outside guides in setting the left and right limits of comfortable navigation in the social sea.

THE RÔLE OF PUBLIC OPINION

Democratic Structure

The democratic structure rests primarily upon popular understanding and support of its institutions and not upon coercion. The democratic life should be coöperative in nature. Acceptance of social objectives and the manner of their functioning are based on popular belief in both purpose and value. Belief indicates an opinion, and so the public belief in a program may also be called the public opinion supporting the program.

Public Opinion

There are two major types of public opinion, one static and the other dynamic. Static public opinion includes the beliefs so strongly held as to be unquestioned, which have grown out of our fundamental customs and traditions and may also be called the social mores. These beliefs, principles, and practices which derive strength and practical sanctity through acceptance by the group mind are a most potent force in directing and regulating individual and group conduct.

Dynamic public opinion is that which is developing at any time toward a specific plan or a specific act. It may arise spontaneously as a translation of the static into a dynamic opinion through a sudden attack on some cherished belief or mores; it may develop as a result of a carefully planned program of education; and it may also grow as a result of specific pressure propaganda. All democratic action rests on the base of both static and dynamic public opinion. It requires a solid majority to make possible social and legal acceptance of a specific plan.

Contrary to general impression, there is no single, uniform public opinion about any particular program. Following the pattern of individual diversity, there is always a series of public opinions which arise out of specific interest groups or alignments of interest groups. The dominant opinion is generally called the public opinion.

Institutional Supports

Democratic social institutions such as the state and public education may be likened to an object that rests on a highly fermentative mass confined within definite physical boundaries. The ferment may be considered both as tradition and custom or static public opinion, and as internal movements toward change. Within this mass is a series of interrelated and competing interest groups each again comprising a group of individual cells that may be likened to yeast. Certain reasonable constants as well as diversities operate within the mass. The constants tend to maintain mass solidarity, but are in themselves progressively modified as a result of the fermentative process. The surface of this active mass has been crystallized into a fairly stiff texture of constitutional and statutory enactments which represent a hardening of the products of fermentation. This hardened surface acts as a protective device for the maintenance and operation of the institution from the vagaries of sudden change. The institution resting on this precarious surface has the same characteristics as the mass itself since it is composed of individuals who operate apart from the mass in only a single technical aspect. The teacher out of school differs little in his conventional attitudes and beliefs from other members of his social group.

PUBLIC EDUCATION
STATUTORY ENACTMENT

Dynamic Public Opinion

Custom and Tradition

Public education rests on the base of public opinion crystallized through statutory enactment.

At irregular intervals the internal ferment may break forth in sudden eruption and disturb the hardened surface. This eruption may be considered as the formation of a dynamic public opinion. If the eruption is sufficiently strong to crack the surface, it changes the protective film by adding to it in the form of statutory enactment or constitutional change. Much of the ferment never reaches the surface and dies without affecting organization structure or functioning. Institutional existence thus rests upon the elastic cushion of custom and tradition, protected against sudden change by the congealed crust or legal structure, but always subject to change if social need expressed by the eruptive fermentative action is sufficiently strong. If the protective crust becomes too strong and does not permit of change by accommodation, a terrific explosion may result from the restricted desires and destroy the crust completely. This condition is revolution.

The successful democratic institution must be thoroughly aware of its own nature; it must also understand the process of social ferment and the means through which public opinion is developed. It must realize that the crust of legal structure can be protective only as it is formed out of a definitely accepted social need which has arisen out of the perpetual ferment of the democratic process. Legal structure superimposed through the use of group pressure from above does not present a desirable democratic method; it is much better to have an idea or practice develop and grow from below through the more gradual process of education.

The mores of to-day represent the dynamic opinions of yesterday that have survived the crucial test of practicality and the apparent satisfaction of social need. They have a conservator value until a better way is found, tried, and proven acceptable. They express themselves as warnings which institutional plans for change and enlargement must always consider carefully if success is a desired outcome. Dynamic public opinion may develop spontaneously or may be directed through the exercise of individual, group, or social leadership. The democratic institution can thrive only in so far as it meets social need, maintains itself in harmonious relations with the beliefs and desires of the people, and promotes greater social effectiveness through the building of an understanding public opinion.

Developing Public Opinion

Public opinion arises out of need, although the need in its initial stages may be neither definite nor clear, but merely an indication of social discomfort or a vague yearning. As a leader considers this feeling and studies its relationship to existing programs, he may clarify and consolidate it into a definite program objective. Thus the process of development begins. Through informal conversation, or specific statement, the movement starts. It may first of all be limited to a single group, but it soon finds its way into the programs of popular groups. The press plays its part in the dissemination of information and the stimulation of discussion. The initial feeling may stimulate study, and research may produce supporting data. The movement now sweeps more extensively to collateral groups. Through conversation, publication, discussion, debate, there is a progressive development of attitudes. The time required depends not only upon the nature, scope, and urgency of the problem upon which public opinion is desired, but also upon its relationship to the deep-rooted static opinion growing out of custom and tradition. The final result is a rejection or acceptance of the idea. If it is accepted, an increasing emotion is transferred to it which finally crystallizes in legal action. Legislation is a terminal step in translating a public opinion into a social plan and action. Owing to the diversity of opinion and differential sectional needs, much of this terminal legislation in public education takes the form of permissive enactments which may be selected by different communities as social acceptance of need occurs through an expression of dynamic public opinion.

Limits to Expression

The very diversity of the democratic organization sets the first limitation to possible perfect expression of a dynamic opinion at any given time. There are many good and sufficient reasons why this limitation should be accepted as reasonable and sound. The country is large, and its needs are diverse. An individual is a member of many interest groups, and it is difficult to secure a complete alignment of individual interest at any given time. Most social and educational problems are decidedly complex in nature and are offered competition from a variety of sources and groups. The size of the various groups is another handicap. Fundamental diversities due to differences in cultural origins and the varying levels of intelligence combine to prevent perfect acceptance and consequent unanimity of opinion. Finally, the limited time which the individual can devote to a single problem makes the process exceedingly difficult. It is doubtful whether it is possible or even desirable, except through coercion in an unusual emergency such as war, to have a completely overwhelming and single public opinion on any specific subject. There is more danger in unanimity than in reasonable diversity. Differences in opinion act as a check upon too rapid or too radical an action.

Forming Public Opinion

Public opinion is formed through the continuous education of an individual or group by factual information that the individual or group translates into those visionary, imaginative, and emotional elements through which he determines value. Presentation of results in discussion and debate may have considerable weight in the actual growth of a belief. Direct and continuing publicity, whether by word of mouth, visually, or through the medium of the press, keeps the subject alive and in the state of fermentation. The actual operation of a social activity under the observation of all interested persons tends also to focus attention directly on the problem. Finally, the interchange of opinions growing out of direct social contacts between individuals and between groups is helpful. Thus, for example, the constant contact of parent and teacher within the parent-teacher association permits a direct and steady focus upon certain aspects of institutional activity.

Although it should be considered desirable to move toward this rational organization for the development of public opinion, the fact cannot be overlooked that conflict and its accompanying high emotion sharply accentuate the growth of public opinion in current life. The technique of controversy is the sharp clash between the poignantly sharp beliefs of the right and left extremes of opinion, characterized by strong emotional sets acting directly and indirectly upon the more placid great central mass of opinion. The desire of either extreme to project its own beliefs upon the entire group results in a direct conflict with the other extreme. Creation of a specific mass opinion on any problem or field of problems will be a compromise resulting from the interplay of these extreme views.

INSTITUTIONAL LAG

A social need arises, and immediately men try to build a machine for achieving objectives and standardizing practices. An accepted facilitating machine is an institution with two definite characteristics. First of all it is a facilitating agency; second, it possesses definite conservator factors. The institution not only operates, but tends to maintain and to enhance the past. In addition every institution is manned by personnel drawn from the general public and having all of the weaknesses and strengths of the cross-section they represent. Thus within the teaching profession on some issues there is as wide a spread of opinion as within the community and possibly an even deeper tendency toward conservatism since the highly educated individuals are apt to be much more conservative than the manual workers. They envision or imagine possible terminal consequences, and they also have a sincere unwillingness to endanger their current economic security. The intellectual may be a left-wing leader as an individual, but this condition characterizes only a minute number of that group.

Social institutions tend to lag behind actual social need as seen by the leader groups. This inability of an institution to adjust itself quickly to change is called institutional or cultural lag and is a normal phenomenon of social functioning.

Change Generally Slow

Any institution that is supported by public opinion in which custom and tradition play so important a part cannot move until the dynamic expression of public opinion is sufficiently broad to permit safe change. It takes a strong working majority to produce institutional change. Once this broad support is determined, the institution may move slowly or quickly to the new position.

Though public opinion has a general tendency to change slowly, there are many exceptions. The quick acceptance of Federal work relief to help depression victims, classified by one authority as merely a transfer of the deeply ingrained American attitude of neighborly helpfulness to the unfortunate, may also illustrate a sudden change in the concept of governmental responsibility. The rapid development of generalized opinion concerning the desirability of old-age annuities is another example which shows that the rapidity of change is determined by the strength of the need or by the effectiveness of propaganda.

The inertia of institutional personnel is frequently so strong that even a majority opinion is resisted in a demand for change. This is the situation in many of our publicly supported institutions of higher learning where outworn traditions and practices obscure pressing current democratic educational need. It is also frequently the effect of propaganda of special interest groups taking conscious advantage of institutional weakness.

The tendency of institutions to crystallize and become statically standardized, plus the need for a wide base of supporting public opinion, makes any institution tend to remain somewhat behind actual social need, but this is less true of democratic institutions. If an institution moves swiftly, conservative opinion will raise objections, and if it moves slowly, the progressive and radical voices are raised in protest.

A democratic institution is never able to satisfy the entire group except in times of danger and stress when extremes of opinion are temporarily telescoped toward the center and when for all practical purposes democracy has been temporarily eliminated by the creation of a dictatorship.

Thus during times of stress such as war variation is forcibly discouraged in the interests of united action. However, even the temporary elimination of democracy is dangerous because by shutting off criticism and free expression of thought, it may not only destroy the leaders, but if frequently repeated, will give validity and strength to coercive strategy. Many people believe that the dictatorship of the World War was prevented from becoming a truly fascist dictatorship during the depression administration of Franklin D. Roosevelt only by the fact that the people were not frightened enough to suppress completely freedom of thought and action. They were willing to be saved by Federal authority but resisted censorship or other throttling of the free press. General Hugh Johnson as the directing head of the N.R.A. illustrated these possibilities. If freedom of discussion and the possibility of judicial review had been stifled, his autocratic methods of administration would have forced every one involved to conform to a strongly individual interpretation of a statutory enactment. Freedom to differ would have disappeared as a result of the power to discipline.

As social institutions the public elementary and secondary schools cannot escape the general implications of social functioning. In a democracy they usually operate at some point near the center of majority opinion. Hence they never wholly satisfy the prophet or reformer, the strong conservative or the violent reactionary. They must sense this position and remain flexible to change when public opinion is sufficiently broad and stable to permit it. In a democratic society sensitivity to changing public opinion and the capability of judging when change is safe is a responsibility of school administration, teaching staff, and parents.

HOW CHANGE OCCURS

If the lag between institutional practice and social need is too great and an institution moves too slowly, exacting public opinion will demand a change in control. This change may be legislative, as in the case of the school board, or administrative, as in the case of the superintendent, or instructional, as in the case of the teaching personnel. These changes, though apparently quite sudden in their inception, may be a long time in the making. The apparent reason for their sometimes explosive suddenness is that the institutional inertia and ignorance of public thinking has been so great that the personnel never sensed the increasing dissatisfaction.

If institutional leaders confuse their own desires with social need and rationalize themselves into action before a sufficiently broad opinion has developed, the final result is the same. It may be possible to initiate the change, but the ensuing conservative reaction is usually more than capable of producing rapid return to popularly accepted patterns. A recent illustration is typical. A progressive-minded superintendent in a certain school district decided to put certain experimental ideas into practice. He was able to convince the board of education and for several years actually managed to keep the parent-teacher association behind the program. However, parental discontent accumulated slowly and forced a change in policy at the end of the fourth year.

The reasons may be diagnosed as a sudden cessation in interpretative technique from teaching to "telling" the parents what needed to be done; an unfortunate and totally unnecessary confusion in identifying new methods in arithmetic and reading, based solely on psychological principles, with radical politics; and an unfortunate assumption by the teaching personnel of the sanctity of progressive methodology.

As a rule, therefore, it is unnecessary to worry much about the institution's being *too far* in advance of social need. The danger is much greater that the institutional lag will be wider than is socially safe, resulting in violent change rather than smooth orderly evolution.

Most of the institutional changes have come about, not through the whole-hearted coöperation of the official personnel, but through intrusion from the outside. Even Horace Mann, now deified by the teaching profession as an educational saint, was at the outset considered a rank lay outsider by the Boston schoolmasters. Careful study of our educational history leads inevitably to the conclusion that the teaching profession, generally, has been unduly conservative and traditional in outlook. Public-school organization has tended to resist essential social change. Our leaders have not been serious enough students of philosophy, the sciences, and the social studies. Neither has the teaching profession made the most of its opportunity for creative leadership. Naturally there are exceptions. Public education has produced able and progressive leaders. However, the implication that in general the profession has failed to live up to the standard of constructive leadership is true.

How Change Occurs

Modifications and enlargements are constantly being made in our educational plan. Changing conditions of life result in new needs. Subjective recognition of these conditions and need is usually first made by industrial, financial, religious, social, or educational leaders. Discussion follows discovery. This is a process of informal education. At first the new implications are challenged or indifferently received. Constant reiteration finally gains tolerance of discussion. Certain more adventurous professional leaders begin experimentation. These experimental results engender further discussion. Public leaders begin to accept and, with acceptance, bring pressure upon the social institution through organized group opinion. Gradually, usually most cautiously, experimental trial is made. Each effort brings further change, modification, and discussion. By direct and indirect means popular acceptance of the new need is established. Finally there is general social acceptance of the need, and it becomes, through legislation, a legal part of the social program.

Since the success of the educational process is conditioned by the closeness of the gap between social need and institutional functioning, the teaching profession must exercise its normal leadership responsibilities by developing plans and procedures through which discussion, understanding, appreciation, and finally dynamic popular support may be given to normal institutional change.

THE RÔLE OF EDUCATION

The democratic educational process has three general functions. The first is the *training* of the immature from infancy to maturity, and the second the *constant reëducation* of the adult to understanding of the changing need. A third may be considered the development of inspiration which should operate on all levels of activity. Until very recently professional emphasis has been almost confined to the first aspect—the teaching of the children. The significance of adult education in the socio-civic field has been almost completely overlooked.

Child Training

The education of the immature is confined primarily to the transmission of the social heritage in knowledge, skill, and customs, plus a technique of variation from the social heritage. The individual child should not only be trained to develop his inborn capacities to the greatest extent in terms of their individual and social values, but also educated to develop a civic consciousness whereby he will be stimulated to make the greatest possible contribution to the welfare of the group. A flexible personality capable of adjusting intelligently to changing social need and practice is one of the desirable educational outcomes.

The partnership concept in American education means that the parents participate to an appreciable extent in the framing and carrying out of the instructional program. Home and school must work together with greater understanding and coöperation to realize the full possibilities of the educational process. Popular control of public education also means that the parents will not permit changes in educational objectives, method, and content unless they understand and approve of these changes. The adult will not permit the exploitation of children.

Adult Education

Institutional efficiency, beyond the area of mere mechanics of operation, will be determined specifically by the degree of intelligent adult understanding. Orderly progressive change in the educational process will be conditioned by the effectiveness with which the adult can be reëducated to changing need. The basic problem in institutional interpretation thus becomes a problem in the second aspect of education—the adult field.

The professional educator's leadership influence in improving public education rests upon his ability to create and to direct public opinion. Since the educator has no legal power to make or to change policies, leadership must be exercised through recognition of the partnership concept and through excursions into the field of adult education.

DIFFICULTIES IN FUNCTIONING

Diverse individual and group interests competing actively for the extension of specific ideas and programs generate a conflict of opinions and so make institutional functioning difficult. At the best these differences express themselves in sharp divisions of opinion and at their worst in serious conflicts between interests and between groups. The institution functioning on the supporting base of favorable public opinion plus a certain amount of fairly neutral opinion is always in difficulties with the conservative and the progressive elements. For the conservative it moves too quickly, and for the progressive its snail-like pace is exasperating. Even at its best the public school cannot expect complete agreement with its policies and practices. Success in functioning may be achieved if these two types of extreme opinions are kept dissatisfied.

The area of social and community conflict presents the greatest problem. Since many of the community differences have nothing to do with education in the beginning but are simply carried over by the process of transference, further difficulties arise and seriously handicap smooth institutional functioning.

The administrative problem is the study, classification and isolation of these conflicts so that rational attempts toward harmony may be made. Conflicts may be classified by type as the economic, political, religious, cultural, racial, man-woman, parent-child, child-school, parent-school, and geographic. Any of these conflicts may be intentional or dishonest, irrational or emotional, and rational or reasoned. Each of them represents a different type and a different method of treatment. Sometimes conflicts extend themselves and unconsciously develop in unexpected areas from unsuspected sources. A man-woman conflict in the home may frequently find its ultimate expression in a parent-school difficulty. Careful analysis of type is necessary to successful solution.

Intentional Conflicts

Intentional conflicts are frequent in the political field; some are deliberately started to secure an effect. The unscrupulous politician decides to expand his personality and his publicity at the expense of organization. Realizing that conflict is news, he deliberately enters the lists as a perennial critic by using the tools of innuendo and implication. He is good copy, takes care of "the boys" or reporters, and merrily makes political capital. If the school community is intelligently aware of conditions, it is safe to allow him sufficient latitude to insure ultimate political failure; if the community is not well informed, this type of conflict may be extremely dangerous to institutional welfare. The dishonest conflict of the professional politician should not be confused with the highly desirable exercise of the critical attitude by both conservative and progressive members of the board of education. The conservative member should be intelligently critical of new and untried schemes until they have been proven experimentally to be worthy of consideration, whereas the progressive members should seek means for improvement and call for their experimental trial. The remedy for intentional conflict is to maintain silence and so reduce the culprit's news value, to interest the individual in a more profitable activity, and to attempt to change his attitude through the constructive influence of friends.

Irrational Conflict

Emotional conflicts develop from a sense of distorted values arising out of high cultural and racial differences. They may be of a temporary nature, but they may also be deep rooted and permanent.

Conflict between a foreign-born parent and a teacher is the most frequent example of the temporary irrational conflict. Another is the difference between liberal and strict sabbath observance which frequently becomes drawn out and almost permanent in nature, moving at times into other fields of problems in terms of the same differences. In one mid-western community a liberal manufacturer with a love for stirring up trouble and a highly emotional preacher got into a conflict thirty years ago. The manufacturer gave the community a recreation field with the direct proviso that it be used for Sunday baseball. The minister emotionally translated this competition into sin and began to preach vigorously against it. The community quickly took sides, and soon a merry liberal-conservative, cavalier-roundhead battle was in operation. After a while the manufacturer became tired and attempted conciliation by giving the church an organ. The minister's attitude changed completely. Not being able for long to control an impish desire for conflict, the manufacturer next openly subsidized teams that played only on Sundays. The battle was on again. This personal conflict raged for ten years until the manufacturer died and the minister was called to larger fields. The community forgot the original conflict, but the same groups have since carried on the struggle by taking opposite sides on every question before the community. At present an intelligent superintendent is gradually pushing it into the background through the technique of friendliness and is taking advantage of time in changing the original values.

Since high emotion characterizes this type of irrational conflict, it cannot be harmonized through counter argument or further conflict. Its solution proceeds best through use of the encircling technique whereby friendly listening is substituted for opposition. The cultivation by neutrals of friendly relations between the different leaders and the use of time as an equalizer and harmonizer are extremely important.

Rational Conflict

Rational or reasoned conflict is a definite part of the democratic process of building public opinion and need not be feared. The technique of harmony is also the technique of education. Rational conflicts arise because of misunderstanding, the placing of different values on different facts, and the ensuing terminal differences in interpretation. Illustrations may be differences of community opinion concerning the value of two reading methods, the grade placement of mathematics, the value of home work, the types of public expenditure, or any other field where differences may quickly arise.

Harmonizing these differences may proceed through the definition and delimitation of the subject; through the consideration of different values; through the securing of facts, experimentation, or giving adults specific experience. The story of the small community that was carried away by the feeling that "the schools were not teaching spelling as well as they used to" is probably well known. The superintendent and teachers decided to let the children carry their own program. When the controversy was at its height, a group of children challenged the parents to a spelling contest to determine who was right. The parent-teacher association picked its twenty self-admitted best spellers. The children picked their own team from the elementary school. When the evening was half over, only one adult was left out of twenty, whereas the child mortality was only five. There was no need for further discussion. A humorous announcement by a parent of the final results rocked the house, and the conflict was over. As a by-product the community was convinced of the children's ability to spell, and the reasonableness of institutional method. The contest actually didn't prove anything except that the golden halo placed upon the adult past was badly tarnished.

The experimental technique of settling rational conflicts is highly desirable, but it requires time and is not always usable except in schools where it is constantly employed as a phase of the creative technique for improvement. Ironing out different points of view by panel discussion, specialist question-and-answer methods, or the development of group-working techniques is a possibility. If a group of doubting parents can be induced to work directly with the teachers in the solution of a moot problem, the experience will be educative to both, and the conflict can usually be ended.

In general conflicts are to be avoided through institutional observation of trouble spots and the development of preventive measures and by bringing them into the open for rational discussion. Where conflicts exist, they should be studied carefully with respect to type, and steps should be taken toward a harmonious viewpoint.

SUMMARY

The democratic process is a constant struggle between the encompassing and compelling desires of the group and the need for the individual to resist in order to grow, achieve his reasonable ambitions and to make his contribution to progress. The group desires conformity and tends toward a static condition. The individual is the agent of social fermentation and through his projection of personality stimulates other individuals to the point where group plans and patterns may undergo change. The ideal is that point where the interests of the individual and of the group are in harmonious balance. However, this condition can seldom exist in a dynamic democratic culture. Democratic procedures result in extreme diversity of opinion, and these shades of belief are essential to a well-balanced whole. The function of the conservative is to act as a stabilizer, whereas that of the radical is to produce explosive thought to stimulate recognition and consideration of problems. Neither the ultra-conservative nor the ultra-radical should ever be in complete control. The result is social difficulty and loss of function.

Democratic institutions rest upon a broad base of static public opinion or custom and tradition, reasonably reinforced and protected by legislative enactments. Statutory patterns are primarily stabilizing institutional devices, protecting the institutions from sudden change. The public school, like any other institution, cannot operate much in advance of or too much behind majority public opinion. Either practice may result in violent community upheaval. Institutions may retain flexibility and a satisfactory relationship to changing need if the professional personnel accepts its leadership responsibility, and proceeds through adult education to assist in the formation of a public opinion that recognizes the need for and is willing to accept and support change. The problem of maintaining the institution in a dynamic flexible state through the activity of adult education is a continuous and time-consuming process.

Chapter 3

PROPAGANDA AND THE SCHOOLS

ORIENTATION of the public school in its broad relation to social organization and the brief description of the general processes of democratic life may now be further enlarged by specific analysis of certain problems confronting the public schools. These problems arise from the attempt of special interest groups to extend their influence and program by direct or indirect propaganda methods. Propaganda cannot be talked or laughed away, but must be considered in the broadest sense as a definite means, or device, that has considerable permanence in human relations. In both its direct and indirect forms, it is not new but goes back into the dim past of man's history, even before the days of the ancient Pharaohs and the haughty Assyrian despots. But though the practices are as old as mankind, modern knowledge and invention have developed new techniques and created new problems.

DEFINITION

In the generic sense any effort to influence the opinions and conduct of others is propaganda. Thus all educational activity that attempts blindly to condition its subjects to a specific point of view may be considered as propaganda. However, the use of this method by governments during the World War to justify their conduct and to develop sympathy of other nations has resulted in restricting the application of this term to a much narrower meaning. Regardless of academic subtlety or hair-splitting technical differences as to the potential meaning of the term, it is necessary for practical purposes to accept the modern concept in preference to the generic. In the modern sense, then, *propaganda may be considered as those individual or group efforts, including attitudes, opinions or actions, that seek to convert other individuals or groups to the maintenance of old or the acceptance of new attitudes, opinions, beliefs, or actions through open or secret methods for the purpose of helping or injuring a person, cause, or an institution.* Propaganda involves all those efforts that seek to attain their objective through the presentation of half truths or carefully selected facts organized to support a specific view. Some authorities even go further in their definitive restrictions.[1]

Acceptance of this modern definition makes it possible to state by way of illustration that the completely state-controlled schools of Germany, Italy, Japan, Mexico, and Russia are at present restricted to the dissemination of special propaganda in contrast to the schools of Great Britain, the Scandinavian countries, and the United States with their wider, freer, and more diversified programs under both state and voluntary effort.

Propaganda is, therefore, accepted as the conventional and widely used device whereby individuals or groups seek conversion of other individuals and groups to a point of view that is of special interest and profit to the propagandist.[2] It is of peculiar importance in international relations and causes much difficulty to the thoughtfully reflective individual. Through direct control of news agencies and censorship a government can be assured that only desired information sifts into the world press. Propaganda is also the methodology of partizan politics and institutional religion. Unfortunately much of the current institutional interpretative activity in state and local government can be called propaganda, and in recent years the public schools have been guilty of permitting the interpretative process to degenerate into propaganda. Functionally the processes of social interpretation and those of propaganda are at opposite poles and need not be confused in practice.

[1] Lumley considers that: "Propaganda is promotion which is veiled in one way or another as to (1) its origin or sources, (2) the interests involved, (3) the methods employed, (4) the content spread, and (5) the results accruing to the victims—any one, any two, any three, any four, or all five." Frederick E. Lumley, *The Propaganda Menace* (New York, D. Appleton-Century Co., 1933), p. 44. Quoted by kind permission of the publishers.

[2] *Propaganda Analysis,* Vol. 1, No. 1 (October, 1937), offers the following wider definition of propaganda as: "Propaganda is expression of opinion or action by individuals or groups deliberately designed to influence opinions or actions of other individuals or groups with reference to predetermined ends."

As one of the most important social agencies of organized democratic life, the public school has always been and always will be subject to pressure and pulls. In the broad definitive sense propaganda is nothing to become disturbed about, but should rather be considered as the means employed by individuals or groups to project their views and to extend their influence over other individuals and groups. If propaganda methods are open and above board, if the source of information and purpose are known, it is quite easy to take the use of propaganda as a matter of course. But when the source of propaganda is hidden and the ultimate objectives are clothed in false garments of bright and attractive hue and the *modus operandi* exceeds that of good democratic sportsmanship, then a social institution is confronted with problems that require serious attention.

Both Good and Bad

Propaganda as a whole cannot be considered completely good or bad. Each type must be judged according to source, purpose, and value. The propaganda both for preparedness and for peace has distinct value since national life in a disturbed and power-mad world requires reasonable defense against the conscienceless attempts of certain national wills to power. Unintelligent as the procedure may finally seem, it is still desirable to spend money on battleships, sailors, soldiers, and guns. A difference of opinion might arise as to what constitutes adequate national defense lest the myopic specialist —in this case the professional soldier and sailor—should develop the means out of all reasonable proportion to need. Similarly no sane person will question the value of peace and the utter senselessness of war. Intelligent education to prevent war is highly desirable. However, the neurotic extension of the peace concept into its more extended phases of complete non-resistance under current international conditions, characterized by a complete absence of moral principles, should be subjected to rational review. Here is a striking example of propaganda for war, and counter propaganda for peace. If the interplay of these opposed propagandas results in heavy democratic discussion and makes possible the development of a sensible, compromise public opinion and terminal action, both propagandas have performed their duties. However, if either side attempts through bribery, intimidation, use of physical force, blasting of leader reputation, or other sinister coercive means to secure its complete objective, then the condition may be considered bad regardless of which side is the offender. The end cannot be considered as justification of any means.

Value of Propaganda

New ideas are developed by the individual, extended through propaganda of some specialized type to consideration by others; acceptance by a group leads to more extensive and intensive group propaganda until there is a possible general social acceptance and incorporation in the general cultural patterns. The case of the low-priced automobile is a good example. Henry Ford had an idea. Every one laughed at him as he confined his experimental work to a barn in a secluded alley. But the experiment was successful, and he developed his propaganda sufficiently to convince a few men of the automobile's economic feasibility. They united financially and produced an automobile which through the intensive propaganda of direct advertising, racing, and street demonstration convinced others sufficiently to sell cars. The propaganda of manufacturer and customer rapidly progressed to such avalanche proportions that the culture under which the progenitor of the cheap automobile had grown up was very much changed. Henry Ford probably had no intention of changing the life habits of millions of people. He simply had an idea that was accepted by large numbers of people. To-day the genius of Dearborn is spending many hours and much money to reconstruct as a museum plaything in Greenfield Village some of the living habits that he was chiefly instrumental in destroying. This illustration might easily be multiplied a hundredfold, so frequently does it occur.

Because of their conservator characteristics and the natural resistance of their operating agents who are conventionalized individuals upon the whole suspicious of anything that is new and out of the beaten path, institutions normally resist change through inertia. Inadequate concept of institutional function and neglect in the development of an intelligently critical attitude that is absolutely essential to change and progress do not greet with favor the desire of single-minded enthusiasts for new things. Although our economic and social life has undergone astounding revolution within a generation, the major civil and educational institutions still operate blithely and unconsciously through inadequate machinery and methods. Having substituted the worship of form for substance and methods for principles, the institutional agents appear content. A reasonably large share of public taxes is still consumed by inefficient, cumbersome, and completely inadequate forms of local government. The development of an efficient and well-balanced modern system of taxation complemented by modern methods of collection and administration has been estimated as capable of providing sufficient funds to satisfy improved and expanded current governmental needs. No increase in taxes would be necessary if the government could count on savings from its own efficiency.

The nature of the social institution and its resistance to change make it currently necessary for ideas to come from the outside. It is actually possible for an institution to be alert and flexibly responsive to social change, but the widespread achievement of this state may be considered as a future possibility rather than an immediate probability. However, even a socially alert institution cannot be expected to furnish all of the ideas. The broadest possible conception of efficient democratic social functioning still needs the stimulus that comes from the individual whose vision is not cramped by institutional or professional patterns.

The need for change in the character of the elementary schools in the seventies was apparent to many serious students both within and without the schools. The academic use of the graded system, a desirable instructional device, to produce individual conformity to a single standard of performance with no regard for individual differences had created unrest both in Europe and the United States because of sterile methodology and frequent brutality toward small children, parading under the sanctified name of discipline.

Then Froebel had an idea, and the kindergarten grew out of it. This idea crossed the Atlantic to the United States, as ideas have a habit of doing, and made an impression on many people. They talked to professional educators about it and suggested trial. Their reception lacked warmth, so they started a little propaganda movement of their own by establishing kindergartens under voluntary support. They talked about their experiments, demonstrated results, and slowly converted many people. These individuals in turn worked upon the educator and school-board members. The pressure of public opinion soon forced many educators to change their minds. Some of the more creative individuals now felt it safe to hold these opinions without fear of professional reprisal. In several centers, experimental classes were accepted, and gradually institutional resistance was worn down so that the kindergarten became a part of the public school. However, academic negativism was still so strong that, though gradual approval was secured, the actual integration of this activity into the elementary program has not been completely attained even to-day, half a century later.[3]

The same story might be repeated with the case of manual training, the subject which finally evolved into vocational education; cooking and sewing which are gradually developing as a sensible program for home-making; special attention to atypical children, a service that may progressively modify all educational methodology; expansion of the fine arts from "sissy education" to a realization of their fundamental cultural importance; and many other innovations and changes. More changes, enlargements, and improvements of the institutional aspect of public education have come about through the influence of outside forces than from within. These changes were made as a result of individual and social propaganda and in some instances the employment of significant pressures. They may be added to the credit side of propaganda.

In summary, propaganda in its generic sense is any attempt to create or conserve attitudes and beliefs. In the narrower current

---

[3] The National Kindergarten Union still exists (1937) as an aggressive interest group with the objective of providing kindergarten opportunity for all children. Its separateness is still apparent.

connotation of the term, propaganda represents more frequently a perversion of the true educational method in so far as it selects only favorable materials; uses techniques that emphasize and capitalize the emotions of fear, pity, and love; and stimulates the animal urges of cupidity, self-interest, sex, and the exploitation of others. Truth may be and is often propagandized, but this device is much more frequently used in extending only one side of a controversy in which opinion, not truth, is the issue. Some ideas are subject to factual proof such as the economies achieved through standardization and mass production, but many ideas and accepted principles are not subject to complete factual analysis, such as peace, democracy, and religion, but rest upon the acceptance and belief in them as values that produce emotional satisfaction.

Since some propaganda is definitely good in terms of its objectives and outcomes, certain voluntary social agencies like the church, ethical organizations, groups engaged in social betterment, and professional organizations including teachers, may be justified in its use.[4]

Public institutions, however, are in a completely different category from voluntary interest groups. They belong to the people, and the power to direct them must remain in the people. The agency created to serve all the people, such as the public schools, cannot be allowed to use methods which will enable institutional personnel to control the people. Such an arrogation of authority would represent a perversion of function completely incompatible with the concept of the limitation of democratic institutions.[5] The people are entitled to all of the truth regarding their social efforts.

Propaganda, even when good, is such a dangerous instrument that it should at no time be consciously employed by the public schools. The immediately accruing gains may be definite losses over the long span.

Propaganda is and will probably continue to be a problem in human relations. Adults and children will be exposed to it prac-

[4] See also Chapters 4 and 14.
[5] See Chapter 1, pp. 12-13.

tically every waking moment of their lives. Commercial propaganda affects our living habits and creates many new patterns of taste. Through newspaper, billboard, radio, and direct mail the bombardment goes on continuously. Economic and political propaganda seeks constantly to create and to maintain specific points of view toward institutional change. The school as a social institution cannot escape and can less afford to ignore propaganda. There appear to be two institutional responsibilities: first, to know propaganda so thoroughly that the institution may be protected from its most baneful effects, and second, to teach both children and adults its nature, methods, purpose, and means of recognition so that their social effectiveness may be increased.[6]

Current propaganda to which the public schools are normally subjected will be considered in greater detail in the following pages from the standpoint of: (1) types of propaganda, (2) propaganda methods, (3) institutional techniques, and (4) teaching controversial issues.

TYPES OF PROPAGANDA

The public schools are exposed at different times to at least seven types of propaganda including conservator, economic, professional, political, racial, religious, and social. Although the methods of attack differ, each general classification has a common purpose in so far as it seeks to develop specific points of view in those individuals or groups to which it is presented. Since this analysis is concerned only with description and not evaluation, only significant examples of each type will be reviewed.

Conservator

Propaganda for the purpose of conserving real or assumed values in the economic, social, and political life of the nation, comprises this division. Certain organizations like the Sons and Daughters of the American Revolution, United Daughters of the Confederacy, the Constitution League, and interest groups dealing with conservation of wild life and natural resources confine their major efforts

[6] See also Chapter 24.

to conservator activities, whereas organizations like the American Legion and certain economic groups devote only a portion of their efforts to this work.

Their major propaganda is built upon the assumption that certain beliefs, ideas, and practices accepted as distinctively American should be passed on in all their virility to posterity. For this reason they are particularly anxious to maintain relations with public education and to insist that their materials be placed in and used by the schools. Their efforts may be simply educational, as the heavy advertising by public utilities during the depression warning against the dire effects of projected New Deal legislation to the American tradition of free individual enterprise. They may include the preparation of certain patriotic materials for readings in the elementary and secondary schools whereby the legendary ideals of American heroes may be kept constantly before the children or, again, may include the organization and use of speakers to present certain points of view to school audiences. Sometimes their propaganda takes the form of presentation of flags and pictures to act as a constant visual influence. Open propaganda of this type is easily handled and is reasonably simple. When conservator organizations go below the ground and attempt to achieve their aims by the censoring of textbooks, regulating the conduct of teachers, belittling and undermining the reputations of public officials by the popular method of name-calling and radical labeling, propaganda becomes extremely difficult to combat. Another favorite method of the conservator group is to apply pressure to the legislature and secure the passage of bills that include everything from teachers' loyalty oaths to mandatory curricular requirements in the selection of subject-matter for social studies.

There is a definite place in the scheme of social organization for either positive or negative types of conservator propaganda provided that it operates in the American manner of open and fair play. The function of the reactionary and conservative is to oppose change and is therefore of some importance as a social brake. When it passes the point of warning against change to use coercive measures, its worth is dubious. The will of the great mass of people, allowing normal protection for minority differences, must ultimately prevail.

Economic

The economic groups include all interests from insurance, public utilities, chambers of commerce, bankers, construction interests, builders, farmers, labor, processors, manufacturers, distributors, retailers, service interests ranging from cosmeticians to morticians, and professionals including architects, engineers, doctors, and teachers. Their number is legion, and their direct and indirect influence is great. Probably every individual has membership in one or more of these groups in some relationship or activity.

The surface efforts of commercial groups are easy to distinguish. They include giving samples, offering prizes, sponsoring contests, furnishing free educational supplies with direct advertising on the cover or throughout the material, furnishing athletic equipment, preparing brochures or expensive monographs describing their processes, preparing charts of their products, giving motion-picture films, providing lectures, offering exhibits of their plants and specimens of their products, and performing a multitude of other services whereby the children will be exposed to their products and their claims to superiority. These open attempts to introduce material directly into the schools may be dealt with by a flexible blanket policy that will permit the institutional agents to appraise the worth and value of the material and make wise selection. Much of this material, though obviously commercial advertising, has an intrinsic instructional value that need not be cast aside because some special interest has prepared it for use. Commercial interests must also be credited with extending worthily the limits of human knowledge through direct institutional research or the disinterested subsidy of independent research in institutions of higher learning. Certain descriptions of productive and manufacturing methods are not available in textual material and are desirable supplements to the always starved classroom. The charts of animal cuts are valuable in cooking classes; presentations of automobile chassis, tools, and machine processes are essential to the shop; and the story of various extractive milling processes actually enhances the teaching process. It is, moreover, questionable whether by these contributions the already world-known materials prepared by General Electric, General Motors, Henry Ford, International Harvester, big mining companies, and certain processing corporations have much to gain except good will.

The indirect efforts of wider economic groups, as distinguished from specific commercial organization, to influence teaching in the schools are much more subtle. Telling the story about the electric light is one thing, but the attempt of the utilities to direct university and secondary-school teaching and thinking through influencing teachers and textbook authors by subsidy in one form or another is an entirely different matter. Efforts to distort the truth about public and private ownership are definitely restrictive propaganda. And when governmental agencies are denied through subtle practices the right to tell the people of the relative values of certain types of food, another dangerous situation has been created.

Professional

At times the teaching profession also employs propaganda methods in the classroom. To the extent that the children are exploited to extend the physical and financial limits of institutional functioning and advance personal and professional interests, the teaching profession is using propaganda practices just as any other outside interests with similar purposes and practices. A teacher who weeps before a classroom of immature children because he does not believe his salary is large enough, who works on child sympathy for either retention or promotion, incites sympathy strikes, or otherwise comports himself non-professionally in violation of his teaching trust, cannot be excused on the grounds that "improvement of the teacher means improvement of the child."

Teachers who, in their institutional aspect, violate the classless spirit of the American public school by the suppression of the fundamental civil rights of children or fellow-teachers, who attempt to impress their personal views and beliefs upon the children, who neglect to present all points of view impartially, belittle certain religious beliefs, or preach Nordic superiority, cannot escape the charge of being propagandists.

Teachers interested in the education of atypical children have formed an effective nation-wide special-education-interest group and through the use of open propaganda have been attempting for several years to influence Federal legislation with respect to special appropriations for subnormal and crippled children.

Individuals interested in the expansion of vocational education have designed a heavy pressure group that is considered by professional politicians and newspaper men as the second strongest pressure lobby at the national capital. Through high-powered propaganda this group is furthering and enlarging the scope and financial support of vocational education somewhat out of its normal relationship to the balance of the curriculum. The legislation secured and maintained through its efforts is slowly changing the entire character of local control of public education so far as vocational education is concerned. The public schools need as much protection from the narrow and selfish interests of certain sections of the teaching profession as from commercial and conservator agencies.

Since the World War the War Department through the Reserve Officers' Training Corps in secondary schools and institutions of higher learning has built up a powerful propaganda technique for furthering its own organizational interests. Not only has the R.O.T.C. been an agency for the training of reserve officers, which is its natural function, but its teaching manuals have gone far beyond their normal military function and seek by preaching specific points of view to cover fields and subjects that may be confined more safely and rationally to uncolored treatment in the social studies.

The medical and dental professions are also engaged in the projection of specific professional points of view through propagandizing in their several official publications and through speeches. Many so-called health practices which are debatable in the opinion of any disinterested member of these professions have crept into public-school teaching.

Political

Political interests include the major political organizations, minority groups, economic groups in certain aspects of their program, and conservator groups. Political propaganda may be directed either by groups open in their purpose and affiliation, by interests working through and motivating the political group, or by organizations that merely use the strong-arm legislative method to attain a certain objective. Their methods are generally indirect and frequently very difficult to trace. They form an ever annoying activity because of their surface elusiveness.

Political propaganda may be confined to local, state, or national problems, or through carefully organized high pressure and highly skilled professionals it may bring the schools within the range of international propaganda. In the early stages of the World War, long before the intervention by the United States, British and French interests played a very important part through pamphlet, poster, and speakers in creating in the child mind a picture of German barbarity and brutality, at the same time painting the Allies as glorious crusaders on white horses. Lafayette always rode a white horse, and the Galahad implication of the Allies' purpose was obvious. Who will ever forget the steady stream of English doctors and American doctors in British pay who told the children about Belgian children spitted on bayonets or poisoned by German candy? Ever since the war the schools have been constantly bombarded by many types of cleverly disguised foreign national propaganda. Teachers sometimes exhibit much excitement over free pencils and paper given the children by advertising concerns as reprehensible practice without realizing that much more important conditioning is taking place through control of textual material or by international propaganda. Teachers of modern languages, desirous of favor, recognition, and possibly foreign decoration, frequently become, through their eagerness, the unconscious agents through which the smooth foreign propagandist works.

Racial

That high racial sensitivity of Europe and Asia is also present in this country and securing recognition of racial equality, superiority, or admission of cultural achievement is the purpose of many interested groups. With watchful eye on the school program, they attempt quietly to eliminate any material that might reflect on their particular race and also to furnish colored examples of heroic achievement. Skilful and unobtrusive Jewish propaganda succeeded within a decade in removing *The Merchant of Venice* from the required reading lists for university entrance and also from secondary-school English courses in most states. Negro groups are almost neurotically active in preventing any discrimination or assumed derogation of their claims, whereas the Poles, French, Italians, and Germans are distinctly alert to possible slights. On the positive side through recognition in statue of their national heroes or individuals involved in the American War for Independence, special birthday programs, and the naming of school buildings, these groups seek to instill in childish minds the contributions of their fellow-countrymen.

Religious

The major religious sects present both positive and negative propaganda problems to public education, but on the whole these activities are generally most serious in the smaller centers. Religious propaganda is so effective in the typical small town to-day that religious qualifications for teaching positions actually form a part of unwritten criteria for selection. In some sections of the country only members of certain Protestant sects are permitted to hold teaching positions. In the larger population centers the propaganda of one religious point of view is balanced or offset by that of another group, and a much greater spirit of tolerance is noticeable.

A democratic school system can operate functionally only as long as a complete separation between church and state is maintained in spirit and fact. Religion is not and need not be divorced from the public-school program, but its organized sectarian beliefs and practices must be. Propaganda demands of aggressive sectarian groups in small communities tend to negate this principle through the stimulation of a community public opinion that quickly transmits itself to the board of education.

Other types of religious propaganda prevail. Despite the fact that numerous religious persuasions exist in this country, there is an insistent demand in many sections for the reading of the Bible in school. The edition selected is always the Protestant King James version which does not appeal to the Greek or Roman Catholics, to the Jews, or to other numerous Christian and non-Christian persuasions. Propaganda for the dismissal of children from school for special religious instruction is frequent; attempts to restrict health education because of sectarian attitude is felt in the city schools and in legislative enactment; efforts of Catholic and Protestant interests for state aid in maintaining their voluntary schools is met by counter propaganda from certain other groups who are attempting to maintain the traditional separation of church and state.

In some small communities the dominant Protestant sects have developed such a proprietary interest in school activities that a fairly large number of districts has reported the insistence of the minister on having public-school commencements in the church in order to give them the benefit of religious sanction. Certain ministers must appear in their official capacity at other school programs and are always given a prominent official place. In general the pressure of special religious interests and their emotionalized propaganda are not very difficult except in many of the smaller public-school systems. The day of the revivalist who could within a month make a Sunday School superintendent out of a free-thinking metropolitan school superintendent has apparently passed.

Social

Social groups of various types, including those interests whose programs are self-constructed, such as community-improvement, bring pressure upon the schools through the prestige of their influence and the desire of non-members to appear worth while and correct in their attitude. Like the religious organizations they operate indirectly upon the institution through pressures developed within the community. These groups include such organizations as the Anti-Cigarette League, the Anti-Saloon League, the Women's Christian Temperance Union, and a host of others. Temperance groups frequently operate through the legislature and upon textbook publishers. No science or biology text can to-day have successful sale in the public schools anywhere in the country unless it meets the propaganda requirements of the temperance groups in the same manner that certain patriotic interests censor history texts for sectional consumption.

Sometimes these social groups go further and attempt to destroy the classless concept of the secondary school by insisting on certain program differentiations. One reported instance was the insistence of certain groups for differentiation in social activities of the schools and even different quality of bindings for the school annual "so that our children will not be forced to mix with the offspring of foreigners and hand laborers." The influence of social propaganda is frequently seen in the failure of secondary parent-teacher organizations.

PROPAGANDA METHODS

Propaganda varies with program and type of group and may include casual, direct, and indirect methods. These several methods may be further subdivided as educational, social, defamatory, intimidating, and bribing. There need be little concern over educational methods that are open and above board; under-cover types are the greatest cause of trouble and frequently offer extreme difficulty.

Casual Propaganda

Included in this method are the occasional suggestions that may come to the school from individuals or groups, expressing a point of view, an interest, or possibly a demand on the institution. There is generally no specific program either for the direct education of the institution to these suggestions, no pressure or use of specialized personal techniques for achievement. From one aspect these efforts may be considered merely as suggestions, and treated accordingly.

Direct Propaganda

Methods of direct propaganda include those efforts which seek first to influence the institution directly through presentation of group viewpoints as frank and open expressions of opinion. They may take the form of hearings before the board of education, interview, speaking, discussion, presentation of visual material, pamphlets or textbooks, contests of various types, and the radio or newspaper. These forms of propaganda have a wholesome value for the alert administrator and teacher in revealing the variety and scope of community opinions. The purpose is to create a public opinion for a specific idea through the democratic method of discussion and conviction. The source of information is generally clear; its purpose is obvious to all involved; and its general method is educational. The weakness is that presentation depends on the selection and coloring of certain facts. In some cases the sources of information are readily available and form a basis for desirable counter propaganda; in others they are well veiled, and the emotionalization of issues makes objective consideration a little more difficult. In general, the direct methods of propaganda represent the democratic method in operation, and need cause public education little trouble.

Indirect Propaganda

Indirect propaganda methods may be extremely difficult to meet and are generally responsible for the large part of institutional difficulty. They may be personal or social in their nature. The general theory underlying their use is the desire to stimulate promotion of a program through fear or special pressures. The individual or group conceiving and benefiting from the program remains discreetly covered in the background, working through obvious stooges and "fronts" who are apparently high minded and altruistic about their demands. Sometimes they are. Frequently ministers, doctors, dentists, college professors, and idealistic visionaries are stimulated to action for an idea the ulterior motive of which is unknown to them. The professional "fixer" or indirect propagandist considers the clergyman and the physician the easiest individual to dupe. This view is also held by high-pressure specialists in "wild cat" investments.

Indirect methods may be trained on the newspaper, and realistic as the professional journalist must be, he is still capable of considerable gullibility where really smart professional efforts are involved. These groups frequently operate through the local political bosses to influence the legislators for quick statutory enactment before the state is aware of what is taking place. Sometimes a state awakens almost too late to the fact that an enterprising equipment broker has almost committed them to state publication of textbooks and over a million dollars' worth of mechanical equipment.

Indirect methods may operate in a similar way to prevent legislative action by the addition of apparently innocent "riders" to fiscal legislation. Again, they may simply work through friends to secure a favorable point of view or create a hysterical attitude on the part of parents through the use of fear. Censorship may be used as a negative means of achieving or preventing achievement of a program. Those interests that seek selfish advantage or personal profit are frequently just as keenly interested in defeating as in promoting a program. Railroads, utilities, insurance companies, real-estate boards, publishers, manufacturing associations, and farmer interests—all maintain what might be termed "watch dog" lobbies to forestall legislative action that might affect their interests.

The methods of indirect propaganda may be those of attempting to establish a point of view through friendly relations, or they may include much more sinister types such as indirect bribery through the promising of favors in securing better jobs for superintendents and principals; direct bribery of political bosses, community leaders, and members of the board of education; destroying public confidence in leaders through labeling them as "radical," "unpatriotic," "non-coöperative," "knocker," and "immoral"; threatening loss of position and blacklisting with other boards of education; carrying on whispering campaigns with respect to the leader's sex life, home relations, and financial probity, and offering social favors to ambitious wives.

Pressure propaganda may be direct or indirect, representing chiefly a variation in method of procedure. Pressure may be applied through direct bombardment by literature or dynamic speech or progressive interview, by threat of consequence, by hope of reward, by friendship demands, or by calling in political obligations. Since both direct and indirect methods have already been considered, it is possible to present several significant examples to illustrate some of these pressure techniques.

"This Community Needs ———"

Some years ago a smartly dressed and very presentable woman, armed with extremely favorable credentials, used to appear on the educational programs of the women's clubs in moderate sized but only fairly prosperous communities. She lived at the best hotels or clubs, entertained tastefully, and spoke on the beauty of child life and changing concepts of education. She usually ended her series of free lectures by leading the women to make an appraisal of the physical condition of the local school plant. Stressing both the need for educational change and new facilities, the possibility of danger in non-fire-resisting school buildings, she was usually able to start a definite community movement for better schools. If her program was completely successful, the women's organizations proceeded to convince the school board of the need. If not, another skilful woman speaker followed the first speaker and kept the pot boiling. During the course of these talks the speakers always managed to couple innocently the name of a certain architect with the new era of better schools in this country. Naturally the women's lobby wanted their community to have the benefit of this genius. He was later invited to appear before the board of education, and after he spoke and radiated improvement of the schools, nothing remained except to sign the contract. His organization relieved the board of education of such annoying details as preparing and campaigning for bond issues, and if need demanded, he generously invited the outstanding local architect to colleague association, which really amounted to job inspection or clerk of the works. The board of education received a standardized plan built on the mass-production basis which did not always provide good curricular fit. Sometimes the community found itself with buildings too large or poorly balanced for local need, and a staggering debt. Few communities ever seemed to connect the altruistic and socially charming lady speaker with the completed new building.

"Do Me a Favor"

The superintendency was open in a fairly large community, and a certain textbook publisher wanted to name the candidate. A careful survey indicated that three votes were lacking. The member favorably inclined stalled for time by suggesting and setting up an involved procedure for selecting an executive. In the course of several months careful examination of the personal and economic relations of these dissenting members by the publisher's "attorney" resulted in having one member reverse his stand because a prominent relative of national importance asked him to "do me a favor"; a second negative vote was reversed by the following roundabout process of interrelated interests. A large stockholder in the publishing company was also a relative of a director in this second member's corporation. By friendly suggestion over a luncheon table the second director was ready to grant his publisher friend an innocent favor. It cost him nothing. He didn't live in the community and cared less about it. The director talked to the board member who was in his corporate employ, and this man saw a distinct personal value in meeting the director's wishes. The third vote was secured through the pressure of a social group that appealed to certain ambitions of a third member. The candidate favored by the publisher was elected accordingly, and a long line of prospective candidates attracted by the apparently impartial method of selection sent in their expense accounts and called it a day. The new superintendent happened to be an unusually capable man, and it has never been obvious that the publisher reaped any direct benefit for all of his expense and labor. Possibly he saved changes in textual adoptions, but no rival company has yet complained of favoritism in the purchase of books.

"Buy, or Else ———"

A manufacturing concern that may well go unnamed was interested in placing its equipment in a new urban high school. An amenable architect wrote "cold specifications." The superintendent studied the situation carefully and came to the conclusion that something was radically wrong. It looked as if certain individuals might profit personally by this selection and that the cost of the building might be increased. He brought the problem forcefully to the attention of the board members and insisted on open specifications. As a leader he was highly respected in the community and had behind him the force of strong public opinion. The board concurred, but the producer did not and proceeded by a very indirect and complicated method to "frame" the superintendent by starting a whispering campaign concerning the superintendent's alleged relations with a woman teacher. This story ran its whispering length to the board of education, and several members nervously felt that it might be better to change the specifications and save the reputation of their superintendent. That individual surprisingly refused to accede and offered to bring the entire scandal into the open by running down the responsible individuals and starting suit for slander and defamation of character. The board overcame its attack of jitters, agreed to stand by, and this threat alone was sufficient to kill the whispering campaign within a week. Contractual estimates under conditions of open competition actually gave a cheaper building, and careful supervision gave an honest one.

The "Crown Prince"

Sometimes a pressure group finds the superintendent unintelligently adamant in refusing to accede to pressure propaganda. The interest then proceeds slowly to undermine his reputation and to build up one of the principals or a colleague outside of the system as a successor. Incidents are readily produced when the time is ripe just as they are in international situations, and a change in officials permits the achievement of the desired program. Superintendents worry much about the "crown prince." The low standard of professional ethics makes this practice fairly easy.

"Have You Heard———?"

Pressure propaganda is used not only by interest groups outside of the school but also by members of the teaching profession itself to gain an immediate objective or vent a spite. In a medium-sized city a few years ago the superintendent was up for his third reëlection on a three-year contract. In the operation of an involved merit salary schedule one teacher had been given repeated annual salary increases, whereas another teacher's pay remained stationary. The general personnel policy was one of "hush" that did not permit principals to disclose the reasons for these awards. Despite the fact that a teacher's contract is a public record and so open to inspection by any resident of the school district, the superintendent steadily persisted in this silly policy of silence. The slighted lady proceeded to make propaganda. Six months before the time for consideration of the new contract, whispers spread from several of the city's schools to the effect of "have you heard that our superintendent is intimate with Miss Y. [the capable teacher who had received regular annual increases]? Of course, don't tell a soul, but———." Apparently the other teachers had not heard, but some of them lost no time in telling their friends and neighbors. Within a few months the whispers reached the board members through a serious-minded banker who felt that "the board should protect the morals of the children, etc." Several board members became worried and had their wives make some discreet inquiries. Yes, it looked bad since "every one" believed the story. The superintendent sensed something wrong, but no one told him the truth. When it began to look as if it might be necessary to refuse another contract, a shrewd member of the board of education consulted a physician friend. Fortunately it happened that the physician also knew the young lady in question, not as a patient however. As a special case she had attracted some medical interest. When he informed the board member that sex relations between the teacher in question and the superintendent were impossible, it was easily possible for this board member to start counter propaganda and completely change the opinion that was crystallizing. The citizens' committee, headed by a minister, that was about to make certain demands of the board of education, lost a prominent member. He had heard and did not care to undertake a foolish mission. The committee quickly dissolved. However, this board member was a curious individual and made further investigation of the dissemination centers and traced the original rumors to a certain group known for close friendship to the teacher who never got a raise. Then he informed the superintendent and suggested that he change his personnel policy and salary schedule as well. That particular superintendent is now a firm believer in automatic salary schedules and was heard at a state meeting a year later to condemn roundly any system of merit awards as "impracticable." The original trouble-maker is still teaching but knows why she doesn't get a raise.

"Wouldn't It Be Nice?"

The use of social pressure is familiar to all who have studied the realistic operation of politics in Washington. This same technique of approval or disapproval through the use of female stooges working on the men and more particularly their wives is very effective. Many a board member and superintendent accede to certain pressures because their wives are directly ambitious for social recognition or are too sensitive to withstand snubs from social leaders. Human relations are delicate and complicated areas that furnish fertile ground for the smart propagandist.

"Never Mention His Name"

Censorship or punishing through silence is a much more infrequent measure. A democratic leader must have access to his followers, and the radio and press are therefore essential instruments of communication. During the World War the newspapers generally combined to eliminate from their columns the speeches of Robert La Follette and the other "wilful men" who dared to vote against President Wilson's war program. Except in Wisconsin, the people generally forgot that such men existed and were still acting courageously in accord with the dictates of high principles. They came to life only slowly after the armistice. Sometimes a newspaper that is thwarted in its desire to bend the public schools to its personal ends still uses the "blacklist" method of censorship to achieve its purpose. Editors have discovered that though it may be good tactics to fight a man, there is too much danger in fighting a woman even if she is a member of a legislative body. They adopt the safer method of ignoring her. In national politics censorship is difficult to overcome, but it is not too effective within a school district since the stronger avenues of personal contact are always open.

INSTITUTIONAL TECHNIQUES

The school as a social institution need not be considered as helpless against these constant propagandistic barrages. It has available a number of techniques of varying worth which from many aspects places it in a most advantageous position. Recognition of the propaganda activity as a normal phase of democratic functioning makes it desirable to consider the use of a few generalized principles that will be helpful in developing an institutional set toward any propaganda problem that may arise.

Above all things the public school should always keep the propagandistic issue clear and out of the confusion of emotional by-paths and social fog. The best means for accomplishing this objective is the development of a scientific attitude toward every problem, including an objective approach, a time sense to prevent hurried decision, a willingness to wait until all of the evidence is available, and harmonization of the diverse viewpoints in terms of such evidence. The scientific method avoids senseless struggle and fighting on an emotional basis which only tends to provide more fuel for deeper conflict. It is also essential that the institutional attitude be devoid of finality and dogmatism, maintaining instead, like the individual, an open mind and an always reasonable attitude.

Refusal and Acceptance

Two extreme institutional techniques are those of refusal or acceptance of the pressures of interest groups, standing unbending as a rock against the repeated waves of specialized opinion or bending like a reed before every zephyr in acquiescence to each and every demand. Neither extreme is intelligent for a democratic institution. Inflexibility or subservient complacency are both so lacking in value that they may be discarded except as extremes in emergencies arising from lack of institutional preparedness.

Experimental Technique

An institutional attitude of interest and receptiveness to new ideas, suggestions, and demands pointing always toward the values of experimental trial and objective determination of need is much less dangerous. It prevents the building of an overpowering emotional pressure possible as a result of direct refusal and prevents also the overwhelming of the institution by any demand regardless of its worth. The experimental technique may be considered as a step in the direction of more scientific institutional functioning and also as a cushioning device whereby time, the most valuable element in social administration, may be used as an ally.

The purpose of experimental consideration of ideas by public institutions is to bring the idea or demand into the open, submit it to careful scrutiny through providing means for its trial, permit public examination of the demand by all interests, and so direct it into the path of normal democratic functioning. At no point is conflict necessary because the institution neither accepts nor rejects but simply projects the demand into the laboratory arena of fair play where all may see, observe, and form conclusions as the evidence objectively develops. During the experimental period there is time to smoke out the hidden purpose of undesirable demands and to bring sponsors into the open. Whispers of the "they say" technique must be replaced by specific responsible sponsorship. In many instances institutional willingness to experiment quickly causes withdrawal or modification of demands developed by certain types of pressure or indirect methods since many cannot stand the bright light of publicity. If the idea or suggestion is considered worthy, it may be readily financed by the institution; however, if it is vague and somewhat unreasonable, it may be good tactics to request the supporting interest to pay for independent experimentation.

The outcome of the experimental technique is possible acceptance or rejection. In the meantime a lot of water has rolled down the stream since the first demand was made; much general popular education has been possible, and the outcome of experimentation will either have the support or non-support of public opinion. The institution is then in an entirely different position with respect to making decision. The demand may die of its own weight before trial or fail at the end of the experimental period. If it does succeed, it may be considered by the institution in the light of legal requirements, personnel, plant, and finance just as any other desirable extension must be.

Adoption of the experimental technique and its attendant publicity may serve a better purpose than the older and more dangerous practices of building fires behind the demand and thus stimulating counter propaganda or by a direct appeal to the people. Both of these practices possess certain inherent dangers since the source of counter propaganda is always easy to trace, whereas direct popular appeal cannot be safeguarded from emotional clouding. Publicity incidental to experimentation produces the same results without the same complications.

Preparation

The capacity of an institution to meet open and covert propaganda is conditioned by the degree of ability through complete command of the situation. The best equipped school system is one in which the activity of social interpretation is so thoroughly understood and practiced that the institution knows its community with a greater thoroughness than any community segment or section knows itself. This knowledge may be secured only through the development of a continuing community survey through which information about background, habits of thought, conditions, and deficiencies are kept constantly up to date by a simple system of reporting, paralleled on the other hand by just as complete a knowledge of the institution itself in terms of program, personnel, plant, and finance. Only as the institution is itself prepared through exact knowledge is it capable of operating efficiently in a democratic pattern.

TEACHING CONTROVERSIAL ISSUES

The public school must be realistic in both program and functioning. The democratic process, both as it is and as it might be, must be taught the children at those periods when they are reasonably capable of benefiting from such teaching. The pattern variation in functioning imbedded in individual civil liberties which form the key-stone of the democratic arch makes such teaching possible. Since the school is supported by public opinion, the first requisite to realistic teaching is the creation of an intelligent adult opinion concerning democratic needs. Unfortunately the school of the past generation so completely ignored the orientation of its product in the area of social and political relations and methods that it is necessary for the current institution to make amends by a reëducation of the adult to the meanings and implications of democracy. Once that task has been accomplished, it will be possible to improve the instruction of the immature. Any attempts to push the school frontier forward by starting with the immature instead of the adult is fraught with considerable danger both to the institution and to the teacher.

The first weakness in this field is within the teaching profession itself. The teacher talks much of democracy, but, judging by attitudes and actions, appears considerably handicapped through intellectual and emotional inability to reduce generalities and slogans to concrete practice. The teacher must first become consciously democratic, understanding and sympathizing with democratic problems, able to use the democratic technique, and willing to submit to democratic appraisal.

The second step is directing adult education to democratic problems and really developing an attitude of tolerance and support of its methodology.

The third step includes teaching the children the meaning and methods of democracy so that they will recognize the value of variation as well as uniformity. In this division falls teaching the nature and value of propaganda, its types, methods, and techniques both for recognition and control. Understanding the nature of method and process and the development of a critical attitude until all of the evidence is available and the establishment of habits of reasoned thought can do much to inculcate in the minds of the children desirable methods of social operation.[7]

After these three steps have been achieved, it is possible to proceed to the actual teaching of controversial issues by presenting all points of view related to a problem, evaluating them according to source and purpose, and generalizing without presenting hard conclusions or placing dogmatic emphasis upon specific beliefs. The teacher must be able to divest himself of his own personal points of view and act in a completely judicial attitude toward all aspects of a problem without becoming disturbed or emotional. Adult understanding, supplemented by child realization of processes and problems and the judicially minded impersonal teacher, forms a trilogy through which the presentation and consideration of controversial issues may be safely accomplished.

SUMMARY

The public schools are faced by constant demands from all quarters of the social compass and subjected constantly to intermittent or continuing pressure by special interest groups. The method of individual or group projection is through propaganda which, of and by itself, cannot be classified as entirely good or bad. It is not easy to generalize about propaganda honestly conceived and openly presented. Each demand must be considered by itself and judged as to social worth and value. Interest groups use propaganda for advertising themselves or their product, impressing their own views on other individuals and groups, securing personal or organization publicity, extending the normal limits of their power, increasing their membership to improve financial strength and mis-

[7] See *Propaganda Analysis,* Published by the Institute for Propaganda Analysis, Inc.

sionary power for the purpose of raising men and women to an assumed improved status and for pure altruism.

The public institution has an advantageous position in recognizing and harmonizing the diverse propagandistic demands of interest and pressure groups if it develops administrative competency through intelligent understanding of community, institution, use of the experimental method, and if it prevents emergencies from arising by being forehanded. The direct methods of propaganda are easy to discern and fairly easy to meet, but it requires time to bring the indirect methods into the open and subject them to experimental consideration during the course of which the normal processes of democratic discussion may be developed.

Too much current attention is paid to the efforts of manufacturing and retail interests to secure a little free advertising through the schools while the less obvious but infinitely more important underground methods through which large demands are made and frequently secured escape notice.

Chapter 4

THE TEACHING PROFESSION

THE teaching profession occupies a unique and at the same time the most difficult position of all agencies in the field of institutional interpretation. In their individual institutional relationships members of the teaching profession act as agents of the state, and in their professional relationships as members of an interest group. These two aspects of functioning are frequently confused by the layman and are not always clear to the educator. Clarification is essential to efficiency in operation and to prevention of possible loss of popular confidence. The teacher's relation to public-school organization and his place and responsibility for institutional interpretation are fully covered in other chapters. This discussion will attempt to define and orient the teachers as members of a professional group from the standpoint of: (1) function of the teaching profession, (2) current views and practices, (3) professional organization needs, (4) professional responsibilities, and (5) difficulties in functioning. Programs of professional organizations will be treated separately under their classification as a specific community and state agency.

FUNCTION OF THE TEACHING PROFESSION

The classification of teachers as a profession connotes by popular definition a difference between physical and mental means of making a livelihood. There is no fundamental assumption of superiority implied between the brain and hand worker but rather a relative difference in possible responsibility and form of social contribution. Both manual and mental effort are fundamentally labor. However, much more is expected in contribution to social welfare from those who have been gifted by nature and in addition given all environmental advantage to develop native capacity. The assumption of responsibility for improvement over and beyond the prescribed work and the unselfish contribution to social improvement should be considered as the hall-mark of distinction. Only as an interest group rises to the challenge of social obligation and makes unselfish, unpaid contributions to the advance of civilization is it worthy of being classed as a profession. The physicians make this distinction clearly in providing for the social use of discoveries in the field of medicine without profit to the originator. Failure to conform means expulsion from their professional organizations.

If the public-school teachers of the United States are determined to develop a true profession, they must be willing to accept the social responsibilities which such choice entails. Many of them have inherited richer gifts of mental capacity than the average and wider social opportunity to develop them, and their consequent debt to society is greater than that of those groups that do not aspire to professional levels.

Improvement

The primary function of the teachers as a professional group should be to serve the people by making improvement of the public schools their primary objective. Methodology will be considered later. Attempts to improve the schools may possibly require the assumption of certain group risks which might also result in temporary personal penalties. However, a professional group which does not possess the courage of maintaining its convictions has little right to this presumptive classification.

Our social organization is so complex that the average individual's ability to maintain and to express himself is conditioned, with notable exceptions, by his direct affiliation with one or more interest groups. He maintains his religious freedom by affiliation or non-affiliation with the church, his political right to express his views by attachment to an organized party or by remaining an independent, and his economic interest by membership in the specific organizations designed for those purposes. Since the teachers do not differ in their social aspect from other individuals, it is also desirable that they organize as an interest group to protect and advance their economic status and afford to the individual the protection of group organization. The welfare of its members is the second function of a professional organization. It must provide protection from the punitive actions of other interest groups, aid in securing work and maintaining the freedom of the individual to express himself.

Since the improvement of the schools demands ever increasing personal efficiency through advance in knowledge, a third function of the teaching profession is to provide means and stimuli whereby every member will become more consciously aware of the need for self-improvement. Personal improvement is the third obligation of the teaching profession.

The teaching profession, in summary, includes these specific objectives of acceptance of responsibility for the improvement of the educational function, welfare of its members, and provision for self-improvement. The first and third objectives are directly involved in the process of institutional interpretation.

Functional Organization

On the basis of these objectives and in light of the peculiar position of teachers as agents of the state rather than individuals engaged in private enterprise, the question of organization assumes paramount importance. The easiest means of clarification is a review of the theoretical basis for such organization in terms of objectives, relationships, and long-time values.

Teacher Aspects

Teachers have three aspects: as individuals, as teachers, and as members of a profession.

As an individual, each teacher undoubtedly has the same right as any other citizen. In theory he can make his own religious, political, economic, and social choices. In theory he can direct his personal life in accordance with his conscience and his beliefs. For these choices he must assume sole responsibility since a choice indicates a potential outcome. Outcomes, again, lead to certain reactions on the part of the individual. Since it is difficult in practice to find always sufficient elbow space in which to make free choice, specific professional limitations upon individual freedom appear traditionally. These are not inherent in the situation, but are mentioned simply because they have evolved out of tradition and must be considered.

The teacher, as the operating agent of the school as a social agency, must reflect the character of the institution itself. He is more than an individual, becoming for all practical purposes its operating agent. The public-school teacher in the United States occupies an essentially judicial position. In the classroom he must divest himself of personal prejudice and emotion; he must be non-sectarian, non-partizan with respect to current political programs operating through an organized or informal party, non-doctrinaire, and non-missionary.

The state also expects positive qualities of its servants. He must be loyal to democracy and genuinely moral. He must inspire confidence in the parents, or he will be discarded by these partners in social enterprise. No amount of statutory enactment will prevent such expression of democratic choice. The total effectiveness of the public-school teacher in the United States depends not only upon his ability as an instructor but also upon his ability to gain and to retain the confidence of the people. As a teacher he will never be free to perform at will in terms of his specialized personal beliefs, fancies, or phobias. The limits of freedom will be conditioned at any time by the specific beliefs of the specific community and type of institution which he serves. As soon as he steps out of his judicial rôle, he is in danger of reprisals from individuals, special interests, or the community as a whole. When the teacher falls under suspicion of political, economic, or religious partizanship, the impartial character of the school also suffers. In practice teachers have been partizan to the most powerful community interest groups, and this fact has certainly conditioned the social effectiveness of the schools.

The teacher should become a member of a professional interest group to protect and improve the school, to provide for personal growth through mutual stimulation, and to protect himself. Membership in the teaching profession entails a moral responsibility for interpreting the value, conditions, failures, and needs of public education to the people. The effectiveness of this group interpretation is conditioned by the confidence the people have in the teachers' unselfish, judicial attitude. If a profession means anything, it includes the responsibility for improvement. Our highly specialized society provides better protection for the average individual when he is reinforced by the strength of the group. Here arises the question of technique or strategy whereby greater protection may be secured. There appear to be three divergent choices.

Shall the teachers join the chamber of commerce, affiliate with organized labor groups, or shall they remain as an independent profession close to their official rôle as agents of the state, impartial and non-partizan?

In his individual aspect each teacher theoretically has full freedom of choice and of consequences. In his professional relationship the field of choice cannot be so wide. Since the fundamental strength of the teacher lies in his impartiality and his position as social referee in a classless school, any action which reduces essential social confidence is something to be pondered carefully. Professional affiliation with capital or management groups is ultimately extremely dangerous and unwise. It naturally decreases the confidence of other groups and interests. Affiliation with organized labor, as a specific interest group, also destroys the confidence in teacher integrity of groups normally opposed to these specific interests. In a similar way, affiliation with certain fire-eating militarists will dampen the enthusiasm of those who do not believe in war, whereas direct affiliation with extreme pacifists would certainly cause questioning on the part of other groups more realistically inclined. The teacher in his professional relationships cannot disassociate himself from his limitations.

There is no attempt at disparagement of any agencies mentioned as possible affiliates. Each one of them has its purpose and place in democratic organization. Nor is there any assumption that the individual teacher is bound to restrict his *personal* affiliations to the professional group only. In fact, the reverse may be true. Teachers will probably become better teachers in so far as they broaden their field of interest and group contacts. Personal membership in interest groups other than the teaching profession does not indicate that the results of these affiliations will be reflected in classroom teaching.

The conclusions presented refer merely to affiliation of the teachers, *as a profession,* with special interest groups.

It is doubtful whether the teaching profession, as a group, can drop its traditional rôle of impartiality and still retain the popular confidence as the impartial teachers of all other groups. Nor can the teaching profession make specific inter-group affiliation and remain disinterested in other spheres. Treaties and affiliations demand *quid pro quo!* Society offers little without demanding its price. Teachers as a group do not rise much above any similar cross-section of the people. There is no need for self-delusion in this respect. The profession should not bind itself to the possibilities of achievement of their objectives through up-to-the-present unexplored possibilities of effective independent and impartial professional organization.

Democratic life is a constant struggle between robust interests. It evolves through struggle and through compromise. In certain aspects it always needs a referee. The state for political life and the school for child and adult educational life should furnish a means through which diverse groups and interests can harmonize their differences and progressively learn the greater lessons of coöperation. Democracy cannot be achieved by wishing for it. It can come only as we are willing to work for it. To safeguard human liberties and human rights, and to protect all of the children of all of the people is a program worthy of the teacher.

CURRENT VIEWS AND PRACTICES

Three current major practices have arisen out of the traditional and current problems confronting the profession. The first of these, confined largely to institutions of higher learning and to voluntary schools, is that the members of the teaching profession should remain independent in all of its aspects, limiting membership only to learned societies whose sole object is the advancement of human knowledge. The other extreme is represented by an increasingly militant minority, drawn from elementary and secondary schools, colleges and universities, and voluntary institutions, who believe that the salvation of the teachers lies in direct affiliation with the labor movement either through the craft union of the American Federation of Labor or the vertical union of the Committee for Industrial Organization.[1] The third and largest group is committed to the traditional independent organization of teachers into state and national organization as members of a teaching guild. Approximately half of the teaching profession is affiliated with these independent state groups, 20 per cent with the National Education Association, less than 2 per cent belongs to the teacher-labor movement, and the balance is either independent or affiliated only with learned societies whose activities are limited to the advancement of knowledge. The majority of teachers in both sectarian and non-sectarian independent schools have also their own professional groups.

Although the current problems of teacher organization grew directly out of and became acute during the depression, there was already a significant movement toward teacher-labor affiliation as early as 1902 when the San Antonio Public School Teachers' Association, the Chicago Teachers' Federation, and two other county associations in Illinois received charters from the American Federation of Labor. The great stimulus to membership came after 1929. Membership is confined chiefly to the larger industrial cities and to certain other areas where labor organization is strong. According to statements of these early officers the teacher-labor movement rose out of generally low salaries, autocratic administration of school systems by boards of education and superintendents, the cramping effect on teaching of local alliances between school boards and corrupt political organization, insecure tenure for teachers, and domination of the teaching process itself by industrial and financial interest groups. To these reasons might be added the fact that professional teacher organization was weak, because it was designed to provide for control of policies by administrators and to remedy the general lack of protection given to its members.

The objects of the teachers' union may be summarized as the desire:[2]

[1] See *Proceedings* of the National Education Association, 1937; and *The American Teacher*.
[2] James W. Welsh, *A Brief History of the Union Movement Among Teachers in the Public Schools of the United States*. Unpublished Master's Thesis, University of Michigan, 1930, pp. 100-101.

... to establish freedom in teaching and to defeat attempts to set up censorship in the writing and publishing of textbooks, to build among teachers a professional spirit based on professional self-respect, to develop interest in experimental education among teachers and among school officials; to eliminate political and ecclesiastic influence, and to uphold merit as the basis of appointment to positions in the school systems.

The work accomplished by the teachers' unions cannot be lightly passed by. They have contributed very definitely to the improvement of educational and teacher conditions in certain centers. Their outstanding weakness is the attempt to carry over from labor practice into professional organization a separation of teaching and administrative activities as analogous to the labor and management divisions in industry. This unfortunate policy, unless completely reversed, will do much to retard movements that are now tending toward more functional and hence more democratic methods of administration.

The ever increasing dangers to the welfare of teachers through non-affiliation and through diversion of interest brought the problem to the attention of the Department of Superintendence Committee on Longer Planned Programs which, in its report to the 1936 Convention, advocated study of the possibilities of developing a unified professional guild.[3] The Educational Policies Commission gave the problem its serious attention and published in February, 1937, the results of a preliminary survey of its study.[4] It submitted certain questions to its 2,000 consultants and also to 2,000 classroom teachers selected at random and proportionately representative of all sections of the United States. From the opinion expressed in the returns received, the Educational Policies Commission prepared the following seven recommendations for consideration by the teaching profession:[5]

I. *Purposes*
    The purpose of a national professional organization in the field of education is the maintenance and improvement of the

[3] See *Proceedings of the Department of Superintendence*, 1936.
[4] *A National Organization for Education*, The Educational Policies Commission (Washington, D. C., National Education Association, 1937).
[5] Educational Policies Commission, *op. cit.*, pp. 36-37.

educational service. In order to achieve this purpose it is essential that there should be: continuous study and research with respect to the process of education, the conditions under which the process is carried on, the results achieved, and the means of its improvement; promotion of all movements which will give stability and progressive character to educational undertakings; provisions which will insure the continued professional growth of those engaged in the service of education; and the maintenance of such relations with the public as will secure economic welfare, social security, and civil liberties for those who serve the public in carrying on education.

II. *Membership*

Membership in professional organizations should be wholly voluntary.

III. *Socio-Economic Activities*

A professional organization should be concerned with programs calculated to improve the quality of educational service. Although avoiding partisanship on general social questions, the national professional organization should call public attention to the educational aspects and implications of existing socio-economic conditions and of proposed social, economic, or governmental changes.

IV. *Protection of Members*

The national professional organization should define and publicize the civic and professional rights and obligations of teachers. It should also, in certain important selected test cases, investigate or assist state and local associations in investigating apparent infringements and engage in efforts to secure judicial rulings in defense of these rights.

V. *Branches of Educational Service*

The national professional organization should provide a department for each important branch of educational service. Membership in a department should require and carry with it membership in the general organization. The departments and affiliated organizations (to which latter group the requirement of individual membership may not apply) should be integrated through representation in the governing machinery of the general organization or in some other effective way.

VI. *Local, State, and National Membership*

Membership in any local and state or territorial organizations should, so far as possible, be made co-inclusive with membership in the national organization so that membership in one would carry with it membership in the others.

VII. *Lay Affiliations*

The national professional organization should welcome the active cooperation of lay groups in measures designed to inform the public on educational matters and to improve educational conditions. In no case should it enter into organic affiliation with any lay organization which has as its primary purpose the promotion of interests outside the field of education.

PROFESSIONAL ORGANIZATION NEEDS

Much of the recent discussion and criticism concerning professional organization results from the feeling that these groups have not been effective during the recent crisis. The critics fail to realize that the effects of the depression on public education resulted from causes beyond the scope and power of any single interest group. The economic debacle was the result of many selfish and short-sighted practices by numerous interest groups owing to lack of both vision and a fully developed sense of social responsibility. International conditions resulting from the World War and post-war national functioning also contributed heavily.

Reasons for Weakness

However, the professional groups have been sick for a long time but for very different reasons. It was not until the depression produced real despair that the dissentients found courage to take action. The causes for weaknesses in professional organization may be summarized briefly as follows: The method of organization, consciously imitative of corporate administrative technique in which the actual control rests with a small directing group and the professional secretariat, is too autocratic to meet the needs of the teaching profession and accounts for the dissatisfaction of the classroom teachers. There is also little real integration between the state and national groups. The development of huge and special interest divisions around either a subject-matter or a technique interest has drained much of the power from both state and national organizations. The attempt to overcome lack of instructional interest by use of "administrative pressure" to secure memberships has developed cumulatively bad feeling.

Existing professional organizations have permitted two codes of ethics to operate: one for the teachers, and the other for administrators. Teachers have been forced to watch rewards follow unethical conduct on the part of administrators without having the profession take a step against it. They have seen intellectual dishonesty rewarded and faithful service penalized. There has been little concerted action to arouse public opinion against injustice to individual teachers or the effects of the venal political alliances of boards of education.

The Guild Plan

The teaching profession needs better and more effective organization. One of the many suggestions for improvement that may have merit is the guild plan. The first characteristic of this type of organization is that teachers, principals, and superintendents all join together equally in their capacity as teachers. The guild spirit is the colleague spirit. It recognizes no higher title or position than that of teacher. All organization differentiation is considered as merely representative of essential specialization to facilitate the supreme function—the instruction of children. This fundamental guild principle states: There is no higher position than that of teacher, and all teachers are essentially in a colleague relationship to each other.

The second characteristic of the guild is that it starts as a primary democratic unit in each school district, self-governing in every respect. It must carry on its business and its constant study of local educational needs in order that the people may be kept completely informed of their schools. As an organized professional group it becomes, along with the parent-teacher group, an extralegal advisor of the local board of education upon problems of professional import. Through local news agencies or its own publications each primary unit has the power and the responsibility to turn constantly the full power of the brilliant white light of publicity on educational deficiencies and questionable practices.

The guild could operate under one code of ethics for all, and this code would grow naturally out of experience as an ethic should, rather than be superimposed from above. The code would be reasonable but strict. It would call for trial and disbarment from membership for proved unethical conduct. Adverse action against an unworthy individual might result in license revocation by the state. The prestige of the organization would be strong enough to force unethical and unscrupulous individuals from employment and would maintain a standard of qualification for membership and for performance that would gain the respect of the general public. Through this means it would be possible to maintain a strong professional discipline.

It would also have the power through close and well-knit organization to protect its members from exploitation by politically minded, interest-subservient, and crooked boards of education. The power that would accrue from the strength of many, operating on a sound ethical basis, would prevent much of the chicanery and peculiar tactics now so prevalent in certain localities. So long as the people felt that the teacher guilds were operating on an unselfish social program, the guild would have popular following.

The organization of the teacher guild offers two definite problems, one in relation to the mechanics of organization and the other to professional (technical) interests. The guild may start with local chapters organized around the primary interest of the members—the school district or the institution. These local chapters in turn will create the state federation or association by electing representatives to a state assembly. The national organization will then become a federation of state associations.

Since public education is organized legally by states, the greatest strength of the teacher guild must be within the local district and the state. There is to-day much greater need for powerful state than national groups in the field of social interpretation. Protection of the teaching personnel must also be accomplished through the state. The national organization is much too remote in terms of organization problems. Organization emphasis may therefore be very properly first laid by building a unified profession around the major immediate professional interest—the school district—and expanding this interest to cover the legal area of functioning.

To meet the technical or professional interests there may be organized special interest or program groups for exchange of experience and general professional improvement regionally or for the state as a whole. In turn these state groups might also be consolidated into national groups. Such groups would include teaching and administration with refinements or specialization within each group to meet all professional requirements. Thus any department could start with regional conferences, organized in turn into state conferences, and finally culminating into the present national conference. This type of coördination would make for more effective professional organization.

The Federation Plan

Another plan now receiving some consideration may be classed as the federation type. The realistic assumption underlying its possibilities is that there are existing certain professional organizations so diverse in their secondary interests as to make it impossible to bring them together under any single plan like that proposed by the guild.

A number of professional interest groups have developed gradually in this country. These include the national and state education associations comprised largely of the public-school teachers, the American Vocational Association, the Progressive Education Association, the several associations of teachers of independent and voluntary schools, the American Association of University Professors, the American Association for the Advancement of Science and other learned associations in the field of higher education, and the American Federation of Teachers, including membership from both public schools and institutions of higher learning. In addition to these major organizations there are numerous small independent groups each organized in terms of its special professional interest.

The realist feels that it is impossible to bring all of these diverse interests into a single guild. He also feels that it may be democratically undesirable to attempt to unite all teachers into a single group because American educational organization tends to become a distinct pressure group, no different in its levels of functioning from any other pressure group. Current practices of certain existing groups give some basis for this fear.

The federation idea has been slowly developing as an alternative plan. This proposal would bring all current professional organizations first into state and then into a national federation under a type of organization that would permit complete freedom of individual action by separate groups and coöperation only in those areas where in the opinion of all of the interests united action was necessary.

Other Plans

Other suggestions indicate the desirability of permitting professional organization to develop as in the past and regard any attempt to bring diverse interests together either in a guild or federated organization as of little merit. There is a genuine feeling among proponents of voluntary independent organization that the possible danger ultimately accruing to the teaching profession through strong organization offsets the possible dangers of continued independent organization.

PROFESSIONAL RESPONSIBILITIES

As members of a profession teachers have a definite responsibility for leadership that requires primary consideration. When acting as individual agents for the state, they are necessarily circumscribed and limited in their actions by popular understanding and the policies of the school district. If organization provides no means through which they may reasonably differ with existing policy, they have the choice of conforming or resigning. In case of either conformance or resignation it should be possible for them to supply essential information of undesirable conditions or unsatisfied institutional needs to the profession itself which may then exercise its responsibility of informing the people directly. The teaching profession cannot remain a quiet and non-objecting spectator to inefficient methods of teaching, through the evil effects of partizan political control or incompetent leadership. The leadership responsibility means that the profession must always be ready to present to the people complete and unbiased information concerning the conditions and needs of their educational institutions.

It is also the prerogative of every interest group to enter the competitive lists with any other interest group to present and seek by ethical means the attainment of those needs which are judged essential to existence and improvement.

The usual means through which competing interest groups express themselves is specialized propaganda and the use of political pressure lobbying technique or legislative lobbying. There is nothing essentially undesirable in the lobby activity. It is merely the exercise of the constitutional right of petition by the people to their representatives in legislature and should be zealously maintained. Group lobbies have succeeded personal lobbies to the same extent that interest groups have replaced the individual. The exercise of the constitutional right of petition may be soundly or poorly expressed by the professional lobby. When functional lobbying degenerates into professional pressure lobbying and maintains its effectiveness through the abuse of political power, threat of personal blackmail, and outright bribery, it cannot be too completely condemned. It is an ever present danger when the careerist enters the field.

The teaching profession must continue to function on high level. Certainly members of the profession may appear before legislative bodies to present their points of view and program, but the greater professional effort may be more successfully expended in the extension of its teaching technique into the field of adult education, creating public opinion through convincing the people of rational educational needs. Because of close relationship of the school to the state, great care must always be taken not to overstep the ethical bounds and create in the minds of the people a feeling that advantage is being taken of institutional position. The teaching profession will remain on safe ground so long as it is willing to coöperate unselfishly with all other interest groups who are working for improvement of the educational process and so long as it operates as a public-opinion-forming group through the dissemination of the complete truth of educational needs devoid of concealment or secret propaganda motive.

DIFFICULTIES IN FUNCTIONING

These statements of possible methods of functioning as a professional guild lead immediately to consideration of the normal difficulties in functioning. The current programs of interest groups are fundamentally propagandistic in concept and practice. The entrance of group interests into the arena of conflict with a program based on unselfishness and the full truth, using the persuasion technique in developing a progressive public opinion, is so novel in itself that it might be some time before a basic popular confidence could be built up. The further spectacle of a group that is willing to place its responsibility to the people above its personal interest would also raise considerable initial doubt. A group supremely confident of its own function and responsibility to stand alone for the long view when apparently immediate results could be secured through mutual alliances with other groups or questionable political entanglements, would certainly be a novelty among interest groups. Yet, unless the teaching profession can develop that breadth of vision and lay its plans accordingly, it will never be possible to realize its full possibilities or to make its full professional contribution to the people of the United States.

In exercising professional responsibility the teacher group must avoid many pitfalls that have ensnared and reduced the power and prestige of other groups. It must develop greater understanding of the democratic process and tolerance of differences in point of view. However desirable changes in structure, objective, and methodology may be, they cannot be achieved overnight. The democratic method is slow and often cumbersome. Changes depend on the full-hearted acceptance of need by the people. Once the people have been convinced and adopt a plan of action, it is reasonably certain that it will be fairly permanent in character. The teaching profession should possess greater understanding of the group mind and the need for constant learning from as well as the presentation of information to the people. Petty grievances or dislikes should never cause professional tactics to include personalities at the expense of program, to employ the whispering technique of reprisal or the boycott of agencies with whom differences of viewpoints may develop. Tactics of this nature are two-edged and impede rather than accelerate the attainment of professional objectives. Tolerance for the views of one's opponents is an essential to democratic functioning.

SUMMARY

The teaching profession has a definite responsibility for the improvement of public education as well as for the protection and improvement of its individual members. It is only to the extent that the teaching profession is willing to accept and carry out this responsibility that the educational function may be progressively improved and adjusted to social ends. As an independent professional group the teachers are definitely entrusted with keeping the people informed of the value, conditions, failures, and needs of their educational institutions. Since the strength of the professional position depends on the degree of confidence that the people have in the sterling disinterestedness of the teachers, the character of professional organization becomes extremely important. The school cannot operate as a classless agency in democratic society unless the teachers are willing to assume and carry out their functional responsibility for remaining impartial agents of the state.

As agents of the state the teachers are confined in their interpretative activities to keeping the people informed of the value and needs of public education through normal and accepted means of communication. They are definitely constrained, however, to working within the confines of the existing pattern and are professionally enjoined from using the schools as a means of advancing their own interests even when these interests may be in harmony with the increase of efficiency within school organization. Only as teachers and administrators perform their official duties in accord with the high tradition of disinterested service already established can they retain the full confidence of the public.

Organized as a guild or as a federation teachers may act in their second relationship as members of other interest groups. As a guild the teaching profession is entitled to present to the people continuously the requirements of public education and their own rational demands for adequate rewards, recognition, security, and freedom in teaching. Acting in a professional capacity, the teaching profession thus transcends the difficulties and possible restrictions of local organization and becomes a dependable extralegal appraisal agency for the people.

As a guild or federation the teaching profession has the responsibility for determining its own standards for membership and for improvement. It must develop a rational ethic as a basis for operation. It must offer protection to its members and at the same time be ready to discipline them for unethical conduct. It must protect both the institution and its members.

The difficulty facing the teacher is attempting to keep overlapping personal, teaching, and professional activities as distinct and clear as possible. The strength of the teaching profession is through the projection of its influence in the extension of the teaching technique to the adult population and the consequent creation of a rational public opinion, understanding conditions and willing to supply the needs of public education.

PART II

EDUCATIONAL POLICIES

Chapter 5

PRINCIPLES OF INTERPRETATION

EDUCATION as a social function is eternal. So long as the race reproduces itself and requires social institutions to expedite smooth achievement of desirable goals, it will be necessary to provide activities whereby each generation is exposed to the accumulated and current experiences of mankind. The educational process is primarily one of social reproduction. In its institutional aspects it parallels the home by operating in the rôle of social parent. Although the function itself is a constant, its institutional expression is highly transitory. There is no particular merit in any specific institutional form except as it serves to promote social need at any time. Hence there are different institutional concepts in different cultures. The philosophy and organization of the German schools differ greatly from those of the United States. Japan and China are moving in different educational directions. Even in our own country there has been considerable change in both organization and extent of education within the past hundred years. There will probably be many more changes within the second century.

The formal institution under which the education of the immature proceeds is not the entire expression of the educational process. It represents only a fraction of institutional and generalized stimuli constantly before both children and adults in their daily lives. The home, the church, the state, the economic and social community life —all play a definite part in the progressive process of individual adjustment to efficient social functioning. The professional educator is prone to place too much stress upon the final importance of a mere fraction of a large process and to pay too much respect to the conventional institutional forms. Closeness to the job produces myopic vision of the entire problem. It is the old case of the forest and the trees.

The orientation of the institutionalized educational process to the entire spread of social activity is necessary to the consideration of generalized principles of institutional interpretation. These problems will be discussed as: (1) definition and goals of social interpretation, (2) principles of institutional interpretation, (3) interpretative programs, and (4) difficulties in interpretation.

DEFINITION AND GOALS OF SOCIAL INTERPRETATION

Since democratic social institutions belong to the people and are means through which the group may more easily achieve its objectives, it is essential that the people be kept intelligently informed of the reasons for institutional existence, the desirable extent of functional limits, the value of operation, and the needs for improvement. Institutional programs arise out of cultural needs and must change as old needs are enlarged or replaced by new ones. Flexibility is an outstanding characteristic of the truly efficient democratic institution.

Definition

The activity of social interpretation arises from a functional institutional demand and is justifiable and essential so long as it remains within functional limitations. From a definitive standpoint *social interpretation may be considered as that activity whereby the institution is made aware of community conditions and needs and the factual informational service whereby the people are kept continuously informed of the purpose, value, conditions, and needs of their educational program.* Its purpose is not selfish, and its motives are not ulterior. It is merely recognition and acceptance of the legal and moral responsibility to render a constant account of stewardship to the community. The actual methods of reporting have changed from simple to highly complex problems to the same extent that the community life has undergone change. Specific activities are highly flexible and subject to quick change, though the nature itself remains a permanent element in the functioning of a democratic institution.

Social interpretation is an all-inclusive activity which includes the two major subdivisions of community and institutional interpretation. In the first category are those activities through which the institution develops understanding of community conditions and needs, whereas the second is concerned with that group of activities by which the people are made aware of institutional conditions and needs. The two aspects are complementary and integrative in nature.

Definitive Differences

Carrying the definitive idea a step farther, any contacts between an institution and the people may be considered as public or institutional relations. In a functional sense the term *public relations* describes a condition more accurately than it does a program. It is neither sufficiently broad nor descriptive to designate the activity which has for a fundamental objective the translation of the community to the educational institution and the translation of the educational institution to the community. Though it served well in the developmental stages, its continued use should be restricted to its descriptive concept.

In like manner publicity considered functionally is only one activity aspect of the total program and should be restricted narrowly to materials which appear in public print, in motion or talking picture, or are transmitted over the radio.

The terms *public relations* and *publicity* are unfortunately used interchangeably by educators. They are not synonymous.

The proper use of descriptive terminology in this field should be carefully observed because of the reflective value in popular connotation. Thus publicity, even if it were completely adequate, has been so misused by professional specialists that it has a sadly negative meaning both to the newspaper man and to a large portion of the public. The commercial exploitation of public relations by professional counselors employed by individuals and corporations to direct their propaganda programs has made this term synonymous with propaganda. Stage and radio have further caricatured it beyond institutional value.

As a functional concept social interpretation offers not only a description for a field of activity but also implies directly an institutional philosophy respecting community and institutional responsibilities. It is entirely free from connotations that are functionally untenable.

Social interpretation and propaganda are at opposite poles. Social interpretation is recognition and satisfaction of institutional responsibility for locating, defining, and crystallizing unexpressed and undefined social feelings, desires, and wills. It seeks clarification and definiteness in expression of the social will through methods of democratic education which include presentation of all known facts and complete freedom of discussion of these facts by the people. Propaganda seeks to attain its special objectives without reference to the social will. Thus, although it is possible that the objectives of social interpretation and propaganda may be the same in certain instances, the methodologies of achievement are completely different.

The sources of information used by the schools are public records and may be easily inspected. The directors and participants in the activity are always known. Whether board member or superintendent, teacher, clerical worker, or custodial agent, the professional man's past and present, his background and relationships, are available to public view and inspection. The methods of interpretation are the methods of teaching and may be kept completely in the open. The purpose of the activity is social, and change is expected through the formation of public opinion based on free and open discussion which may terminate in conviction. If these conditions are maintained, there is no need for confusing social interpretation with propaganda.

Objectives

The interpretative activity has definite objectives which may be considered as ultimate and immediate. The ultimate objective is to develop continuing public consciousness of the importance of the educational process in a democratic social organization, to establish confidence in the functioning institution, to furnish adequate means to maintain its efficient operation, and to improve the partnership concept through active parental participation. The immediate objective at any specific time might be the enlistment of parental or community support in some health measure such as education in safe living, improvement of physical facilities, specific extension of an educational policy, or innumerable other desires. The long time objective should always be kept in mind and current objectives coordinated and fitted to the ultimate purpose.

PRINCIPLES OF INSTITUTIONAL INTERPRETATION

The relationship of the democratic school to the social order, the nature of the democratic process, and the responsibility of the teaching profession make it possible to set forth certain principles and guides in the formulation of policy and the preparation of detailed plans. These principles may also be used as criteria against which the worth of the proposed program may be judged. They include the following:

1. Democratic social institutions are merely facilitating means for the achievement of a social purpose and have no fundamental value apart from purpose.
2. The educational function is constant, but its institutional organization must be considered as a purely transitory expression of the function.
3. Democratic social institutions rest on public confidence which depends ultimately upon the honesty and sincerity of institutional functioning. The democratic public school is limited in its institutional effectiveness and breadth of program by the confidence and understanding of the people and cannot rise far above the popular concept and understanding of function. Informational material must be adjusted to the interest and intelligence of a culturally complex adult audience.
4. The public school as an impartial democratic agency operates on the central tendency in public opinion and will always be subject to criticism by reactionary and radical opinion.
5. The theory of democratic institutional authority definitely limits both purpose and method of interpretation and considers the enlargement or contraction of institutional activity to be a function of the people. The interests of all of the people are superior to the interests of the teaching profession.
6. The public school acts as an institution for harmonizing cultural differences and must avoid the creation of social conflict. Institutional interpretation must avoid all implications of a propagandistic

motif. Institutional interpretation must be based on the larger objectives of public education and be truthful, sincere, and simple.
7. The partnership concept of public education in the United States requires the active interest and intelligent participation of parents in the educational program.
8. Institutional interpretation is a process of adult education to the purpose, value, conditions, and needs of public education. Interpretative methodology demands the application of the laws of learning to adult education and information that is constant and regular in character.
9. The process of social interpretation is coöperative in nature, and its success is contingent on the active and intelligent participation of every institutional agent and can be ultimately effective only to the extent that all participating agents conceive of their functional responsibility for participation in a functional activity.
10. The legal responsibility for determination of interpretative policy and the approval of means for making policy effective is a function of the educational legislative body—the board of education.
11. The use of children in the interpretative program is limited to the development of understanding and appreciation of the purpose and value of all social institutions.
12. The teaching profession as an interest group may make normal attempts, in accord with sound democratic practice, beyond institutional limits to convert other individuals and other interest groups to the support of normal institutional enlargement and betterment or their own personal interests.

INTERPRETATIVE PROGRAMS

The purpose of a program is to secure ultimately a definitely crystallized public opinion on a specific problem. The first step in the program is the providing of information through which, second, appeal is made to the adult. Discussion follows as a third step, and finally there grows out of these three steps the resolve or will to approve or to do. To be successful every program must be easily understood, satisfying in emotional audience appeal, with repetition at frequent intervals and reaching every community group. Competition of other groups and agencies for popular attention makes it necessary to point the program to an emotional value close to individual interest or the child. Recognition of child need is distinctly a feature of democratic organization. Expressed in another way, it is provision for the nurture and protection of the immature so that they may grow into strong and well-integrated personalities, each capable of exercising his civil responsibilities. The program appeal must be emotional in so far as it creates definite interest, but sloppy sentimentality and pathological super-emotionalism must be ruled out immediately. It is possible to present factual information so that it is interesting and emotionally satisfying. It is possible to emphasize child needs without tears or sobs. Both institutional and professional appeal must have common-sense values for the normal individual.

Objectives the Base

The objectives of public education must form the base of any well-conceived long-time program of interpretation. The objectives arise from cultural need and are not necessarily the sole responsibility of the teaching profession. As a professional interest group the teachers may and should participate in the process of interpreting the popular will as expressed in statutory enactment refined and interpreted through judicial review in coöperation with other social groups and, when necessary, to reinterpret these crystallized objectives in the light of changing social conditions. Fundamental educational objectives will probably vary little within the limits of a generation, but the same attitude of flexibility and cold appraisal must be applied to them as to the more mechanical institutional practices.

Since the public school cannot rise above the social concept of function, it is essential that the broad program make every provision for constant presentation of major objectives. The question may be asked whether it is possible so to organize these objectives that they may have popular acceptance. The coöperative experiment of the State of Michigan in 1934 furnishes a good illustration.[1] The state leaders in agriculture, industry, finance, labor, education, and women's interests were brought together in a popular planning group. Out of this group effort came a state-wide program, the first phase of which crystallized the goals of public education in Michi-

[1] See also Chapter 19.

gan. These goals are presented here as illustrative of possibilities since they represent a terminal product of lay group planning. They include the following nine aims:[2]

The Goals of Public Education in Michigan

In order to preserve and improve our democratic civilization, and to provide educational advantages for all, in accordance with the American principle of equality of opportunity, the state of Michigan has the right and the obligation to provide a system of public education at public expense. In such a system it should be the aim to seek to achieve the following nine goals at the appropriate levels of the public school system —elementary, secondary, and higher.

One. To cultivate a deep regard for democracy and an intelligent appreciation of democratic institutions

This goal implies that effective democratic institutions constitute the best means for insuring justice and liberty; for maintaining the equality of political, social, and economic opportunities; for fostering growth and progress; and for furthering truth and honesty.

Two. To develop those qualities of character which are of special significance in a democracy

This goal implies that citizens in a democracy must possess certain qualities of character that are not required in other forms of society. The preparation requires the development of a personality that will find expression in responsible self-direction, self-control, and self-appraisal in both individual and cooperative endeavor. This goal implies emphasis (*a*) on understanding and appreciation instead of blind obedience; (*b*) on fair and honest dealings instead of exploitation; (*c*) on investigation instead of thoughtless acceptance; (*d*) on openmindedness instead of prejudice; and (*e*) on the promotion of the common good instead of selfish advancement of the individual.

Three. To develop the willingness and the ability to cooperate effectively in a democratic society

Democracy succeeds in proportion to the capacity of the people to solve their problems through voluntary self-directed cooperation. This goal requires a system of education, in organization, materials, and method of instruction, which will provide in the school an environment that will most nearly approximate an ideal democratic society. In such a school pupils and students may participate actively in the life of the school, molding it to their needs and aspirations and adjusting themselves to it.

---

[2] *The Goals of Public Education in Michigan,* as adopted by the Michigan Educational Planning Commission, Lansing, Michigan, June, 1934.

Four. To develop the ability to use the most effective and reliable methods in searching for truth as a basis for the discovery and solution of problems

In a democracy, new generations should be prepared to discover new truths and to revise their practices accordingly. The training proposed in this goal will furnish necessary preparation for the cooperative discovery and solution of the problems created by the complexity and interdependence of our social, political, and economic relationships. It will also increase the power of citizens to cooperate successfully in creating the best conditions of living for all.

Five. To develop the effective use of the fundamental knowledge and skills required by all

This goal demands effective training in the arts of reading, writing, spelling, language, and arithmetic. Such arts are essential tools of common understanding and communication.

Six. To insure an abundant social and individual life in accordance with each individual's capacity and ambition

This goal involves provision for proper and adequate training in problems of health, in desirable home membership, and in the worthy and constructive use of leisure time. It also calls for the general and specific vocational training required for economic sufficiency.

Seven. To provide training in the specialized and professional services which are requisite for society

Society must have the services of persons specially equipped in the preservation and further development of the knowledge, skills, and techniques vital to the advancement of society as a whole. This goal recognizes that the valuable and useful accumulation described as "the social inheritance" must be preserved and transmitted from generation to generation. Through research and experimentation this inheritance should be increased.

Eight. To provide for the enrichment of adult life

This goal is receiving attention because our increased leisure demands provision for continued education for adults, and the changing social and economic conditions require the provision for retraining for both the vocational and avocational aspects of life.

Nine. To plan for the continuous appraisal and readjustment of the educational program to fit changing conditions

When scientific discoveries and inventions force us to set aside old ways of living, the schools should provide new activities which give definite practice in making adjustments to new situations in order that society may be modified through the process of orderly change rather than through revolution. This goal is important in a democracy because social and economic conditions change and education must also change accordingly in order to make its contribution at each stage of social progress.

Within these objectives lies the entire program of interpretation. Complete popular familiarity with their implications and acceptance of their normal projection into action would provide a broad and potentially capable institution. However, the final instructional efficiency will be determined by the character, motivation, and skill of participating executive agents. That is not the province of the people.

Detailed consideration of program variation for the board of education, the teaching profession, the child, the parent, and the community will be considered in later and more specialized chapters devoted to specific group interests.

Program Activities

The continuing community survey offers a means for appraising community conditions and needs; analysis of the instructional program will permit the school to determine how well it is responding to them; plans for the progressive improvement of the schools may be projected, developed, and presented to the people for discussion and consideration. This process of surveying, appraising, planning, and interpreting is a constant cycle. The means through which the people may become conscious of these needs are the numerous interpretative activities.

Classification of program activities must be more or less arbitrary. Except for ease in consideration such organization is of relatively little value. The nature of the work performed is such that many phases could easily fall into several categories. The major program activities may be considered in five divisions: (*a*) individual contacts, (*b*) group contacts, (*c*) direct publicity, (*d*) parent education, and (*e*) adult education.

Individual contacts include those between teacher and child, teacher and parent, teacher and community organization, and intra-institutional relationships. They comprise the largest program unit and are both beginning and end. Institutional relations start with individual contacts and proceed through group contacts back to the individual in an attempt to develop and improve the partnership concept in American education and to focus more attention on institutional provision for individual difference.

Group contacts include relationships between the institution as a totality and various types and classifications of organized interests. From the institutional aspect they include all school programs and gatherings in which adult audiences participate, ranging from athletic contests to commencements. In their social aspect they include all institutional relationships with organized adult groups within and without the school.

Direct publicity may include those activities which are concerned with oral or written publication including the press, school reports, house organs, special bulletins, lectures, and visual presentation.

Parent education is primarily the organization of adult groups for the mutual study of child problems and self-improvement through specific training for parental duties. It may be carried on within the institution in a formal organized way or may be stimulated and directed within lay organization such as the child study groups of the American Association of University Women. It is a vital but relatively unexplored field.

Adult education forms the fifth category. This activity may be either institutional or extra-institutional. It includes all of those formal and informal activities through which the adult is made conscious of socio-civic responsibilities and problems and is given opportunity to hear presentation and discussion. Opportunity for the development of self-expression through the cultivation of leisure-time interests is primarily an institutional activity that has received wide stimulus in recent years.

Program Methods

Methods of organizing and presenting programs should follow the principles of the laws of learning. Material must be adapted to audience intelligence and interest, starting with the familiar and proceeding to the unfamiliar. Material may be coördinated purposively to capacity and interest. There should be definite provision for repetition. In general the development of method in interpretative programs should follow the same principles and practices that accompany curriculum construction. In many senses the program of interpretation is merely a curriculum for adult education, characterized by much more flexibility than is true of the child curriculum. It should be designed in units of learning rather than time-credit units.

A great difficulty in this field is that the teaching profession as yet knows little about adult learning. It is handicapped by the formal academic set of "telling" instead of teaching, a prevalent weakness of both elementary and secondary schools. The autocratic organization of the classroom tends to develop in the typical teacher a pontifical attitude of superiority and complacency that is definitely handicapping in child education and fatal in the adult field. The adult curriculum must be designed in the spirit of equality of personality where a group is attempting understanding and finally coöperation through presentation of information, discussion, and interchange of experience. The interpretative program must be specifically adjusted to varying community differences and needs. It is undesirable even to suggest a standardized pattern.

DIFFICULTIES IN INTERPRETATION

There are numerous difficulties that arise in institutional interpretation. The definite spread of area affects both type and size of audience. Our culture is a composite and includes many diverse racial and cultural groups. The range of educational community levels or intellectual capacity and the time limitation that operates both on the institution and the individual are great. Competing interest groups vie for individual and group attention. Then, too, the school problems themselves are complex. The goals as understood by a large portion of the profession are vague. It is difficult to demonstrate absolute tangibility of results despite the positive efforts of certain individuals to prove the dollars-and-cents value of education even down to the fine point of a week of schooling. Programs of expediency outnumbered by far long-range planning. "Activity" is frequently confused with and substituted for intelligent practice. The apparent indifference of large sections of the public press to anything except "sex, money, and crime" news concepts is not helpful in the large communities. Political pressure against the school to maintain or secure control for patronage purposes has caused either professional subservience or timidity. The public has been exposed to so much group and institutional propaganda that it is difficult to remove their normal suspicion that all interpretative effort is simply propaganda. The weakness of the teaching profession's organization in acceptance of the professional responsibility for institutional improvement and the great indifference of the typical teacher to the entire activity encompass some of the difficulties.

The greatest weakness appears to be within the teaching profession itself. The autocracy of the academic tradition, both in teaching and in administration, interferes to an appreciable extent with the normal operation of democratic teaching. If some of the difficulties earlier considered could be eradicated, the community problems might be slowly but successfully overcome.

SUMMARY

The constancy of the educational function is paralleled by the temporal nature of institutional form and practice. The institutional need is to remain dynamic and flexible. This condition may be achieved through the development of understanding and through the two-phase activity of social interpretation—understanding of the community by the institution and understanding of the institution by the community. Social interpretation is all inclusive and carries within it the phase of public relations and the activity of publicity. The principles governing the operation of social institutions within the democratic pattern apply directly to the basis for educational interpretation. The basis of interpretation is naturally the crystallized expression of institutional objectives. These objectives arise out of cultural need, and in their formulation the teaching profession plays a part. The methods of social interpretation are the extension of the laws of learning to adult education, and the process is just as critical and continuous as curriculum planning and development in the formal educational process. Numerous difficulties present obstacles to the perfect easy expression of the interpretative activity. The most serious is that furnished by the teaching profession itself. Overcoming the professional obstacles is the immediate task confronting the institution.

Chapter 6

FUNDAMENTAL POLICIES

SO far this discussion has been concerned with a brief survey of the public school functioning as a dynamic social institution in a democratic society, the nature of the democratic process, the operation of pressure groups, the teaching profession's responsibility for the interpretative process, and the general principles involved in social interpretation. It is now possible to proceed to a consideration of the technical aspects of the process as operating within the institution and the community.

This chapter will consider the several aspects of policy development as a basic planning need. Institutional planning starts with legal authority sanctioning the gathering, interpretation and use of essential information. This authorization may be defined as a policy.

Since education is a function of the state, the officers in charge of the administration of the schools in local districts are at once state as well as local officers. The state exercises authority in planning the program in accordance with social need and in appraising the administration of the plan by the local district. It is also inherently responsible for high leadership and stimulation of local effort.

The beginning of a broad policy for social interpretation is therefore a state responsibility. The state authority must first recognize the need for interpretation of the existing institution and then provide, either by administrative ruling or through recommended legislation, for general authority to engage in activities of this nature. Every state already has legal authority for reporting directly to the people on either a mandatory or permissive basis. Statutes concerned with the publication of board of education journals, financial reports, budgets, competitive contracts, and more extended written reports to the people have been in existence for many years. However, the existing state legal policies with respect to interpretation are highly conventional in type and still retain many of the characteristics of earlier need, when the institutional character was much simpler. They are of the pioneer type.

Since in many states there is considerable legal doubt as to the validity of much interpretative activity and considerable confusion with respect to the limits of authority, the first general step in planning appears to be the inauguration of a specific state policy upon which local policy can safely rest.

Comparatively little attention has been given by state educational authority to amendments and enlargement to bring these earlier reporting policies up to date. Even during the depression, while state authority increased somewhat its own area of activity in the field of interpretation, little was accomplished in changing the fundamental power to act. State authority in general has also done very little to encourage the formation of policies within the local districts. It has therefore been easy for extralegal agencies to step in with propaganda programs. Where the states did develop and use lay advisory groups, there was a tendency to use them as devices for immediate and fractional action.

However, the failure of the state to perform its duty in this respect need not interfere fundamentally with the implied powers already possessed by local district authority. The power to execute the educational program has been legally delegated to the district. The detailed interpretative activity must therefore take place within the local district. The state's responsibility will be more general in character and more restricted in type.

Specific emphasis will therefore be given in this chapter to the question of local policy through which orderly interpretative activity may be carried on. Policy-making will be considered from the following aspects: (1) the nature of a policy, (2) method of policy development, (3) types of policies, and (4) current difficulties.

NATURE OF A POLICY

An educational policy is a legal definitive plan of action in which general purpose, objectives, authority, and means are stated. Policies may be customary or written. The customary or unwritten policy is now most generally in use, but this type has so many obvious weaknesses that it need not receive detailed consideration here. This discussion will be limited to the written policy.

A policy is the legal plan, in terms of its orientation into the structure, through which public education operates. The will to have education rests in the traditions and customs of the people supplemented by constitutional mandate, statute enactments and judicial interpretation. Within the limits of the legal pattern the authority to operate the schools rests definitely with the local board of education. By its authority the mandatory state requirements are definitely carried out. It makes selection of permissive legislation either directly or with majority approval of the school community electorate. It also has in many instances the power to carry on experimental activity not contemplated even in broad permissive legislation.

The approval of the board of education in regular meeting assembled is legally essential to the carrying on of general educational activity. The board is the state's instrument for consideration and approval of all save the minimum program which is carried automatically through the mandatory laws. Any plan for studying or solving a problem must first of all be given official approval by the board of education before it possesses any assumption of legality.

As a legally definitive plan a policy should include in its first expression a succinct statement of purpose. Totality of general purpose may be considered in two phases. The board of education has a legal and moral duty to keep the people thoroughly informed of institutional needs and on the other hand to keep the schools thoroughly informed of the needs and problems of the community.

A policy should also possess a clear definition which determines the limits of the activity under consideration. In the case of social interpretation a recommended definition is that activity which seeks to keep the community fully informed of the purpose, value, conditions, and needs of public education.

A policy should always contain a general statement of means of achievement so that it may be easily possible for any one interested to appraise their desirability. It is a protection against charges of propaganda. Methods and agencies may be considered although that is not always essential. So long as the possible avenues through which purpose is to be achieved are made obvious, one might consider the criterion satisfied.

Objectives are frequently only implied in our educational policies. They may also be ascertained occasionally by piecing together certain different policies. A general objective should be considered in each policy, stating clearly the goal toward which purpose and method tend. The objective of an interpretation policy might be the education of the people to the point of consciousness so that a dynamic public opinion would be operating constantly with respect to the purpose, value, conditions, and needs of their schools.

There should be definite evidence of the real authority on which policy enactments are made. If the policy is part of a general code of policies and procedures, authority may be given at once. If the policy is considered separately and independently of other existing or contemplated policy, special reference to legal authority is desirable.

An illustration of a generalized social interpretation policy is reproduced here:

Suggested Social Interpretation Policy

Since the successful operation of a democratic educational institution depends upon the coöperation and participation of the people in its functioning, and since the ability to coöperate depends upon the confidence in and the understanding of the purpose and value of the institution, the Board of Education of Idealia shall consider it both a legal and a moral obligation to interpret the schools to the people.

The Board of Education shall consider that the limits of legal and moral responsibility have been reached when it presents continuously information concerning the conditions and needs of the schools together with recommendations for improvement. Final approval and support must be furnished by the people.

FUNDAMENTAL POLICIES

Social interpretation shall be considered as that activity through which the people are fully and completely informed of the purpose, value, conditions, and needs of public education.

The Board of Education recognizes fully that the problem of continuing interpretation is twofold. The community and its needs must be interpreted to the schools, and the schools must be interpreted to the people.

Although the Board of Education recognizes its fundamental responsibility for the act of interpretation, it also considers the problem so involved, intricate, and technical, that much of the specific operation of the activity must be delegated to those professional agents who, as a totality, are responsible for the actual execution of the educational program.

It shall be the policy of the Board of Education to provide for full information to all of the people through: (1) complete factual information, (2) frequency of contact, (3) continuity of information, and (4) adjustment to the various levels of understanding essential to any community.

The ultimate objective shall be the development of complete understanding by the people of the conditions and needs of the schools to provide for their intelligent support so that public education may ever serve the needs of democracy more effectively.

Authority is hereby delegated to the superintendent of schools to develop means of procedure whereby this policy may be made effective.

Publicity

Since a policy adopted by a board of education is a public policy, it should be given full publicity both in its consideration and discussion and through official promulgation after adoption. The people and the executive personnel are all entitled to know exactly what the policies of the board of education are. Any policy considered in secret, thereafter kept under cover for emergency purposes, is of little value and possesses many dangerous elements. Such practice is pernicious and should be completely discouraged.

METHOD OF POLICY DEVELOPMENT

There are seven steps in the orderly development of a policy which deserve sequential treatment. These include: (*a*) statement of need, (*b*) authority to determine facts, (*c*) interpretation and presentation,

(d) education of the board of education, (e) discussion and deliberation, (f) legal approval, and (g) authority to develop means.

Statement of Need

Though the power to adopt policies and to provide means for making them effective rests legally with the board of education, the leadership responsibility for the determination of need and the development of the plan to be used in policy formulation is the distinct responsibility of the professional executive or, more specifically at the present time, the superintendent of schools. Need may be determined autocratically or democratically. The superintendent may start with a mere "hunch" or feeling or may have at his disposal unusually complete information. The general information developed for the board of education at this step should have for its sole purpose the securing of recognition of the problem by the legislative body and a resulting willingness to study it more intensively. Since no action is required, the presentation can be most informal and generalized. Since time is required in policy development, presentation of need may be considered as only a first step in the general process of educating the board.

Authority to Study

Recognition of need by the legislative body should result in authorizing the executive to determine the facts through the survey method. The activity in this instance is the social survey of the community, essential as a base for the organization of the interpretative program.

Interpretation and Presentation

Interpretation of facts gathered by the executive personnel concerning the community and the schools in summary form, indicating conditions and problems, will represent the third developmental step. This need must be interpreted by the executive and presented to the board of education in a series of generalized statements for consideration and discussion. Since the ultimate policy should represent a long-time plan, it is highly desirable that the tentative plan present only generalized objectives. Details may be cared for in supplementary data and discussion. Policy should be reasonably constant for a long period of time. It is desirable that this material be presented without any time limitation for action. It is merely the second contact, from a slightly different approach, with the possible need for doing something in the future.

Education of the Board

The fourth step is the education of the board members, as individuals and as a whole, with respect to the existing need. In this phase of development the detailed data derived from the sociological survey will be of unusual value. It will enable the executive to point out to board members what community attitudes towards the public schools are and some of the difficulties involved in the development of better understanding and coöperation between home and school. Many prejudices and doubts on the part of board members must be erased; traditional concepts of school and community relationships must be overcome. Both the too frequent pontifical attitude of the teaching profession and the conventional highly emotionalized appraisals by the community need definite modification. The success of policy development depends on the skill with which the executive carries out this phase of the program.

During the process of education the board members will engage in discussion and deliberation. It is highly desirable that the period of education and of discussion run simultaneously. The best procedure is consideration of the program in committee of the whole where full and free discussion is possible without commitment. Time is a vital element. The executive must have patience, not hurrying the decision and not expecting immediate action. The time element will vary directly with the type of board and the skill with which the members are being informed concerning the need for action. It may take only a few weeks, or it may require several months before action is possible. It is highly desirable to secure unanimous support to a proposed policy and to wait until this is possible rather than to have only partial support by forcing the issue too rapidly. Unless policy is unanimously adopted, there is too much danger in carrying on subsequent activity, and the popular mind will be disturbed by the apparent division of opinion on the board of education.

Legal Approval

When the stage has been reached where all members feel the need for a policy covering the problem, the individual members of the board of education will be ready, without outside pressure, to take action and to adopt a policy at the same time instructing the superintendent to formulate means of procedure for consideration and approval.

Developing Procedures

Major emphasis has been purposely laid on the technique of developing a public-relations policy. After the board of education has adopted a policy, the superintendent will be directed to prepare essential procedures. These represent the technical plans whereby the general and specific objectives are to be achieved. They should be experimentally developed and custom-built for each community. It is desirable that representatives of all groups of agents involved in the program take part in its development. The coöperative method of building is by far the most effective not only in experimentation and development, but also as a means of training the key agents who will later participate in the activity.

TYPES OF POLICIES

The purpose of establishing a policy is to secure legal approval for carrying out plans and programs. The terminal outcome should be understanding, appreciation, interest, and intelligent participation in the educational process by parents of children and other adult members of the school community. All of these outcomes are conditioned by the degree of institutional confidence which both policy and program are capable of creating. As a result, the types of policy selected are of great importance.

Periodic Information

The first major choice is between periodic or high-pressure activity or a continuous campaign of community education. High-pressure campaigns had their inception in war time. This method is also extensively used in many industrial and commercial selling plans. It is still almost universally used in community money-getting activity in the field of social work such as community fund drives. In the past, high-pressure campaigns have been most frequently used in the presentation of school-plant programs. Sometimes high-pressure campaigns to present the school-plant program are conceived, directed, and operated directly by the superintendent and staff. More recently professional direction, operating either under the direction of the architect or under professional campaigners who make the collection of funds their specialty, has been appearing in the public-school field. This method has also been popular in securing general financial support.

The high-pressure or periodic method is based on the ability to arouse a conscious public opinion through an emotional appeal. Public sympathy is created through the exploitation of the needs of the child or the teacher, generally in a manner all out of proportion to the actual situation. It usually represents an attempt to overcome at one stroke ten years' neglect in planning. It presents a catch-up program as an overwhelming need that has just been magically discovered. It seeks to cover all previous errors of commission and omission by a highly colored presentation. It has a specific objective. Its success depends on skilful timing and planning the vote at the psychological moment when a fever pitch has been established and before the opposition can get organized. A miscalculation of a week and, in some cases, even days in timing may result negatively for the program. As a rule, the greater the emotional intensity of the campaign, the greater the subsequent reaction on the part of the conservative element. Many an executive has discovered to his intense sorrow that "go-getter" qualities are not valued so highly by the board of education and community after the final reckoning is made as during the progress of a campaign.

The selection of high-pressure means in social interpretation is to be condemned because it is unfair to the people and unsafe for the executive and board of education, decreases confidence as a result of post-campaign reaction, results in much exaggeration during the heat of the campaign, furnishes a rallying point for reactionary elements in the community, and does not provide for the intelligent education of the people.

The evils of propaganda are always present in emotional presentation no matter how careful the safeguards. It is generally expensive because of the different printed and visual devices essential to the creation of interest. Since it is confined to very specific objectives, the larger goals of the normal interpretative process are very frequently lost sight of. It upsets the school, tires the personnel through excessive time demands, lowers the instructional efficiency, and in reaction, tends to lower the general morale of the functioning institution. Its use to-day generally shows a lack of careful planning.

Continuous Information

The second policy choice is for a continuous program of community education to the purpose, value, conditions, and needs of public education. It presupposes that the problem of developing a healthy public opinion toward public education is relatively no different from the process of educating the children. The intelligent support of the community must be developed through understanding and appreciation based on confidence. The best way to establish such confidence is through constant contacts between parent and teacher, community and school. The adult cannot be hurried in this developmental process. Again, time is a very vital factor. Facts may be presented, problems considered, and conditions revealed, but until the parent has digested and has developed understanding through constantly recurring contacts, it is very difficult to secure intelligent support. The school program must be made meaningful to the adult not only in terms of general social needs, which may be more or less academic and far removed from the general understanding of the average individual, but more particularly through the values accruing to their children who are progressing through the schools. Five and even ten years of continuous education may be necessary before a fairly complete community opinion is fully established. The length of time will vary with the type of community and its traditional set. Though it requires much more painstaking effort and less show than the high-pressure type, ultimately much more lasting results will be secured from the program of continuous education.

The finally effective social-interpretation policy is one which will reach all of the people all of the time, and will have developed so completely with respect to information that both understanding and appreciation accrue. Every effort must be made to eliminate the propaganda motive and the advancement of selfish individual or group professional interests. Institutional and child welfare must be paramount.

Policy Method

The second selection under policy represents similar choices for either of these two basic plans, including the cover-up, the partial-fact, the unorganized-fact, and the organized-fact policy.

The cover-up policy is one under which all facts, except the bare minimum required by law, are either completely suppressed or toned down to imperceptibility.

Since the suppression of essential facts requires a special mode of presentation, the cover-up policy leads quickly to emotionalism and "uplift." With the selection of facts generally delegated to the executive, it is perfectly natural that this type of policy soon degenerates into publicity of a propagandistic nature. If for a period of time an institution tells only that which it considers worthy and superior, there is no valid basis for rational judgment by the people. It is also the normal habit of the individual who looks only "for the good" that the protective coloring of personal partiality will enter and cloud professional judgment. The school is not a perfect institution and should not be presented to the people as such. It can be kept much more human and close to the understanding of the people if the low as well as the high spots are given consideration.

The cover-up policy is most frequently employed in conjunction with high-pressure campaigns. It has been possible to achieve considerable immediate success by the employment of this method of deliberately concealing vital and pertinent facts and meeting all opposition on a subjective and emotional basis. However, the final price has been high, as many superintendents and school-board members have discovered to their personal discomfiture.

Partial-Fact Policy

The practice of using "selected facts and information" is a second type of policy that has for its purpose the presentation of the school as a social institution in its most favorable light. It may be essentially honest in concept, but seldom remains so in practice. The reason is obvious. No person can over a long period of time be entrusted with the selection of certain facts and the suppression of certain others, especially where personal promotion or safety is involved. At its best it represents a judgment of what the executive or board of education considers "good" for the public to know. At its worst it is personal propaganda of the most selfish type for superintendent and school-board member.

The operation of this policy gradually extends itself to all phases of the school sytem. Superintendents are frequently tempted and quite frequently succumb to the temptation to withhold information from the board of education. Principals and teachers, also seeking to protect themselves, withhold information from the superintendent in a like manner. The terminal result is a vicious circle of partial information and decreasing popular confidence.

The most frequent excuse for the selection of either of these policies is that the educational process is much too technical for the people to understand. If this is true, it is unfortunate. In all probability it is merely the inability or lack of desire on the part of the professional in education to attempt the difficult process of making a highly technical process intelligible to the lay mind. Educational aims and practices can be made intelligible, but the job requires painstaking effort and much experimentation.

Unorganized-Fact Policy

Many who have no faith in either of the foregoing policies go to the other extreme and favor the complete presentation of all facts without regard for organization. The best that can be said concerning this policy is the complete honesty of motive. However, it must be understood that a democratic society includes many diverse elements. Its outstanding characteristics are diversity of points of view and strong emotional sets. The educational process is highly intricate and complicated, possessing certain technical aspects not easily comprehended by the lay mind. The broadcast method of dissemination of all information may have disastrous results in so far as isolated items may furnish means for reducing rather than advancing the increasing effectiveness of the institution. Although tenable in theory, by assuming a rather high understanding and capacity on the part of all of the people, it must be considered of dubious validity in practice.

Organized-Fact Policy

The board of education has a legal and moral responsibility for institutional interpretation to the people. It should tell the complete truth in so far as it is possible to ascertain it, but this truth must be organized so that intelligent interpretation is possible. The collecting of facts and their interpretation is essentially the responsibility of the professional specialist. Since all of the facts are presented, questioning and curious individuals can ascertain for themselves whether the interpretation is valid. No attempt is made to hide anything. While it is true that the same set of facts may be interpreted differently by any one who has the desire and capacity for doing so, the ability to analyze and check upon an official interpretation is limited to a relatively small minority. This fact does not invalidate the principle involved.

It is extremely difficult for practices under this policy to degenerate into propaganda. Since conflicts of opinion with respect to conclusions may be harmonized objectively in terms of the basic facts, unjustifiable interpretation by board of education or educational specialist can be too quickly controverted by examination of data to make the risk profitable.

Desirable Policy

In the final analysis all public as well as private activity rests on the basis of *confidence*. Into public activity enter also the legal and social responsibilities of the people's representatives. The selection of policy method, which will operate over a long period, should be considered in these terms. In some instances, particularly when high-pressure methods are used, it has been possible to achieve immediate success by using the cover-up method and deliberately concealing vital facts and meeting questions on a subjective and emotional basis. The final price, however, has been high. In other instances it has been possible to achieve immediate progress through the partial presentation of some facts and the deliberate concealment of other facts. So far as the layman is concerned the use of completely unorganized facts leads to confusion and doubt because of his inability to understand and interpret statistical data. The last policy, that of organized factual presentation, satisfies both legal and moral requirements and, over a period of time, will probably produce the most satisfactory results.

If the adoption of the fourth procedure is new to any community, it may require considerable time and some personal hardships until it is accepted. Once community confidence has been established, the result will be well worth the effort.

The adoption of the policy of organized factual presentation is conditioned by the vision of the individuals involved. Generally speaking the tenure of superintendents in any given district is usually so brief that they can afford to give little attention to long-time planning. They are most immediately concerned with pressing current problems. The future success of school administration and the progressive building of socially more efficient school systems is contingent on the vision displayed in planning for the future on a broad and effective foundation. If we are considering the immediate situation of a given superintendent, emergency conditions may point to the acceptance of an emergency policy. On the other hand, if the ultimate welfare of the public-education program is accented, then the choice of informational policies narrows to the fourth—the presentation of all of the facts carefully organized.

CURRENT DIFFICULTIES

There are many difficulties in the way of policy development. These arise from lack of thorough understanding of the nature of a democratic social organization with particular reference to public education and a peculiar concept of the superintendency. Some of the difficulties are psychological, and others arise from lack of professional efficiency. The average executive does not appear to realize the value of written policies as a protective shield against emotional reactions within a community. The typical board member, without the essential education that intelligent professional leadership constantly furnishes, tends normally to follow the traditional political practice of not placing himself on record.

The average board of education is not able, without good directive leadership, to understand the complexities of the work it is supposed to do for the people nor the actual limitations of lay direction. Unless this leadership is furnished by the professional executive and advisor of the board, it is difficult to see where the board can get it. It is not reasonable to condemn boards of education out of hand for social inefficiency but rather to examine the reasons for the deficiencies in professional leadership and the apparent failure of the professional to meet squarely the responsibilities which training and position credit to him.

The typical executive is extremely shy of written policies. He prefers to operate on a hand-to-mouth basis or in terms of opportunism. Neither certain of himself nor his assumptions of program, he desires above all personal protection. To him a written policy is like a leash to a dog. It constricts his field of activity and cramps his range of action. He therefore prefers the *laissez-faire* method of operation, constantly ready to father another line if immediate social approval lies in that direction.

Current difficulties in the path of constructive educational policy development, such as professional inertia and lack of vision, the expression of expediency in an effort to prevent specific commitment, the low level of institutional and community functioning, can be solved only as the educator becomes more completely familiar with the nature of his specific area of responsibility and is both capable of and willing to operate functionally. There must be greater realization of the fact that education is truly a partnership between home and school, that the board of education is the responsible legislative body, and that the professional educator is responsible for the technical administration of the plan and for the furnishing of leadership to the lay board. Considered functionally, the development and acceptance of broad plans or policies means that the school community, through its legal representatives, has approved certain plans and practices and thus assures the professional of organization protection in carrying out these plans.

Planning and Expediency

A striking example of the outcomes of operation with and without consistent policy and plans is possible through evidence derived from the study of two school systems in different states. The accelerating factor in this instance was the depression, but the same results might also accrue under typical economic conditions.

COMMUNITY

Functional Operation	Opportunistic Operation
Community A is the industrial type with a large portion of foreign born of diverse nationality. It is characterized by many serious racial, religious, and economic conflicts. There were many instances of financial irregularity both in the schools and the community.	Community B represents a more diversified economic pattern and is predominantly second- and third-generation American-born families. Its deepest differences are economic and social.

SCHOOLS

The schools were the poorest in the state with respect to holding power and adjustment to the	The schools were considered to be superior in academic attainments. A strong educational

FUNDAMENTAL POLICIES

needs of the children. Owing to a definite lack in educational leadership the quality of the teaching staff was poor and professional morale hardly visible. There was no community tradition for good education. The people merely tolerated the teachers.

tradition insisted on a one-track secondary-school program that had college preparation as its goal. The teaching staff was capable and progressive as individuals, but several strong-minded superintendents had definitely limited its expression. The community regarded its teachers highly.

POLICIES

There was a complete absence of written policy. The state requirements were barely met.

The community had operated on the basis of vague customary policies for several generations. Current practice was always assumed to be correct.

CHANGE

Community leaders gradually brought about an educational revolution because of dissatisfaction. By some political planning a new board of education was gradually elected and at the beginning of this comparative study possessed five college graduates out of a possible seven. The new board, assisted by community leaders, looked for a new superintendent. They asked advice of the state department, state and local leaders. They wanted a strong man.

There was no community dissatisfaction. One superintendent followed another, after fairly long terms. One of the primary elements in choice of a new superintendent was social availability. The community expected the superintendent and his wife to be social leaders and apparently took educational competence for granted. Sometimes their selection produced good educators, but more frequently good golf players.

NEW SUPERINTENDENTS

The new superintendent was a large man physically and mentally, endowed with tremendous courage. A deep student of the social processes he believed ear-

The new superintendent was capable mentally and of impressive physique. His training beyond the minimum professional requirements was spotty

nestly in the democratic way of life and lived in accordance with its best traditions. He was an able scholar and had achieved the doctorate in social studies. Pleasant, tolerant, possessing a good sense of humor, he was a friendly person. He possessed a splendid nervous system and was capable of a remarkable self-discipline.

and consisted largely of attending those training institutions whose publicity was most attractive and whose placement bureaus were admittedly effective. His name was on the active placement list of three major institutions. He had "calls" every year that were usually good for a salary increase. Temperamentally he was nervous and high strung, frequently developing "temper tantrums" when things went wrong.

First Appearance

Appearing before community leaders and board members shortly after reaching the community, he declared that he knew nothing about the schools, but felt that a big task was ahead of the community, the board of education, and the teaching profession. He asked for support and cooperation. Several leaders present expressed themselves as disappointed. He had not "viewed with alarm" or made promises.

At a large reception and dinner after his second month on the job, the superintendent told his hearers that Community B had the best schools in the state and that his job was merely to preserve and safeguard what was already in existence. This statement pleased community complacency, and he was immediately considered a good choice.

Work

Superintendent A started to study intensively the community and the schools. At the end of the first year he informed the board members in executive session of actual conditions and the need for change. He recommended further study, improvement of existing personnel, instructional program, plant, and requested authority to proceed. It required

Superintendent B played the country-club clique on the theory that the superintendent must know the leaders. Lacking scholarly thoroughness he paid little attention to initial appraisal or to the need for community and institutional inventory. Efforts to introduce scientific methods of research were quietly discouraged. At an early meet-

FUNDAMENTAL POLICIES

six months of serious effort to educate the board to a realization of its position and responsibilities. Progressively, this legislative body gave less attention to pencils and paper, held meetings weekly, and spent hours discussing educational problems. The process of development continued, and at the end of two years there emerged a completed plan of written policies and procedures for an educational program adapted to specific community needs, one of the most intelligently operating boards of education in the country, and a progressive reorganization of instruction that in many respects was a distinct contribution to general educational practice. He built up a staff of strong men and women who possessed not only professional capacity but wide vision and courage as well. The schools quietly began to exercise a dominant influence in the community and for the first time in their history received the active community support. The board members were regularly returned to office, despite minority attempts to substitute more pliable men.

ing with his staff he stated as a policy: "We'll meet problems as they arise. Telling the people or the board of education too much merely means trouble, and I never have trouble." Socially adroit, he was able to let things drift and permit the board of education to piddle along, spending hours considering whether paper towels should be twelve or fifteen inches wide. As replacements of personnel became necessary, he never selected a strong man. The capable executives already in the system were always urged to move if another district offered more money. He surrounded himself with complacent female assistants so that no "crown prince" would develop. He always said nice things at banquets, school gatherings, and to the Rotarians. Skilfully weaving in and out, he played the game of expediency. When more thoughtful leaders and parents questioned certain practices, he waved them off with "we have the best schools in the state. I can prove it." But he never did.

INTERPRETATION

Superintendent A believed that the success and stability of the schools depended on the ability of the community to understand. The board's policy made specific pro-

Superintendent B did not believe in taking the people or the board into his confidence. It was the job of the superintendent to run the schools. There was no policy

vision for interpretation, and every individual in the system from board member through janitor was expected to carry a share of the burden.

and no general practice. His work was considered sufficient. When the local chapter of the teachers' association suggested the need for educating the community, he tactfully recommended that they confine their attention to teaching problems since his was the sole responsibility for keeping the community informed.

The Depression

Although Community A felt the depression quickly and heavily, the popular attitude to the schools was such that teachers' salaries were not reduced until after the third year. The teachers responded quickly to changed needs by accepting heavier loads, and the schools became the center of sensible community relief activities. Children were fed and clothed and kept in school; teachers were paid in cash, owing to foresight in placing currency in safety-deposit vaults when the banking structure became shaky. It is true that the board of education neglected to pay interest on its bonds during this period because, as one member stated, "the needs of the children came first." To-day (1937) this community has restored its salary schedule, increased it in some respects, and has recovered completely from the depression.

Community B had given only casual attention to its finances. It had a large bonded debt and a moderately large floating debt. When the effects of the depression were felt and the pressure of the taxpayers' league became strong, Superintendent B became panicky. He suffered that terrific emotional agony that usually accompanies indecision and uncertainty in a crisis. Some nights he never slept at all. Without consulting the board of education he allowed himself to be persuaded by members of the taxpayers' league and speculative realtors and actually forced upon the board of education an unnecessary recommendation for a large cut in teachers' salaries, at the same time recommending that all bond interest be met as usual. The morale of the staff went to a new low. Capable personnel quietly sought positions elsewhere, and certain dissatisfaction began to develop among more thoughtful leaders. A citizens' committee made pointed inquiry, and the board was helpless because of lack of understanding due to the absence of complete information. At this juncture Superintendent B was "called" elsewhere and left with glowing recommendations from a board now well pleased to have matters terminate so peacefully. His successor is wallowing in a highly disorganized school system in which the major depression salary cuts are still in effect. A recent survey indicated that it will require five years to bring the schools back to where they were, to say nothing of needed improvement.

SUMMARY

The purpose of this discussion as a preface to a more detailed subsequent statement of its direct application to social interpretation is to demonstrate that high-pressure tactics are of doubtful value and that the presentation of educational conditions and needs must be prefaced by a long period of community education to a general understanding and acceptance of possible needs. It is obvious that a social-interpretation program cannot be built successfully over night. It requires at least five years of consistent and intelligent effort to make any deep and lasting impression on community thought, unless the recognition of need has risen from the community itself. Programs should be developed and built upon a sound foundation. Under such a policy development as described here the legal responsibility is placed upon the community and the technical responsibility on the educator.

Chapter 7

THE COMMUNITY SURVEY

THE effectiveness of institutional interpretation depends upon the effectiveness of community interpretation. Understanding of the community is essential to sound interpretative methodology. Both policy and means of procedure must be built upon certainty instead of on guess work. True knowledge of and feeling for a community can be obtained only through actual living within the local pattern, maintaining normal social relations with its people, and studying carefully its methods of operation. The outsider, with Jovian complacency, may secure technical information and professional understanding, but only those who become definitely and fully a part of the community can hope to be successful in the administration of its activities and institutions. Knowledge of a community cannot be garnered over night, but requires the consistent accumulation of information and its constant interpretation. The means through which this knowledge may be secured is the community survey.

Survey activity is not new to public education. It has been in operation since at least 1845 in the instructional field. Only within the last two decades has this method been extended to study of the community itself. Social-survey technique has been developed by both geographer and sociologist. From the viewpoint of the geographer the community survey is primarily an inventory of land use, resources, and economic life. The sociologist places much greater emphasis on the people, their condition, needs, and aspirations. The teaching profession should probably combine both viewpoints and methods as a base for the extensive and continuing program of adult education which is essential to the understanding and support of democratic education.

In the past the lack of definite community information has retarded considerably the development of a curriculum more closely adapted to community requirements. The absence of knowledge concerning community habits and thought has often forced educators to resort to propaganda in attempting to maintain the schools. The inability of educators to produce reliable and complete information has certainly played a part at times in undermining the confidence of the press, community leaders, and legislative groups in the ability of the schools to know themselves. Lack of accurate information of community needs has led to patchwork, makeshift legislation, and to the frequent embarrassment of state departments of education.

Although the community survey is treated here as a separate activity to emphasize its immediate relationship to the interpretative process, it possesses much greater general value.

Curricular adjustments to specific and real community need are dependent upon knowing these actual requirements. The survey also provides means whereby services now neglected by the school may be given more rational consideration. Community financial attitudes, considered in relation to ability, determine the practical financial ceiling at any time. Many a desirable change in the school program has been sadly crippled because of absence of community attitude, and lack of institutional interpretation has caused emotional and conventional reactions to enlarged budgets. Complete knowledge of the community must form the base for local planning for public education. The total knowledge derived from the combination of all community surveys is essential for the formation of a sound state policy of both education and interpretation.

The technique of the community survey will be considered here in terms of: (1) essential information, (2) organization, (3) methodology, and (4) pitfalls. The presentation will attempt to sketch the broad outlines of this activity rather than furnish an exhaustive detailed treatment.

ESSENTIAL INFORMATION

Some of the earlier school surveys pointed out the value of a sociological analysis of community life. Later, specialized surveys in the school-plant field have presented a partial study of the community with special emphasis on land use. All of these studies and suggestions have been quite fragmentary in character. It is essential that the educator know not only land use and its social effect but also the cultural composition of the district, its means of making a living and of using its leisure time, its political functioning, its aspirations and ideals. For collection purposes the required data may be classified in eleven divisions. In practice the actual collection of information might be secured simultaneously and from the same sources. These divisions of information include: (*a*) land use, (*b*) racial and cultural composition, (*c*) family social conditions, (*d*) economic life, (*e*) ethical life, (*f*) community life, (*g*) political organization and thought, (*h*) leisure-time activity, (*i*) leadership studies, (*j*) history of past community efforts, and (*k*) analysis of social conflicts.

Land Use

Progressive studies of land use are essential to understanding of the community. The growing American community produces almost revolutionary changes in land use each generation. From subdivision to home-building, through the progressive stages to boarding-house and submerged or slum areas, may take less than thirty years. The community land-use patterns follow a rather definite pattern. The small town with its single business district, lone factory, and residential area becomes magnified and reproduced many times in the large city. The metropolis is fundamentally a collection of small communities, featured by a greatly enlarged central business area and by greater economic diversity.

Land use conditions living to such an extent that it is difficult to understand cultural variations unless the character of basic use is fully known. Since land use changes rapidly, the value of this phase of study lies in its continuity.

It is easily possible to determine land use by reference to community records checked against actual survey. If the elementary attendance district is used as the primary survey collection unit, large-scale maps for each district can plat vacant and used land.

THE COMMUNITY SURVEY   141

By means of different shadings, significant use may be indicated, supplemented by written records that provide much more detail.

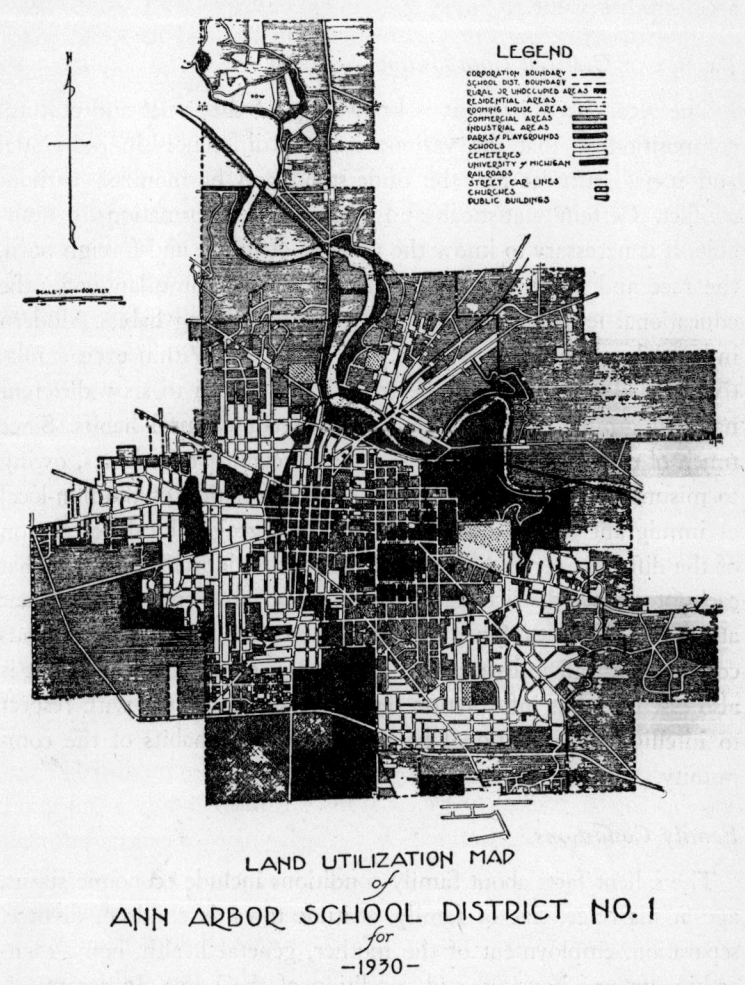

LAND UTILIZATION MAP
of
ANN ARBOR SCHOOL DISTRICT NO. 1
for
—1930—

A land-use map as a basis of community planning.

These district maps may be quickly assembled to furnish a total picture.

Certain authorities favor making land use a part of local inventory projects whereby the children become acquainted with neighborhood and community through survey of actual community conditions. Under certain administrative safeguards this plan has good social-studies value.

Racial and Cultural Composition

The second requirement is knowledge of the racial and cultural composition so that the various cultural differences in individual and social attitudes may be understood and harmonized without conflict. Certain statistical and geographic information is desirable. It is necessary to know the number of native and foreign born, the race and color, the citizenship status, the home language, the educational levels, the intelligence, and the reading habits. Modern industrial communities are complex culturally. Within even a relatively small city there may be from half a dozen to sixty different national groups, each representing different cultural habits. Since much of our social conflict is in reality a conflict of cultures, owing to misunderstandings and lack of the appreciation of the non-local or immigrant way of life, a statistical and geographical description of the different racial and national groups is desirable in order that each attendance district may analyze, understand and consider their attitudes and views. Since it will be necessary to make continuous contacts with all individuals in the process of adult education, it is also essential that information be progressively secured with respect to intelligence, educational levels, and reading habits of the community.

Family Conditions

The salient facts about family conditions include economic status, age at marriage, size of family, attitude towards children, divorce, separation, employment of the mother, general health, home ownership, type of housing, and condition of the home. In communities with large numbers of foreign born, conflicts between school and parent and between parent and child are frequent. Its base, as a rule, lies in the fundamental differences in attitude towards the children as exemplified by the American and the continental cultures. The immigrant considers the child as an economic asset to be exploited reasonably by the parent; the American feels and insists that the child is all important and reverses the age-old attitude of a peasant culture. These conflicts are among the most serious in our school systems and will not be solved until the basic cultural differences are understood, appreciated, and intelligently harmonized. Again, size of family and economic status may be very definite factors in determining parental attitude towards the children. The difficulties arising from broken homes and the employment of the mother need no elaboration here. Home ownership is an indication of the relative stability and permanence of the group. The type of housing and the crowding ratio are indices of significant social conditions.

Current school records may offer much information concerning basic family conditions, but it is necessary to supplement this source of information by use of social-service records from the court and public voluntary organizations. Such organizations as the Visiting Nurses, the Family Welfare Bureau, Sociological or Settlement Centers, the Red Cross, and Community Chest Clearing Houses have extensive records available.

Economic Life

The economic study should indicate how the people make their living. The survey includes the geographic location and classification of industrial, commercial, and transportation activity. Location of industry affects housing directly. A secondary economic grouping is the retail service of various types carried on within the neighborhoods throughout the city. Although secondary in type with respect to numbers employed, the social significance of retail outlets to a district or area may be immediately far greater than that of the large manufacturing units.

Information concerning types of employment, stability of employment, and wage conditions is highly desirable. Neighborhood banks are excellent barometers of economic conditions. Periodicity of employment may have an important bearing upon a social-interpretation program.

It is also highly desirable to ascertain the several types of economic organization. These include business men's luncheon clubs, the chamber of commerce, neighborhood economic or improvement associations, employers' leagues, labor organizations, and other similar groups. Wherever organization exists, there is an immediate social nucleus around which educational activity may eventually be organized. Each of these diverse organizations has a definite value and a real place in community education.

City directories, chambers of commerce, Federal census reports, the Department of Commerce, and the Department of Labor are prolific secondary sources for quick and accurate information.

Ethical Life

The ethical life of the community may be studied in terms of institutional religious activity and through observation of ethical movements outside of the church. The second group is much more difficult to analyze because of its lack of organization. However, it is necessary to recognize the fact that to-day much of the ethical life of a community exists outside of the church. This condition is particularly true in large urban centers.

Knowledge of churches by location, type, size, economic status, and specific beliefs is desirable. The social and educational programs of the several denominations must be studied and considered in relationship to public-education activity. Where possible, parish membership should be geographically placed on spot maps. There is much difference in viewpoint and social aggressiveness and solidarity of organization between the closely knit neighborhood parish and the scattered metropolitan parish.

Since our industrial communities embrace within their limits to-day almost every type of organized religion, the public school's adult-education program must give consideration to these conditions.

Community Life

The survey of community life will include all of those coöperative activities which the people carry on for health, for safety, for advancement, or for pleasure. They may be classified as health, welfare, government and public safety, cultural agencies, poverty, and crime.

Health work in the community would include study of preventive measures to protect the people, such as milk and food inspection, garbage and refuse collection, general sanitation, water supply, isolation of contagious disease, hospitalization, mortality, morbidity, and general health conditions.

Welfare studies will include both private and public effort to alleviate poverty, care for the aged and the unfit, and provision for reconstruction agencies of various types.

Survey of civil government will consider analysis of type and quality. The legal and extralegal machinery of governmental organization should be studied.

Cultural agencies include both public and voluntary agencies. Knowledge of the libraries, museums, art centers, and similar organizations, representing the informal educational agencies, is essential. Professional and amateur music and dramatic groups are important agencies.

Poverty and crime, particularly juvenile delinquency, need continuous study. Geographical case location is important. These can be related to other fields of problems already considered, such as housing, crowding, family size, economic status, and periodicity of employment. Careful and serious consideration should be given to these related fields.

Means for securing and maintaining information of this type is possible through definite and close coöperation of public education with public and voluntary community agencies. This recommended coöperation is one means by which the school may become more closely integrated with the wider community life.

Political Organization

There is a naïve assumption on the part of many educators that the school as a social institution must be kept free from the political life of the community. Since politics is the art of government, the public school cannot ignore it any more than it can ignore life itself. It is better to distinguish in this area between politics as an essential activity and the work of the extralegal political organization with its frequently low level of partizan operation. Political organization is the motivating power of visible legal government and cannot be ignored except to the grave danger of any public institution. Study of community political activity should include the party organization within the precinct, the ward, city, and the county in smaller communities.

Party personnel is important. The capable precinct lieutenant wields a power and acts as a molder of official public opinion to an extent undreamed of by one unfamiliar with this field. The ward, city, and county boss are important, but the precinct worker may be of material value to the school. From the study of political organization the school may learn much. The professional political machine is worth studying as an American phenomenon for its own sake. Its efficiency in maintaining power through continuing primary contacts, its flexibility and merit system and internal discipline are educative.

Use of Leisure

Study of leisure time use may include three aspects. The first is to determine what facilities are available (public and commercial) for recreation purposes, both quantitatively and qualitatively. The second consideration is to investigate how the people actually do spend their leisure time upon a seasonal basis. The third is to secure, if possible, a general survey of what the people would like to do if choice and opportunity were both available. Since the intelligent use of leisure is one of the most important problems confronting any community at the present time, there are immediately many other uses for these data.

The leisure activities of the boys and girls should form a large part of this sectional survey. Detailed study of recreational facilities for the youth is indicated.

The Leader Group

Except for purely academic purposes, no social survey is of much value without a careful study of the leader group. The primary, secondary, and small bloc leaders should be carefully studied, analyzed, and classified. In our highly diverse democratic organization, there is also much specialization in the leader group from the bottom, or neighborhood group, to the most outstanding and powerful individuals. These leaders follow the trend of specialization and may be powerful in one phase of life or organization and almost unknown in another. They may be roughly classified as political, social, publishing, financial, commercial, manufacturing, labor, ethical, and medical. These again may be considered as native and foreign born, and further subdivided into the verbal or obvious type and the silent, or under-cover leader. A leader-group survey that includes only the figures who appear in the public eye, figuratively beating the drum or carrying the flag, will probably miss the much more powerful motivating group that seldom appears in public and is scarcely known save in limited circles.

Since none of the leader group are in any sense free individuals in the social organization, study of them must include all of the ascertainable factors that, taken together, will account for their attitudes and actions. In a number of instances men in public position vote for something in which they heartily disbelieve or in a reverse case desperately fight a movement with which they are personally much in favor. In other words, every leader is motivated and moved not necessarily by his own convictions, but often by outside forces that exercise a determining influence. Sometimes these forces are visible, but more generally they are not. Leader groups and leader contacts may run a wide gamut of activity. It is wise, therefore, to analyze each leader in terms of all possible pulls and ties. As an individual, certain factors come into play. Blood and legal relatives may determine actions to a surprising degree. The church, because of its presumed institutional power, undoubtedly exercises influence upon many of these individuals. His economic activities and banking affiliations will probably determine many decisions. Locally, political parties may have little influence, but the invisible machine boss does mean much, and the leader in public life may find himself a much modified personality.

It is impossible to know too much about the leader group. It is very essential that the background, the affiliation, the weakness, the strength, and the emotional tendencies be understood. Without this fundamental knowledge many good amateur plans go astray, and many an optimist is destroyed.

Means for collecting information concerning the leader group may present some difficulties and requires a very high degree of confidential coöperation among all agents. Preparing general descriptive specifications of what constitutes a leader and discussion of these criteria with the teachers may result in the collection of an unusual number of reports on individuals. These initial reports may be further studied and specifically checked by indirect means against the opinions of well-known community leaders and the daily newspapers. Careful study of economic, social, political, and ethical activity is also indicated in developing this information. Again, the elementary attendance district is best suited for this purpose since both principal and teachers are more intimately familiar with the influential personalities within their immediate area. These bloc, precinct, or district leaders are extremely important agents in the development of public opinion and may have more immediate directive influence than the better known and apparently bigger community leaders.

After the leader index has been developed, the detailed information may be transferred to cards of convenient size on which are indicated the individual's totality of influence through his direct affiliation with different interest groups, including only specific factual information. Space may be provided on the reverse side whereby the record of each individual's participation in different community programs is chronologically noted.

The record should contain family relations, religious affiliation, educational background, economic activity and relationships, social and fraternal contacts, social and political beliefs, and significant friends.

History of Past Effort

Every community has its share of coöperative failures in economic, social, educational, and ethical activity. In each of these failures, some people were disappointed, and others were hurt emotionally or financially. Since their future attitude will be colored to some extent by their past experience, it is well for the school organization to know definitely and completely the history of these past failures that were rapidly withdrawn from the social stage. Without such information, serious errors may be made in arranging for future projects.

Social Conflict

Out of our coöperative society arise many conflicts. Whatever their specific classification, they form stumbling blocks to any constructive activity within given areas or limits. They may arise from political, economic, social, religious, or general cultural differences. They may have their inception in a neighborhood fight between two boys which finally spreads to a huge parish feud. They may arise from different time concepts of leisure-time activity, such as late practising on a brass horn, radio, or vocal demonstration. They may have been carried over for a generation in a particularly large, powerful, or very emotional family until the original reasons have been lost to view. Public manifestations may range from "non-talking" to twelve-foot spite fences. They may be humorous or maudlin, but they cannot be neglected. Whatever the cause, whatever the group, these conflicts play an important part in community life and politics. All of them should be known and should be tabulated and recorded in some form so that the school may not only be aware of them but also develop means for harmonizing them so far as they affect the technical operation of the schools and their community relationships.

SURVEY ORGANIZATION

If the social survey is viewed as one of the many executive activities in which the professional executive, using that term in its most inclusive sense, must engage, the method of organization and administration will normally follow established channels through which other activity takes place. Survey includes collection, tabulation, and maintenance of data. It is essential that each school community have thorough coverage. Since knowledge is essential to use, that type of organization which employs its executive agents most successfully will tend to secure the best results.

Organization to make the social survey need not be obvious or receive general publicity. It may be quite informal in character although effective in functioning. In communities where the activity is new, progress should be made slowly. It may take a year or more to get really under way.

Centralized Organization

The general survey plan and organization may be prepared by the superintendent and his staff and developed as a centralized procedure. This form of organization will probably prevail in those school districts where a high degree of staff specialization has been developed. Under the centralized organization responsibility for conducting the survey may be placed in the research division just as other fact-finding activities are. The process of securing information may then be carried on under highly technical direction and only carefully selected and trained agents used in the process. Centralized organization might follow the pattern frequently employed in curriculum revision in which a large number of representative committees are used.

Decentralized Organization

Since the success of the interpretative activity will ultimately be conditioned by the primary field contacts, the entire teaching personnel needs experience in both collection and use of social information. A more desirable organization is one in which the general outlines and procedures are promulgated by the superintendent and the responsibility for achievement completely delegated to the individual building and its staff. Complete coverage of a community may be most easily secured through its elementary attendance districts. Teachers and principals may be more effectively used if they are given complete responsibility and latitude within their area of influence. The activity should be so organized that it may be carried on by existing agents, close to the people, who are in direct and continuous contact with the field. There is already existing in every school organization of any size an excellent field organization. The best plan for this work is to divide the district sociologically upon the basis of elementary building districts. These districts cover every square foot of territory. They are relatively small in size, and even the larger districts include little more than one square mile. They are generally the most homogeneous units socially, economically, and racially. The school has direct primary contact with the parents through the children. The school may be made the social nucleus for the district. The types of information, the method of tabulation, the geographical studies of other factors may all be planned to meet the needs of the entire district. This program can then be divided geographically by elementary-school districts and the district responsibility delegated to the elementary principal. Some training in survey technique may be necessary in the case of the principal and also for teachers. In planning and executing this program, the implication should be clear that the elementary-school principal is the responsible community leader in his specific district and that he must be so familiar with all activities within the district that feelings and attitudes, movements and activities, can be transmitted to the superintendent to keep him informed of the community. Through this activity, the principal also becomes more capable of interpreting the community to the school, which is quite as important as interpreting the school to the community.

Since the secondary attendance districts are merely a series of elementary units, it is desirable to avoid duplication of effort and have the elementary schools furnish continuous information to the secondary units. High-school principals and teachers have a special job in securing specific information, especially in the area of parent-child and parent-school conflicts, that pertains only to their own problem. The elementary school remains the most important social survey unit.

Size Factor

There is fundamentally little difference in survey activity between the small and large community. The extent of information is the same. The primary difference lies in detail and diversity of personnel. In the large community the executive organization represents a high degree of specialization; in the small district there is much more generalization. However, even the same community, especially where reorganization has taken place on either an arbitrary or natural area basis, is developing greater specialization. The visiting teacher and nurse, the agricultural specialist, and community clinicians are increasing in numbers each year. Possibly more of the survey responsibility will fall on the superintendent where the principalship has not been developed extensively. It is important that the executive in the small district realize the relative similarity in educational problems between small and large communities rather than the differences. The conventional assumption that small towns are radically dissimilar from large centers may be merely a translation of emotional experience created by lack of elbow room and the consequent closer social relationships than to real differences. The large city is merely a collection of small towns.

SURVEY METHODOLOGY

The effectively functioning school must be a friendly and human institution. The reaction of the adults and children to the institution will be determined by the degree to which the executive personnel is able to develop confidence through individual and group social contacts. The success of any venture undertaken will be conditioned directly by community attitudes. The first requirement of sound methodology in the social survey is to avoid all possible emotion that might be aroused if the institutional effort is construed as unwarranted prying into the personal affairs of individuals. In the field of social relationships the school should recognize the confidential nature of its child and parent relationships and maintain inviolate personal information derived through this relationship. The terminal outcome in school-community relationships is the reflection and resultant of the effect of the totality of institutional effort and practice. Hence understanding, friendliness, and coöperation must be the basis for all technical methodology.

There is considerable difference of opinion regarding the use of written records in the social survey. Personnel indiscretions, possible misinterpretations, non-recognition of responsibility for those who come afterwards, and unpleasant personal experience all combine in a traditional reaction against the written social record. It was not so many years ago that city principals transferred from one building to another conceived it to be their duty to destroy all existing records so that the incoming principal would not be handicapped or annoyed. This protective technique grew out of the professional dangers of a politically controlled school system. It quickly crystallized into a working policy.

There may be a few individuals endowed with a photographic mind who can retain accurately a tremendous volume of detail. Unfortunately for organization, however, their number is too small to be significant. The normal time limitation makes it impossible to use these individuals efficiently. Considering the need of present-day organization, there can be little question of the value of written records. If the information is essential to social functioning, it is also possible to organize it in written form so that it will be available for all. Intelligently developed written records need not necessarily be a source of embarrassment.

There are two general aspects to survey methodology. The first is the initial collection of information, and the second is the means of maintaining it in usable up-to-date form.

Sources of Information

Much of the essential information is already in usable form in the records maintained by the school, governmental, and economic agencies. Race, country of birth, citizenship status, economic condition, home language, and family size should all be available from the continuing school census. Federal, state, and local records will supplement and check school records with respect to racial and cultural conditions.

Land use may be ascertained by actual field survey, by study of city or county land records, and through departments of public works. Information on family conditions is easily available through school, social-service agencies, and the courts.

In general a church organization is willing to coöperate in furnishing information concerning affiliation. The conditions of economic activity may be secured from Federal data and from local economic organizations such as the chamber of commerce. Economic affiliation of parents is available in the more complete school records. Information concerning type, number, and location of retail outlets may be most easily secured by field study within each community area.

City license records indicate type and location of commercial recreation facilities.

The political organization is not always so obvious. Though there is occasional publicity of plans and practices, there are seldom easily available records of district, ward, city, and county leaders. Study and observations are recommended in this area.

In small communities the history of past efforts generally comes by word of mouth. In large cities, patient and constant study is necessary to discover sore spots and delicate areas.

Conflicts, as they arise, will be discovered either from newspaper publicity or direct contact. Information concerning deeper cultural and political conflicts of long standing must be gradually discovered through the time-consuming process of listening.

Current thought and attitudes can best be ascertained through child reporting, continuing contact with significant news disseminating centers, boarding-house contacts in small places, letters written to newspaper editors, editorial comment, and school discussion programs.

Significant parental beliefs are quickly transmitted by the child to the classroom. In analyzing and reporting these opinions, the teacher is the responsible agent. The retail outlet is an important news-disseminating and opinion-forming center. The general store in the small town; the corner drug-store in every community; the neighborhood tobacco shop, poolroom, barber shop, and beauty parlor cannot be overlooked as agencies for the collection of significant information. Friendly relationships established with the owner-manager are generally productive of constant news, and these individuals may be very helpful if intelligently used. The small-town boarding-house is so significant that many superintendents place teachers there rather arbitrarily. Pressure is of dubious value. The center must be covered, but it requires intelligent appreciation of the situation, together with interest, if the contacting personnel is to use this agency constructively.

The more recently developing techniques of furnishing parents within any attendance district with a safety valve through organization of open discussion sessions has high potential value. There are many ways of carrying out such a program, but that form through which patrons are permitted to ask questions of a panel of individuals appears to be worth while. Since this type of discussion program is best when organized and directed by the parent-teacher association, it will be discussed in greater detail later. The questions asked should furnish for the social survey a definite indication of individual and social thought within the attendance district and supply a base for the development of later programs.

The summation of all this information should furnish a fairly complete composite view of the school community condition and mores.

Records

The question of types of records maintained in this survey will vary with community. Provided that the information is written, the exact form is not specifically important. Wide flexibility and record diversity may be encouraged. In general, the information that cannot be easily translated graphically or on maps should be kept in written form.

A quick means of studying conditions is through the development of district maps. These may be of wall size or reduced to cap or letter-head size in loose bound books. Larger maps permit greater display of significant detail. Land use and housing conditions are best shown in map form. Vacant property and its use may be shown. Population spot maps according to race, economic conditions, and religious affiliation are extremely worth while in giving general information at a glance. Tardiness, absence, sickness, and delinquency may all be quickly noted by use of colored pins or permanent spots. Concentration of these problems in certain sections furnishes possible clues for their progressive solution by determining fundamental general causes as well as purely individual-institutional relationships.

Leadership studies should be tabulated as both written and visual records. The use of different colored pins can designate the location of different types of leadership.

Maintaining Information

Although the work of initial collection of social information requires considerable application and effort, the maintaining of this information up to date is not so difficult. It is quickly and easily routinized without becoming too burdensome. Methodology in this field is largely a process of organizing reporting units for constant and current information. Most of the immediate information will probably come from the children and parents directly to the teacher. Thus the teacher becomes the most important reporting agent. Custodial and clerical personnel is also available for this purpose. Much information is consistently gleaned through study of community and neighborhood newspaper opinion, from social contacts with community leaders, and by maintaining relationships with the neighborhood retail outlets. In addition current publications of other types of community survey are readily available.

PITFALLS

Though the primary purpose of the social survey is to secure deep knowledge of the community background, beliefs, and aspirations upon which to build an intelligently adjusted program of interpretation, it also furnishes a means for developing machinery through which the plan may be put into effect, and for prevention of difficulties between institution and community by knowledge of what may and may not be tried at any specific period. In the organization and development of this survey procedure extreme care must be exercised to avoid doing anything that will tend to arouse suspicion and create community sore spots. All information should be quietly and unobtrusively gathered. Above all the ringing of doorbells to find out what is going on in the house must be discouraged. The American family is highly sensitive and jealous of its traditional privacy. Intelligent social administration secures information without annoyance.

Another pitfall to be most studiously avoided is creating the impression that certain professional personnel with a low degree of social sensitivity are agents of uplift and reform. In many instances this difficulty is created by class-conscious individuals. The problem has already been considered earlier.

Careless use of confidential material may raise a storm that will be disastrous to the success of the school. Every member of the teaching profession will do well to remember that in a democratic society doctor, teacher, and priest are equally responsible for maintaining personal confidences. Under no conditions should these intimate relationships be violated.

Though it is extremely desirable to establish coöperative relations with voluntary agencies of different types, every safeguard must be taken to prevent the schools from being brought into questionable relationships to commercial activity or to permit the use of certain types of school information for private benefit. It is possible to be friendly with political leaders without furnishing them with lists of teachers or patrons for circulating political literature. In a similar manner, it is not desirable to furnish aggressive clergymen with lists of children or to permit a state building to be used to advance sectarian interests.

SUMMARY

The social survey, so essential as a base for the development of an institutional interpretation program, requires the use of all organization personnel to make it effective. Social sense and discretion are absolutely essential to its employment as an information-securing device. Its initiation requires careful planning, and its execution takes much work and time. Once the initial survey has been complete, its maintenance is relatively simple. Time must be considered as a vital factor in this activity. Finally, the following principles should be consistently followed in both planning and execution:

The community survey should be so organized and conducted that essential information is secured and used without arousing any emotional antipathies.

Personal information gathered by the institution through this method should be held completely and permanently confidential.

The application of the general technique of procedure or methodology must be so organized that it will result in an increase of confidence on the part of the community to its educational institutions.

To be of real and lasting value in the development of an adult-education program, the social survey must not only be all inclusive, but also continuing in type.

Surveys should be so organized that primary information is secured by those agents who have constant and intimate contact with the community and who, by nature of their responsibility, will be required to use it continuously.

PART III

INSTITUTIONAL AGENTS

PART III

INSTITUTIONAL AGENTS

Chapter 8
THE BOARD OF EDUCATION

AS the legislative and appraisal body for the school district, the board of education occupies a unique position in social interpretation. On the one hand it is responsible for the entire plan, its means of execution and its judgment or appraisal; on the other, both because of the nature of its organization and its composition, the scope and range of its direct participation in social interpretation is considerably limited. Some executives are inciined to the opinion that the less a board of education does in community relations the better for the schools. The other extreme belief appears to be that there is some magic quality inherent in the board, and its possibilities appear to be without limit. Neither view is of much value. There is a very distinct, if somewhat limited, value of the board in social interpretation. The purpose of this chapter is to explore these possibilities and establish some concrete field of endeavor and to suggest certain logical activities. Since much of the value of the board of education lies in its actual functioning, the problem will be considered from the following aspects: (1) the nature of the board of education, (2) responsibilities, (3) secrets of success, (4) plans and procedures, (5) community contacts, and (6) conflicts.

NATURE OF THE BOARD OF EDUCATION

It is essential first to understand the peculiar nature of the school board in the United States plan of public education. Though the education activity is legally organized as one of the major prerogatives and efforts of the state, the actual execution of the specific plan is delegated to small local units, or quasi-corporations most commonly called school districts. Thus the people of the state as a whole, through their legislative assembly, create general policies under which the training of both children and adults shall be carried on and then, through much smaller and more compact community organizations, provide the actual machinery through which the general plan is carried into effect. Centralization of policy-making and, theoretically, general appraisal are accomplished by the state, but the execution of the plan is secured through decentralization for local planning and for direct execution within the confines of these artificial units or districts. The local board of education is a state as well as a local agency operating within a specific area. In this respect it differs quite markedly from many other governmental agencies. In actual practice few boards fully recognize their true relationship and have come to think of their function as purely that of serving a particular local community interest. Local execution has been one of the valuable elements in the United States plan, but it has also been one of its greatest weaknesses. Too little feeling for its responsibility to the entire state is one of the outstanding characteristics of the average school board.

The Legal Plan

The function of the district board as the direct agency for the promulgation of the state plan may be considered as that of a specialized legislative body whose activity is confined to one major field. Operating under the state statutes relating to education, each board is required to carry out the mandatory minimum program of education irrespective of local attitude. Beyond this point each board possesses fairly wide powers of a permissive nature which enable the district to provide for certain types of educational activity over and above minimum essentials that are necessary to its peculiar cultural needs. Even further, local boards of education frequently are granted authority under the permissive powers to experiment and to push their activities beyond the specifically enacted statutes.[1] The legal organization of the state educational plan into two ranges of activity—the mandatory, involving the absolute essentials required by the state as a whole; the permissive in two divisions to

[1] For one illustration see *General School Laws, State of Michigan* (Revision of 1927), Part I, Chapter 6, Section 15 "... and in general to do anything not inconsistent with this act which is necessary for the proper establishment, maintenance, management and carrying on of the public schools of such district."

meet generalized need in different centers and extending far beyond the minimum essentials into the area of experimentation or the trying of new activities to permit quick adjustment to essential change —represents the most unique organization of legislation in any field of public activity. The state recognizes the fact that the social needs of different sections within a state vary greatly. It permits flexibility to adjust to the differentiated area requirements, and it provides for the ability to grow and change as the general cultural needs change.

This sensible development of the legal plan also brings with it numerous problems pertinent to the field of social interpretation. The execution of the minimum mandatory essentials must be carried on without choice. As an illustration, every board of education is required to carry out the provisions of the compulsory education laws regardless of local attitudes and reactions. Since the permissive range of powers is fairly well understood, the fact of the board's mandatory responsibility is often confused in popular thought. Many conflicts arise because these mandatory requirements are not completely understood, and few boards apparently make any attempt to interpret them. Popular reactions and differences of opinion are most frequently passed off with a shrug of the shoulder and a vague statement that "the state requires it."

Interpreting Community Needs

The permissive powers bring the situation into quite a different setting. Here it is a question of knowing the community and interpreting its specific needs. The actual application of these permissive powers means not only the actual interpretation of needs but also the development within the community itself of a recognition and understanding of these needs together with the desire to achieve them. Here the board of education faces a real problem in social planning.

The schools are one of the few public efforts in which the executive function has been distinctly professionalized and which the state has protected from the popular assumption that election to office automatically insures executive ability. Other community projects are only tardily following the lead of the schools in this respect. It is therefore natural that the professional executive, trained to recognize and provide for social need through its organized program, should be the first to recognize and to urge its satisfaction; he is generally far ahead of the community in educational thinking. The board member, like the typical adult, is prone to accept unquestioningly that which has the stamp of traditional respectability. He looks with some suspicion upon new and, to him, untried ideas. This gap between the layman and the professional must always be considered as one of the real problems of professional administration. Since the acceptance of the operation of the permissive aspects of the educational program depends largely on the popular recognition and acceptance of the need, the board of education is in a delicate position. It cannot harmonize the natural inertia and tradition of the typical community within the community needs as determined by the professional except through some specific means of two-way community education. The condition created by natural divergence of these viewpoints is at once its responsibility, its danger, and its opportunity.

Possibilities of Experimentation

In the third range of activity, the field of experimentation, the situation is even more delicate. Though the average adult does not consider himself essentially expert in law and medicine, he does have a feeling that education is more or less an open book, extremely simple for any adult to master. Experimentation also involves change from traditional acceptance of some practice that has been in operation for a long period and therefore in many respects endowed with venerable qualities regardless of worth. Change of attitude means effort, the overcoming of a series of emotional relationships to the things as they are. It is particularly dangerous to undertake change except as the ground is prepared for social acceptance.

Community Education

In the primary discussion of the nature of the board of education there are three fields of possible activity in the immediate promulgation of the educational plan that require recognition and study.

Since popular education rests on the will of the people and upon a recognition of need and a willingness to meet that need, the immediate development of the basic educational plan involves a series of problems in community education that have rarely been recognized by the specialized legislative bodies.

The carrying out of any plan requires finance, and the United States tradition has been to provide for fiscal independence in the majority of school districts so that assurance of adequate finance might be had apart from the stress and partizanship of general politics. The smooth application of the power to tax rests distinctly on the active acceptance by the people of the purposes for which these moneys are to be spent. The actual supplying of finance to carry on the required and assumed program cannot be accomplished easily unless the people are willing to contribute. The problem of community education is again involved.

RESPONSIBILITY OF THE BOARD OF EDUCATION

A summary of this brief discussion indicates that the board of education is a specialized legislative body acting as the agent of the state and of the community it specifically represents. This legislative body is empowered to make the state educational plan effective in its own locality. Since only a small part of this plan is mandatory, the actual development and execution of a complete educational plan for most communities must be conditioned not only by the interpretation of community needs but also by the development of a community consciousness of these needs. The local school board has as one of its specific and distinct responsibilities the interpretation of the community it represents to the professional group and the interpretation of the professional group to the community. In other words one of its major social functions is to act as buffer or equalizer between the professional will on one hand and the social will on the other. To perform the most important activity of stabilization without being stalemated, the board of education must understand both community and the schools. As laymen, the members are often at a loss to understand the schools, and this inadequacy is frequently the cause of much trouble. The problem of interpretation is necessarily difficult and complicated. It requires large areas for continuous contact and a great diversity of personnel. The board of education, as a board and as individual members, is therefore necessarily restricted in its program of interpretation and must enlist the services of the entire professional group as its authorized executive agents. Because of these inherent limitations the board should not sit back with a "let George do it" attitude, but should recognize its responsibility as well as its limitations and make intelligent provision to overcome the latter and discharge the former. Unless the board of education does recognize both problems and requirements and makes complete provision for them, it is not acting in accordance with its inherent responsibilities as a social agency.

Must Provide Means

In addition to interpretation the board of education must also provide means for keeping the community fully and constantly informed of the purpose, value, conditions, and needs of its schools. As indicated earlier, the individual part played by members of the educational legislative body is not the primary one in this field. Its chief responsibility consists in recognition of the complete problem and making adequate provision for its solution through the professional personnel.

SECRETS OF SUCCESS

There are several elements in operation of this specialized legislative body that must be recognized to insure success. The first of these is recognition of its actual nature and its real limitations. The second is an understanding, however general, of the nature of the task and the major problems involved in its success. The board of education should therefore develop a functional viewpoint, a philosophy both of purpose and of achievement. The third element is the development of a philosophy of control through which these democratic social ideals may be effectively achieved. As the legal source of authority, the board of education must consciously recognize the need for proper allocation of functional activity, operating as a planning and appraisal body for the school district and delegating the execution of the technical plan to professionals qualified under the laws of the state. Recognition of its position as the community social parent, the subjection of personal profit and ambition to the welfare of the children and the community, its responsibilities for the betterment of its own community life as well as serving the state, are essentially secrets of its successful functioning. There should always be full recognition of the social nature of its services and the consequent complete elimination of the vagaries and peculiarities of partizan politics. The schools are not the responsibility of political parties but a coöperative activity carried on by all of the people in terms of social and individual needs. The United States tradition of unpaid unselfish services by school-board members to the welfare of the community, though violated in many instances, still remains one of the fine ideals inherited from our pioneer past. It is worth while preserving.

PLANS AND PROCEDURES

The effectiveness of the board of education hinges on the extent to which it is conscious of those responsibilities, the will to meet them and the methods selected for achievement. The first requirement is a knowledge not only of the social situation but also of the basic nature and needs of the educational activity. Secondly, in order to carry on successfully as a board each member must be thoroughly acquainted with every other member. The best start may be made in this field by each member adopting at the beginning a completely objective and impersonal set toward every other member, considering each other as individual units involved in the execution of a vital community project and not traditionally as either friends or enemies. Such an attitude does not necessarily preclude social relationships. In fact it may ultimately tend to stimulate them. It does set forth specifications for successful operation and the elimination of individual conflicts in terms of prejudice and passion. Each fellow-member should be considered as equally zealous in the recognition and the performance of duty and should study every other member and become familiar with his background, his associations, his philosophy, and his desires. It is only as the motivating forces underlying individual action are understood that adequate consideration and tolerance may develop. No two individuals will probably consider every phase of a question from the same standpoint. Appreciation of background generally tends toward an objective tolerance to individual expressions of opinion. There will always be essential differences of opinion in any board as an expression of the democratic method. Objective consideration of these differences need not develop conflict if there is understanding, appreciation, and tolerance of individual attitudes.

Educating New Members

The membership of the typical board of education shifts rapidly. Old members retire, and new ones are added through popular election or appointment. The process of study and understanding is therefore continuous. To these new members the board of education has a twofold duty. It must not only appraise them as individuals, but it must also educate them to the conditions within both community and schools and to the need of the schools. Though the superintendent plays a definite part in the training of the new members, the board of education must also consider the process of orientation as one of its responsibilities. Sometimes the training of new members is not easy. Frequently their election is based on some fancied or real difference of opinion on policy in operation. Sometimes the election is achieved through opposition to a specific personality, a principal, a superintendent, or a board member. Campaigns conducted on these platforms tend to become bitter. Unfortunately people do not take politics objectively enough to distinguish between a conflict between different policies and a conflict between personalities.

The typical new member joins the board with a grave suspicion of his colleagues and their practices. He wants to "view with alarm," to find something that will justify his campaign utterances. He also frequently objects to dropping out of front-page prominence to the anonymity of group activity. The individual or individuals who have been assailed during the campaign are also bitter. Their stand is far from being non-emotional and friendly. Yet it is absolutely essential for the well-being of the schools that the new member be accepted without quibble or argument as the representative of public opinion at that specific occasion, and that the board gradually and intelligently orient him into the pattern of group activity. Each situation should be studied by the board in terms of the specific problems involved and means developed to bring the new member into harmonious relationships to the whole.

Know Your Schools

The school board must also be aware of actual conditions within the schools. The methods of securing this information have been considered in another section.[2] Knowing general conditions, it is possible to select points of attack and to make specific determination of need through constant survey activity.

Policies Essential

Since the most effective method of action is in terms of a broad but well-defined plan and carefully determined objectives, the next problem of the board of education is to adopt policies in accord with the legal requirements and the social needs of the community.[3] Written policies represent a charted plan to be followed and tend to eliminate confusion and conflict. These working policies will naturally be the result of professional interpretation of need further correlated by the board of education on the basis of its interpretation of community conditions and need. However, policies represent only a general plan and must be supplemented in functioning by adequately conceived and intelligently administered plans of procedure. Here again the board plays a distinctly legislative part by receiving, considering, and approving essential executive plans.

Finally, there must be adequate provision on both the executive and legislative levels for means of judging the effectiveness of the plan and making provision to correct inadequacies and to meet new needs to provide for essential growth. The results of appraisal should be constantly presented to the people in simple but com-

[2] See Chapter 7.
[3] See Chapter 6.

prehensive form so that the social group will also be in an understanding relationship to the educational activity.

The Board Meeting

These plans and programs are formulated principally through the mechanics of regular and special gatherings of the board of education. The principal means through which the board of education operates are the regular meetings provided by law and such other special meetings as may be required. This legal working device is also a very important agency in the program of community education and should always be organized and carried on with this end in view.

In the first place, the board's business is community business, and one of the primary principles of community relationships is that all public business should be transacted in public regardless of whether or not it suits the convenience of board or superintendent. No other procedure can be upheld because of the nature of public activity. There may be certain discussions and problems that should not be considered in public for the personal welfare of the individuals involved. There is a method for taking care of such exceptions in executive session, the occasional occurrence of which does not weaken the principle of open meetings by one iota.

Board meetings have a series of purposes, and organization should be provided to meet all of them. The first purpose of the meeting is to disseminate information and allow free and open discussion of vital problems. The second purpose is to provide adequate means for the taking of action in accordance with the law. The third purpose is to provide means whereby adult members of the community may meet with their representatives, present their viewpoints, and observe both manner and method by which their own business is accomplished.

Discussion Technique

Unified action results from consideration and discussion of problems. Since the board of education can and should function solely as a board instead of as individuals, the best device for securing proper discussion conditions is by the technique known as the committee of the whole. The well-organized board may provide for one or two complementary discussion periods preceding each regular meeting. Sessions of the committee of the whole may be held at regularly advertised intervals in the official meeting room of the board of education and be open to the public.

Operating under an elected or rotating chairmanship the board may have routine and other essential information informally presented to it through the superintendent. Since the committee of the whole is a discussion device, members are not immediately confronted with the necessity for placing themselves on official record as for or against any plan or project. Properly conducted under parliamentary procedure and on an impersonal basis, there is freedom from strain and pressure. Much more unhurried attention may be given any plan. All aspects may be considered and discussed until every member is thoroughly familiar with the situation and is ready to form a group opinion.

As a discussion device, it has all of the advantages of a generalized forum. The superintendent presents his data and his reports together with his interpretation. These reports in all instances should present a deep study of the problem together with all of the available evidence. Discussions may then be restricted to the problem and to the facts. The average board may react in three different ways. The extremely conservative and extremely progressive opinions will be predominant in early discussion. As the play of opinions weaves back and forth and both extremes are presented, there will gradually develop certain common areas of thought in which the different shades of milder viewpoints will gradually emerge. The required elements are tolerance, open-mindedness, and flexibility. If a presented solution arouses too much emotion, some substitute should be quickly found. Many a promising development has grown into conflict because of insistence on a particular solution. It is necessary to be able to distinguish quickly and smartly between principles and practices that merely look like them. Under good leadership, the discussion may be stimulated and adequate hearing given to every phase of reaction. There is no occasion for hurry. It may require one or a score of discussion sessions before a generalized opinion is developed that will permit harmony between all viewpoints and a unanimous acceptance of the modified plan. Discussion is the only means by which harmony of different viewpoints may be achieved.

For the public discussion by the committee of the whole is a valuable means of securing an education respecting problems and needs. A well-balanced board of education will tend to represent most shades of opinion found in the community. The individual hearing his own and other ideas and beliefs discussed rationally and without heat gradually tends to undergo a similar transformation as do members of the board. He begins to appreciate other viewpoints and by following thoroughly the complete discussion accepts the fact that no individual's opinion has prevailed but rather that the result is a pooling of the best of each viewpoint. The mere fact that everything is open and all cards are on the table is of itself most convincing in developing confidence.

The open-door discussion is also of value in eliminating suspicion on the part of purveyors to the schools that all bidders have a fair and equal chance. Though the technique and activity of purchase may be delegated to the professional executive, the actual receiving and opening of bids for tabulation should be made in open meeting, either in committee of the whole or at a specially advertised time in the presence of the officers of the board. The safest procedure is to receive bids only in public and open them in public. This plan prevents actual dishonesty in the treatment of "favored bidders," and it also gives each individual and corporation the feeling that they have been dealt with honestly. Too much emphasis cannot be laid on the avoidance of conflict and suspicion arising from purchasing.

Regular Meetings

Once the board of education has determined on any line of action, it may be reported at the regular meetings. The journal of the committee of the whole may be presented, considered and approved in relatively short time, routine business quickly dispatched, and opportunity and encouragement given to the public to present its requests or air its grievances in formal fashion allowing the board to consider them at leisure later in discussion by the committee of the whole. Despite the best intentions plans sometimes go wrong. Controversial issues involve deep emotions, and though the board may have come to a definite and satisfactory conclusion in committee of the whole between these sittings and the regular meetings certain interested elements may have brought pressure on some member to change his mind. It also frequently happens that a board of education will have one or two members who are easily swayed by dominant personalities. When previously considered discussion plans are presented for approval and legal action, one or more members may object so violently to something heretofore agreed upon that it must be obvious what has happened. It is desirable in this case to give every impression of non-hurry, of calmness, and of dignity. The best device is a motion to lay on the table or to recommit to committee of the whole. Such procedure involves time, but it must be constantly remembered that time is the best equalizer and harmonizer of conflicts. In spite of the feeling of the high-pressure specialist in any field, time is not so limited an element that its function in solving social conflict can be ignored.

Community Demands

The same procedure should prevail with respect to community demands through petition or personal presentation. The right to differ is fundamental, but the right to impress the views of a militant minority on an entire community is not tenable. Minorities of this description are generally not only militant and extremely aggressive but also tend to operate by raising emotional issues. A board of education, dignified in its procedure and refusing to be bullied, can, by commitment of popular demands to the committee of the whole for study and consideration, eliminate largely the emotional pressure of small well-organized groups, thus avoiding conflict, which is always desirable, and protecting the schools, which is absolutely essential.

To meet these requirements the meeting room of the board of

education should be commodious enough to provide space for a fairly large number of interested individuals, in such a manner that the board itself will be completely segregated from the public. The room may be tastefully furnished in a manner to emphasize the dignity of the activity. Good insulation is desirable to prevent echoes and to permit speech of reasonable volume to be heard easily in all parts of the room. A harsh, hard room tends to excitement and vociferous expression on the part of a speaker since it is necessary to use volume and greater effort to secure an effect. Sooner or later this condition stimulates him beyond rational need. Speeches made before the board of education should on all occasion be courteously kept by the chairman to the subject under discussion and steered away from personalities.

The Executive Session

The third device of operation is that of executive session. There are very few occasions demanding executive sessions. The mere fact that a discussion is held in secret breeds popular suspicion rapidly. If the use of the executive session is limited to consideration of social problems involving the protection of the children and of the personnel it may possibly avoid suspicion. Executive sessions need not be advertised, but it is well to have the press represented after pledging the reporters to secrecy regarding the publication of the discussions. By including the press, it is possible to establish in the newspaper offices the feeling that nothing is hidden save where a personal reputation is involved, and any attack by outsiders on these sessions will usually fail to secure publicity. If the press is prohibited from attending, seeds of grave suspicion are immediately engendered in the editorial mind.

Report Meetings

Since only a small number of the public can regularly attend the meetings of the board of education, it is highly desirable that the discussions in committee of the whole and in regular meetings be reported by all of the newspapers. Reporters should be invited to each session. If a newspaper is not represented, officers of the board of education should see that the city desk receives a full report of all action. Widespread publicity in the press is another excellent means of keeping the board and its business constantly before the public. Objection to this procedure is often made by board members because newspaper reports of action are frequently distorted and trifles are featured whereas the real serious business is neglected. Method of reporting does vary with the paper and its peculiarities of management. This defect is inherent in a privately owned and operated press. In general, the reporter writes what to him is news. Conflicts, wide differences of opinion, and personal disagreements are grist to his mill. Most frequently it is the board of education rather than the reporter that is at fault. A logical, dignified, and open procedure; a decent consideration by individual board members of their position and responsibilities; procedure on an objective and impersonal basis with attention to the needs of the schools rather than the personalities of board members will tend to create a situation that will not lend itself readily to distortion in the reporting of meetings.

However, if the press situation is such that despite all efforts on the part of the board news is consistently and regularly distorted, it may be desirable to contract with all of the papers and print regularly the full official proceedings of the meetings in order that the intelligent reader may have both accounts and reach his own opinion as to the validity of the news presentation.

Board Records Vital

Since the work of the board is laid up in permanent form in official records, these agencies form a vital part of the interpretative responsibilities of the board of education. The official records of the board should be as complete as possible and so organized that they are always available to the public. In well-organized and larger school systems it may even be desirable to set aside a convenient room in headquarters where individuals who display interest may see and read all of the records. In addition, copies may be placed in all branch libraries and in school libraries so that the board journal will always be available for public inspection. Board records are public records and to have full value must be located where they are of easy access to the public.

Apart from the journal itself the most important records are those through which the financial activities of the board are carried on. These records should be complete but so simple in their organization that they may be easily understood by the layman. Purchasing records, bidding blanks, specification sheets, accounting records, and the budget may all be organized with the fact constantly in mind that they are essentially public records and as such should be readily understandable by the people. Much difficulty arises because of inadequate, incomplete, and too complicated records. It is the tendency of every specialist to complicate his procedures and activities unnecessarily, and unless all finance records are constantly appraised in terms of their interpretative as well as their functional values they will tend to become complicated. This condition is unnecessary. The highest effectiveness may be secured through simplicity, provided that social need is always kept well in mind.

Interpreted Tax Statements

The means through which the educational plan is made effective is finance. One of the difficulties involved in any scheme of taxation up to the present is the fact that services have never been correlated with payments. Coöperative community service is given constantly with very little effort to keep its relatively low expense constantly before the people. Tax bills are rendered as generalities without any correlation to service. It is perfectly natural for the individual to react to this condition negatively. Taxes are too high! They always have been and always will be until the true relationship of these expenses to service rendered is intelligently established. There appear to be two easy ways to eliminate these emotional reactions. The first is the budgeting of taxes as a modern need by distributing them in twelve payments and urging upon the householder the desirability of budgeting them monthly just as he does his other bills. The present traditional procedure of lumping them in one payment is so contrary to all other current practice in every line of business and imposes so senseless a burden upon taxpayers that their reactions are logical and rational. The second means that boards of education might adopt is to develop interpretative tax bills in which the service rendered is fully correlated with payments, showing the purpose for which every part of the tax dollar is used. Although this procedure may be legally difficult in certain states, it is also possible to interpret services which taxes bring through other agencies.[4]

Audit Desirable

A final desirable activity is the periodic audit of all finance records by reliable professionals outside of the board of education and also by state educational authority. Fiscal appraisal should not be merely a check of the current records to determine mechanical accuracy of the books but a much deeper study of the actual disposal of all services. When completed, the audit should be translated from the technical report into easily comprehended language and simple tabulations, published so that the layman may be kept thoroughly familiar with conditions. With full community coverage through the schools, distribution of such material may be easily and inexpensively obtained.

COMMUNITY CONTACTS

Though the board of education will operate in the interpretative activity chiefly through its collective aspect, the individual responsibility and scope of individual activity cannot be overlooked or minimized. As a representative of the people each board member is morally obligated to render an account of his stewardship. If the board operates in the manner outlined above each individual will be thoroughly informed regarding the purpose, value, conditions and needs of the schools, and it may be reasonably expected that he will be capable of translating his information to the people. This process of translation will be continuous and may be achieved through informal as well as formal contacts. As an official office holder, the board member will be in demand at many school and

[4] See Chapters 18, 20, 21, and 22.

community gatherings. He usually has a chance to express himself officially under these conditions. It is an excellent opportunity for him to bring before the people certain essential facts, and their promulgation by him lends to the situation a certain official atmosphere that is quite beneficial. On these occasions he may translate in his own language, for his audience, the information received. The chances are good that these informal talks will come closer to popular understanding than many carefully worked-out professional efforts.

Individual Contacts

The widest range of activity in which the board member engages is through individual contacts. In family gatherings, in social relationships, through church activity, in fraternal contacts, in economic and political relationships he has frequent and almost constant opportunity to present in concrete form certain problems and certain needs of the schools. Through these contacts the board member also receives much gossip and much distorted information from members of the community. If thoroughly informed, he may easily counteract these situations by presenting the facts quietly and effectively and offering reference to them in published form. Much baseless gossip may be quickly stopped if the board member is informed and is therefore not caught unawares and placed on the defensive. In meeting these charges and correcting viewpoints he also has the means for keeping the executive continuously informed of possible trouble spots, of incipient conflicts, of differences in opinion, and of lack of understanding. The efforts of the organization may therefore be directed quickly to a correction of these difficulties. Since the board member hears many things that seldom if ever come to the professional ear, his community contacts form an invaluable part of any interpretative program, both as a corrective and as a reporting agent.

One of the pitfalls against which the individual board member must guard in his individual capacity is never to forget his position or his relationship to the entire plan. As an individual he has no legal authority. Though the activity of inspection is one in which he may and should constantly engage, it is always necessary, from a lay standpoint, to bear in mind his limitations and the province of the superintendent, principals, and teachers in carrying out the policies of the board. He should immediately report these opinions to the superintendent in writing. He may listen but need not express himself with respect to any direct or indirect gossip, never committing himself in advance with respect to the action the board may contemplate since it tends to place every other member on the defensive and also creates considerable suspicion and jealousy. He must constantly bear in mind that the operation of a highly complicated social plan involving numerous personnel and operating in an intricate social order is an extremely delicate situation that demands the utmost in official tact and in the maintenance of complete coördination. He must realize the unusual social value of the service rendered to the community and the necessity for subordination of himself as an individual to the welfare and the need of the board as a whole.

CONFLICTS

There are few school districts without serious conflicts which have arisen out of situations created by the board of education either within its organization or in its relationship to the professional executive or the community. Further, it must not be expected that even a high state of effectiveness in the operation of the procedure here outlined will attain the millennium and cause the proverbial lion and sheep to lie quietly with each other. There will probably always be differences of opinion, and there will always be individual personality conflicts. All that may be reasonably hoped for is that the gradual development of a rational plan for the recognition of problems and difficulties in the way of coöperative action will just as gradually tend to minimize some of the major current difficulties and gradually provide for much more effective modes of procedure. It is now possible to recognize and minimize the bad effects of certain types of conflict.

Conflict Within Board

The first classification is that of conflict within the board of education itself. Perfectly rational differences of opinion carried on for a long period on a personal basis result always in bitter antagonisms and enmities. These conflicts in their original form are not essentially irrational, but are due primarily to group activity operating on a low form. If they have continued for a long period, it is practically impossible to harmonize the clashing personalities. Since they result primarily from poor method of operation, the primary remedy appears to be the development of an objective procedure as outlined above.

Individual Conflict

The second group includes the "rugged individualist," the egotist, the mild paranoiac, the bigot, and others. Evidences of conflict in this group are exhibited by assumption of superiority on the part of the individual member by grandiose newspaper interviews, by embarrassment of the board through press statements of plans which tend to place them on record before adequate consideration and discussion had been given, by pseudo-eloquence or "playing the gallery," by long-winded and sometimes bitter personal speeches at board meetings, by attacks on members of the professional personnel, by assuming executive functions in the operation of schools, and in many instances, by personal criticism of superintendent and board members for their actions. Almost every board of education has or has had a conflict of this type.

Remedies

The remedy is not easy. A suggested generalized procedure might include the following attempts at solutions. It is first necessary to analyze and classify the conflict. First of all find out what the individual wants and give it to him if it may be done without danger to the school program. If his demands are impossible of satisfaction or are dangerous, the second best solution is to furnish more freedom and allow him to stand in his true light before the community.

Although they seem to make progress for a time, eventually these irrational "loud speakers" achieve their own destiny—political oblivion—at the hands of the community. Though the average individual enjoys a good fight, marathon battles and dances have little sustaining interest. Time is an excellent ally and ultimate comforter. Many a potential politician has talked himself back to private life. A third method might be considered the policy of developing isolation by the psychological device of "building a fence" around him. Since this type of conflict depends chiefly on replenishment through placing the board of education on the defensive and apparently forcing it to defend itself, a most excellent procedure appears to ignore the dissenting personality and to refuse to be drawn into an argument. A one-sided battle is most unsatisfactory as news. Interest soon languishes. The majority prefer the quiet and decorous behavior of the balance of the board to the raucous shoutings of the "lone wolf," and he is soon forgotten. Another possible solution is to further his political ambitions, if they exist, by assisting him to higher or more personally profitable office. In this attempt the individual may be badly beaten and thus doubly out of the running, or he may win and transfer his peculiar gifts to another field of activity where they are not so potentially dangerous.

One caution is essential. The board of education should never attempt to gag such an individual by restriction of his constitutional right to free speech. It is the worst possible procedure. Although the storm of criticism and abuse may be hard to take with bowed shoulders or unwilling cheek, the danger of using the "gag" will quickly react against the board and in favor of the individual, however irrational his attitude. He quickly achieves martyrdom, a most unsatisfactory state for the rest of the board.

The Executive Member

Many conflicts arise when board members forget their functional relationship to the general plan and assume executive duties. The instant a board member steps into the executive activity, he has short-circuited the authority of the professional executive. The distance between the old days of political preferment in public education and the present trend toward professionalization is still too short in many places to have built up a firm ethic with respect to personnel and board of education relationships. As a result there are numerous teaching and operating persons within a school system always ready to give a straying and eager board member the exact type of information he desires, expecting promotional favors in return. Gossip of all types is carried to him. Essential administrative discipline is broken, and favoritism prevails.

The type of conflict engendered by the meddling board member is also a difficult one for the executive on account of the relationship between a member of the legislative body and the hired professional. If the professional ethic is strong enough, the meddler type will make little headway. If it is not, the problem is one for the board of education to solve. Recognizing the need for functional relationships in order to insure success of the plan, the intelligent board will, as soon as the situation is sensed, proceed to educate the member to his error. If the board of education is operating in terms of clearly defined written policies, reference to this policy may be easily made. If the difficulty continues, a resolution condemning the practice and giving notice to the profession and the community of the stand taken by the board of education should be salutary. In general, the last suggestion should be used only in a final emergency since it places the individual involved in a very unpleasant situation. It is highly desirable that conflicts of this type be cautiously solved without forcing the individual involved openly to lose "face." Though the condemnatory resolution and the official repudiation of his acts may terminate his activities, the result is a disgruntled and emotionally disturbed individual. The pricking of his ego has not made him friendly, and the termination will either be retirement into private life or the beginning of a long political grudge fight.

Vendor Conflicts

There are numerous conflicts arising out of relationships between the board of education and vendors of supplies, materials, equipment, and construction service. These conflicts develop on the part of the board through suspicion of the selling technique of the manufacturers' agents and on the part of the field representatives because of suspicion of unfair procedure on the part of boards of education. The outcome of many of these conflicts is the elimination by the board of certain individuals and firms from future bidding and abstinence from bidding on the part of disgruntled purveyors. They may also result in much neighborhood conflict and sometimes drift into politics. In any case loose talk and gossip result, breeding trouble spots that may develop into serious problems at other periods.

Careful study of these conflicts indicates that both parties usually have their share of blame. However, the serious factor is that the aftermath of conflicts and difficulties in one place is reported back to the sales division, and gradually there is built up in the minds of all field representatives a deep-rooted suspicion of all boards of education, and the trouble spreads. Many of these present-day conflicts had their origin years ago and are received by inheritance.

Competition among the purveyors of materials is keen and sharp. High-pressure and quota salesmanship places undue and unintelligent pressure on field representatives. Central office stimulation, motivation, and rather superficial appraisal in terms of current sales force the field representative to extend himself. He seeks to build good will and to secure a favored position by rendering services of a personal and political nature to board members and professional personnel. Less frequently, direct gifts and bribes are used. Fully cognizant of his own peculiar methods of salesmanship, this type of salesman naturally regards his competitors as operating on a similar basis.

Purchasing procedure employed by many boards of education is frequently sketchy, archaic, or so devised that even the simplest acts may create suspicion. The result is bad and not very helpful to the school program. Community suspicion of business methods by its representatives leads to many difficulties.

The ultimate solution lies in the recognition of fault and the taking of steps to remedy it. The board of education may assist greatly by development and approval of a procedure whereby all purchasing is so open and straightforward with respect to method and public visibility that no suspicion may be attached to it. Suggestions for accomplishment were considered earlier in the chapter. The purchase of all material through standard specifications and public notice, the elimination of the board member from all share in purchasing as an individual will also be very helpful. A board of education may also promulgate definite rules forbidding its executive agents to accept favors, discounts, and gifts from manufacturers' representatives. Summary dismissal is the desirable penalty for violation of these rules.

The board of education may also assist in attempting to bring the fact before all purveyors that it is unnecessary to "buy" business on any other basis than merit and quality of material. The manufacturer and sales organizations might be of great assistance in attempting to develop a higher ethic in their sales programs. However, since the raising of commercial ethics will probably be a long process the immediate responsibility for elimination of this type of conflict and difficulty appears to be in the hands of the board of education.

Press Conflicts

Press conflicts may be generally classified in three types. The first may result from an original basic disagreement on the part of the owner of the paper with the policy of the board of education. An original difference of this type quickly evolves into the "spotting" of outstanding personalities and playing the "news" against them. It is fairly well agreed among professional journalists that conflicts between personalities and drives against individuals are much more satisfactory from the newspaper standpoint than a crusade against a general principle or a specific application of that principle. As time passes the original conflict is forgotten, and the policy of the paper may be determined by tradition or by the suspicions engendered and developed during the conflict.

The second type of conflict with the press, particularly in smaller communities, results from some personal disagreement of the editor or reporter with individual board members. It may be the outcome of an earlier conflict, a fancied wrong to the editor's family or children, or just an expression of partizan politics or religious prejudice. Gradually this disagreement is also shifted to the board of education as a whole and then to the school itself.

The third type of conflict results from the inability of the board members to withstand criticism of their acts by the press. Forgetting that one of the serious functions of the press is to act as an extra-legal appraisal agency and that two parties are required to develop and maintain conflict, the board of education retaliates by replies in a rival paper or by other means, generally so emotional that the original cause of conflict is quickly forgotten in the current fight. The offending reporter may be barred from meetings, or news deliberately withheld from him or his papers in retaliation for his temerity to criticize or disagree.

It is extremely doubtful whether these conflicts may be completely eliminated. However, harmony is readily possible in most instances. Several elements are involved. News lives on conflict. If a difference arises, it is well to analyze the difference fully and attempt first of all to harmonize it in terms of actual facts, instead of on a personal basis. Sometimes a friendly conference with editor or reporter after a luncheon or dinner will furnish a means for recognition of the merit of both sides of the controversy. All discussion of these differences should be kept on a non-personal basis. Let the practice or the principle involved be the permanent basis for adjustment. Cutting off the reporter from his news sources endangers his livelihood. Such procedure will not make him more friendly or inclined to coöperate. It is a most unintelligent procedure. Through it an initially small difference may develop into real suspicion and permanent difficulty. Finally, in all conflicts with the press it is well for a board of education to remember that all of its business is public business and that one of the functions of the press is to act as a popular appraisal agent. The individual who undertakes public business must expect to have a strong light shining on him and his work at all times. He must be prepared for criticism. The practical condition that an individual newspaper often falls far from its true function does not condemn the principle but rather implies that the situation requires more study and more intelligence in the proper orientation of the problem. Though difficult, these conflicts are not insurmountable.

SUMMARY

The board of education plays a peculiar part in the development and execution of the social-interpretation program. As the legislative and appraisal agency for the district its first duty is the study of the needs of the community and the adoption of policy and approval of means of procedure. The activities of the board of education and the technique of discussion and meetings form the next most important phase of its participation in this activity. The major requirement is a technique that will keep the work of the board and the needs of the schools constantly before the people—full publicity at all times. The activity closely related to and growing out of board procedure is that of journal and finance records, one of the most delicate fields in which the board operates. Further, there is the necessity of correlating much more closely the taking of money by taxation with the purposes for which the public revenues are spent. As individuals the members of the board of education are in relatively the same relationship as other organization personnel. Their responsibility lies in furnishing the people facts of the actual conditions, discovering and reporting conflict and trouble spots to the executive. One of the most valuable contributions the board may make is the perfection of a technique which will tend to reduce conflicts between members to a minimum.

Chapter 9

THE SUPERINTENDENT AND STAFF

THE orientation of the superintendent of schools in the interpretative activity is conditioned to a large extent by the existing concepts concerning the nature of this office. The two fundamental practices in operation to-day conceive, first, the board of education as the legislative, executive, and appraisal body; the second, growing out of specialization of function, considers the board of education as only the legislative and appraisal body, with the executive activity delegated to professional specialists. Under the first concept, the standing committees of the board are in reality the multiple executive, and the specialists operating directly under them in instruction, finance, and buildings have relatively little authority. The dual or multiple executive operates more in a secretarial capacity to the specific committee than as a fully responsible executive. The delegation of the executive function completely to professional personnel requires the consideration of this functional activity as a totality or a unit. Under the dual or multiple concept, the board of education acts as the coördinating body; under the unit concept of the executive, the superintendent of schools becomes the coördinator.

For purposes of this presentation the functional viewpoint will be chosen and the executive activity in public education considered as a unitary totality delegated completely to a group of educational specialists under the administrative direction of an officer known most commonly as the superintendent of schools. The superintendent's relationship to and responsibility of social interpretation will be discussed in the following sequence: (1) the superintendent's totality of function, (2) methods of organization, (3) relationship to the board of education, (4) relationship to the professional colleagues, (5) relationship to the people, and (6) appraisal of the program.

SUPERINTENDENT'S FUNCTION

The primary function of educational organization is the execution of the instructional program. The executive activity includes every agent who has a part in making the plan effective, from superintendent through principal, teacher, custodial and clerical personnel. By legal definition the superintendent is only the executive officer of the board and chief executive agent. This legal allocation of authority does not separate him from his coöperating professional and non-professional colleagues.

The general responsibilities of the superintendent of schools are the facilitation of the instructional process by: (*a*) putting the adopted educational policies of the state and of the board of education into practice, (*b*) appraising the practice in accordance with executive needs, (*c*) supplying the board of education with means for keeping the agents and the people fully informed of conditions and needs of the schools, (*d*) furnishing creative leadership to the profession and to the board of education, and (*e*) acting as professional adviser to the board of education.

Under the unitary concept, each of the specialized agents (staff and principals) which become essential as a school system grows in numbers, is regarded as operating under the general executive authority and, for purposes of organization, under the administrative direction of the superintendent. The superintendent is held completely responsible for the successful operation of the educational program in accordance with the means of procedure adopted by the board of education. Limitation of responsibility is conditioned by the totality of financial and other essential means made available at any specific period in relation to program requirements.

As professional adviser to the board of education and responsible for furnishing leadership, the superintendent is also responsible for the determination of need and the building of the plan.[1] It is his duty to develop detailed plans of procedure through which policies may be made effective.

The superintendency is an involved job. He is, first of all, a

[1] See Chapter 6.

state officer and responsible for the carrying out of the mandatory educational program of the state. He is also the executive officer of the board of education. As such he is definitely the eyes and ears of the board and is required to bring before this body all information concerning the condition of the schools. It is doubtful whether he has any moral right to withhold information from this popular legislative body, even if damaging to himself. His fundamental relationship to the board is also a direct relationship to all of the people. On the other side he is a member of the teaching profession and owes a professional duty to his colleagues. The socially astute superintendent conceives of his function in all of these aspects and wisely subordinates self to organization. Tersely expressed, the "we" supplants the "I" feeling.

The superintendent who can quickly gain the confidence of his visitors gains an important advantage in interpretation. He should be friendly and cordial without being familiar or personal. Understanding of the layman and his thought process, tolerance for the other man's point of view, and mental flexibility to shift with need are important qualities. Above all, it is desirable in social relations to avoid all impressions of aloofness, coldness, and academic superiority. Insistence on authority, minutia of detail, and routine processes create many an unnecessary conflict.

ORGANIZATION

Organization is determined by need. The problem of interpreting the schools to the people is a group activity and not the sole responsibility of the superintendent. It is impossible for one person to attempt to carry the burden even in a reasonably small community. If the fundamentally coöperative nature of the work is accepted, certain questions of organization are easily answered.

Decentralization

Though the superintendent is responsible to the board of education for results, his first job is to build an organization that will be effective in terms of the total problem and then orient his personal office to the direct service of this organization. Plans of procedure built on adopted board of education policy should provide for the definite decentralization of authority within each sphere of activity. The major part of the program, beginning with the community survey, through execution and appraisal of the plan, should be delegated to the several attendance districts within the school district. Great freedom, under major policy requirements, should be permitted each attendance district to develop specific activities to meet special sectional need. Sufficient central control can be maintained through appraisal of practice.

An early executive responsibility in plan development is the arousing of interest among all executive personnel in the interpretation activity. The coöperative preparation of general plans, after the adoption of a policy by the board of education, is the second step. There is sufficient creative ability in every school system which, if properly organized and directed, will produce a far more effective scheme for operation than could be accomplished by any single individual. These planning committees may be as diverse in character as the degree of personnel specialization within a school system permits. Every phase of interest should have representation. Janitor, clerk, nurse, visiting teacher, classroom teacher, principal, and staff specialists are all involved.

Staff Duties

In larger systems the several phases of executive activity essential to facilitation of the instructional process are administered by staff specialists. In a functional organization the staff member is an activity specialist without managerial authority. His job is to make the work of principal and teacher easier through furnishing information, suggestions, and devices whereby teaching may be improved. Staff organization varies greatly. In some instances the research activity in both instructional and administrative areas is concentrated in one or two divisions. In others there is a wiser placement by the organization of research within each specific area, such as child accounting, instruction, personnel, plant, finance, service of supplies, records, and publications. Whatever the organization, the staff specialists are the centers of all information. Every item of information must pass through their offices for tabulation and interpretation. The staff reports are the primary means through which the superintendent is kept aware of what is taking place in the schools. All of this information should be available to the board of education and to the individual schools as a basis for operation.

Earlier opinion also inclined to the organization of the interpretative activity as a staff function under the direction and control of a public-relations specialist. This concept is perfectly sound for a highly centralized and autocratic organization or for a narrow concept of interpretation as primarily concerned with publicity and social contacts. It is of dubious value for a complete program in the decentralized type of organization now recommended.

The practice of delegating responsibility for all aspects of an activity to each division or department appears much more rational for permanent functioning. Thus each staff division would be responsible for research in its own field and also for the interpretative aspect of its area of responsibility. Instead of a high-powered professional publicist in one division attempting to do all the work of written, oral, and visual interpretation, the more complete permeation of every staff member with consciousness of the importance of the whole interpretative process appears to have larger possibilities for success. Under this concept the superintendent would maintain, as he normally should, direct general control of the interpretative activity, delegating the execution rather completely to staff and to individual school buildings.

Size Differences

The only real difference between the small and larger community is in number of personnel and amount of detail. In the small district the superintendent combines within his own person the staff activities that are delegated in the larger organization. His collection agency includes generally only a clerk and bookkeeper. Hence these problems of staff organization do not immediately affect him. On the whole his organization problem is much simpler although the interpretative activity possesses the same problems and the same complexities in both the small and large community.

Superintendent's Office

As a public official the superintendent of schools is a popular symbol to the people. One of the insistent demands of a democratic organization is for personal contact with their officials, whether to secure favors, present grievances, or offer advice. The superintendent must be easily available to board members, the teaching profession, and the general public. Hence the organization of his office is of more than passing significance in the field of interpretation.

Though corporations may hide their chief executives on the upper floors of tall buildings, the rule of accessibility requires that public executives should be easy to reach. Hence the location of the superintendent's office on the first floor, near the main entrance, is definitely indicated. The public official must rely upon the intelligence of information clerk and secretary in order to be kept free from petty annoyance. He may also be provided with a small working office in a more inaccessible part of the building where he may retire as occasion requires, for uninterrupted work.

Offices of the board of education should be located preferably in a building separate from a school itself. If the superintendent's office is in a school building, it inevitably dwarfs the principalship and may cause definite internal organization conflicts. Wherever size permits, a separate building is desirable. Where separation is impractical, the board of education offices should be isolated as much as possible from the school itself, even to the extent of separate entrances.

Initial contact with public organization is important. A visitor must be able to find his way easily to the desired office. A general information center, maintained close to the main building entrance, is a valuable asset.

Public business must not be done behind closed doors. Some public-building specialists to-day advocate administration buildings in which all offices are in full view of a wide central corridor, separated only by waist- or shoulder-high partitions. Quiet from noise may be secured through careful acoustical treatment. Psychologically this is a perfectly sound idea. Since the majority of school executive

An information station and exhibition cases in the modern style attract visitors.

Clear glass partitions allow the public to see how business is conducted.

offices are located in old school buildings or in sections of private and public buildings devoted to other uses, such open organization may be too difficult of attainment. A desirable modification is the use of clear-glass partitions between offices so that all employees are constantly in full view. Doors between the general and private office should never be locked. It is even desirable to have only latches that will permit closing but not locking. Solid doors and spring locks on private offices are distinct liabilities in public administration. It is sufficient if outer or corridor doors are locked. Valuable papers and records may be easily safeguarded in fireproof vaults or metal desks where they are afforded protection against both fire and theft.

Close to the superintendent's office and board room should be a large room where general current information concerning the conditions and needs of the schools may be displayed in graphic form on wall charts carefully protected by glass covering. This room may be considered as a private office not available to the general public where board members, superintendent, and staff may quickly secure essential information. The value of this informational exhibit lies in keeping the material up to date. Supplementary to this room may be the professional library where all books and current publications of value to superintendent and staff are readily available.

Contact Personnel

In large cities two of the most important posts are those of informational and departmental secretaries. An information center is without value if great care is not used in the selection of personnel. The informational secretary in smaller systems may also be the telephone operator, but in large centers higher specialization is demanded.

In the selection of all "front office" or contact personnel, the first requirement should be an attractive personality. A woman is preferred in all cases. She should be selected on the basis of being a good listener, possessing a sense of humor, good breeding, tact, tolerance, balance, friendliness, reasonableness, a sound time sense, and evenness of disposition. The second qualification is social intelligence, and the third is general intelligence. She must be able to remember names and faces and to respond instinctively to an individual's sense of his own importance.

Knowledge of the school system is important, and other things being equal, a trained teacher is preferred. Much of the secretary's value consists in her judgment and ability to route an individual to those officers who are most interested. Though technically the superintendent is always available, it is her duty to protect him from unnecessary interviews. The second contact by the visitor should be the departmental secretary. These individuals possessing similar abilities are valuable to the extent that they short-circuit all unnecessary contact with the superintendent or staff member, at the same time leaving the visitor completely satisfied with respect to his initial objective. Socially intelligent secretaries are invaluable in satisfying the visitor and protecting the officials.

RELATION TO BOARD OF EDUCATION

As the executive agent of the board of education the superintendent is legally responsible for furnishing full and complete information to its members. His first duty is to keep the board of education completely and continuously informed of the conditions and needs of the schools in order that members may consider and appraise intelligently both policies and means. The second job is to educate the board members to a realization of their office and their responsibilities in carrying on the democratic educational process.

The board may be kept informed through a system of periodic reports on the state of the schools. These progress reports should be condensed as much as possible and carefully written so that the busy layman may quickly secure essential information. For those who desire to delve more deeply, much more detailed information may be furnished in appendix form. The summary of conditions is essentially the superintendent's interpretation to the board. Since differences of opinion may arise among board members concerning interpretation, it is highly desirable to have complete information available with each presentation.

THE SUPERINTENDENT AND STAFF

Instruction

Reports to the board should include first of all analysis of instructional conditions and problems. Initially, the board member will not display much interest in this type of information, but as the true function of the school is kept before him in language that he understands, his thinking may be affected by function rather than supplementary activity. Too many superintendents avoid discussion of instructional problems with the board of education because the field is technical, the interest low, and the difficulty of interpretation great. As a result the board inclines more to giving major consideration to supplies, equipment, plant, and finance—activities more easily understood. Finally, the tail begins to wag the dog. In too many instances the almost complete absorption of boards of education in the so-called "practical activities" may be traced directly to the lack of educational leadership exercised by a succession of superintendents. It is vital that the board of education be educated to the all-embracing importance of the instructional program and the proper subordination of all other facilitating activities. This job is one of the most important facing the superintendent.

Child Accounting

Next in importance to instruction are the child-accounting reports through which the board may become aware of how effectively the institution is meeting its legal responsibility for education. If monthly reports were presented with sensible interpretation, some progress might be made in solving the problem of non-attendance of many children. Solution of this problem is not one for punitive technique, but involves rather the problem of better community education in coöperating to secure these educational advantages for the children.

Plant

Information concerning the use of the plant is important to the board. It is most embarrassing for board members to discover, through individual reports outside of the school system, that the physical plant is not being used to best advantages or is being misused. The physical plant not only represents a large investment, but is a continually obvious monument. There may be good and sufficient reasons for non-use of certain facilities or low use of others. Board members should be the first to know these reasons and thus be intelligently capable of controverting community gossip and avoiding personal embarrassment. Reports of this type may include capacity, use, and explanation of use. By maintaining continuing records in this field it is also possible to prepare years in advance for necessary additions and changes to the physical plant. Progressive understanding of need eliminates senseless emergencies and dangerous high-pressure campaigns.

Teacher

Although the teacher is the most important agent in the instructional process, few boards of education are acutely aware of it. Unless board members and the community are given understanding of this fact, improvement of personnel is difficult. Too many boards of education still consider the teacher as any other laborer, to be secured as cheaply as possible and worked to the limit of physical endurance. There is too little official concern with growth, development, well-being, and efficiency of the teacher. Personnel presents a wide area for informing and educating the board members. Groundwork will require education of the importance of the teacher and the need for growth through effective organization and extended training. Periodic appraisal of personnel conditions should be included in these reports.

Service of Supplies

Price-buying characterizes the majority practice by which educational supplies and equipment are secured. Since little effort is made to present need from the purely instructional standpoint and the building of standards according to instructional requirements, the "lowest bidder" practice, without specific specifications is the rule rather than the exception. From this implication many of our large city districts must be excluded. Where boards of education are politically dominated and controlled, supplies and equipment, along with school-plant construction, represent the darkest spot in educational administration.

The best teaching effort can be easily nullified if the paper, pens, pencils, and ink are of inferior quality. It is doubtful practice to spend money on teaching handwriting if the quality of physical tools is so low that the children cannot perform efficiently. If children are to be taught color recognition, it is desirable that they be exposed to the true colors instead of shades of color which comprise the cheaper stocks in paper, paints, and chalk.

Finance

Since finance is only a facilitating agency, its proper orientation is important. Program should determine finance. It is recognized that so long as our traditionally inefficient systems of taxation are maintained, certain limitations on program are normally necessary. However, the principle is sound and should form a basic part of the board's education. If finance is intelligently translated into instructional results, the development of the functional point of view is not so difficult as it might appear on the surface. Budgets can be developed as the direct impersonal translation of policy and should be interpreted to the board of education from this aspect. Since nothing is so quickly disastrous in public administration as careless handling of money, accounting practice must include safeguards against overdrafts and the incurring of deficits. Hence a system of monthly reports that will indicate appropriations, encumbrances, and balances is extremely helpful in focusing attention on fiscal management.

Community

Community problems and needs are another type of information that needs careful organization. Information concerning community habits of thoughts, conflict and problem areas, and desires is fundamental to a well-informed board of education. Most executives are chary of reporting on community conditions. They apparently feel that expediency is a better policy. However, intelligent board members will quickly pick up stray information in the community. Teachers, parents, and other disgruntled personnel quietly find their way to the source of legal authority. Pre-warning by the superintendent will prevent members from being embarrassed through lack of knowledge. Reports on community conditions should be highly confidential, and there is some justification for the feeling that they may best be presented orally. Selection of means can be determined by the conditions within the community.

The annual report and the house organ, where used, are not primarily pointed to the board of education and will be considered later.

Other Media

The growth of board members in understanding of work and efficiency in functioning is contingent upon how well they understand the general educational problems and are also familiar with the efforts of other communities. For their exposure and stimulation the superintendent must assume responsibility. He may suggest and carry out programs of visitation by members to local and neighboring schools. Wherever good practice is available, such visitation may be planned. He may urge consistent attendance at state and national education programs. Many superintendents plan definitely for these meetings. Board members are advised as to worthwhile programs, and discussion sessions between superintendent, staff, and board members follow each meeting. Questions are raised and discussed, and technical points which may not be clear to the layman are simplified. The results are usually alert and understanding boards.

The superintendent may also furnish board members with professional magazines and certain non-technical books. Since these publications have been prepared primarily for the professional, their interest value to the beginning board member is doubtful. It may be of far greater value to digest and interpret certain significant articles, making the full publication available in the professional library.

Personal Appearance

Board members should carry much more of the burden in social interpretation than is normally the case. It is part of the leadership function of the superintendent to provide the members with opportunities for diverse community contacts and with the materials for speaking engagements. As representatives of the people these members are definitely responsible for giving an account of their stewardship directly to the people.

Board members may be considered as symbols of the state and community at commencement time in presenting diplomas to graduates. The board can also be represented on community question panels held in the schools. There are numerous other opportunities for speaking engagements. Every time a board member presents the problems and needs of the schools, he is not only acting in his fundamental stewardship relationship but also as a definite social shield to the teaching profession.

It may require much time and effort to develop board members as effective speakers, but it is worth much in accruing social values.

Preparation

One safe rule to follow in board-superintendent relationships is for the superintendent to avoid presenting a problem to the board as a whole upon which the individuals have not been at least partially informed. Nothing causes a quicker and more negative action from elected officials than to be confronted with need for a decision on a subject with which they are unfamiliar. It is almost fatal to attempt work with a "cold" board.

Since the effectiveness of board-superintendent relations will be finally determined by the degree of confidence in the superintendent as a person, it is also essential to plan for continuous individual contacts on a social basis with individual members. These contacts will require considerable sacrifice of personal leisure, but the successful public executive must be ready to make such concessions to insure success.

RELATION TO THE PROFESSION

The superintendent's relationship to the teaching profession in social interpretation is as general director of the entire program and a means for furnishing creative leadership. Specific training of the specialized agents, except in very small systems, is the principal's responsibility under the decentralized plan of organization.

As director of the entire program the executive makes general plans, directs the community survey, and builds procedures. Use of the coöperative technique will call for the careful organization of committees which will work on specific elements in the program. Since the functional concept of the interpretative activity is that of a continuing program of adult education, detailed methodology and practice are normally more closely aligned with the principal than with the superintendent. It is the superintendent's job to point out what should be done through translation of the policies of the board of education, suggest means for doing it, stimulate interest and understanding, and then delegate the detailed execution to the responsible agents. He is also responsible for the periodic appraisal of the results and the building of new plans and procedures.

The more clearly the superintendent delegates execution in terms of a broad general framework, the greater the possibility of success. Teachers and principals must be allowed wide freedom and initiative. Social education cannot be hampered by red tape nor can its agents be subjected to detailed and constant supervision.

Contact with professional and non-professional personnel in the small system may be possible through oral means alone. Periodic meetings and conferences appear sufficient for this purpose. In larger centers the occasional oral contact may be supplemented by written means. Occasional bulletins, house organs, and teacher publications are all effective agencies.

Open Channels

The superintendent is definitely concerned in maintaining two-way informative channels within the executive organization. Channels for outgoing information are easily established and maintained.

They exist in every school system. Incoming channels also exist, but are most generally used for routine transmission of information. Every executive needs to know the exact conditions in community and schools. If bad news is distasteful or arouses emotion, bad news soon stops coming in. Too many city superintendents are to-day actually isolated from much essential information because the word has been passed in field administrative circles that bad news makes the chief nervous and causes tantrums. It is always possible for the executive to secure what he wants, so, if only good news is in order, only good news will be reported. The closing of incoming channels for social information is the beginning of incompetency in functioning. Public administration requires an impervious skin and strong nerves. It is no place for jittery individuals.

Balancing the Load

Extreme care needs to be exercised so that the burden of social interpretation does not fall on a few willing and capable individuals. Progressive recognition of the importance of the interpretative activity in improving the institutional efficiency should lead to a careful restudy of its implications with respect to teaching load. Teachers are in too many instances sadly overburdened because instructional activity and interpretative duties have been added to an already full day. The problem calls for a new attitude toward the teacher work-load on a broader base than the currently accepted formalized student-clock-hours of classroom instruction.

Loyalties

Even in a large system it is possible for the superintendent to maintain close relations with professional and non-professional personnel by being accessible to conference and friendly in professional relationships. The day of paternalism in educational organization has passed into limbo. The superintendent and principal are no longer the "educational fathers" of the teaching profession but rather the professional colleagues of fellow-workers. The superintendent or principal whose practices are unethical should deserve the support and confidence of the teaching profession no more than other individuals. Confidence and respect for their professional integrity is the largest degree of executive expectancy. Personal loyalties are neither possible nor desirable at the present; they have no place in educational organization. To secure more complete professionalization and hence responsible functioning, organization loyalties must be built around professional ideals. Appraisal of individuals may then proceed on how well they meet professional standards of performance rather than in terms of personality.

RELATION TO THE PEOPLE

The superintendent's relation to the people in the interpretative program should be confined so far as possible to generalized contacts that will result in creating attitudes and developing confidence. In the small system his popular contacts will be social and oral; in a large system they may be supplemented by written means, including the annual report, the budget, house organ, the newspaper, and possible home contacts through letters to parents.

In general, one of the major executive aims should be to increase the community's confidence in the teaching profession. Too many districts think of the educational process as operated by a big executive with many minor assistants, a normal transfer from their economic experience. Good educational administration has little in common with autocratic business practice. The sooner this myth is destroyed, the better it will be for education. One of the best means of increasing popular confidence in the teaching profession is to bring both teachers and principals forward and permit them to display their ability through speaking and other personal demonstration.

In medium-sized and small communities it is possible to make effective use of specialists in the several fields of subject-matter and service activities such as health and psychology. Initial adult intellectual interest in science, vocations, and fine arts may be progressively directed to specific interest in these phases of the school program.

The beginning superintendent may find it difficult to avoid oral contact with every important community organization. Every group wants top names for its programs. It is an American characteristic not to be satisfied with less. It is also wise for the superintendent to appear personally on different programs as the official representative of public education. However, constant appearances dull popular appreciation quickly. When later demands are made, it is comparatively easy to suggest some principal or teacher who might be equally capable of talking in a certain field of specialization.

Bringing other personnel into the spotlight is not merely a device to relieve the already burdened superintendent but also a means to assert to the community that their educational plan rests not on a whim of a single individual but rather on the coöperative efforts of many persons, each an able and accomplished individual in his own field of specialization. Bringing out and building up the teaching personnel is an indirect means for creating greater respect and confidence for the teaching profession in the community.

Personal Knowledge

Through personal contact, observation, and through information derived from the community survey, the well-informed executive may become acquainted with the strengths and weaknesses of the community and its social, political, economic, and religious leaders. It is extremely important that he know personally as many of these individuals as possible. Many difficulties can be solved through knowing the key men in any situation.

Personal Affiliations

Even the most enthusiastic joiner cannot affiliate with each and every one of the numerous social interest groups so characteristic of our culture. It is necessary to make selection and limit social contacts to certain areas. Church and fraternal and political organizations will probably take care of themselves on a basis of earlier personal choice. Beyond these personal areas, the superintendent, as head of the state public schools, should be extremely careful of the types of permanent affiliations made. In certain communities there is considerable merit in the criticism that the schools in operation incline toward certain group interests rather than maintaining their normal social impartiality. There is no reason why the superintendent who joins a chamber of commerce should not also be closely associated with a labor organization. If this duality is impossible in the one person, every effort should be made to have members of the professional and non-professional staff provide such affiliations. If the superintendent cannot cover all types of major interests, it might be better to maintain personal freedom from organization membership, suggesting more complete association on the part of his colleagues.

The socially alert superintendent will include in his plans means for maintaining complete coverage in social and economic organization through stimulating these contacts on the part of teachers and principals. The more widely the community comes in contact with a good teaching staff, the greater will be the normal confidence in and respect for their work.

APPRAISAL

Continuing appraisal is essential to the success of the superintendent's work in the interpretation process. His is the definite responsibility for the development of means whereby the entire plan of procedure may be judged as to efficiency of operation and the totality of effect upon the school system. Fairly gross appraisal is possible in determining his specific relationships to the board of education, to the teaching profession, and to the public. Devices and methods of appraisal of other activities may be taken from current practice or may be developed to meet the specific needs of the district or activity.

Research methodology in social interpretation is practically an unexplored field. A few valuable techniques exist, but in general most of the work still needs to be done. At the present time, the development of an intelligently critical attitude toward programs and results is the first essential. Some difficulty is apparently experienced in social relations in objectifying one's efforts. It is even more important to stimulate to self-appraisal each individual involved in the process.

SUMMARY

The primary function of the superintendent in social interpretation is as leader and general director. It is not his work to be a detail man. The process of interpretation is so involved and complicated, requiring the services of so many diverse individuals, that attempts at accomplishment by autocratic means and individual executive effort are futile. High-pressure publicity will not compensate for low morale or negative attitudes on the part of clerk, custodian, or teacher. The coöperative nature of this process must be more fully appreciated.

The most effective social leadership is that which recognizes the nature and problems of democratic structure and stimulates others to efforts. Some of the most successful administrators include those whose names appear infrequently in public press and in school publications. The wise superintendent in recognition of the nature of his work uses the board of education as a social buttress in the formation of policy and consequent protection of the profession. He recognizes and attempts to build the popular esteem for and confidence in the teaching profession by building up its members to wider and more successful social participation. He attempts through multiplicity of contact to bring school and community close together. In so doing he astutely avoids the spotlight of temporary personal publicity for the more solid backlog of group achievement. Professional competency needs to be given more complete recognition. Successful subordination of self and elevation of the group are definite hall-marks of successful social administration.

Finally, the superintendent must be aware of the value of time in institutional success. Sound program-building requires more time than flash publicity. Not only is time needed to build plans, train agents, and develop method through cautious experimentation, but it is a definite essential in the development of fundamental confidence in both institution and personnel. Executive success in social interpretation as well as in the instructional field requires that a superintendent remain long enough on a job to understand the community and to be able to give his full and undivided attention to the problem, unhampered by too frequent outside excursions in collateral job-hunting. Too short tenure in a community is in itself a handicap to a comprehensive and wise appraisal of the specific needs of the educational program including the community at large, the teaching staff, and the children enrolled in the schools.

Chapter 10

THE BUILDING PRINCIPAL

PLANS may be projected and perfected by general administration, but they become effective only as they are put into action by the individual school. The building principal is the most important field administrative agent in any well-rounded interpretation program. The maintenance of primary community relationships is one of his major responsibilities. Within the limits of the attendance area for which he is administratively responsible, the principal is in direct control of all aspects of the plan. His duties are similar to those of the superintendent so far as scope is concerned. They differ in area and in so far as the principal is required to place the program into actual operation and to direct specialized agents in their various duties.

In the larger school districts building differentiation is possible. In the smaller districts plant specialization is distinctly limited. Instead of a large number of elementary units and secondary centers, all of the children are gathered into a single building. As a result of building differentiation in large centers the elementary and secondary principalships are also highly specialized. In the single building district the principalship is too frequently a salary title, and his activities are restricted to teaching, maintaining records, and disciplining. By the process of condensation, the superintendent in these centers assumes much of the responsibility for direct interpretation that normally is delegated to the principal. Examination of responsibility and activity will be presented here in its widest scope.

There is no difference in principle or general technique between the interpretative responsibilities of the elementary and secondary principal. Elementary attendance districts tend to be more homogeneous in social composition than secondary attendance districts. The secondary school's sphere of influence is much wider territorially and generally much more diversified with respect to details. The homogeneity of the elementary attendance districts is replaced by wider social, economic, and religious differences. The mother-child relationship is probably closer during the elementary period than at any other time. The onset of adolescence produces a change in these relationships, and the problem of parent contacts presents more diversity and difficulties in the secondary-school program.

Though the general pattern of activity is not subject to variation, differences in program detail change directly with community and cannot be specified minutely in a generalized treatment. The same groups of activities are essential in the small and the large district.

The position and responsibility of the building principal in the social-interpretation activity will be considered as: (1) the totality of the principal's function, (2) harmonizing district conflicts, and (3) methods and devices.

THE PRINCIPAL'S FUNCTION

The building principal is the administrative field officer of public education. His specific functional duty is the facilitation of instruction through: (a) putting into operation the course of study, instructions, and standards of achievement, and supervising of the classroom and extra-classroom activities to see that these standards are achieved; (b) carrying out the adopted policies, through approved means, as directed by the superintendent, that provide physical and educational conditions under which child and teacher may work to best advantages; (c) appraising and reporting educational, social, and physical conditions within the school, preparing reports, and making recommendations for the improvement of conditions; (d) furnishing professional leadership to administrative, teaching, and operating agents by collecting data, conducting research; and (e) maintaining community relationships.

Interpretation Duties

The building principal's interpretation duties may be sequentially expressed as eleven major activities: (a) conducting continuing sociological survey; (*b*) making detailed plans and selecting possible agencies for particular uses; (*c*) surveying and analyzing possibilities of the teaching and non-teaching agents under his direction; (*d*) selecting possible community agents, organized and unorganized, as district nucleus; (*e*) planning the organization of agents and agencies and developing specific programs; (*f*) training the teaching and non-teaching agents; (*g*) executing the program; (*h*) surveying the results of the program; (*i*) appraising the results and modifying the program in terms of this appraisal; (*j*) locating, reporting, analyzing, and remedying trouble spots; and (*k*) making recommendations for improvement.

Community Survey

The generalized procedure for conducting continuing community survey was considered in Chapter 7. It is only necessary here to present certain differentials as they affect the elementary and secondary attendance districts. The elementary principal is responsible for developing the generalized community inventory as well as the analysis of those problems that concern primarily the preadolescent segment of population. This common information can be assembled easily by each secondary school from the elementary attendance districts it serves. Close contact between elementary and secondary schools is necessary since the secondary school should be supplied with knowledge of changing conditions in somewhat greater detail than the superintendent's office. The continuing survey in the secondary school can be confined to the gathering of information more immediately related to its functioning.

Since the success of any program of interpretation depends upon the extent to which the individual school knows its community, the terminal purpose of survey activity should always be kept well in the foreground. The school must be aware of what is going on in its area of responsibility in order to avoid lost effort and to prevent serious errors. An actively functioning survey should inform the school of potential difficulties long before they arise.

Making Plans

Though the general policy may be constant, plans and procedures must be custom-built to meet the varying needs of different sections. School programs should at all times be flexible, subject both to change and shift in emphasis as the information derived from the community survey may indicate. The plan should be designed to provide for continuous information flowing from the community to the school and from the school to the community. It should embrace contacts with the entire community.[1]

Selecting Agencies

After the general plan has been determined, the next step is the study and selection of specific agencies whose existence, interests, and availability have already been determined through the social survey. Each of the possible agencies must now be studied and given a definite part in the general plan. Means for bringing each type into closer relationship and harmony with the public school must be developed. In this specific field the secondary-school social interpretation program differs greatly from that of the elementary school. If the district has been planned logically, it may represent a regional unit with fairly complete social and economic activity. Luncheon clubs, improvement associations, social-service organizations, women's clubs, fraternal orders, youth groups, newspapers, and many other types of activity may be present. Though the parent-teacher association may be an extremely effective agency in elementary education, it is generally not so successful in the secondary field. Possibilities of supplementing the secondary parent-teacher groups with smaller mothers' clubs, home-room groups, or individual parent-teacher conferences must be carefully considered.[2] The chances for success are greater if these mother groups are planned in relationship to the elementary district in which the members live. If the elementary program has been effectively developed, they are already acquainted with each other and accustomed

---

[1] See Chapters 16 and 19.
[2] See Chapter 17.

to the neighborhood group. The transition of this smaller group intact to the secondary school has fewer difficulties than an attempt to create a larger parent-teacher organization from elements that are much too diverse.

After thorough knowledge of the district possibilities has been secured and the general plan roughly developed, the third step is the selection of agents. These will vary with the size of the school district and the policy of organization. In the dual or multiple executive type the agents will probably be limited to the teacher; in the functionally organized unit-executive a greater variety of choice is possible. The widest program might include the following: teachers, librarians, clerk, custodian and cleaners, school nurse, and visiting teacher.

Every one of these agents should be studied in terms of temperament, personality, social background, social interests, special abilities, and interests in order that each may be carefully and intelligently entrusted with the type of activity in which the greatest success is possible. Some individuals are eminently fitted to maintain community contacts through general association. Others will work better in intimate parent-teacher-child conference. Still others have special gifts that make them excellent educational agents through their ability in oral expression. Whatever the specific talent of any individual, there is a definite place for him in the general program if selection is carefully studied.

Initial adjustment of agents is highly essential to success since in these social situations so much depends upon individual initiative, tact, and social skill. If the interest factor is neglected, there is bound to be loss of efficiency.

Community Agents

It is difficult if not impossible to operate an interpretation program with a large measure of success just by dependence upon the institutional agents. There exists a large necessity for the selection, organization, and development of community agents who, once trained, will act as a leader-group nucleus in carrying the program. From a purely psychological standpoint the more non-institutional agents intelligently operating within a district, the more effective the program will be. The selection of the community agents requires rare skill. Probably the safest method for the beginner is to use the available organizations to secure key agents. The most frequent are the parent-teacher associations, the American Association of University Women, and the various types of community clubs. Suggestions for possible experimentation would be the use of the "block-mother" idea, so successfully used in certain other types of social work. Other possibilities are the gradual and progressive enlistment and education of the economic, labor, social, political, and religious community leaders.

Though it is difficult to carry on a complete interpretative program without using community agents, it is also necessary to exercise great care in their selection with due reference to their relationship to specific localities and interests. The best advice in this field is to be conservative and to proceed only when success is practically certain.

Organization

Where a diversified program exists and numerous agents participate, the need for organization arises. It should never be considered, however, except as a facilitating device and developed only to the point of effectiveness required in execution. The same close organization possible in the larger instructional program may defeat its own ends if projected into interpretation. Organization must be inconspicuous. Apparent spontaneity of action and casualness of method is the acme of successful social organization. The principal, however, should have a clear-cut plan and a definite means for achieving it. He must know where to place agents and the means through which they work. He must provide channels whereby the information from the superintendent's office may be quietly and quickly digested and transmitted in the most intelligible form both to the school and to the community. He must also provide for reporting back to the superintendent.

As the responsible director, the principal's primary function in organization is the furnishing of leadership and planning. It is not action in the sense that mere personal activity makes for success. The nature and complexity of the educational process make it increasingly difficult for any individual to assume complete responsibility. The wise executive quickly senses the limits of one-man control and devises plans whereby responsibility for both planning and execution can be widely diffused through both school and community. The secret of successful organization is its ability to operate effectively even in the absence of one or two key individuals.

A good device for school organization is the building of a permanent committee within the organization. Membership may be determined both by interest and by special abilities. The types of required abilities will be determined by the scope of the program. If direct publicity is one of the important phases, then a teacher whose interest lies in this field and who has both the training and skill to carry it out would normally be a committee member. If school exhibits are to be featured, talent for this type of work should be sought. The school interpretation committee may include from three to ten members, depending on diversity of program and size of school. It should be simple in organization and flexible in personnel. There is no reason why non-professional personnel such as clerks and custodians should be excluded from membership. Care should be taken not to overload a single individual regardless of talent.

Those principals who are not enthusiastic about the committee organization may use the creative and key teacher to assist in planning and administrative aspects. For planning, individuals should be chosen who have given indication of having ideas in the several program aspects. For the executive aspect, particularly in the training of personnel and follow-up of program, individuals acting as key teachers should have shown some administrative capacity in different aspects of school work.

Each attendance district has its own neighborhood leaders and its special interest groups. These leaders may be invited to form a district advisory committee to stimulate community contacts and to act as buffers in the prevention and harmonization of conflict.

Certain aspects of the program may be delegated to this group. It is at once a primary unity for direct individual education as well as for community education. There is no reason why there should be only a single community committee. There might well be as many groups as there are special phases of program interest. The education of these members to the realization of the importance of active participation in the American partnership concept in public education, between home and school, is a desirable outcome.

Planning the Program

The principal may now plan the program in terms of exact knowledge of conditions, of possible organized agencies, and personnel. In this respect it is desirable to emphasize the fact that the ultimate objective of interpretation should be the education of each individual to the purpose, value, conditions, and needs of the schools. A well-balanced program will attack the problem from many angles but ultimately should produce closer contact and better understanding between the school and home. The problem of home and school contacts must therefore be featured. The logical procedure is the development of active interest, coöperation, and understanding through parental visitation and conference. The visiting teacher, the nurse, and the socially capable instructor should be capable of encouraging, stimulating, and maintaining effective school contacts. Techniques must be developed so that parental contacts are positive. Conflicts must be avoided.

Though the principal may lead and direct the major work, probably the most valuable suggestions will come from those who are in intimate contact with field conditions. In building the plan it is desirable to sketch first the rough outlines of the entire structure and then proceed slowly to fill in the framework with detailed activities, each specifically pointed to contribute to the major objective.

If the ultimate objective is constantly kept in mind, it will be easier to avoid some of the cheap, unworthy, and frequently distorted views of the public-school program that now grace many of our newspapers. It is not necessary to stress direct publicity. Far more permanent results will accrue from effective and direct home and community contacts.

Training the Personnel

The success of any venture, no matter how skilfully conceived and intelligently developed, depends finally on the attitude, ability, and skill of the personnel involved. The basis for success is the effectiveness of the personnel training program. The agent requires first of all to have an intelligent understanding of the nature of the interpretation activity, its possibilities and its dangers. Each agent must be aware of his individual responsibility for a small section of the program, its relation to the specific school and to public education generally. He should also be aware of its immediate effect upon him as a member of the teaching profession. A good way to prepare agents is through a specific course in this field by which familiarity with the problem and development of skill in procedure is accomplished.

As director of the entire instructional program, of which interpretation is a single phase, the principal must be able to instruct the personnel with respect to the entire field of problems, the basic necessity for the program, and the technique of execution. In this activity he may be assisted by outside specialists and by key teachers or committee members, but the duty is essentially his, and the outcome of the program will depend on how well he performs this task. The details of procedure must be developed by the individual school.

Since the interpretative activity presents a teaching problem even more intricate and under less control than the regular curricular activities, the same degree of skill and attention to detail must be used in the training program. Program outlines, teaching suggestions, bibliographies, and an adequate professional library are indicated as essential. After the general idea has been developed, key teachers may work with different sections and with different types of education. Home contacts, school contacts, building use, development of social nuclei, direct publicity in school, neighborhood and community press—all differ in treatment and method and require different techniques. Every phase of the program must be considered and every phase taught to the participating personnel.

Executing the Program

In the actual execution of the plan it should be constantly remembered that the ultimate purpose is education of the community to the purpose, value, conditions, and needs of public education. Needs can be considered only after a sympathetic understanding of conditions has been developed. There is so wide a gap between the current progressive instructional program and the average adult conception of such a program that considerable time is required to bridge the first gap before considering the possible future. The attainment of objectives will be a relatively slow process. Since the most effective long-time plan discards the highly emotional appeal that characterizes "high-pressure" publicity, the time element cannot be given too much consideration. Final success depends upon how well the ground work has been laid.

The execution of the interpretative program should therefore proceed slowly and by the piecemeal process. It is well to avoid haste and, above all, to escape the suspicion of propaganda or selfish personal aggrandizement. Many serious mistakes have been made through overeagerness and too much speed. Patience is a most vital element in success.

Surveying the Results

Continuing research is essential to the success of the interpretation program. All possible means should be employed to ascertain the change in community attitude, the progressive elimination of conflicts, better adjustment and understanding between home and school, increasing interest of parents in school visitation, better coöperation between teachers and parents, and better support of essential changes in the school program.

There are many avenues through which it is possible to secure this information. Attitudes may be determined through interview, the occasional school question clinic in which parents ask questions and express themselves on various aspects of the program, the number of parental visits to the school, the degree of voluntary activity on the part of community leaders, and analysis of letters from parents to teachers, principal, and to the newspapers.

Appraising the Results

Information secured from informal survey forms the basis for judgment of the effectiveness of the program. Exact appraisal is difficult in so widespread a program. It is the principal's responsibility to judge the effect of the program in his own particular attendance district. In general group appraisal, if the committee method is used, will be more effective than the principal's individual judgment.

The criteria to be used as a basis for appraisal are those which form the basis and purpose of the program. In summary, the end results of the interpretation activity should be a better understanding and appreciation of the purpose, value, conditions, and needs of public education, and an increased community and professional morale, all of which should serve better the vital purpose of the educational process—the production of a well-integrated personality for effective living and for effective contribution to the betterment of society.

Program modifications may be quickly made on the basis of the evidence collected and analyzed.

Locating Trouble Spots

Appraisal and the ensuing modification of program complete the logical sequence, but special attention must be given to a constant study of "trouble spots" or conflict areas. They exist in every community regardless of size. Sometimes they represent healthy differences of opinion, but more frequently they indicate lack of adjustment of the institution to the community. They may have their inception in general community conflicts, community failures, or direct conflict between school and community. They may be due to the professional agents, the principal, the board of education, or may lie completely outside of organization responsibility. They exist most annoyingly in communities where the interpretation activity is still considered as a vague theory, but they also appear suddenly in the best regulated program. Whatever the cause, these "trouble spots" are serious. Every school should be in such close relationship to its patrons that any emotional disturbance or conflict will immediately be reported through either institutional or non-institutional agents. These reports should be considered seriously, analyzed carefully, studied, and judgment made of causes and the possibility of elimination. Each serious one, as it arises, should be reported immediately to the superintendent so that he may, figuratively speaking, have his professional hand upon the community pulse; so that he may be familiar with changes and shifts in group or individual opinion, realize its relative importance, and take adequate steps to secure its solution.

Many of our conventionally administered systems still operate upon the "hush" policy whereby they appraise the effectiveness of their work by the absence of complaints received at the central offices. Principals are quick to realize these situations and adjust themselves readily to this program. If bad news causes emotional peevishness upon the part of the executive, the natural result is a suppression of such news. The autocrat and the weak hear only that which is known to be pleasing to the executive ear. A "cover-up" policy invites disaster. However, the modern executive realizes that the worst possible mistake he can make is to shut off the avenues through which community interpretation returns to the central executive. It is as if a deep sea diver deliberately choked off his air supply. Reports of social "trouble spots" are considered just as objectively as reports received of instructional inefficiency, leaky roofs, and inadequate supplies. He realizes that the safety and welfare of the schools depend not only upon how effectively he interprets the schools to the public but also how efficiently he can interpret the public to the schools.

The community school, completely organized and operating effectively as an interpretative agency, should be to the school system what the nerves are to the body, flexible and capable in the location and reporting of difficulties. Early knowledge permits quick remedy and many a community upset in public education could be prevented if the information, carefully gathered, organized, and analyzed, is reported early enough.

HARMONIZING COMMUNITY CONFLICTS

Conflicts arising within the attendance district may be reflexes of those created in the wider area of the district.[3] More frequently they represent differences of opinion that have grown out of immediate difficulties within the attendance district. These attendance-district conflicts may be classified as arising from the school plant, professional disunity, and social, economic, religious, political, and cultural differences.

Conflicts arising from the physical plant itself will be considered in a later chapter.

Professional Conflicts

Professional conflicts within the building are much more serious and widespread than is generally assumed. They have been accentuated by the depression. Some are emotional differences growing out of autocratic administration, with its accompanying restrictions on the freedom of the teachers, whereas others arise from peculiar interpretations of the personal loyalty concept. High sensitivity, the frequent absence of a sense of humor, extreme emphasis on trivia of administrative routine, and old-maidish supervision combine further to produce conflicts of intensity and virulence. Many of these are particularly dangerous because they are suppressed. Conflicts within the profession result in a lowering of individual and group morale and are quickly reflected in the community. Children are highly sensitive to conditions, and it is surprising how quickly the neighborhood becomes aware of professional differences.

These conflicts must be harmonized before the professional group can operate to its full effectiveness. Both principal and teacher should cultivate a sense of proportion and humor. They must have patience with and faith in their colleagues. Differences between administration and teaching, discussed at greater length elsewhere, must be merged in the colleague concept of partnership. Democratic

[3] See Chapter 2.

methods of administration in which all personnel assume responsibility and are permitted expression of this responsibility through active participation in management have great possibilities. The conditions for professional unity must include freedom of the individuals to grow and to express themselves without fear of reprisal. The unstable neurotic who is consistently a trouble-maker and a disturber of morale may be either transferred to a new environment or eliminated entirely.

Social conflicts include differences between teacher and child, between parent and teacher, and those differences growing out of teacher behavior that is in conflict with community mores. This group of differences is also treated elsewhere and is mentioned here to maintain continuity of presentation only.

Conflicts between teacher and child quickly develop into difficulties between parents and teachers. These secondary difficulties may become emotional and place upon the principal a definite responsibility for their harmonization. Parents who are disturbed and inclined by nature to be emotional about child difficulties should never be permitted to visit teachers directly. Such encounters too frequently result in physical attack such as kicking, biting, striking, and hair pulling. Personal struggles between parents and teachers are much too frequent in our large cities. They frequently make the front page of the newspaper and terminate in court. They are undignified, dangerous, and unnecessary.

Listening Technique

The technique for preventing direct encounter and harmonizing personal misunderstanding is simple, requiring only patience, tact, and the application of certain elementary psychological principles. In the well-organized school an angry parent should make first contact with sympathetic office personnel. The secretary or clerk should be trained as a perfect listener who shows sympathy and feeling. The angry parent wishes relief from pent-up emotions. She should be given an opportunity to tell her story, make her threats, and generally blow off steam until relieved or exhausted, and *never be opposed* at this stage. It may be necessary to have the story told and retold several times before the individual is able to listen sanely to reason. Until the visitor is in such receptive state, the secretary should remain on the job as the new found friend and guide.

When the proper time has arrived, the visitor may be brought to the principal. The continued presence of the secretary as silent observer is still necessary. She represents a psychological ally for the parent. Let the story be told again. The principal must judge when the proper time has arrived for a generalized discussion of the conflict from the institutional standpoint. Later this explanation may be applied to the individual case in question. However, acceptance of certain general assumptions as a basis for discussion is first necessary.

If the parent has been cooled down to rationality and sensibility because of intelligent treatment, it may be possible to bring the teacher into the discussion and harmonize the conflict at this point. If this procedure is possible, the secretary may withdraw and be replaced psychologically by the principal, now also the firm friend and supporter of the parent. In certain cases it may be desirable not to bring the teacher into the first conference but to arrange for a second or third meeting. When the teacher does enter, the final result must be complete understanding. The school as a dignified arm of the state should never permit itself to be carried into personal bickering or struggle.

Economic Conflicts

Economic conflicts within the attendance district grow out of differences between neighborhood retail and recreational outlets and the school. Exploitation of the butcher, baker, and druggist by what amounts to forced advertising in school publications frequently produces reactions that spread to the entire program. Poolrooms and corner drug-stores attract children largely because of their need for friendly meeting places. Refusal to permit students to congregate at these stores not only reduces what the merchants consider as their normal trade prerogatives but places a certain stigma upon them. Resentment against arbitrary school action, intensified by the students' enlargement upon institutional attitudes, increases and intensifies these feelings.

These conflicts require intelligence and patience for their solution. The development of friendliness and understanding between neighborhood merchants and the school may result in both understanding and development of mutual appreciation of problems. Recognition by the school of child need for a "hang-out" might result in the provision for lounging rooms within the building itself.

Religious Conflicts

Understanding, broad tolerance, and patience are essential to the harmony of religious conflicts. Friendly relations with parish heads are helpful. Coöperation to the extent of institutional capacity in recognizing these parallel spheres of interest and influence are extremely helpful in developing mutual understanding. As a state institution the school must be careful not only to maintain complete separation of state and church but to prevent any possible slight to sectarian sensitivity.

Political Conflicts

Political conflicts arise in school systems where the relationship between partizan politics and the school district is close. So long as custodial and clerical personnel are selected because of their political value, there will be lack of harmony between the teaching and operating personnel. These conflicts are seldom capable of solution within the attendance district and require complete separation of the schools from the political machine through the pressure of public opinion and action of the board of education.

Cultural Conflicts

The school that is in conflict with the cultural beliefs and practices of the district which it serves has little effectiveness. As indicated earlier this series of difficulties is one of the real problems of institutional operation. Its solution lies in the field of adult education where acceptances of new practices and procedures are possible through the process of orderly education. The individual school cannot push far ahead of public opinion within its area of service.

It is extremely doubtful whether the principal alone can be successful in securing harmony of conflict areas. It is a problem for the entire teaching profession. The coöperation of every teacher, clerk, and operating agent is essential. Fundamentally it requires a complete change in the traditional institutional set. Any program of community education must proceed on the assumption that both parties, the parent and the school, may be equally right. Starting from that base, harmony of opinion is reasonably possible. The too typical present-day set is that the institution is always right. The academic tradition has unfortunately developed a concept of instructor and institutional infallibility that creates difficulties. The public school exists by no divine ukase and is not a perfect institution. Generally speaking, the chances of being wrong are not completely on the side of the parent. It is good sense to recognize this situation and to attempt to develop the psychological set that "the parent is always right." Starting from this point, it will be much more difficult to develop conflict between school and parent. This concept does not mean that the institution abrogates its authority. It does mean the establishment of the concept that education of both parent and child can only proceed under harmonious conditions entirely devoid of emotional conflict. It represents an attitude and a technique for listening and for conflict avoidance. Recognition of the need of harmonization of opinion and mutual confidence as a basis for effective education is extremely important. Heretofore most of our techniques have been built on the assumption that the institution and the professionals need protection. The underlying psychology of community relations cannot recognize this assumption as valid.

METHODS AND DEVICES

The basic theme running throughout all interpretation programs is translation of the aims, purposes, and values of the educational process to the growth and development of democracy. The immediate problem is the translation of both philosophy and practices into values and terms that are comprehensible to the layman. The methods by which each individual school meets this need are varied. They may include good teaching, school activities, the use of the physical plant, community contacts, and individual contacts.

Good Teaching

The best possible basis for institutional success is the maintenance of an excellent school. There is no substitute for good teaching. It is not only the supreme function of the school but is also the best means for securing community confidence. A school that stresses publicity and neglects teaching cannot long disguise its failure. It is necessary because of the increasing intricacy of our social life to provide supplementary means whereby ability to recognize and value good teaching may be brought to community consciousness. This purpose, together with the need for increasing the efficiency of the partnership concept with the home, should be dominant in all programs and methods.

School Activities

The informal activities growing directly out of the instructional program are so varied and significant that they will be treated in successive chapters. They include school papers and other publications, musical, dramatic, and athletic programs; exhibitions and exhibits; printed and visual material; open house and class visitation.

The Physical Plant

The physical plant [4] has a dual function. The plant itself and its surroundings are the concrete symbol of the material and spiritual values of the activity. Its actual use by children and adults makes it a practical agency of great program importance.

Community Contacts

Community contacts may be considered as two types. The first includes those plans and practices which bring the school into close

[4] See Chapter 23.

Pleasant reception and telephone clerks are an asset in conducting the school's business.

Homelike reception rooms make the school an attractive place for parents to visit.

relationship with community groups, and the second, those related to individual contacts growing out of the first group. General contacts bring the school into close relationship with parent-teacher associations, parent councils, school-improvement leagues, and neighborhood groups. The building itself should be the center for gatherings of this type. Other general contacts include those which bring principal or teachers into close relationship with community organizations, labor groups, service clubs, women's clubs, and other special interest groups at their own places of meeting. Programs for both of these types may include oral, visual, and written presentation.

It is highly desirable that both teachers and principals be well represented in the membership of these interest groups. These affiliations should be broad, arising in general out of a real interest. They should also be sufficiently wide to embrace all interests and points of view. Friendliness and confidence grow out of participation, and it is important that the entire gamut of organization be covered. In the small community this objective is attainable because of the simplicity of community organization; in larger centers the degree of interest specialization by personnel overcomes breadth of organization.

Press Contacts

It may also be considered part of the principal's work to maintain friendly contacts with the public press. If the paper has a school reporter, it is possible to invite him to the school. Routine notices of community meetings, school activities, and other news items may be sent directly to reporter or editor. Before news notices are mailed, it is desirable to become personally acquainted with some member of the news staff so that these items may receive more than casual attention. In general the principal should always welcome reporters to the building and make them feel that every act of the school is open for their careful inspection.

Individual Contacts

Generalized community contacts, though educational and valuable of and by themselves, should have for their primary objective the stimulation of interest to induce individual contacts. Direct contact with the home is possible through the home report, through bulletins or letters to parents, and through visitation.

The principal may well consider the possibility of a monthly letter to parents informing them in very simple terms concerning the work of the school. These letters might be general for the entire system, with the subject and form prepared in the superintendent's office, or they might better be written specifically for the individual attendance district. They should be brief and not in excess of a single page and so prepared that they will resemble closely a personal letter. Mimeographed letters are not very appealing. These letters may also be used in maintaining regular relations with community leaders. Home reports or letters relating to the work of individual students may be effectively delegated to the home-room teacher.

The problem of home visitation is a delicate one to be considered thoughtfully. In large centers it is possible to train specialists including social workers, nurses, visiting teachers, and personnel counselors for this work. In smaller systems it is necessary to use home-room teachers. Caution should be observed to use only those teachers who are capable of sympathetic understanding of home conditions and who can develop time and interest in the activity. The whole teaching staff is not capable of successful contact with the home. The psychology of home visitation should be so developed that the initial invitation comes freely from the home. Only in the case of certain emergencies should intrusion without invitation be considered.

It should be the ultimate purpose to bring parents to the school itself where records and other material are immediately available. Group meeting or social gatherings may precede the individual conferences. It is relatively easy to proceed from general to individual problems if a little skill is used in the organization of programs.

School buildings should make provision for rooms where these conferences can take place under comfortable conditions. The modern school should attract parents who have problems and desire advice in the same manner that they are attracted to the family physician for medical advice. From this aspect the school must be considered more generally in the nature of a social clinic.

SUMMARY

The principal's function in social interpretation is as responsible leader for the entire area of interpretative activity that is assigned to the individual attendance district. In a larger center his responsibility will be wider in scope and include much more detailed planning and direction than in smaller one-principal districts where the superintendent in reality performs many of the principal's normal duties. The principal's job includes at least ten phases from the direction of the community survey to the location, reporting, analysis, and elimination of trouble spots. The entire program is so varied that it is practically impossible to attain success through use of the older and highly autocratic methods of administration. The very nature and demands of the program require the intelligent coöperation and participation of every available agent for this purpose. The development of an intelligent democratic organization is highly desirable. As a leader within the local attendance district the position of the principal is largely one of planning and direction, of remaining well in the background and achieving results through the direction and stimulation of others. The final result of all school programs should be better understanding and appreciation of the purpose, value, conditions, and needs of the school program within the specific area considered. Programs should therefore be organized so that generalized information results progressively in the increase of individual interest and the development of continuing individual contacts through which the partnership concept of American public education can be more fully realized.

Chapter 11

THE TEACHING PERSONNEL

THE personal nature of the educational process makes the teacher the most important agent in interpreting the schools to the public. His immediate everyday contacts are directly with children and indirectly with parents. The teacher determines the success of the school and the degree of institutional effectiveness which is the most vital factor in the creation of popular attitudes. Interpretative programs based on the highest advertising skill cannot for long overcome the handicap of a poorly conceived and operating school. Good teaching will always be the teacher's major contribution to interpretation. His social relationships essential to successful teaching may be considered purely as supplementary. Successful teaching in a democratic order is so definitely conditioned by attitudes of both children and parents that it is extremely difficult to separate the teaching profession from those factors which are also specifically involved in community understanding. It might be possible to neglect many phases of the interpretation program but the school system that overlooks the essential importance of the teacher is doomed to failure as a social institution.

In an attempt to emphasize teacher activities that are generally considered as specifically involved in direct interpretation his work will be considered under the following divisions: (1) function, (2) essential training, (3) teacher-child relationships, (4) teacher-parent relationships, (5) colleague relationships, and (6) community relationships. The general problem—outstanding conflict possibilities and methods of procedure—will be considered under each of these divisions.

THE TEACHER'S FUNCTION

There was a time when the work of the teacher in a democratic social pattern was narrowly conceived as including a certain amount of mechanical activity that took place in a classroom. Fortunately for the success of the institution, that concept has passed into limbo. The teacher to-day must not only be capable in a technical sense but cannot operate effectively unless he also understands the culture in which he lives and the functional problems of democratic institutions. A cloistered existence is no longer possible for the public-school classroom teacher. The school as a social institution cannot be hung in space and insulated from all contacts with real life. It must learn to function effectively in the midst of a very complicated community pattern.

Teacher Duties

In his organization relationships the teacher may be technically considered as the responsible agent for the direct teaching of children within and without the classroom, in accordance with the community policies concerning education as legally promulgated by the local educational legislative body. His specific duties are: (a) putting into operation the course of study, directions, and standard of achievement in all instructional activity; (b) carrying out policies as directed by the principal that provide the educational conditions under which teacher and child may work to advantage; (c) transmitting to the principal information upon physical and educational conditions within the classroom; (d) appraising physical and educational conditions within the classroom by keeping records, collecting data, conducting research, preparing reports, and making suggestions for the improvement of conditions; (e) furnishing through precept and example stimulus and inspiration to other members of the school staff; (f) maintaining community contacts to establish closer relationships between home and school in the interest of more efficient instruction; (g) growing continually in personal efficiency; and (h) proving always by his actions that his conduct is motivated by a professional spirit.

Educational Concept

The American concept of the instructional activity is that of a partnership between the home and the school. The parent has not given up the control and direction of the child to the state. The American public school is merely one of a goodly number of means that supplement the work of the home. Success of the democratic teaching process is contingent upon how well the teacher is able to develop understanding and coöperative relationships between parent, teacher, and child. Under this concept of functioning it is difficult to determine exactly where interpretative activity of the teacher begins or ends. It is a closely interwoven relationship.

As an agent of the state the teacher must reflect the character of its institutions. He is more than an individual, becoming in the popular mind the actual school as an operating agency. As an agent of a democratic state, he must be non-partizan, non-doctrinaire, non-missionary, and non-sectarian. The elementary and secondary classroom is no forum for the expression of personal beliefs and hobbies. The effectiveness of the American public-school teacher is conditioned by his ability to win and retain the confidence of the people as well as through purely technical efficiency in the classroom.

Special Activity

The specific activities and duties of the teacher in the making and executing of plans include continuing participation in the community survey. As a possible member of planning committees under a democratic organization of the activity he is expected to contribute definitely to the entire program. In the continuing community survey he is considered as a primary reporting agent upon the conditions and thought of the community as discovered through classroom contacts. Since prevention through knowledge is a primary objective in social interpretation the degree of success possible will be largely determined by the effectiveness of the individual teacher as a reporting agent. Whatever specific programs are included in the final means of procedure, the teacher as a community agent will be expected to participate. These activities may be considered as those of routine organization although closely related to the four fields of relationships discussed later.

ESSENTIAL TRAINING

The training essential to the teacher in a democratic society, in addition to education in the major disciplines and in methodology, is that which will be specifically directed to give to each individual a definite understanding of the culture in which he lives, the nature of the democratic process, and the nature and functions of the facilitating social institutions. Unfortunately there has been little institutional training of this nature in the past. There are only scattered tendencies to-day, an isolated course or two, but little exists in the way of an organized program in democratic philosophy and practices. The teacher must secure this control of background information either through self-education, in-service training within the school system, or in a few professional graduate schools.

Desirable Qualities

The qualities essential to the teacher come through study and practice. Most important of all is the need for a flexible personality which grows out of developing attitudes of open-mindedness, tolerance, understanding, and vision. In a rapidly changing world, there is little place in teaching for the doctrinaire or the obsessionist. The second requirement is friendliness with all types and conditions of people. The truly great teacher is imbued with a love for teaching and for those taught. Intellectual and social snobberies, those twin liabilities so frequently found in academic life, are also definite liabilities to and limitations upon good teaching. Friendliness and understanding preclude pre-judgment and the "holier than thou" attitude. Above all the successful teacher must cultivate a sound sense of humor. Humor is the safety valve through which rational social balance and perspective may be maintained. One frequent criticism of teachers by the layman is that they take themselves much too seriously. They tend toward pomposity or what is referred to currently as the "stuffed shirt" set. A delicate sense of humor is an excellent safeguard against this form of degeneration

TEACHER-CHILD RELATIONSHIPS

The chief problem in teacher-child relationships is for the teacher to develop and maintain conditions that will permit the smoothest possible operation of the instructional process. The teacher must know each child, his capacities and possibilities, and the chief elements in his environment. The superior teacher has understanding of and sympathy with the child. True learning does not take place in an atmosphere of tension, conflict, and fear. The fundamental teacher-child relationship requires friendliness, confidence, and respect. One of the outstanding characteristics of the superior teacher is the absence of teacher-child conflicts. It leads to the possible conclusion that difficulties between teacher and child may be partial evidence of low efficiency or even gross incompetence.

If the first job is to establish conditions under which the child and teacher may work to best advantage, the second is related to what may be taught children in educational interpretation. In general, education of the child to institutional values and needs should be confined to those civic-social curricular areas concerned with the knowledge and understanding of democratic institutions. Extreme care should be exercised against indoctrinating the child with purely professional concepts of institutional needs. That is a field for adult and not immature teaching. The use of children as proselyting agents for building programs, increases in teacher salaries, extension of the curriculum, and other immediate institutional demands cannot be condemned too strongly. The normal community reaction to these practices will tend to be negative.

Misconceptions

One of the frequent difficulties results from the teacher's misconceptions of function. Certain teachers when in imagined or real difficulties work upon the children to secure their active sympathy and support. Frequently principal-teacher conflicts are carried into the classroom. The child receives a confused impression of the difficulties. The parent's reaction is usually even more confused. If the teacher is well liked, the community may rally to his support; if not, the result is merely unfortunate misunderstanding and even conflict. During the recent depression there were numerous incidents of teachers actually weeping in classrooms before the children to secure sympathy for salary restorations. The discharge of incompetent teachers or coaches frequently results in child strikes and community upheavals. There is absolutely no moral justification for exploitation of children by teachers for personal or professional advancement. Classroom conflicts arise frequently because the teacher arbitrarily and autocratically attempts unreasonable domination of children. Such conditions are inevitable if the teacher places either the child or himself in a position where backing down means loss of caste or "face." The wise teacher avoids these situations and meets disciplinary problems in private conference where the child is not forced, because of possible gang disapproval, to maintain an unreasonable position.

Discipline

The use of physical punishment is another potent reason for teacher-child difficulties. The forcible laying on of hands, the possible damage to wearing apparel, and the physical conflict between teacher and child—all have lasting conflict possibilities. Teachers who find it necessary to throw chalk, erasers, and, in the shops, wood or metal objects at the children have no place in the classroom or the teaching profession.

The superior teacher does not consider physical punishment as a part of the teaching process despite traditional assumption to the contrary. Use of corporal punishment may also be considered as fair evidence of a low quality of teaching ability.

Most of the teacher-child difficulties have their inception in the autocratic organization of the teaching activity. Autocratic concepts of management unfortunately permeate the entire educational organization. However, the greatest degree of autocracy is not in the superintendency as so frequently stated, but within the individual classroom. It is difficult if not completely impossible to teach the democratic way of life through autocratic means. An understanding of the fundamental characteristics of democratic organization and functioning progressively applied to classroom management will eliminate many of the current problems of the teacher. A decent respect for child personality, the development of his progressive ability to coöperate and participate in group activity, the change of teacher status from dictator to counselor and friend are all essential to the ultimate elimination of these conflicts. The transition from undesirable to desirable practice cannot be accomplished over night. It requires first of all a different philosophy of management than is now practised. Effective change is a slow process.

The expected community outcome of teacher-child relationships results in a normal attitude by children to the institution and a direct confidence in the teaching personnel. These attitudes are a direct reflection of teaching method and results. The teacher who displays real interest in the child and does everything in his power to help him progress, both within and without the classroom, is doing the best possible job of interpretation.

Unnecessary Conformity

Sometimes the teacher forgets the cultural diversity of the community and the depth of meaning attached to certain sectarian practices. Insistence on complete conformity by every child because it is administratively the easiest way indicates lack of understanding of individual differences and of the total good of all. It is particularly necessary in the operation of lunchrooms to provide sufficient variety to meet individual tastes and religious prejudices. A pre-primary school-teacher who insisted that an orthodox Jewish boy eat bacon because all the other children did created a conflict that had far-reaching repercussion. A principal who required girls to wear shorts in the gymnasium, contrary to their religious belief concerning the uncovering of the body, brought into existence a religious conflict that supplied the press with several sensational front-page stories and jeopardized to some degree the success of the physical-education program. Another principal who forcibly bathed Mohammedan immigrant children with soap containing animal fat, the use of which was contrary to their religious beliefs, brought on a neighborhood riot. Insistence on the preaching of specific Christian doctrine to children of Mohammedan, Buddhist, and Jewish religious beliefs should be discouraged. Tampering with or belittling cultural beliefs and practices is very dangerous as well as undesirable. Schools must not raise barriers between the children and their parents.

TEACHER-PARENT RELATIONSHIPS

The parent, as a partner in educational enterprise, must be considered by the teacher as a friend and colleague. Intimate knowledge of home conditions, social, economic, and cultural background of the family is essential to successful teaching. Though it is admittedly a difficult problem so long as there is a general tendency toward overworking the teachers and considering class load as the sole criterion of effort, its progressive solution is essential to the improvement of the educational process.

Home Contacts

Indirect home contacts are made through the children and through written reports. The child unconsciously distorts classroom practices, and the first impression of the school through child reporting may be far from convincing to the adult. The parent is also inclined to think of the school in the light of his own experience. The changes in program and method are foreign to him. It is axiomatic that the present can never compete with the past with respect to efficiency. The fundamental problem of the teacher is to develop in parental thinking understanding of the objectives and methods of current education.

Social Contact

Intelligent parental relationships of necessity proceed from an initial basis of confidence in the teacher and the school. Social contact with the parent will furnish the base from which the education of the parent starts. Effective initial contact comes through home visitation or through school visitation by the parent. A fundamental principle to be observed in all teacher-parent contacts is the psychology of parental correctness. If the teacher will adopt the psychological set that "the parent is always right" and then develop technique for indirectly shifting their point of view through flank rather than frontal attack, conflict may be avoided, the parent's sense of competency upheld, and the institutional prestige increased. The conventional attitude of many teachers that the classroom is infallible and the teacher always correct simply leads to difficulties and sometimes unfortunate physical encounters. The modern administrative set-up avoids teacher fighting parent by preventing their conferring together until the parent has been conditioned by the principal to a frame of mind that makes coöperative conference possible.[1] The dogmatism of individual teachers autocratically and irrationally demanding recognition of their authority and complete correctness has led to ruinous results in many school systems.

Home Reports

It is well to adopt the principle that all home contacts shall be constructive. This program means that many types of home contacts must be completely changed. The first of these is the periodic report on work accomplished. The conventional practice is to report indiscriminately on all subjects and activities, but many schools still report only failure more as an institutional protective device than to secure better understanding. It is doubtful whether any of the more conventionalized and standardized methods produce the best results. Sometimes reporting on a more personal basis through the medium of letter-writing seems more desirable. These letters to parents may be social in form and give briefly a simple and positive diagnosis of the child and his progress, measured against the child's individual capacity. Every letter should contain good news, easy to understand and reassuring in nature. It is possible to present bad news without insulting child or parent. Suggestive instead of dictatorial recommendations and simple statements are worth more than display of technical learning. The principal of an experimental school who wrote the parent that "John shows serious indication of an accelerated gastric rhythm" instead of simply noting that he was a rapid eater, brought a worried parent to the doctor instead of to the school. Since the purpose of home reports is to stimulate

[1] See Chapter 10.

personal visitation and individual conference, reports must be pointed in terms of these objectives.

Home Visitations

In recent years there has been a great revival of interest in home visitation. The belief that bringing the teacher to the parent is valuable has caused many administrators to adopt, with great enthusiasm if not too much reflection, a mandatory home-visitation policy. Where the home-room system of social administration is employed and each teacher has a group of children under his care for a long period of time, home visitation is desirable. The possible outcomes are likely to be much better understanding of problems and a greater degree of intelligent coöperation.

There are many drawbacks to visitation as a blanket policy. The American home is suspicious of intrusion. No teacher except nurse, social worker, or attendance officer ought to call upon parents except by invitation. It is simple enough for the socially smart teacher to secure an apparently spontaneous invitation. But where racial or language difficulties enter the problem, visitation is a dubious procedure. Unless the teacher understands perfectly the customs and habits of the foreign born, it may be better to forget about it. Many a foreigner has been unconsciously insulted by an official visitor. Racial supersensitivity is also a factor to consider carefully. Male teachers cannot well engage in home visitation unless they make their contacts in the evening when the entire family is at home.

Mandatory requirements involving social contacts are to be discouraged as much as possible. It is far better procedure to make the home-room teacher responsible for all knowledge of the children under his care, permitting him the freedom of selecting his own means of which home visitation may be one.

Teachers who are adept at visitation generally find themselves well supplied with invitations. In many sections, the alien who likes the teacher expects him to enter fully into his life as a friend of the family. Invitations to weddings, christenings, and funerals, to say nothing of minor celebrations, are often too frequent. Many foreign born have an involved code of highly formalized social conduct, and the visitor must know how to refuse certain favors graciously without giving offense. Otherwise she is likely to find herself in the position of a young and earnest teacher who, as she reeled away from a Polish wedding, murmured, "No one ever told me teaching was like this."

School Visitation

It is essential that teachers make every effort, through individual and group contacts, to secure parental interest to a degree where regular visitation of the school will become routine. Time might be set aside in the teacher's day at regular intervals as a visiting time and parents urged to take advantage of the opportunity. Conferences should be unhurried and sufficiently long to permit survey of the case without being cramped for time. These meetings between parent and teacher, if intelligently directed, may be productive of unusual results in better understanding of child through knowledge of the home and greater appreciation of the value of the school on the part of the parent.

Conflicts

Conflicts between parent and teacher usually arise out of an incident that affects the child. The most frequent are those caused by the martinet, the crude disciplinarian, and the teacher who is always right. For these conflicts there is only one real remedy—better teaching. Good teachers do not raise impossible issues or deify themselves. Though an occasional parent may be the terror of the attendance districts, the fault for teacher-child and teacher-parent conflicts is so obviously caused by professional shortcomings that it is doubtful for the sake of improvement whether any other reason need be considered. If the social intelligence and professional skill of the teacher be improved, practically all of this trouble will disappear.

Another area of conflict, though not so widespread, may seriously affect the entire school system. The dating of secondary-school youth by either male or female teachers is dangerous to the school, especially in the small community. Apart from the questionable professional taste involved, community attitude must be considered. In the typical small town there are a limited number of eligible males. Mothers naturally regard these young men as the normal and logical mates for their growing daughters, and take a proprietary interest in them from early years. If the younger or "trousseau" teachers make inroads, the community mothers consider it as a distinct invasion of property rights. The teacher may be successful in her quest and quit teaching after marriage, but the taste lingers much too long in the community for the good of the school. A thwarted mother is a dangerous opponent to the institution. These conflicts are difficult to avoid since they generally revolve about younger teachers who plan to spend only a few years in professional work. Since the actions lie distinctly within the area of individual choice, the institution cannot make hard and fast rules against them. The problem ought to be covered earlier in the institutional training and field orientation of teachers through pointing out effects upon the school.

COLLEAGUE RELATIONSHIP

Colleague relationships of the teacher include contact with all types of specialized personnel, janitor, clerk, nurse, bus driver, bath attendants, domestics, and teachers. No school can expect to be successful as a teaching center or long maintain community confidence if it is torn by internal dissension. Low morale among the executive agents will spread quickly to both children and community. The worst sins of the teaching profession in this respect are gossip and snobbishness. Gossip may be innocent or malicious; snobbishness is the vice of the pseudo-intellectual. Above all, teachers need to exercise extreme care in their professional colleague relationships, attempting to maintain at all times an attitude of friendliness, refusing always to become an accessory to the spreading of gossip. Only through the continuous efforts of all individuals can this problem be solved or kept within bounds.

Much gossip grows out of disease. The teaching profession has its share of neurotics and high emotionalists. Their wild imaginings and phobias are quickly transferred to fellow-teacher, clerk, and custodial agent with disastrous results. It is not difficult to locate gossip centers among teachers and diagnose responsibility. Many a case of teacher discharge loudly publicized by teacher groups as administrative or community reprisal reveals on careful investigation a high neurotic whose continued presence is a menace to the entire profession.

There are also many highly ambitious and ethically unscrupulous members of the teaching profession. Their technique is that of the stool pigeon varied only by the double control of technique in so far as they first manufacture and spread tales and then report them to their own advantage in administrative or legislative quarters. The "crown prince" fear of the small-town superintendent is not without solid foundation.

Meddling Wives

Another frequent difficulty in colleague relationships is the difficulty caused by the interference of professional wives. Too frequently the teacher or administrator selects a mate from the teaching profession. In many instances ambition, natural aggressiveness, and a desire to dominate brings a wife into professional relationships to the great detriment of teacher morale. Frequently she aspires to social dictatorship; again she may aspire to the "resignation" rôle, both of which have negative value. The remedy for this difficulty is the quick and sensible orientation of wifely ambition by the husband so that it will operate outside of the school. Marriage does not include a joint contract in a public job.

Jealous wives are always problems. A woman who marries a teacher should realize that the major part of his life is going to be spent in the company of women, since the profession is 85 per cent feminine. If this fact is going to be disturbing, it might be better for the lady to consider other mating possibilities. The solution of the problem lies in the field of personal endeavor. It is merely mentioned here to indicate the type of difficulty.

Other Relationships

Snobbishness manifests itself in teacher attitudes toward what the conventional intellectual considers "inferior work." The custodial agents and clerks are involved. Functionally the janitor and clerk are relatively just as important in their sphere of responsibility as the teacher is in his. Their value should be recognized and friendly relations established. Janitors will work much more effectively and be more helpful to the teachers if they are given that essential recognition of worth that every person craves and needs.

COMMUNITY RELATIONSHIPS

Several books and many articles have been written in recent years on the lack of personal freedom enjoyed by the teacher, the insistent demands on her time outside of school, and the unfairness of discriminatory localized contractual obligations. Unfortunately these statements of conditions are true. Reports on the subject convey the general impression that these restrictions affect all teachers in all localities. That generalization is far from true. Most of the personal restrictions appear in rural and small-town areas where there is insufficient elbow room for community and teacher to move freely. Teachers are usually unhampered in their personal sphere of action in the larger cities. The tabulation and rehearsal of these restrictions are appalling, but owing to lack of fundamental diagnosis, the final impression is one of vagueness.

As stated earlier in this discussion the public-school teacher is not a free agent and never can expect to be.[2] He is the reflection of the institution. The people demand certain standards of behavior from their educational agents just as they do from their religious leaders. Since the public-school teacher is definitely concerned with the direction of the immature, there can be little question of the legitimacy of rational community demands.

Fit Community

The successful teacher will place himself in harmony with community standards of conduct regardless of whether he approves of them. To each teaching agent is given the freedom of contract and the selection of a place to teach. Having this freedom of choice he must also assume responsibility for choice. Since the educational institution is part of the normal community life, the community

[2] See Chapter 4.

mores will certainly be reflected in the school. To avoid conflict and difficulty, the institutional agents must maintain harmonious surface relations. Rational conformity without abject surrender is an intellectual possibility. The individual teacher cannot rebel successfully against what may be considered unfair demands, except through the process of resignation since a successful frontal attack on community mores cannot be made by institutional agents.

Current mores must be accepted realistically as the current level of community functioning. Ideas and practices that are now prevalent are probably the reflection of what the last generation's schools taught. The molding influence of McGuffey cannot be estimated lightly.

Change Through Education

Change in community attitudes is, at least in part, the responsibility of the organized teaching profession. Desirable shifts in public opinion may be made gradually. Sometimes outside stimulus is desirable, again consistent internal education is required. The best technique appears to be the education of community leaders to change permitting them to carry the burden with the balance of the people. Only on-the-spot analysis in a given situation can successfully determine procedure.

The second factor of change lies in the possibility of solving the cramped space problem. Size is essential for teacher freedom from petty surveillance by village Mother Grundys. When the teachers become fully conscious of the fundamental relation of spatial organization to tenure, increased rewards, greater personal freedom, and more effective schools, much more rapid progress in these areas will be possible.

Social Contact

Even in the larger school systems teachers are expected to participate in the community's social life. The democratic agent becomes more effective as he knows fully the community in which he is engaged. So far as possible, freedom of individual choice should be granted in making social affiliation. The only desirable requirement is that the teacher shall become a functioning member of the community through social acceptance. The administrative problem is to secure better representation in all areas of interest. A teacher in his personal capacity is privileged to choose his own religious, political, and social contacts. However, these public agents, remembering the all-inclusive character of the institution, should try to secure all types of contact with diverse interest groups. There is no reason why teachers have not the freedom to join the chamber of commerce and luncheon clubs. Neither is there any reason why that same freedom should be denied them in affiliation with labor and other interests representing a different point of view. The democratic process is coöperative and all inclusive. Ultimately the normal sphere of every major interest will be recognized and provided for.

Institutional Requirements

Participation in the parent-teacher association falls somewhat outside of the sphere of personal affiliation. This organization is a means through which the partnership concept between home and school may be carried out. Every teacher can well afford to be an active member as representative of institutional interests.

In working with parents in their organized aspects, the children should view these relationships on a continuing basis. It seems to be better practice to assume a position where unobtrusive leadership is possible permitting parents to hold offices and to remain in the foreground. In many instances these parent-teacher groups must take an aggressive stand on certain problems. Under these circumstances office holding might be embarrassing. Greater success may probably be achieved by the teacher remaining discreetly and effectively in the background and exercising continuing leadership through personal influence and through informal direction of the adult to better understanding of instructional problems.

Legal Contacts

Home contacts in the line of legal duty, such as the investigation of absence, health, and environmental conditions, require a large amount of social tact to prevent conflict. These contacts involve attendance officer, nurse, and visiting teacher. The satisfaction of legal obligation cannot be accomplished on a police basis. It is through education of the community to the value of attendance rather than through use of force in detention of the child and court citation of the parent that satisfactory enforcement of compulsory attendance will proceed. The use of police methods in enforcing compulsory attendance laws should be discarded for the more sensible technique of social education. It is for this reason that many school systems are eliminating the conventional male attendance officer in favor of the trained woman social worker or visiting teacher. A woman is naturally much more tactful and socially capable in home visitation than a man. Whatever the choice of personnel provision for specific training in contact, technique will be needed so that these legal school-home relationships may have more lasting results.

Technical Contacts

In small and rural communities it is necessary to convince the adults of the value in expanded and enriched curriculums. One of the most effective means for accomplishment is the direct participation of technical specialists in the practical life of the community. The knowledge and skill of school scientists, agricultural specialists, shop and home-making teachers may be applied directly through demonstration and advice to assisting in the solution of many rural problems. This activity is essentially adult education, but in conservative centers proceeds through the awakened interest of the child to parent. It is normally more appreciable in the secondary phase of education.

There is a normal professional obligation, in which distinct freedom of choice is still desirable, that the teacher act as community ambassador in those areas that are sometimes productive of institutional difficulty. These include gossip or informal news-dissemination centers such as the corner drug-store, the filling station, the beauty parlor, and the boarding-houses. It is possible to take a narrow view and to consider the village boarding-house as a highly predatory economic interest, but a more rational view accepts the importance of the boarding-house as a creator of community attitudes. As part of the essential information necessary to the functioning of teachers as social agents, it is desirable for administration to point out the accruing values to continuing contacts with these outlets. Suggestions and information may be offered, but decision should in all cases be left to individual initiative.

Though religious affiliation is a personal matter, small communities may provide a narrow range of choice. Teachers should be flexible enough with respect to religious attitude so that affiliation with the existing institutions is possible. It is very dubious administrative practice to insist upon a teacher's participation in Sunday religious instruction after five full days a week in the classroom. The week-end may be better employed as a means of physical and social recreation. Not even a public servant can be expected to work seven days at his trade or profession.

SUMMARY

As the most important agent in the interpretative process the teacher is responsible for work in many fields. The final degree of success will be determined by the effectiveness of teaching which in turn is conditioned directly by his knowledge of and acceptance by the community. The outcome of teacher participation in interpretation should be increased confidence of the community in the value of its educational institution. Appreciation of value and the desire to coöperate by the parent cannot help but improve the educational activity which in turn means again community improvement. Within a democratic social order the entire process of instruction of the immature child and the mature adult really forms an endless cycle. They are so interwoven that except for laboratory diagnosis it is difficult to state where one process begins and the other stops. The teacher's relationships may be considered as those of participating in the building of plans and procedures and of the outcome of relationships with child, parent, colleague, and community.

Most of the teacher-community conflicts arise from violation of community mores, invasion of the local matrimonial prospects, and through social contacts with board of education members. The only progressive solution of these difficulties lies with the teaching profession itself.

Finally, if the teacher fails in his professional obligations as a constructive agent in the continuing process of institutional interpretation, no amount of effort by administrative agents can overcome the deadly effect of negative effort in the field of primary contacts. Neglect or indifference by the teacher ultimately will seriously affect child, community, and teacher.

Chapter 12
THE NON-TEACHING PERSONNEL

NON-TEACHING personnel includes all those specialized professional and non-professional agents whose work is essential to the facilitation of the instructional process. In the professional group are included doctor, dentist, nurse, social worker or visiting teacher, and attendance officer and in the non-professional group clerical, custodial, and lunchroom and transportation employees.

The cross-section of non-teaching personnel is the most neglected group in the entire field of social interpretation. Since one of the interpretation objectives is complete information to all of the people, this neglect leaves a wide gap in community contacts and represents a definite weakness to the total program. Non-teaching personnel will be considered here in the: (1) professional and (2) non-professional categories.

PROFESSIONAL NON-TEACHING PERSONNEL

Professional non-teaching personnel includes a group whose contacts are primarily in the school and another classification whose work in the line of duty carries them directly to the home.

Doctors and Dentists

Doctors and dentists comprise the first division. Their relationship to the school is about the same whether they are assigned by cooperative relation with the health department or employed part or full time directly by the school. Their work includes physical examination, remedial suggestions, supervision of corrective work in many instances, and in some isolated cases advising the teaching personnel in the development of hygiene and health courses. In the majority of cases doctors and dentists make regular routine examinations for health records and also daily inspection to determine the presence of contagious disease. Reports are made directly to the principal and the professional's contact is usually limited directly to the children. Except for a few days at the beginning of each semester the time spent by the doctor in each building is limited to a brief period daily or to several visits a week. Even when employed full time by the board of education, the school physician is seldom attached full time to an individual school building. The same condition prevails so far as the dentist is concerned.

Difficulties

These limited contacts appear to furnish a reason for neglecting physician and dentist as interpretative agents. The area of physician-child relations is one of real importance for several reasons. Professional antipathy to and suspicion of socialized or state medicine is so great that extreme tact must be exercised by the school physician to avoid conflict with regular private practitioners. His direct relations with the children are also important because of their reflex action on the parent and through him to the family physician.

As interpretative agents the doctor and dentist should be kept fully informed by superintendent and principal of the purpose and position of the schools, made aware of social difficulties arising out of community misunderstanding and suspicion, and convinced of the need for great tact in their institutional relationships. Constructive attitudes can only be developed through the art of persuasion since it is inadvisable to issue direct orders to individuals who are so jealous of their independence and prerogatives. The doctor and dentist may be considered primarily as contact men between the organized professional groups of which they are members and the school. It is really their job to keep the medical and dental professions well informed concerning the purposes and programs of the schools to avoid drawing this institution into partizan professional conflict. Many a city school system is bearing the sharp antipathy of the medical profession because of lack of tact on the part of the school doctors.

In many small communities difficulties arise because the board of education tends to favor one doctor and dentist instead of maintaining an attitude of strict impartiality toward all practitioners. Some of these favored individuals presumably use their institutional contacts deliberately to enlarge their commercial practices to the disadvantage of their less favored colleagues. In some instances doctors and dentists are elected to boards of education and then have themselves appointed as school physicians. A few cases have been reported in recent years where these doctors on the board of education have also extended their presumption of interest to the teaching staff itself, the professional group selecting these board members as their personal physicians. This practice is so well known that it is common assumption that in many instances a physician seeks membership on the board of education as a distinct method of enlarging his practice. The ethics of the procedure in both cases are dubious, but the situation is one with which the professional code of the American Medical Association is well able to cope. Apart from the ethical aspect, these practices also represent such distinct dangers to the educational institution that they should be avoided through the process of prevention which is so much simpler than cure.

Nurse and Social Workers

Unlike the doctor and dentist the nurse and social worker, also known as the visiting teacher, make direct contact with the home through visitation in the line of duty. These are not social contacts in the strict sense of the word, but are contacts necessary in the investigation of absence from school. The relation of nurse and social worker to the home is a delicate one fraught with danger of resentment and conflict unless very smartly administered.

Both nurse and social worker are chosen for social and personality qualities as well as for professional competency. They should be cheerful, pleasant, and friendly without being at all familiar, exercising great tact in securing much of their required information through indirect questioning. Effort is required to overcome the obvious implication of their official affiliation. By being friendly and helpful to the many times distracted, annoyed, or sick parent, it is possible for these agents to develop such friendly relations that technical difficulties may be easily corrected. All school-home relationships should proceed on the assumption that the school is an educational and not a coercive institution, using continually the teaching rather than the commanding technique. As confidence in the institution is established through these required home contacts, active coöperation is more easily possible. The desired objective is solution of home problems through coöperation.

Technique Description

A recently reported technique may be considered descriptive of these relations. In a midwestern community that includes a large percentage of foreign born, truancy was an aggravated factor. Appraisal of this condition led the superintendent to begin changes in a highly academic secondary school that would provide for better adjustment between school and child, and also to examine the nature of home contacts. Male attendance officers were replaced by women teachers who had also had some training as social workers. The visiting nurses and teachers were instructed to make friends with the people instead of showing official authority. One particular family produced an annoying amount of non-attendance. On her first visit to this home the nurse discovered on Monday morning a disorganized family of eight; the mother had a black eye which had been donated by a drunken husband in the course of a postalcoholic debate; two children were sick; and the others were just languidly sitting around. As a further expression of his opinion the father had generously smashed a few dishes and some of the furniture before taking his hangover to work. Under these conditions questions of why John, Henry, Pete, and Eddie were not in school would have been beside the point to the somewhat discouraged mother. The nurse went to work, prepared some breakfast for the family, sent a boy for some meat with which to treat the mother's eye, put that sadly disorganized individual to bed, and then cleaned and straightened up the house with the aid of the children. She made three calls that week and helped around the house. The mother quickly became friendly and soon made the nurse her confidante. It was not until the fifth visit or third week of contact that the question of school relations was broached. After some interval the mother, and later the father, became seriously interested in the school; non-attendance of the children dropped; and the mother later joined an adult class in cooking. It took some time to eliminate this difficulty, but once it was settled, there was no further problem. This type of procedure has possibilities in home-school contacts.

Attendance Officers

Fortunately the traditional attendance officer is disappearing. The retired policeman and the casual layman who would like "something to do" have no place in the enforcement of compulsory education requirements. The social technique of the social worker described above is far more effective than that of the male visitor who puts his foot between the door and the jamb, shows his badge, and truculently demands the presence of the offending child. It is even highly debatable whether the male is fitted by training or the underlying social conditions to serve well in this capacity. Many educators are rapidly shifting to the opinion that specially trained women are much more capable as contact and indirectly as interpretative agents. The school should also be chary of taking cases of non-attendance to court without first attempting to educate parents to the American point of view. A policeman's club and a judge's official correction are very poor educational agencies. Although technical compliance with these decrees may be secured, the fundamental result is a deep and bitter resentment against the school and its personnel. As a truly educative agency the public school must transfer and use its teaching technique in home contacts as well as in the classroom.

Census Enumerators

One of the weakest links in the chain of home contacts is the taking of the school census. In general periodic enumerators, devoid of training in the art of asking people personal questions without creating suspicion or actual distrust, are still employed both for political and friendship reasons to make annual contact with every home. Census operators, unlike certain gadget salesmen, have nothing to offer the housewife. In many instances family heads definitely resent questions that they consider of no concern to the state. To the casual operator it is a part-time job at so much per capita. Unless a minimum of time is spent on each name, there is no decent recompense in the job. Haste is the rule. There is little if any interest in avoiding social conflict.

There is no question of the need for this information, but the collection technique certainly requires improvement. Many school systems have already recognized this fact and now employ teachers as enumerators, permitting them to do the work in late afternoon and evening. If the teachers are carefully selected, this plan has many advantages over use of the casual and frequently immature enumerator.

Even more effective means of eliminating possible census difficulties is through the gradual establishment of a continuing census kept up to date within twenty-four hours by a system of child- and block-mother reporting system. This procedure makes the elementary attendance district the local reporting unit, and population shifts are quickly noted. When operating effectively, it permits easier control of non-attendance than through a more centralized procedure. It does not do away with the central census office, but delegates to the individual school the problem of reporting and investigating these problems. Under the decentralized plan the central office becomes chiefly an inspection and appraisal unit. The real value of the continuing census from the interpretation point of view is the elimination of annual "bell ringing," an inadvisable procedure in this country.

NON-PROFESSIONAL PERSONNEL

Clerical, custodial, and special-service personnel is essential to the success of the teaching process, and much more important than the traditional professional attitudes indicate. In any plan of interpretation they furnish a group of contacts that cannot safely be neglected. Since the secretarial type has already been considered, this discussion will be limited to the secondary contact or "back office" personnel.[1]

Political Factors

The chief value of non-professional personnel lies in the understanding and performance of duty. This is clearly a problem in personnel management and need not be enlarged upon. However, some of the conditions that lower their effectiveness have significance here. Three of these problems are concerned with the too frequent political nature of these employees, their recompense and recognition. Janitor, clerk, bus driver, and lunchroom manager are still considered as perquisites of the regular political organization. They are employed not on account of their direct ability to perform the task but because they have performed service in the political field or are related to some one who has. It is a difficult situation since the professional executive has little real control over them. He knows it, and they know it, so unless a great deal of tact is used, conflicts are certain to develop here.

The remedy for the politically appointed employee is not a direct attack on the individual involved. They are merely part of a system that must gradually give way to appointment on merit and ability just as has teaching. Attack upon the politically controlled board can be made through the education of community leaders to its dangers. Leadership in this field appears to be a responsibility of the teaching profession in its organized aspects. The professional's job within the system is to accept the realistic implications of current practice and through education attempt to improve the personnel which political accident has foisted upon the schools. Among them are usually many potentially capable individuals whom friendliness and training will develop into capable performers.

The baneful influence of the political janitor or custodial officer is most frequently encountered in the small community. Although political preference still exists in several of the larger cities, their direct influence is not so great. In many a small town, the janitor is actually the local political boss who takes for himself a school job

[1] See Chapter 9.

as an easy way of maintaining life between elections. He is sometimes known as a superintendent-maker, being able to influence the board of education and community to change. Teachers are frequently moved from these small towns without realizing that it is the terminal outcome of some snub given to this potent under-the-stairs personality. The best solution is to make him a friend and try to increase his pride in the job. It is impossible for the professional within the organization to fight this condition successfully.

Recompense

In school organization where a system of civil service or merit appointment prevails, the second problem arises out of the small recompense granted clerks and janitors. Though the salaries of teachers are themselves quite low, they still remain high from the standpoint of the non-professional employee. In many institutions these individuals are shamelessly exploited on wages much too low for decent existence. It is a part of the professional's responsibility to educate the board to the value of these supplementary services and make every effort to improve these conditions. There is a definite relationship between the salaries of teachers and unskilled and semi-skilled labor that cannot be overlooked. The active interest of the professional in the economic welfare of these individuals will do much to create more friendly relationships between teachers and other employees and a correspondingly better attitude toward the job.

Recognition

The third problem is need for recognition. The professional superiority too frequently expressed in snobbish disdain of the "inferior manual employee" is quickly sensed and resented by these individuals. Like every other human being they crave recognition and are entitled to it. It does not cost the professional much in time or effort to adopt a definitely friendly attitude toward these essential helpers. By so doing, social recognition is given to the man and his work. He will generally respond better to the job and find helpful things to do. Except in the South, where racial differences prevail, it is entirely possible and even desirable to include the clerical and custodial personnel in staff meetings where general problems relating to the school are considered. Technical discussions of instructional problems may be considered at more restricted gatherings.

Custodial and clerical contacts with children and parents are somewhat limited due to the nature of their work. However, in many instances the janitor is still supervisor of toilets during mass recess and helps on the playground during recreational periods. His main efforts are never seen except in their effects.

Custodial Contacts

In the community outside of the school, custodial contacts are made in areas that the professional seldom reaches because of lack of interest or inability to comprehend the thought and language of these groups. Certain neighborhood news-dissemination centers, groups of fraternal orders, and community clubs are included in this category. His social friends include those closely aligned with the professional political organization who take their voting duties very seriously. They represent a group that may make itself felt in no uncertain terms if grievances arise. It is therefore extremely important to the school to have intelligently informed custodial personnel, friendly to the institution and its personnel, acting as contact agents in these quarters.

Bus Drivers

The bus driver is also, unfortunately, too frequently a political appointee. Numerous accidents with attendant fatalities can be traced in a large degree to the fact that driving competence is not the primary factor in employment. Public opinion is bound to change this situation quickly since the safety of the children is involved. The drivers of school buses should be as high a type of personnel as the operators of commercial passenger lines. The work can be made important and attractive enough to bring into the school a much higher type of man.

Like the custodial agent the bus driver covers a field of social contact not open to the professional. In addition he is in daily contact with the children, knows what they are thinking about, and frequently offers them his views. It is quite desirable that this individual be familiar with the purpose and plans of the school so that he may quietly correct some of the distorted views that the children may have acquired. He may also be used in a manner similar to the custodian as a reporting agent on community conditions and thinking. Only home-contact personnel and classroom teacher get as much first-hand community news.

Lunchroom Operators

Many student and community difficulties grow out of lunchroom management. Many school systems are much too inflexible in their organization of this activity by assuming institutional correctness in all instances and forgetting that the child consumer has a very definite interest stake in what he consumes. Menus are frequently quite correct in caloric value but definitely lacking in child appeal. Institutional insistence on use of the lunchroom irks many children, and a good appraisal of the school eating facilities may be found in the patronage of the corner drug-store and "hot dog" stand. Most school lunchrooms are too noisy, stiff, and factory-like in their appointments and administrative routine to carry the greatest child appeal. The school should recognize the validity of child claims and provide for more flexible and sensible practices. Lunchroom personnel, particularly counter- and clean-up girls, might be chosen for friendliness in their contacts with the children. A dour face does not improve a child's attitude toward his food. Under no conditions should lunchroom personnel be permitted to engage in argumentative discussion with the children. It is their job to maintain pleased and satisfied customers.

Adult Use

Care must always be exercised that essential educational service activities, such as the lunchroom, are not exploited by the adult community or by the employed personnel. Community suppers under the direction of the parent-teacher association and other community groups may be rightfully encouraged, but regular general adult use of lunchroom facilities because the cost is lower may be objectionable, particularly if the school is brought into competition with private enterprise.

Book-Store Personnel

Many secondary schools are developing book and supply stores to meet student need more efficiently. The idea is good and can be used to distinct community advantage by pointing out the activity as an economy to the parents. However, the temptation to use book-store balances as supplementary budget revenue is unfortunately not restricted often enough. There is no justification for the school to operate a service activity at a profit.

Book-store employees have the same obligation to the customer that exists in the lunchroom. Conflicts with children should be avoided and the policy of the school explained as often as child questions concerning its merits are demanded. Mere telling is not sufficient. Rather, the opportunity should be taken to convince the child of the value of the service and the reasonableness of its operation. By adopting the same attitude that any normal business activity requires much friction in the book store will be eliminated.

Training Employees

Although the general policies respecting the orienting of personnel to their work will be developed by the board of education and promulgated through the superintendent, it is a primary responsibility of the principal, except in the very small school system, to provide means for training both professional and non-professional employees to their work. Since social institutional interpretation is distinctly a logical demand upon all executive agents, there should be definite provision for in-service training. Fighting the customer has a very low service value.

The nature of the school, its relation to the community and to the larger aspects of society, the manner in which it maintains itself and provides for essential enlargement, and the important part that every agent plays in maintaining and improving community institutional confidence form essential parts of a training program.

Exact method and time required must be determined according to the needs of the particular school.

SUMMARY

A well-balanced plan of institutional interpretation requires that constructive contacts be maintained with every phase of community life. The teaching personnel is distinctly limited by nature of its training in the sphere of social influence and relationships. Non-teaching personnel beginning with the school doctor and ending with the charwoman must be considered as a definite part of the plan and so oriented and trained for their work that the larger social implications of their institutional relationships will be fully realized. The specific part played by these non-teaching agents will be limited to the need for constructive contacts within the school and the maintenance of a rational interpretative attitude for the institution in their diverse social contacts. Failure to include the non-teaching agents in the general plan and to use them on their several levels of possibility will result in a great weakness in the general program, one that may have extremely important results in a severe economic or institutional crisis.

PART IV

INSTITUTIONAL AND COMMUNITY AGENCIES

PART IV

INSTITUTIONAL AND COMMUNITY AGENCIES

Chapter 13
THE STATE EDUCATIONAL AUTHORITY

PUBLIC education is a state function and its institutional apex is the state educational authority. The organization variation runs from a state superintendent, elected by partizan ballot, through provision for a complete administrative university with a popular directing body and capable professional executives selected solely for their professional capability. This central organization, whatever its form and scope, will be called the state educational authority in order to avoid possible confusion. The state educational authority as an agency in social interpretation will be discussed from the standpoint of: (1) function, (2) program and problems, (3) activities, and (4) difficulties.

STATE EDUCATIONAL AUTHORITY FUNCTION

Although the United States scheme provides for legal organization of public education by states, specific state organization shows much variation both in form and in method of operation. Central authority is provided that may have merely supervisory and leadership responsibility or that may be an extremely active and powerful directive agency. It may be a unit or may be divided into three or four independent segments each responsible for some area of functioning. It is not uncommon to have one authority for public education of elementary and secondary grade, and other separate authority for the state university, the land-grant college, the teachers' college, and specialized independent controls for other specialized state institutional activity such as schools of a corrective nature, institutes for the blind and for those low in intelligence.

State Function

A generalized description of the state educational authority's function might be considered as responsibility for furnishing educational leadership to the entire state; appraisal of the operation of the state educational plan; interpretation of the purpose, value, conditions, shortcomings, and needs of the public schools; long-range and short-term planning, including the making of specific recommendations to the legislature; and the exercise of certain regulatory authority. The specific executive authority for making the general state plan actually effective, except in a few narrow areas, has been delegated completely to the local school district. The exercise of state authority has for its general purpose the maintenance and improvement of the total educational activity.

Leadership

The theory underlying state educational organization is that this central authority is responsible for the leadership in the discovery, promulgation, and discussion of educational problems both to the teaching profession and to the people of the state. In one sense this expression of leadership is an aspect of social interpretation. It is mentioned separately for the sake of emphasis.

Appraisal

The state educational authority is legally responsible for judging the working of the complete educational plan in the local administrative areas or school districts. The bases for appraisal are the accepted educational objectives and the statutory enactments that form the legal frame through which these objectives may be realized. The activities basic to appraisal include the receiving, tabulating, and interpretation of reports from local districts and the actual inspection of the schools in operation. State-wide examinations or testing programs may be also considered as appraisal devices.

Interpretation

The state educational authority has a direct stewardship responsibility which is legally expressed in its mandatory requirement for reporting the institutional conditions and needs to the state legislature and the moral obligation to make additional reporting to the people themselves to increase understanding and appreciation of need. It is with this vital but much neglected area of state functioning that this discussion is primarily concerned.

The state-wide central educational organization is separated from the people. Both its area and methodology are restricted on account of its position in the general plan. Its personnel is highly specialized and relatively few of its relationships are expressed through popular contact. It does not concern itself immediately with either children, parents, or teachers, but is confined to regular organization channels through the local board of education and superintendent on one hand and with the legislature, the governor, and other executive agencies of state government on the other.

Planning

The dynamic nature of the American culture makes the state legal plan for education constantly subject to modification and enlargement as new needs are felt or as the experimental trial of plan extension requires statutory sanction and protection.

Planning presupposes exact knowledge of conditions and needs and is based upon appraisal of existing conditions and practices. In any continuing cycle of functional activity planning is both the first and the last step. It grows out of appraisal and is itself the criteria by which subsequent appraisal for improvement is made. The steps leading to the making of technical plans include inspection of existing institutions, research into their operating conditions through receiving, tabulating, analyzing, and interpreting reports. This inspection will normally include all phases of the educational process such as instruction, personnel, plant, service of supplies, child accounting, and finance. It will also include verbal information received directly from professional and lay groups. Survey and inspection of this nature determine institutional conditions and needs.

Similar analysis of general problems and needs within the state that are currently beyond institutional functioning are an essential complementary requirement so that the preparation of technical plans may proceed in harmony with both social and institutional requirements. Technical plans may be prepared through use of state executive specialists, the employment of outside technical specialists, and coöperation with committees selected from representative local organization interests.

Long-Time Planning

The state educational authority in coöperating with other state planning agencies is responsible for the development of long-time plans for improvement and enlargement of the educational function. Popular education to establish a general understanding of the need for these periodic changes and extensions in the legal structure is a primary state interpretative obligation.

These projections into the future evolve from interpretation of changing social needs and current institutional levels of functioning. They form the general framework which may be progressively filled in with enabling legislation and extended support as sustaining public opinion is developed with respect to their acceptance. In one sense the long-term plan for education may be expressed popularly in the desirable goals for public education. The constant reinterpretation of these goals for the people will create a public consciousness that will prepare the way for progressive achievement. The long-term program has no time pressure and permits continuing leisurely and objective discussion.

Progressive Achievement

From its analysis of state opinion and institutional conditions the state educational authority in coöperation with the state educational advisory commission,[1] recommended as representative of general popular interests, may prepare specific, piecemeal legislation that will fit into the outlines of the long-time pattern.

To the extent that state educational authority recognizes its leadership and planning responsibilities, carefully directing lay and professional thought and action into harmony with orderly satisfaction of need, it may be possible to prevent sporadic and unbalanced pressures by independent groups and cliques. Many current difficulties and much restrictive and hampering educational legislation may be

[1] See Chapter 18.

traced directly to the inadequacy of state educational authority in exercising essential leadership in its proper area of functioning. This condition will continue to exist until there is fuller realization of responsibility and more complete development of technique for achievement. The improvement of public education within any state is conditioned by the extent to which state authority increases in efficiency.

Regulatory Activities

The state authority has specific regulatory responsibilities in areas common to the entire state. These include the direction and control of teacher certification, child accounting, state and Federal financial subventions, transportation, and removal of local school officers for misfeasance or malfeasance in office. In certain states the administrative control of specialized state educational institutions is directly under the state authority. However, the United States administrative scheme does not contemplate direct administrative authority over local functioning, and except in a few states, the local school district is given wide powers to make the state educational plan effective through its own independent organization.

Tendencies

In recent years there have been strong tendencies toward the actual increase in the central authority's direct control over local functioning. Changing tendencies in taxation have resulted in financial plans that include large increases in state aid to local districts. These increases normally carry with them greater authority to determine both educational program and personnel. In certain states, notably North Carolina, the assumption by the state of complete responsibility for the mandatory program has practically shifted administrative control, in the larger sense, from the local district to the state. This tendency will probably continue so long as an increasingly large proportion of financial aid comes from the state instead of the local district.

The stimulation of vocational education by both Federal government and the state under the provisions of the Smith-Hughes Act has resulted in the past twenty years in definite increases in central state and Federal control over the policies, organization, size of class, type of work given, selection of personnel, determination of salaries, and general domination of local instructional and administrative practices. These controls in certain sections have even been extended to the actual insistence upon the local employment of individuals specified by the state and to the abnormal orientation of vocational education to the general educational program.

There is also a very noticeable tendency for the state educational authority to make the state educational program subservient to the desires of the governor. This tendency is probably the logical outcome of the practice in certain states of permitting the governor to appoint the state superintendent of public instruction for a length of term that may coincide with his own. The governor naturally considers the state superintendent under these conditions to be simply an appointee and henchman of his own, subject to his political needs and operating merely as a gubernatorial executive assistant.[2] This tendency is extremely dangerous to the traditional plan of maintaining public education close to the people and beyond the control of partizan politics.

Many current tendencies toward greater centralization of power within the state authority to the detriment of local responsibility represent very doubtful and dangerous ventures which, if continued, may destroy almost entirely the concept and practice of the independent school state.

PROGRAM AND PROBLEMS

The state authority's responsibility for social interpretation cannot be avoided. Unless it does accept and perform essential duties within this area, the local district is going to be severely handicapped. Failure of the state to act does not, however, furnish an excuse for the local district to neglect its aspect of functioning. Local interpretative activity may and should be carried on regardless of the

[2] Even under conditions of appointment by the governor there are notable instances of independence and statesmanlike programs in a number of states. Apparently the character and vision of the incumbent is a very large factor. However, too few governors appoint strong men.

efficiency of the central authority. However, state inefficiency naturally lowers the possible level of functioning within the local district.

Securing Information

The state's first need is to secure adequate information with respect to the functioning of the educational plan within the district. The conventional means is through regular reports on the several aspects of the educational problem, supplemented by direct inspection of the schools in action. In some states the inspection is confined to casual and infrequent visits; in others it is shared with one of the state institutions of higher learning, particularly in secondary schools; and in others it is carried on completely by the state. Inspection may be supplemented by research activity on a state-wide basis on some specific problem or field of problems. In rare instances exact information is secured through specialized inventory survey made generally by specialists outside of the organization. Occasionally the state executive or legislature becomes uncertain of the efficiency of educational operation and authorizes a special survey of its own. Since the extent and validity of information from the smaller administrative districts within any state are distinctly inadequate, it is difficult to secure complete information at any given time. The internal organization of most state departments of education is so weak that it appears to be impractical if not completely impossible to compile and publish essential information until long after it has lost its current value and has become merely archival in nature.

Some Weaknesses

Some informational weaknesses of state educational departments may illustrate and support this assertion. The legislature in each state has provided for determination of legal responsibility for compulsory attendance. It would be extremely difficult to find a current state report that presented to the legislature the exact efficiency in the operation of compulsory attendance laws, the amount of nonattendance, the number of children totally escaping institutional training, and the amount of legal and illegal child labor. The question of teachers' salaries and the improvement of efficiency in teaching personnel through increased training is conditioned by the relationship of demand for and supply of teachers. Without this information and specific state control of teacher supply through control of training and certification, it is impossible to prevent heavy dislocation between supply and demand such as was in process of making even before the depression. Yet not one of the forty-eight state authorities produces annually a statement of teacher need and then attempts adjustment of supply to need. Less than six states even made an attempt at such analysis during the depression. The adjustment of the school program to child needs is reflected in part by the elimination of children from school. It is exceedingly difficult to find in any state publications continuing reports on lack of curricular balance. The number of children in each state who are deprived of their educational birthright on the secondary-school level because of economic inadequacy is large; yet there is a practical dearth of information on this score available to either the legislature or to the people. The inescapable conclusion appears to be that state educational authority is not adequate in its current collection, analysis, and publication of vital information concerning general levels of educational efficiency.

Possible Improvement

Improvement in the state educational authority's efficiency in gathering and reporting vital information is essential. Much of the technical need can be corrected only through extension of professional and clerical personnel to make state coverage possible. There are other means, however, by which the state might secure much more information and establish a greater awareness of state and institutional needs. These devices for the improvement of interpretation will be briefly reviewed.

Organization Coöperation

Much progress has already been made in the area of state coöperation with institutional organization. Through the establishment of a definite program of relations with boards of education and departments of superintendents, general means of securing information of local need have been established. The extension of the influence of state authority in interpreting conditions and possibilities within the state as a whole to these organizations has received insufficient attention.

Professional Coöperation

The organized teaching profession may be considered as general advisors to state authority. The teachers as a group should be aware of the inadequacy of current functioning and are able to point out grave weaknesses. In a direct advisory capacity they may be of great service to the state. However, the organized teaching profession certainly needs some agency outside of its own membership to educate it to the totality of conditions within the state that place a possible current limitation on complete functional improvement. This area again presents an excellent means for two-way education.

Educational Interests

All of the institutional and voluntary educational interests within a state make possible the organization of a state council on educational problems through which much information may be secured and a correspondingly large and valuable information given. Though different in character from other agencies, it may serve as a clearing house through which those phases of educational problems that are not always clearly recognized by the state institutions may be considered.

Parent-Teacher Coöperation

The state parent-teacher association as an agency for improving the partnership concept in American public education furnishes another excellent possibility for coöperation with a lay group. Probably more than any other state agency, with the bare possible exception of the teaching profession, this organization is aware of the educational need and to an appreciable degree of the conditioning social, economic, and political factors that retard more highly perfected institutional functioning. The parent-teacher association has an advisory value to state authority that is not yet even partially recognized.

Lay Educational Advisory Commission

The organization of a lay educational advisory commission composed of representatives of the various interests within the state has strong possibilities as a coöperating agency in the formation of legislative plans. It represents also the partnership concept of the people carried into the state educational plan, furnishes means whereby the state can secure a typical cross-section of popular opinion, and offers ample opportunity for the education of the lay members to educational need.

Program

The interpretation program of the state educational authority divides naturally into three parts. The first division is concerned with continuing reports to the legislature and to the state executive officers on the conditions and needs of the schools. The legislature is responsible for the enactment of educational need into legal form. It is therefore highly essential that its members be made thoroughly aware of the specific needs. The state executive officers have a large share in influencing legislation, and the governor may be instrumental in accelerating or retarding legislation for the schools. It is not sufficient that the legislature be kept informed only during the time it is sitting, but in off years as well. That a large number of representatives and senators may not be returned to membership in the succeeding session is little excuse for neglecting this area.

If the state authority is actually exercising its true leadership responsibility and developing coöperative relationships with professional and lay groups as discussed earlier and maintaining close relationship with local organization, if the interpretative programs of the local districts are themselves effective in establishing an intelligent sustaining public opinion, then the members of the legislature will probably be well informed themselves and start their work with an intelligent opinion toward the subject.

The second phase of the state program includes those essential relations with the people of the state in their interest organizations, embracing all of the activities essential to the two-way educational process of coöperating with lay and professional groups. Both state authority and the representatives of these leader groups are kept informed of popular desires and state requirements.

The third division of the state interpretative activity involves those generalized contacts with the people of the state as a whole through the medium of press and radio and the personal contacts made by appearance on local programs. The responsibility for direct and continuing relations with the people in the local districts belongs to the local district and cannot be delegated. State relations in specific localities must be considered chiefly as supplementary to local effort.

ACTIVITIES

The activities of state authority will be determined by the nature of the program. The process of educating legislature and governor to educational need may be accomplished by the preparation of periodical reports, occasional official bulletins for the record, and very completely through personal conference. If state authority can create in the minds of the legislature confidence in its motives and plans, the battle is half over. Such confidence existed to a high degree between the New York State authority during the gubernatorial tenure of Alfred Emanuel Smith to the great benefit of the public schools. It is a continuing possibility within every state.

The education of the lay and professional groups to both the needs and the possibilities of the educational problems may best be carried on by regular reports and discussion within the group. The informal conference is the best device for this purpose. Monthly intervals are none too frequent for a continuing program.[3]

The teaching profession and legal organization may be kept informed through frequent news letters or bulletins prepared weekly or bi-weekly. These may be either printed or mimeographed, depending upon the funds available for this purpose. Appearance of state staff members before teachers' institutes, school officers' meetings, and regional professional meetings permits personal contact

[3] See Chapter 22.

and effective oral presentation of conditions and needs. Some member of the state educational authority should be represented on every major professional program since this is one of the few means of bringing the state into direct relation with the large body of teachers. Generalized local relations may be maintained through regular press releases, intelligent use of the radio, and through occasional simple, well-illustrated bulletins.

Tell the Truth

The question is frequently asked concerning the type of information that is desirable for popular consumption. There can be only one answer in a long-time planning program and that is to tell the truth. The people of the state through legislative enactment have provided a certain type of educational opportunity. These legal enactments may be considered as criteria for measuring the functional efficiency of the organization. If 10 to 25 per cent of the children are escaping schooling because of local and state educational inefficiency, the people are entitled to this information. If it is withheld, there is no reason to assume that the people will do otherwise than believe that the policy which has been enacted has also been carried out in practice. If the maintenance of pioneer school districts much too small and inefficient for current needs is hindering the educational function, the people should be made aware of this fact. If a partizan political machine is interfering with the popular educational process and attempting to levy its conventional toll of patronage and graft, there is no more certain means of discouragement than by bringing the people to a watchful and protective attitude. Whispering about it in secluded corners does not help much. There should be no hesitation on the part of state educational authority in telling the people of the shortcomings of their educational institutions. If the truth is consistently told, the people and the legislative authority may be in a far more receptive attitude toward needed changes and enlargements.

It is difficult to offer perpetual praise of the public schools for eighteen months out of every two years and then "view with alarm" only during legislative sessions. It is little to wonder about if many desirable bills fail to become law. Appraisal of the operation of educational activity may be followed by analysis of the general problems and needs of the state. There is sufficient capacity and competence among the several divisions of state government plus the information available from Federal sources to furnish a base for interpretation of changing need. Study of need is naturally followed by the development of extended means. The actual planning for change should be done at least a year in advance of legislative meeting in order that a supporting public opinion for plans may be developed. These plans evolved through the suggested method of coöperation with lay groups should be prepared sufficiently far in advance of possible enactment so that they may be extensively publicized and discussed within each local district by the people, the teaching profession, and the legal organization. Under a continuing method of planning and interpreting a public opinion is prepared in advance.

DIFFICULTIES

As the harassed state educational authority might say, it is considerably easier to write about the responsibility of the state than it is to carry these suggestions into practice. In a large measure such current criticism would be valid. It is impossible for the typical state educational authority to achieve within the course of a few months the program that has been considered here. Some state departments have already made considerable progress; others would need to start from scratch. Current inadequacy is due in large measure to the state of organizational competency and its relation to politics. The majority of state superintendents of public instruction are still elected directly by the people by partizan ballot. So long as this practice obtains it is difficult to separate education from practical politics. The state official so elected is under obligation to his party and meets his obligation by the appointment of "deserving workers." There is a very low correlation between political efficiency and professional competency. Since a popular election is decided by organization effort and the vote-getting personality of the candidate, there is little assurance except for a few fortunate accidents that competent professional educators will be selected. The short term of the typical state educational executive makes it extremely difficult for even a competent and conscientious man to devote his attention to educational improvement. Much of his time must be given to building personal fences or helping his brother office holders to prepare and carry on campaigns. Even where the state executive is appointed by the governor and the term of office is short, little improvement can be noted. The high degree of professionalization of the University of the State of New York and the traditional gubernatorial attitude toward the office of the state commissioner of education in New Jersey are exceptions.

Although it is very doubtful whether the state educational authority can achieve its highest stage of development until the entire central educational organization has been completely reorganized, there are still many possibilities for improvement of current levels of functioning. The accidental presence of strong men in some of these offices indicates that there are possibilities. Michigan and Pennsylvania have offered striking examples in support of this contention.

Current Practice

A recent sampling of the current interpretative activities of departments of education in twenty states indicated that nine made no provision for direct interpretation except through publication and limited circulation of the legal annual report; eight states provided for a partial program with special emphasis on continuing relations between the local school organization and state, whereas only three reported fairly complete continuing programs of both professional and lay interpretation. Of these, Michigan was the only state using the coöperative method with both lay and professional interest groups.[4]

Since many of the states reporting partial programs represent also

[4] The Educational Policies Commission reports as of October 15, 1937, that at least nine states have organized educational councils or planning commissions. However, all of these have developed out of the recommendations of State Education Associations and are, in practically all instances, a professional instead of a state department activity.

areas where partizan politics play a large part in determination of state office personnel and tenure, it still appears to be possible to do some good work despite the obvious limitations of the system.

Annual Report

The principal publication of the state educational authority is the annual report. Since this has been required by law for many, many years, it generally has much of the mustiness and literary deadliness that tradition and bureaucratic personnel have built into it. Its traditional circulation is limited to state officers, local school organization, and libraries. It is usually from one to two years late in appearance, making its value purely archival. Though distinctly limited as an interpretative agency it could through modernization be made much more effective and increase its possible reading circulation to leaders in the numerous interest groups. Much of the archival statistics should be either boiled down to reasonableness or prepared in separate form in a limited number of volumes for the state record.

The state authority's annual report should contain in as brief and terse a manner as possible a survey of the educational conditions in the state during the past year. These appraisal studies may be organized by functional activity such as instruction, child accounting, plant, and finance. Illustrations are desirable whenever possible.

At the beginning of each report the state executive may summarize in a few hundred words the significant and outstanding high and low spots in the educational plan and present specific recommendations for improvement through enabling legislation. This summarized introduction may well be accomplished within three thousand words. It is also possible to print this extract of general popular interest separately for wider circulation than is feasible for the entire report.

If finance permits, an even more popular presentation of the purposes, conditions, and needs may be evolved from this annual report through the preparation of well-illustrated booklets in which many pictures and few words are offered to the state leaders and particularly to women's organizations. Mass circulation of any state

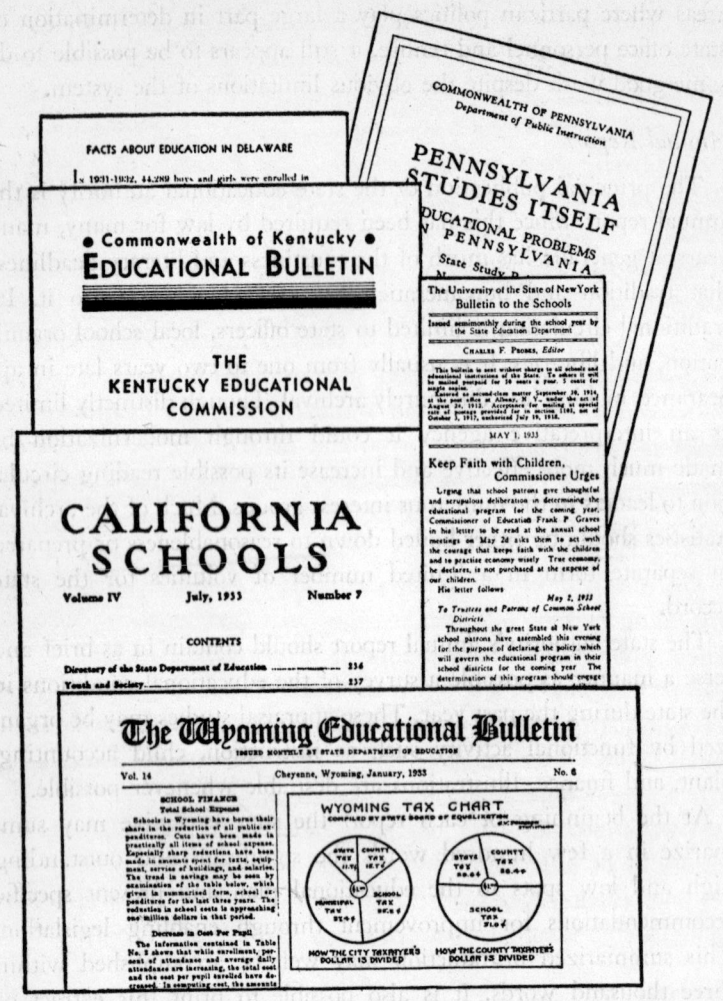

Bulletins published by state departments of education.

publication is too expensive in terms of possible results to justify it. That type of contact bulletin may be better allocated to the local district.

Time is a definite factor in the value of the annual report. There appears to be no good reason except conventional organization routine why the central authority should not be able to furnish complete information to the state within a three months' period after the close of the year. If complete publication is not considered feasible within this period, fractional publication is certainly possible. Incidentally, this method represents a good means of securing from six to twelve good newspaper releases on the individual chapters where only one story is generally possible through complete publication.

Size is also a factor in the interpretative value of the report. A desirable maximum is one hundred pages. Those tomes that cannot be read without table support will not as a rule be read at all.

Conventional type fonts used in state reporting present a page too crowded, too hard to read without strain, and unattractive in make-up. Modernization of type and format will be of material assistance to the reading matter.

News Letters

The weekly or bi-weekly news letter offers further opportunity for presenting current information in a brief and attractive manner. These publications are also limited in circulation to local school officers, state officers, and a few thousand outstanding leaders. They serve primarily as the state house organ and furnish direct informational contact between state and local organization. These news letters appear most frequently today as monthly bulletins, but the four-week interval is too long since much of the news has become history or of little value, and the size does not encourage general reading. Eight pages twice a month or once a week will receive more careful attention than thirty-two pages once a month.

Publicity

The state's means for mass contact is through direct publicity by newspaper or radio.[5] The public press furnishes good means for the dissemination of general information to all of the people. The larger papers and news services have personal representatives in every capital who should have regular access to state educational officers for the securing of news. These releases may be either

[5] For discussion of radio, see Chapter 20.

verbal or written. The metropolitan press does not like "hand outs." Since much of the news coverage is actually made through the small daily or weekly paper that cannot well afford expensive news service, it is desirable to mail news releases at regular intervals directly to the editor. If this material is developed as straight news or feature stories without propaganda motive, much of it will be available for publication.

SUMMARY

The state educational authority has within its area of functioning a direct legal and moral responsibility for social interpretation. It is responsible for the appraisal of the operation of the educational plan and for its improvement. The planning function is one of its most important tasks. Despite the handicap of partizan political influence which lies heavily upon too many of our state organizations, it is possible to expand and improve the range of activity in the interpretative field. There is no reason why state authority should not capitalize upon the partnership concept in American public education and expand this unique idea by continuing coöperation with representative lay and professional groups through which information with respect to popular opinion may be secured and whereby the state leaders may be informed and support rational extensions of the educational plan. The effectiveness of interpretation in the local district may be greatly enhanced by supplementation and support through the more generalized state program. Failure of state authority to fulfill its obligations cannot serve as an excuse for neglect within the local district. The local and state areas of functioning are complementary.

Chapter 14

THE TEACHING PROFESSION: PROGRAM

THE function and desirable organization of the teaching profession as a socially responsible interest group has already been considered.[1] This chapter will attempt to consider program as methods of functioning in terms of: (1) program policy, (2) methods, and (3) activities.

PROGRAM POLICY

Program policy arises from function and objectives. The professional objectives include the improvement of the educational process with emphasis on its institutional aspects, the welfare and growth of the teachers. The immediate importance of the teaching profession in institutional interpretation is as an interest group operating outside of the legal organization of the schools. It is the responsibility of the teaching profession first of all to point out to the people the value, conditions, and needs of their public schools in a much more aggressive manner than is possible within organization. The legal organization may be operating under a "hush" policy by which the people are given little or only partial information, or it may be keeping the people completely informed. Working within the limits of the principle of institutional limitations, the schools in their operating aspect are distinctly limited in the degree of urging changes. The teaching profession is under no such limitation. As an interest group it is fully qualified to present to the general public the specific changes in type and breadth of structure that its professional knowledge makes evident. This promulgation of program is part of the democratic process of functioning. Each interest group may present its own views and attempt through sensible means to convert other interest groups to that opinion. Out of this presenta-

[1] See Chapter 4.

tion and arguments for defense of position will finally emerge a public opinion in favor of or opposed to the change. If the opinion is favorable, legal action by the legislature is correspondingly easy; if the opinion is unfavorable, the process of education goes on until a favorable opinion is formed or the professional interest group is ready to change its position and immediate demands.

Educate Lay Groups

The strongest possible policy of popular education is one by which a general opinion is secured through the direct education of one or more lay interest groups which in turn will act as agencies in the convincing of others. Thus the forming of a specific opinion concerning the needs of the schools in the Parent-Teacher Association, the League of Women Voters, and the Federation of Women's Clubs may result in these groups in turn convincing certain male interest groups in a similar way to educational need and gradually extending the range of favorable opinion until a majority is secured.

Independent Action

In its relation to other interest groups it should be the policy of the teaching profession to remain aloof from entangling alliances and partizan effort. Since the schools belong to the people and not to the teachers, it is relatively easier to maintain this independence in operation without being subject to the pulls and stresses of the groups operating around only a specific group objective. There is considerable temptation for a teacher group, particularly when dominated by administrators who desire quick action, to consider the short view and enter into reciprocal relationships. Such policy may secure immediate results, but is dangerous for the long pull.

The teaching profession should take the point of view that the educational process has as long a life as social organization and that any single generation of teachers is only the contemporary agency for the improvement and enlargement of the educational function. The teaching profession in its interest-group aspects should differ from all other interest groups in the extent of vision and the unselfish desire to subordinate self to the achievement of ultimate purposes. The pressure of time becomes of less importance as part of the operating policy if the nature of the democratic process and the need for vision and long-term planning is recognized. Many of our institutions, particularly the more strongly organized authoritarian churches, have a more sensible feeling about the value of time which certainly conditions the effectiveness of their functioning.

The public schools belong to all of the people, and the teaching profession is merely a group of individuals who are fortunate to have a share in the operation of the process. As individuals and as members of an interest group they, like all other citizens, have a share in the process and a right to be heard. If the people are not willing to accept the professional program at any time, it may be possible that the program is not adjusted to popular understanding or the requisite popular confidence is lacking. The professional is frequently far ahead of the popular mind in his thinking and is further handicapped by a lack of understanding of the popular mind. Either one or both of these difficulties may limit the effectiveness of the group at any time. Again, it is not always certain that the teaching profession is always completely right and the people always completely wrong. The professional's lack of realistic knowledge of social functioning and sometime strangely myopic group view should be given more consideration.

Unselfishness is part of the formula for improvement of education. So long as the people are convinced that the welfare of the children and of the social order are first, there will be a greater ensuing confidence. On the other hand, the presentation of a program of teacher welfare thinly disguised and emotionalized as a need of the children may cause popular doubt. The schools have no need to pose as charitable institutions dependent on popular dole. Their appeal will be stronger if the institution is considered as one of the social coöperative activities from which the participants receive a direct value and return that is measurable both in the individual and in the group.

In this process the teacher has certain needs and legitimate desires such as adequate recompense in terms of training and value of the work, security in position from the vagaries of partizan politics

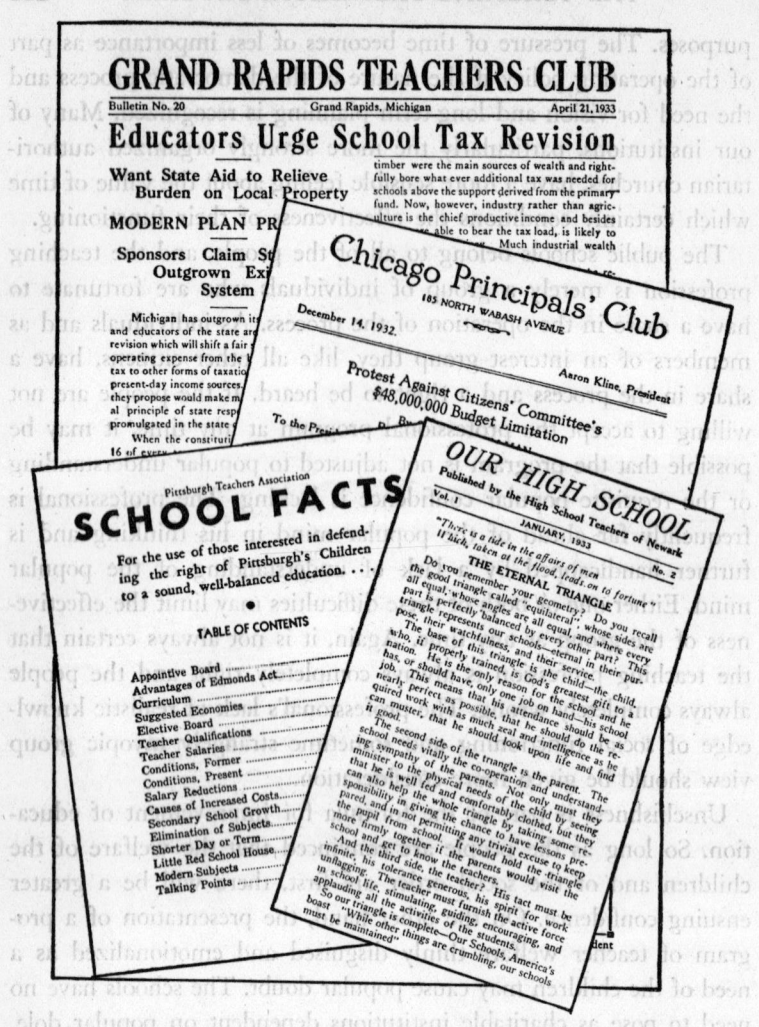

Publications of local teachers' associations.

or vindictive interest groups, freedom without personal penalties to teach the truth as it is progressively revealed. These are legitimate needs and may be legitimately expressed and struggled for without wrapping them up hypocritically in the welfare of the child. The teaching profession should be just as careful not to exploit the immature as it is to keep other groups from doing so.

Adult Program

It should be a definite part of professional policy to recognize that the educational process includes the education of both the immature and the adult. To the immature there must be the highest type of unselfish responsibility, whereas in the case of the mature individual an adult technique is possible. The educational institution operates through the support of public opinion; therefore, essential institutional changes must be preceded by educating the adult to the value of these changes so that they may be legally or experimentally made in the education of the children.

In carrying out its long-range program of keeping the people informed of educational needs, the professional may wisely reject sentimentality and high emotionalism as a policy. This does not mean that the straightforward presentation of bare facts alone will be effective and convincing and that the people will be moved by an appeal to pure reason. It suggests rather the desirability of building up in the popular mind an appreciation of the value and need for improved education and creating just as strong an opposing attitude against exploitation of children by selfish interests for personal profit; it means creating an alertness with respect to protecting the child and general community interests and strengthening the American concept of fair play so that the great dream of educational equality of opportunity in accord with inborn capacity may be progressively realized. Though there must be an appeal to the emotions, this appeal should be rationally organized and developed on the basis of sound teaching methodology instead of emphasizing neurotic sympathy and pity.

Avoid Propaganda

While it was stated in Chapter 3 that an interest group may be justified in using propaganda, although a public institution is debarred from its use, it is still desirable as a long-time policy that the teaching profession also eschew propaganda in the interests of full and complete presentation of all of the facts. An informational policy will require much more study and time than the use of the propaganda technique. As an illustration it might be worth while to recall much of the depression campaigning for better school support. The emotional appeal was based on the educationally submerged rural child and teacher. The general impression created was that some powerful interest was holding out and crushing this educational sector. Low salaries and short schooling were brought into the limelight, even into a presidential campaign. Was it true? Did the additional appropriations change the rural situation? Not much, and to the serious student of educational problems it is quite obvious why they did not do so. The low level of rural education is due to the inadequacy of structure, inadequacy in the training of the teacher, the economic interest of the farmer in the district teacher, the low level of popular control as evidenced in the typical rural board of education, the absence of even rudimentary supervision of sub-marginal teachers, and the labor income level of the leading members of a rural community. Pouring more money into a sub-marginal area without solving the fundamental problems essential to true improvement of educational service is hard to defend from any rational viewpoint. There is no solution for this problem until all of the facts are definitely brought out and a public opinion created to make fundamental change possible. This technique merely used the plight of the rural child as a stalking horse in campaigns for increased support and was too often used knowingly by state teacher organizations as a bait for increased rural teacher membership and for legislative support by the Grange and Farm Bureau.

Avoid Pressure

The policy of continuing adult education is preferable by far to a high-pressure policy which may achieve an objective but will gradually bring upon the teaching profession the suspicion and distrust of the competing interest groups.

It is desirable that the policy of progressive popular education supplant many dubious and dangerous current practices, such as the calling of names, decrying the programs of other interest groups, or use of the martyr technique of the "poor teacher." Very little is accomplished by starting a fight. That luxury may well be left to other interest groups. Conflicts are a long time healing and are generally unnecessary. A calm, confident attitude and sane presentation of program are much more effective.

PROFESSIONAL METHODS

The professional responsibilities for social interpretation cannot be evaded. Every member of the teaching profession is responsible. Neither can they be delegated to a small group of professionals in the full-time secretariat. Professional success will ultimately be conditioned by the degree of completeness with which every member does his part in the general plan. Since acceptance of responsibility is normally conditioned by active interest, professional organization must be designed to secure the greatest possible continuing interest. One of the only satisfactory means of accomplishment is through the progressive democratization of professional organization so that there is much greater possibility of participation by every member. A primary need is the building of strong local groups which in turn will produce a well-integrated state federation. There must be opportunity for full and free discussion of all problems and the development of professional policy as a result of recognition and acceptance by all of the members. Other possibilities exist in special services that may be offered members with respect to securing employment, protection from political and economic pressure groups, and consistently developing means for the normal advancement of teaching as a profession.

Membership Standards

Ultimately it will be necessary for the teaching profession to make selective standards for admission of teachers instead of using all too frequently pressure methods and program modifications to attract larger numbers and greater revenue. It is questionable whether the trousseau teacher, the sub-marginal quasi-teacher, or the casual who uses teaching as a stepping stone to some other work, should be considered as part of the professional group. There should be qualifications not only for training but for purpose and a probationary period during which the individual is studied in terms of capability. Until the teaching profession does set standards for memberships, it will be difficult to secure the greatest degree of public confidence and the real interest of the truly professional teacher.

Planning Board

In developing policy and studying long-time plans, it seems desirable that each organization provide from among its most capable leaders a continuing planning board which would prepare programs and methods of achievement for the local chapters and the state directors. Membership on this planning board should be staggered so that it will form a continuing means of program and program direction for the entire professional group. Membership on this board might be determined by vote of the board of directors or direct election by the members of each large district division within the total organization, the method depending entirely upon the desire of the members. It is advisable that the planning board be without administrative power, acting only in a creative capacity to the regular organization.

The first program requirement is that the members of the profession should be kept fully informed of general economic, social, and political problems as well as the implication of educational problems. The first requisite of the alert professional is intelligent orientation to the general cultural problems out of which will rise a much better and broader understanding of educational problems. The day of seclusion and monastic retirement of the teacher from active life has fortunately passed.

The second demand is for greater integration of the teaching profession around a broad program of objectives which is sufficiently understood in all its implications to secure a continuing interest. The teacher must be fully educated and ready for a program before it can become really effective.

The teacher should be educated to see that teacher improvement is inseparable from institutional improvement. The people will pay more for better things.

The direction of the professional program should always be in terms of the value of the schools to the people and to the children. These are immediately understandable values. For the long-time program the improvement of the schools may be definitely stressed. The teaching profession must therefore be itself prepared to consider improvement as a vital point in policy. The people are not primarily interested in the welfare of the teachers *per se,* but only in relation to their contributions to instruction and its improvement.

Research

Another important work is the securing of complete information in all essential areas, which may best be accomplished through the employment of competent research specialists. The professional organization may secure the services of a full-time individual to whom would be entrusted all activity of an investigative nature; a variety of research specialists may be used to work only on special assignments for which they are particularly competent, returning to their own school systems upon completion of the problem; or coöperative relationships may be established with institutions of higher learning within the state, and the services of their faculties and graduate research students utilized. The important need in this field is that the research be both valid and competent in order to insure greatest popular confidence in its findings. Since it is the normal tendency of administrative officers to interfere somewhat in terms of policy motives with the independence of the research specialist, the third method appears to offer the best advantages and, in addition, will probably be the least expensive.

In general the methods used in educating its members and the adult public should be an extension of the teaching technique and will involve application of the laws of learning to adult education, simplicity in form, continuity in presentation, and fairness in approach.

PROFESSIONAL ACTIVITIES

The first activity includes the education of its members. The conventional method is through a series of district and regional meetings usually held once a year. These programs are primarily professional in character with what may be termed "inspirational efforts" in the general sessions. Some of these state meetings are unusually high in program caliber, and others are more representative of the conventional county institute. They offer an unusual opportunity for excellence when properly organized and projected. Problems of technical interest to specialized aspects of teaching might well be confined entirely to sectional meetings. Educational problems of more general interest may be considered at divisional meetings holding the general sessions completely free for presentation of different social, economic, and political problems in which different points of view are represented. Balance is highly desirable. It is far better to consider one problem in all of its aspects than to "highspot" the field. If the managerial or capitalistic point of view is presented, labor should also have a chance to present its side of the case. The economic theoretician should be balanced by the political and social specialists who can demonstrate the effects of applying new theories and practices. If properly organized, the general session may be of real educational value. Annual meetings focus unusual emphasis through the press on the teaching profession, but their value as an educational device is extremely limited unless the theme of the annual meeting can be carried over and continued throughout the year in local study groups. The second step in the education of the teachers should be the building of a study program around fields of problems not directly involved in education. They might be modeled on the study plans of the women's organizations. Small study groups meeting regularly will probably be more effective than occasional large gatherings.

Professional Publications

News may be presented continuously through the professional publication which in practically all instances takes the form of a monthly magazine. These teacher publications could be much more effective in the continuing education of the teacher if they were better adjusted to major audience interest and were completely free and open to permit the expression of different points of view by members of the profession. Their editorial policy is too frequently

THE TEACHING PROFESSION: PROGRAM 289

Bulletins and handbooks published by teachers' professional organizations.

dominated and cramped by the state secretary. The teacher's magazine should offer to the directing heads of our professional associations opportunity to maintain continuing contacts with the members and offer to the teachers a medium of free expression of opinions. Certainly professional publication should be one place where the teacher might exercise his civil right of freedom of speech.

The annual meeting and the professional magazine are probably in need of additional supplementation so that significant information concerning educational conditions and need may go steadily to the teacher. Occasional terse, simply written bulletins are a possible means of stimulation.

Local Leaders

The great professional need is for the development of strong local leaders who are capable of planning and directing local programs. If the local chapter is to function effectively as an advisory group to the board of education, a much better understanding of state and local educational problems is desirable. Group leaders should be chosen with care and maintained over a period of years. It is impossible to develop effective local professional chapters without much effort and time.

Lay Relationships

The professional group's relationship to the lay groups may be determined as a general state policy and again made the executive responsibility of the local chapters. The real work of an interest group is accomplished within the radius of the most intense interest, usually the job or the nearest problem. The most effective lay contacts by the teaching profession will be those made locally.

Lay contacts should in all possible cases be made on the basis of direct participation. Teachers have sufficient collateral social interests to make it possible to maintain a complete membership coverage in practically all significant associations. Through affiliation initial confidence is built and influence exerted. There should be a teacher on the program committee of every community interest group so that the organization may take advantage of teacher skill, and the teacher may offer suggestions for a reasonable time to be allowed educational programs. Through the teacher members it is possible for the state educational associations to place their general publications and specialized informational bulletins effectively within the group.

Since the public school is a classless school, it is desirable that the teachers have the widest type of lay affiliation. Care should be exercised to see that rural interest groups draw as much membership as executive luncheon clubs, that labor organizations are as close as chambers of commerce. The democratic school must be universal in interest and in its community relationships.

The success of professional-lay relations is very completely dependent on the effectiveness of the individual teacher. The state organization may be stimulatingly helpful, but it cannot make effective contacts as a centralized unit.

Direct Publicity

Generalized contacts are possible through direct publicity. The state organization can maintain a news service that will go to every paper in the state when the association really has significant news to send. The regular stereotyped publicity "hand out" is undesirable because it so quickly degenerates into propaganda or what a professional news man considers "prattle."

Newspaper men look upon the teachers' organizations just as they do on any other interest group and suspect a hidden motive or an ax to grind in the most sincere type of interpretative news article. This reaction is the natural result of their daily experience. Consequently it is good sense for the state association to send out only routine news of names, places, and events.

Though newspaper men may discard the state news release as propaganda, the same idea expressed and sponsored by a local leader will be accepted as sound news by the paper in the local community. It would therefore appear to be much better practice to use a decentralized plan for keeping the newspapers supplied with educational news.

Suggestions for news and feature stories may be developed and sent to the local chapter for transmission to the press. The local chapter is much closer to the circulation interest of a newspaper than the headquarters in the state capital. Through the selection of a smart committee on publicity, the state "hand outs" may be rewritten from the local publicity angle or the facts of the story given the local reporter for his own writing. The newspapers in all of the states should carry much more general educational news than they do. The study and improvement of the press relationship is desirable in the interests of better interpretation.

In addition to the public press other methods for direct publicity are open to the teaching profession. The radio may be considered as the twin of the newspaper with possibilities for direct contact with the mass of the people that are just beginning to be realized.[2] The dramatization of educational values and needs through pageants and exhibits offers much opportunity. The teaching profession may also secure greater representation of public education in the programs of lay groups by suggesting both topics and speakers. Whereas the state organization may outline possibilities in this area, contacts with local lay groups will probably be more effective if confined to the teacher members in each locality.

Much of the effort and most of the interpretative activities of professional organization take place during the legislative year while the interim is dormant. If the educational policy is employed, it seems more desirable to maintain a steady program of informational service than to concentrate on a pressure basis just prior to and during legislative sessions.

Lobbying

The lobbying activity is perfectly justifiable if maintained on a petitional and informational basis. Every professional organization should watch through a legislative observer legislation that affects education and the welfare of the teachers. It should not be within the scope of this observer's duty to direct legislation. The best method of securing favorable legislative action is to build a public opinion in the members' community through the educational method recommended for contact with lay organizations. If legislative hearings are desirable, educational and lay leaders may be called upon to appear before either committee or the legislature

[2] See Chapter 20.

itself. A professional organization cannot be too careful about its legislative activities.

It is also questionable procedure whether the professional organization should canvass candidates for public office to declare their attitude toward some projected change in the general educational plan if that proposal represents solely the effort of the organized teaching profession. It may be desirable for lay groups such as the parent-teacher association to canvass major candidates with regard to their general attitudes, policies, and plans for public education. Although the claim is frequently made that this preëlection canvass is merely to place the candidate on record, the practical politician looks upon any attempt to secure his support in advance for a specific detailed plan as a pressure-group threat. He may react in a satisfactory manner publicly, but his private attitude toward the teaching profession's demands will be entirely different. Certainly the teaching profession should not be guilty of attempting to modify the principles of representative government by securing specific promises in advance of election for a specific plan, the merits of which must normally be subject to legislative review in light of all conditions prevailing when this body meets in legal session.

As a result of these unjudicial attempts to "record the candidate," the professional politician already has, by ways well known to himself, created newspaper suspicion of these methods in too many states and in the national capital and started the press writing about "teacher lobbies." These reactions of both legislator and newspapers are dangerous for the better interests of public education and for the teaching profession itself. All group activities should above all things eschew all possible implication of becoming a pressure group or a partizan body. Success achieved through this method is bound to be short lived.

SUMMARY

The program of the professional organization as a direct agency in institutional interpretation should be educational in nature, directed entirely to the adult population, continuing in type, adjusted to all population levels, and operating as far as possible through the stimulation of lay groups who in turn may act as public-opinion informing agencies in community and state. The work of the professional organization includes the development of policy, provision for continuous planning, the education of its members, and the carrying on of various activities of an oral and written nature through which a continuing program may be operated. Owing to the nature of educational organization and community interest, it is very desirable that the execution of the professional informational program be decentralized and the responsibility placed on the local chapters. The state organization may develop generalized plans and skeleton programs permitting the details to vary with community need. The professional organization must take pains to keep its work on a level where it is impossible to astigmatize the group with either partizanship or pressure lobbying. The most effective professional program is one that takes the long view and is willing to wait patiently for results. Time is an important element in final success.

Chapter 15

THE CHILDREN

THE public school in the United States is an extension of the family and supplements the home's sphere of activity. As a social institution it has a responsibility not only to the child but to the group as well. The general efforts of the public school should be directed to the constant improvement of both program and methods. The happy and contented child and the satisfied parent are direct reflections of institutional effectiveness. Generalized child and parental reactions grow out of the feeling of satisfaction derived from the totality of program.

There has been a great deal of loose thinking and dubious institutional practice in school-child relationships during the past decade in the name of "public relations." It is therefore desirable to analyze these relationships functionally and to establish socially defensible perimeters of institutional action. The problem will be considered in the following divisions: (1) institutional responsibilities, (2) institutional limitations, (3) formal curricular activities, (4) informal curricular activities, (5) post-school relationships, and (6) difficulties and dangers.

INSTITUTIONAL RESPONSIBILITIES

Formalized public-school relationships are specifically set by custom, tradition, and statutory enactments. The educational process cannot be conceived narrowly as limited merely to those exercises which provide solely for mental growth, but must be concerned more generally with considerations of all aspects of personality which result in a well-balanced, well-integrated, and socially capable individual, concerning itself with those areas which are involved in the interrelated physical, mental, social, emotional, and spiritual aspects of growth. As one of the agencies for social reproduction the school is responsible for the direct conditioning of the immature to the democratic organization of life. Since the democratic process makes its own specific provision for variation from current functioning by providing specific techniques and methods through the exercise of civil liberties whereby orderly change is possible, there is sufficient freedom and flexibility within the pattern to prevent arbitrary and rigid social indoctrination. These provisions for variation make possible emphasis on the development of the individual as well as the social needs.

The American ideal of democratic education may be expressed as equality of individual opportunity in accordance with inborn capacity. The American public school is presumptively a classless, nurturing agency for all of the children of all of the people in which individual and group welfare are evenly balanced. In so far as the public school falls short of this ideal, it is due to imperfect understanding by the people of institutional shortcomings, imperfect organization and personnel for the facilitation of the function, and imperfect machinery for its financial support. Existing inequalities may be corrected as better social comprehension, means, and greater technical skill are developed.

INSTITUTIONAL LIMITATIONS

The school as a social institution must recognize its current limitations. Since it rests on a broad base of supporting public opinion, it is limited in its current translation of the democratic process by the beliefs of the adult population. As a social partnership with the parents public education can only change and improve as the parents and other adults become conscious of need and are willing to support the change. It is therefore very difficult and dangerous for public education to change the teaching patterns without adult approval. Apparent inability of many members of the teaching profession to grasp completely the American educational scheme accounts for much lack of harmony between school and community. What the teaching profession believes desirable and what the adult community may be willing to accept may be a long distance apart. The solution does not lie in name-calling or viewing with alarm, but rather in realizing the fundamental nature of the process of democratic change and the extension of the teaching technique into the field of adult education.

As an institution public education has no moral right to attempt to overcome institutional inadequacy through the exploitation of the immature individuals confided to its care. It is even questionable whether the child should be permitted to convey adult interpretative information directly to the home. There is only an extremely narrow area in the education of the child where the professional agents may venture in carrying out the educational process. The child must not be used as a propaganda agency to advance either the institutional or teacher interests. Excitation of children to action beyond their limits of functioning whether in expressing sympathy for a teacher through non-attendance strike or working upon the sentiment of adults to secure teacher financial or social advantage is entirely unworthy of the teaching profession. Violation of the ethics of teacher-child relations would, if teaching were really a well-organized profession, result in quick and decisive punitive action by the balance of the profession.

Upon the whole the majority of American public-school teachers do have a definite understanding of the delicacy of these relations and refrain from bringing institutional or personal problems into the classroom. However, certain "go-getter" administrators and a very small number of non-professionally minded teachers desiring quick results apparently do not hesitate to exploit the children to their personal advantage. These unfortunate transgressions usually bring their own results in decrease in popular confidence and in the growth of suspicion toward the teaching profession. The oft-repeated lay indictment that the teachers too frequently consider and use the schools for their personal aggrandizement is not entirely without sound foundation in fact.

The public school is distinctly limited in its indoctrination of children to the teaching of the school as a social institution and its importance in the democratic plan. The history, ideals, and immediate aims of the educational process are definitely capable of curricular translation to the same extent that all other social institutions are. It is merely a part of the learning process whereby children become familiar with social organization as a convenient means through which fundamental values are expressed and the process of living together becomes easier. The degree of realism in teaching will vary directly with the maturity of the individuals. Study and analysis of institutional values and methods must perforce differ considerably in the elementary, secondary, and institutions of higher learning.

FORMAL CURRICULAR ACTIVITIES

Teaching the school as a social institution has a definite place among the varied patterns of the formalized curriculum. Except for the most casual treatment this phase of instruction has been conspicuous by its absence. The reason for this omission is difficult to determine. It may have been due to an earlier generation of teachers leaning over backwards so that it might escape the charge of propaganda, or it may have been due to the lack of exact knowledge of the realistic functioning of the democratic process. Regardless of the cause, the omission is too great to be overlooked at the present time. Though the major emphasis in institutional study probably deserves placement in the socio-civic curricular division, there are many other possibilities and opportunities for specialized aspects of study.

Socio-Civic Teaching

In the socio-civic division the school should be normally treated along with other social institutions. The importance of the educational function in any culture will be followed by the special importance of free education under the democratic plan of life. Comparative study of the educational objectives of foreign countries is well worth while at the same time.

It is not particularly desirable that too much emphasis be placed upon the current institutional expression of the educational function except to show changing organization purely as a means for achieving a social purpose. Too much emphasis and elevation of institutional form may result in a rigid conditioning in the future adult that another generation of teachers will find difficulty in changing to overcome social lag. Thus the continued loyalty of the adult to the three R's as a complete education is probably derived from the earlier institutional emphasis on the socio-civic character building values that were expected to accrue from mere literacy. The educational process is eternal, though its institutional expressions are purely temporal. Excessive emotionalization of the institution results in the development of a rigid alumni such as we find at class reunions in colleges and universities. Partly because of the emphasis on the emotional aspects of "alma mater," the typical graduate firmly believes that institutional adjustments to changing need are merely signs that the old school is slipping. "It isn't as good as it used to be" is the reunion theme song. The obvious answer is that it never was.

Fine-Arts Teaching

In the fine arts the value of institutional forms and facilities in the integration of beauty and use offers unlimited opportunity. The effect of a well-designed and beautifully landscaped school plant as a stimulus to general improvement of community life furnishes an excellent educational theme. Even the simpler cultures pay minute attention to the harmonization of beauty and utility. It is a functional necessity since art without practicality in the larger sense is socially meaningless, and utility without beauty ignores the esthetic yearnings of mankind.

Mathematics Teaching

The entire field of public finance, of which education is only one aspect, may well be integrated in mathematics. Possible understanding of the true nature of taxation and the profitable pooling of common resources for the achievement of social purposes might produce a generation whose blood pressure would remain constant when taxation is the subject of discussion. The cost of education, methods of budgeting and accounting, divisions and types of educational expenditure, the dangers of long-term borrowing, the relation of salaries to work performed, and many other aspects might well be given consideration in arithmetic.

Language Teaching

The languages, especially English, offer supreme opportunity for the study of the lives and works of our educational leaders as well as for the glorification of those who excelled in battle. The arts of peace need not be subordinated to the arts of war. Horace Mann, Henry Barnard, Elizabeth Peabody, Jane Addams, Charles H. Eliot, William Rainey Harper, William T. Harris, James B. Angell, and scores of others are as important in their educational contributions as George Washington, Benjamin Franklin, Thomas Jefferson, James Madison, James Monroe, and Abraham Lincoln. Some of these famous educators' writings on democracy and the value of general free education rank high as literary effort.

A realistic socio-civic education of the children in the aims, processes, and responsibilities of the individual in democratic functioning is within the scope of the school and is one of its highest responsibilities.

INFORMAL CURRICULAR ACTIVITIES

The informal curricular aspects are currently called *extracurricular activities* by the teaching profession, and this unfortunate connotation has created in both child and adult mind the feeling that the most dynamic phase of instruction is something given free, if time allows, like the premium idea in certain types of merchandising. Until the profession drops this peculiar terminology and proceeds to the consideration of these dynamic socialized aspects of learning as an integral part of the program, interpretation for both child and adult is going to be difficult.

During the recent depression popular demands for curricular restriction resulted in the careful preservation of curricular deadwood and the scrapping of new ideas and practices. The fault did not lie with the people since the teaching profession had itself labeled these movements as "extras." The community took the schools at their own word.

Because of their social nature and the problems involved, the informal curricular activities result generally in some display or exhibition that has audience value—hence their importance in direct institutional interpretation. Without desiring to straitjacket them to innocuity, the institution has a natural responsibility in maintaining these activities in channels acceptable to the community and in accord with its patterns of thought. Many a dramatics teacher fresh from the campus has selected examples of sophisticated drama in a community conditioned to *East Lynne*. Informal curricular activities which have inherent interpretative aspects include the school paper, music, drama, exhibitions, contests of all types, commencements, and social gatherings.

School Paper

The school paper is one of the most abused and exploited child activities. In many instances it has become merely a propaganda sheet for adult institutional interpretation to the detriment of child interest or is used in smaller school systems as the personal publicity organ of superintendent and principal.

The school paper is fundamentally a terminal product of learning in several formal curricular fields and represents at the same time practical training in the field of written expression. It should represent to the children what the free press does to the adult. Since it is directly concerned with child interest, there is no reason why the school paper should become a servile imitator of daily press form or mechanical make-up. As a means of conveying news of interest, the school paper may be expected normally to give a balanced view of school life. There is no occasion for the allotment of 20 to 60 per cent of a four-page paper to competitive athletics.

As a terminal instructional project the school paper may be considered just as any similar activity. It should be a charge against instructional supplies and furnished to every child without charge. Considered solely as an instructional activity, its form and expense may be adjusted to institutional possibilities. It may be printed in the school shop; half-tones and zincs may be easily developed as a laboratory hobby interest in either chemistry or physics; linoleum cuts may be made in fine arts, which leaves paper as the only heavy expense. In elementary schools the mimeographed or duplicated forms are possible, particularly if stencils are cut from machines with large type. There is no occasion for ambitious imitation of commercial venture or the extravagant use of money for impressive layout. The school paper is essentially a child product.

The normal direction of the paper appears to fit best in the English instructional division. Each school can afford one teacher who is trained in journalism as well as the more technical aspects of the subject. The teacher's work is similar to that in other instructional activity except with respect to formality of organization. The children may secure incidental instruction in the nature and value of the free press to democracy, specific training in the gathering and presentation of factual material, and practice in the art of written expression. It is not desirable to censor all child ideas and to rewrite them according to adult form. Censorship is an excellent means of destroying child interest. Adult expression or competence is not expected in formal classroom work, and there appears to be no valid reason for a reversal of policy with respect to the school paper. The closer the paper is adjusted to child interest and the more nearly it represents a child product, the more effective it will be as an instructional instrument.

There is a logical place in the paper in terms of child interest for stories of the school as a democratic social institution. Possibilities of child appraisal as to deficiencies and need may also receive consideration. There is no stronger incentive on the part of the child for coördinating his subject-matter than to find that his history theme or his discussion in mathematics is valuable as a piece of news for the school paper. Intelligent direction to maintain news balance, good taste, accuracy, and interest are all that is required of the faculty guide.

The school paper as a child product has only an incidental appeal to the parent. Since it is good policy to allow each contributor to sign his articles, both child and parent interest may be increased in pride of authorship. The adult will read his offspring's efforts and may occasionally glance at items of adult interest such as news of parent-teacher or parent-council meetings, changes and improvement in the physical plant, and news of other audience activities.

Imitation of the commercial press gives rise to strong conflict possibilities. There are two interpretative dangers: the first resulting from a feeling of economic inadequacy when charges are made for the school paper, and many children thus excluded from participation; the second resulting from passing the burden of expense to the neighborhood through advertising. The professional advertising specialist is well convinced that paid advertisements in the school paper have little if any economic value to the advertiser. They are classified as either "pressure" or "good will" advertising. The major sources of this form of revenue are from the neighborhood stores including butcher, baker, drug-store, small notions, and beauty parlors. The merchant realizes the low value, but generally contributes because he feels the danger of child ill will. There are many instances where the children have been taught by faculty sponsor to impress on the unwilling local distributor the possibility of parental boycott if they fail to support the paper by buying space. Because of the combination of circumstances the school gets the revenue and runs the risk of creating much silent ill will that may be easily capitalized in times of emergency. Solicitation of neighborhood advertising also brings the school into competition with commercial enterprise and forms another possible area of conflict. Exceptions may be made in small communities that do not possess a newspaper. Here the school paper frequently combines the instructional with the community function of communication and publication. Such combination is debatable in an institutional organ specifically limited in its news coverage and treatment. This extended treatment of the school paper is essential because it represents an activity that is both misunderstood and misused and has many possibilities of becoming a distinct handicap to constructive interpretation.

Fine Arts

Both music and drama offer unusual opportunities for the stimulation of community interest in the fine arts. The development of vocal and instrumental music in the public schools in the past twenty-five years is one of the most startling phenomena in curricular extension. So firmly has music been intrenched that scarcely a school of any size to-day is without a band, and many secondary schools also possess unusually good orchestras and various types of instrumental choirs. The greater appreciation of dramatic expression that has stimulated the development of the school auditorium into a well-equipped theater is significant. Both of these esthetic expressions have a tremendous emotional appeal to the adult and are excellent means for direct translation of certain aspects of school work. They have not yet reached their possible peak, and their cultural possibilities have just begun to be explored. Only a few cautions are desirable. In general, if admission is charged the adult, the price should be kept so low that no family will be barred from attendance, and the grave amateur fault in timing the length of a performance needs correction. It is much more satisfactory to keep amateur programs shorter than professional performances and have the audience depart in a state of high stimulation and satisfaction than have them watch the clock and become restless during the last half hour.

Exhibitions

Periodic display of terminal curricular products within the school building is an excellent means for concrete explanation of the school work. Care should be observed that these exhibitions really comprise child products and are not loaded with faculty productions in order to bring up the standard of achievement. There is plenty of opportunity for adult exhibitions of work by both community and teachers, but they need not be mixed with those of the child. The display of child work may be made the reason for adult visitation during special open-house occasions and at the time of any adult gathering. Possibly these exhibits may be made more effective if organized, directed, and explained by the children. The child guide has many attractions for the adult. Exhibitions may be easily made an integral part of the visual program maintained constantly and changed at regular intervals.

Contests

There is definite value in contests. Competition among individuals and groups has the possibility of creating unusual emotional interest.

Parents as well as children enjoy such activities as puppet shows and the construction of miniature villages.

In many high schools children discuss and appraise current photoplays.

Herein also lies its danger. Excessive emphasis on the championship idea is causing many schools to realize that they are holding a bear's tail, with the school rapidly following the bear. Rational areas of contests include intra-school athletic events and debates. Many others are currently included but their diversion from performance to competition is dubious. The championship concept is a real danger to long-time institutional interpretation.

Commencements

The commencement program is the institutional ritual of terminal achievement. It has interpretative significance in both the lower and higher divisions of secondary education. There are two distinct choices in this field. The occasion may be made a colorful pageant and ritual in which the children form the background and the program is completely planned and carried out by adults for adults, or it may be organized as a distinctly child production whereby the graduates and possibly other students actually use this occasion to dramatize for themselves and their parents the meaning and value of public education. The choice of type will probably depend upon the attitude of the community to this event. If highly traditional in character, the parental group may not be weaned quickly from its conventional desires. There are undoubtedly values in both practices, and the terminal appraisal must be in community reaction.

Certain specific requirements are indicated for both types of commencements. First of all, the occasion should be one of dignity without becoming pompous or stilted. In one sense the termination of institutional control is a direct initiation of the individual to adult life. This fact is particularly significant in the upper secondary school. The state confers its rewards upon the successful students and bids them godspeed into a more realistic life. For a large proportion of the children and parents this occasion does mark the end of formal institutional control. Certainly a dignified termination is desirable. The second requirement is time sense in both types of programs. As a general rule no amateur performance should exceed one hour and a half in length, and any extension of this time must consider the risk of boring an audience loaded with an unusually high quota of small and restless children. The third requirement is that either type of program may be definitely planned around a specific idea. If an outside speaker is invited to make a formal address, his subject should be furnished in relation to the program objective and his time of delivery definitely limited to twenty minutes or less. In a mixed audience of the commencement type no impression is made after the first twenty minutes. If a speaker cannot confine his efforts within these limits, another choice should be made. The heavy-worded college president who recently spoke for an hour and a half to a commencement audience comprising fifteen different nationalities on the value of putting things in their proper places, concluding with the significant statement that "if we place things of primary importance first, things of secondary importance second, things of tertiary importance third, and other things in the relative order of their importance," may have felt a certain self-satisfaction, but half of the audience was drowsing after the first quarter hour, and the balance centered their attention on possible events of the morrow. The typical American audience is docile and gentlemanly; it has developed a protective attitude of listening while the mind roves afield into pleasant dreams, accompanied and assisted by the sonorous words of a ponderous speaker.

Social Events

The social events of the school frequently give much institutional difficulty. The oncoming generation consistently imitates the more sophisticated procedure of the "younger set." This tendency creates conflict between the children and their parents. The result is many an institutional headache and much community disapprobation. Much difficulty may be avoided and the interpretative problem simplified if the institution would invite the coöperation of the parents in planning and directing these events. Placing the responsibility on the parents is not to be considered merely as a means of escape but rather as the active enlargement of the partnership concept and the means of offering the parents an opportunity for some realistic adult education. The parent eagerly passes this responsibility for harmonizing the inevitable conflict between parents and children to the school.

The school unfortunately is only too ready to accept the challenge and gets into difficulty. The children appear to be the only ones who really enjoy themselves. Joint planning and active supervision through the parent-teacher association is indicated.

POST-SCHOOL RELATIONSHIPS

It is an American custom to emotionalize and romanticize institutions of learning. By a process of direct indoctrination colleges and universities begin to work upon the entering student, developing a high state of "school spirit" so that after graduation the individual will always have a definite feeling of loyalty toward his Alma Mater. The American university alumnus represents a type that is foreign to the higher institutions of any other country. The institutional purpose is to develop a strong body of friends, supporters, and possible contributors. So extensively has this process been developed that an alumnus may now be considered as an individual who by accident of registration and graduation becomes a life contributor to his college.

The alumni idea has been carried over into secondary education and probably reaches its highest degree of emotional effectiveness in voluntary institutions of college-preparatory grade. There is sufficient evidence on the various campuses of the non-public school in building and endowments to indicate reasonable success in the undertaking. In the public secondary school the alumni organization has had varying degrees of success. Many of the larger city schools maintain alumni groups. Under the leadership of a small group, effort is made to maintain periodic contact with graduates and to build up scholarship funds whereby capable individuals who are economically handicapped may have the benefits of higher education. The record of these scholarship loan funds is excellent.

Large city attempts to maintain a close social organization of alumni is doomed to failure by the diversity of interests and time demands upon the adult. In the small community with a simpler life closer social solidarity may be effected, and there are numerous examples of the high-school alumni association which has become the center of the younger generation's community life. Little attempt has been made to organize these post-school interests as a phase of interpretation.

The secondary school may easily provide institutional means whereby regular communication is maintained with those graduates who remain in the community. In its poorest expression the alumni idea is merely a mailing list for school publications, but in its possible form it is the basis for continuing institutional contacts through the appeal of adult education. To the non-college graduate of the secondary school there can be sufficient interest in the continuing of his training in direct vocational areas, in socio-civic fields, in recreation and the fine arts. The status of the student changes specifically upon graduation, and for institutional purposes he may be considered as a responsible adult member of the community. His understanding and appreciation of the school as a valuable social institution may be continued through inclusion in and exposure to the general pre-interpretative program. The secondary alumni field is important and needs careful exploration.

DIFFICULTIES AND DANGERS

From some aspects public secondary education appears to be slowly disintegrating into a series of championships. Teachers and laymen alike are beginning to look with serious misgivings on the uncontrollable giant that administration has unconsciously developed.

Athletic championships are too frequently the exploitation of the immature secondary-school boy and girl to satisfy a carefully nurtured communal desire for a winner and to enhance the reputation of the coach. Championship ventures into new areas do not appear so significant to the casual view and have not been massed to receive the same spectacular attention. The current list includes regional, state, and national championships in performance on academic achievement tests, state educational round-ups, regional and state debating, all publications including weekly papers and yearbooks, instrumental and vocal music, state and national spelling contests, and special prize contests sponsored by commercial or propaganda organizations outside of the school system.

These championship contests are theoretically assumed to be purely amateur performances and, with the exception of athletics, had their inception in the field of interpretation of the school to the community through the always dramatic element of individual or group struggle. At the same time interest groups beyond the school recognized the publicity values accruing from sponsorship and found their services in demand. Where the professional had some real doubts as to the educational value of these activities, a little pressure was sufficient to force the issue. If the value of these contests lay in their educational and interpretative values, it may be well to examine the results.

If the purpose of education is the instruction of all individuals in terms of their inborn capacities by methods that stress the scientific and social aspects of the educational process, then heavy competition, stimulated by the institutional urge to win, is hardly in accord with this philosophy of instruction. The urge to win further complicates the instructional problem by placing on the individual teacher the responsibility for producing winners. Faced with this immediate need teachers naturally adjust their "aim" from the instruction of all in terms of capacity to the stimulation and coaching of those who show the most promise. The state and national spelling contests are examples. Visits to any of the elementary schools in any participating state from January until the spring contests will show that the teaching technique is pointed completely to developing the "winning speller" while the rest of the class receives little attention. Elimination rather than growth and development of all students is the general rule. The children, through rallies and "pep" talks, are placed under the same unnatural emotional strain that championship athletes are. From the standpoint of mental hygiene the immature children are frequently stimulated beyond reason, emotionally disturbed and shaken, and their normal orientation distorted by unbalanced publicity and ballyhoo. Since in some school systems teaching is appraised in terms of championships won, the teachers also become disturbed and jittery.

In music contests, the preparation of bands, orchestras, and glee clubs for "prize contests" eliminates from teaching practically all of the fundamental values of music as a fine art. Again, emphasis is naturally placed on the more capable, and the rest are either eliminated, or just "sit by and toot." Mechanical perfection is developed with certain compositions practised to such a degree that even the participants cry out in revolt against the process. Field days and contests in music in several states are now ranked with hog-calling contests and are exploited through regional or state fairs.

In debating, the spirit of amateurism has so obviously broken down that every one except the lay audience is aware of it. For the most part the speeches are written by the debating coach or "speech teacher." Strategy and techniques are worked by these coaches just as the football mentor devises plays. Different closing arguments and rebuttals are developed and learned. Coaches in the audience signal change of pace and selection of alternate material. The use of tricks, including names spelled backward to represent ostensibly foreign authorities, is classified as strategy. In reality most of the contesting debaters are simply puppets operated by a professional coach.

The first step in securing a publication championship is to contract for a good printing teacher (if the school has its own shop) and a seasoned instructor in journalism. If the latter has had professional newspaper experience and has a flair for mechanical make-up, so much the better. Thus the spontaneous and amateur terminal expressions are immediately frozen into standard and conventional patterns highly imitative of commercial publications. They may win championships, but they amount to little educationally!

From the standpoint of amateurism, the academic field days more closely approach this spirit than the other contests. These at least are apparently mass contests, and, although of very dubious validity educationally, are certainly far above the others in honesty of execution.

The outside sponsors profit through these championships. Newspapers have made athletics and spelling bees their own as circulation stimulators, and the school becomes either a conscious or unconscious tool in advancing the private interests of commercial papers. Institutions of higher learning, including both universities and teachers' colleges, in different sections of the country exploit the secondary schools in publications, debating, and music championships. Sometimes these sponsorships are conceived as higher institutional public relationships to attract students. Special teaching divisions, such as speech and music, in other places stimulate the contests while certain professional fraternities, particularly groups in "journalism," are overzealous for their place in the sun. Many other interest groups are also involved in different places. However, the profession seems to be a little skeptical concerning them. The university that attempts to serve its own interest by exploiting children in championships is no more worthy than the power utility that seeks to stimulate the use of more electricity through "better lighting" contests. The difference between them is one of degree only.

The championship cult is decidedly a liability to the school as a social institution. Once a community has become inoculated with the championship germ, it will not rest content. There must be winners every year. The village poolroom, the chamber of commerce, and the service clubs insist upon it. The long train of teachers departing annually from positions because they could not produce "champions" is a situation that tenure-minded groups should study more carefully. Educationally, the emphasis on championships is hazardous. As an activity, it does not conform to modern educational philosophy or methods. It is progressively disintegrating as more and more emphasis is made within the institution to point for these championships. If these practices are analyzed in terms of their interpretative value to the schools, the answer must be strongly negative. It is a high-spot appeal that finally evolves into a vicious attack with the institution strictly on the defensive. Good interpretation demands that the school overcome these weaknesses.

The exploitation of children is not a legitimate activity of interpretation. The championship cult has a very minute, if any, place in a solid program of adult community education. It should be discouraged by the teaching profession since its promotion and continuance hold nothing but danger to the future of educational practice.

SUMMARY

One of the responsibilities of the teaching profession is to protect the child from exploitation by selfish interests outside of or within the school. There is a very definite limit to the use of children as agencies of interpretation. The area of possible use is the teaching of the worth of the school as a valuable democratic social institution in the same manner and to the same degree that other institutions are considered. The means for accomplishment lie in the formal and informal curricular activities. Since the informal activities have an immediate audience value, they require careful orientation with respect to the adult community. There is a distinct difference between the school and post-school relationship of the child to the interpretative process. In the first phase he is subject to the general institutional protection against exploitation, and in the second he may be considered as an adult capable of participating in the general community life. Care must also be exercised in the financing of informal curricular activities so that they do not exclude any child from full participation and so that they do not act as a drain upon already strained family resources. Many a high-school student has been forced to leave school because of the unequal opportunities created by a non-democratic concept of school activities. The reaction of the community to financial demands upon the children may result in a definitely negative attitude toward the institution itself. Good teaching should be a fundamental policy in school-child relationships—not preaching. Ultimate satisfaction of the value of the public school will be determined by the degree of satisfaction derived from the program. An efficient, friendly institution is the most desirable development. A happy child or a satisfied parent forms the best possible base for institutional understanding and support.

Chapter 16

THE PARENT-TEACHER ASSOCIATION

THE parent-teacher association is a comparatively new social force in public education. Organized in 1897 as an agency for the education of mothers, the National Congress of Parents and Teachers has gradually widened its scope and membership until in April, 1937, it included 2,056,777 parents and teachers in its active membership and celebrated its golden jubilee. An association with the emotional stimulus that the parent-teacher organization contains represents a potency or a power that rises far beyond that of the typical interest group. The unusual efforts of its members during the late depression were responsible in no small measure for the maintenance of the school program in the face of great opposition. Since this is a force to be considered in our local, state, and national life, it is desirable to examine its status, its relationships, some aspects of its program, and its proper relationship to the public school. This discussion will successively consider the parent-teacher association on the basis of: (1) history, (2) character of organization, (3) purpose, (4) relationship to school organization, (5) types of parent-teacher associations, (6) programs and means, (7) methods of organization, and (8) conflicts.

HISTORY OF THE MOVEMENT

The early kindergarten movement required a very definite public opinion to maintain itself against reactionary educators. As early as 1865 leaders in its development and extension started mothers' meetings as a means of bringing before the maternal parent the rather dubious procedure (at that time) of permitting a child to enjoy himself in school. In many communities these meetings gradually evolved into mothers' clubs, and by 1894 the movement had gained so much momentum that it was possible to effect a national organization. The first national meeting held at Washington was possible through the joint efforts of Mrs. Alice McLellan Birney and Mrs. Phoebe A. Hearst.[1] The number of delegates from local organizations was so far beyond the expectation of the organizers and so enthusiastic that the National Congress of Mothers came into existence on February 17, 1897. The original purpose of this Congress was to act as a clearing house for child training and welfare.

In the meantime there had been growing up locally a variation of the mothers' club.[2] Stimulated by the interest in child welfare, progressive principals and teachers in many centers organized coöperating groups of parents and teachers to meet occasionally and to discuss problems related to the child. Many of these were at first confined to the kindergarten and the first and second grades.

Movements Combined

The new clubs were not confined to mothers but admitted fathers as well. Finally two movements were integrated in 1908 when the national organization changed its name to the National Congress of Mothers and Parent-Teacher Associations. In the interests of clearness and brevity the name was again changed in 1924 to the present title of National Congress of Parents and Teachers. As the origin might indicate, the national organization has objectives wider in character than those fostered by the typical local parent-teacher association. Neither have its organizations been confined entirely to schools. Independent parent groups and church groups have been continually stimulated. The National Congress has always taken an aggressive stand on reform legislation affecting both the woman and the child. Early support of the juvenile court system of the probationary plan for young offenders greatly assisted these trends to become established practices. Since then the Congress has consistently supported the Sheppard-Towner Maternity and Infancy Bill, the proposed Child Labor Amendment to the Federal Consti-

[1] For more extended history see *Parents and Teachers,* edited by Marion Sprague Mason (Boston, Ginn and Co., 1928), pp. 113-118, 281-294.

[2] A well-known and widely publicized local parent-teacher club was organized and operated in the Hancock School, Detroit. Its founder was Miss Harriet Marsh, an elementary principal. See *Public Education in Detroit,* by Arthur B. Moehlman, p. 148.

tution, the Jones-Miller Anti-Narcotic Bill, and the successive education bills through which Federal aid to education was urged.[3] So consistent and determined have been the efforts of the National Congress, with its real strength in the state branches and the local associations for developing public opinion at home, that the professional politician refers to it frequently as the "mother lobby." In its national policies and program, the Congress has consistently supported the National Education Association and has maintained close affiliation with state educational organizations.

CHARACTER OF THE ORGANIZATION

In one sense the National Congress of Parents and Teachers is a very democratic organization. Each individual member belongs to a local association, to the state branch, and to the National Congress. The National Congress is governed through the annual convention at which plans and policies are made. The convention includes the board of managers and voting delegates chosen proportionately by states on the basis of total membership. The association is primarily national in organization and control. Although the local and state units exist as a means of carrying out the program more easily, the real and primary organization is national, and all general policies and programs are developed and promulgated by the National Congress in convention assembled. The basic character of the organization may be described as Federal. Local and state units are completely subordinated to national policy and practice, although there are few restrictions on local activities so long as the principal national policies are carried out.

Executive Control

The executive organization operating between conventions, through which the will of the Congress is executed is called the Board of Managers. Included in its membership are the twelve national officers, forty-eight state presidents, six national bureau managers, and the national committee chairman. Since the Board of Managers is a large unwieldy body for executive action, the

[3] The Harrison-Black-Fletcher Bill must be excepted.

actual executive control is vested in the Executive Committee, consisting of the national officers and the bureau managers. The Executive Committee is responsible directly to the Board of Managers and acts for it between meetings.

Method of Organization

The organization starts with the local parent-teacher association, study circles, or other child welfare organizations. The authority to organize comes from the National Congress, and the object of each of these local organizations is primarily "to promote the objects and interests of the National Congress."[4] Each local branch is authorized to make rules and regulations for the transaction of its own business provided that these rules do not conflict with those of the National Congress or the state branch.

After at least twenty local organizations belonging to the National Congress are in active operation in any state, it is mandatory upon the National Congress to organize them into a state branch. After creation, the state branch is authorized to admit members to local organizations and to make rules governing its general procedure so long as these do not conflict with the national by-laws and procedures.

Subsidiary Councils

Within the limits of the patterns set by the National Congress, the state branch becomes the legislative body for the local associations within its jurisdiction. The primary object of the state branch[5] is "to promote the objects and interests of the National Congress." Each state branch holds its own state conventions as well as participating in the national meeting. The state branch has permissive authority to organize its local organizations into city councils, county groups, and district groups for ease in administration and for the development of greater program unity and effort.

[4] See By-Laws, Article XI, Section 1.
[5] See By-Laws, Article XI, Section 5.

THE PURPOSE

The objectives of the National Congress of Parents and Teachers are much wider than those commonly associated with the typical local parent-teacher association. As stated in Article II of the By-Laws of 1928 they include:

1. To promote child welfare in home, school, church, and community; to raise the standards of home life; to secure more adequate laws for the care and protection of women and children.
2. To bring into closer relation the home and the school that parents and teachers may coöperate intelligently in the training of the child, and to develop between educators and the general public such united efforts as will secure for every child the highest advantages in physical, mental, moral, and spiritual education.

Wide Objectives

Child welfare is considered not only from the aspect of the home and school but also in relation to the church and to the community at large. A distinct improvement program may be noted in the expression of purpose "to raise the standards of home life" and a possible pressure interest "to secure more adequate laws for the care and protection of women and children." Thus two major planks in the program of the National Congress are concerned with matters outside of the immediate jurisdiction and scope of the public school. The second major aim is devoted primarily to education, and here may be found the expression of the more immediate relationship to the institution of public education.

Expressed from another aspect, the purposes of the National Congress are to develop coöperation with the school, to act as an agency for the creation of public opinion, to promote child welfare generally, to stimulate and elevate home life, and to take a significant part in the development of essential legislation for this purpose. Taken as a whole the general program is extremely worth while although the school cannot accept or participate in all of its aspects.

Objectives in Practice

The purposes officially promulgated by the National Congress of Parents and Teachers to become effective must be translated into actual practice by fifty-one state and territorial branches and by innumerable local associations under all types and abilities of leadership. It is possible that in the course of distance, time, and the play of individual differences, actual field practices may not be completely in harmony with the official pronouncement.

Several illustrations may suffice. The national purpose says nothing about acting as a supplementary agency to public finance. Yet one of the most frequent local activities is the raising of money both for school and association purposes. There is no expression of becoming a "school political pressure organization" in the national purpose, but so many associations have allowed themselves to become so involved in local politics that numerous criticisms have been raised and local movements sometimes sadly weakened. Other variations and deviations from national purposes might be mentioned at length. The situation does not represent anything new or novel. Every translation of purpose is dependent on the quality of leadership and the strength of the local program. The typical local parent-teacher association has not in the past had the best of either educational or lay direction, and these questionable tendencies are the result. The confusion, conflicts, and inadequacies resulting from the combination of all of these factors have been the concern of educators interested in the development of the movement.

Valid Local Objectives

In a consideration of valid objectives for the parent-teacher association in its public-school relationships, one must recognize the differences existing in a national organization that operates as a lobby to secure desired legislation for women and children and that now has six major divisions and a number of bureaus covering many phases of activity not directly related to public education. In calling attention to the generalized objectives of the National Congress and the specialized objectives of the local parent-teacher association, no question of criticism or disparagement arises. It is merely a realistic recognition of a factual difference between national and local programs in a large organization. Public education has no argument or difference with the national objectives as expressed in the By-Laws of the National Congress. It is more primarily concerned with the possible better adjustment of program to the schools. Neither does it presuppose that the local association may have no other objectives than those related to public education, nor that the Parent-Teacher Association should be controlled by the public schools.

With this differentiation well in mind, the local parent-teacher association may be considered as a direct social interpretative agency, whose generalized objectives may be divided into six groups, considered in order of their chronological importance.

Social

Any plan that includes an extralegal organization in the functioning of the public school starts with the initial need for confidence between the professional and lay groups. Since confidence depends on the attitudes developed through observation and contact, the first objective in a coöperative plan is the development of machinery through which confidence, sympathy, and understanding may be attained. For this reason the first objective is considered as social and includes those activities or means by which parent and teachers may become thoroughly acquainted with each other. School and home visitation, social gatherings, and personal conference are all means through which the social objective may be attained.

Educational

Since the ability to do rests on the degree of understanding, the second objective should be concerned with those activities essential to an understanding of the community as well as of the functional relationship of the school to the community. The work involves consideration of the economic, religious, social, and racial background of community life and study of the child and child life in the totality of its institutional aspects, of which the school is only one. This objective has already been classed as one of the problems of adult education. Before it can function effectively, a parent-teacher association must not only have confidence in the professional organization but must understand what it is all about.

Coöperation

Out of confidence and understanding grow the ability and the willingness to coöperate with the community and the institution for a better attack on the very complicated problem of carrying the child through the various developmental stages to maturity. After all, the primary purpose of this joint venture of parents and teachers is the welfare of the child. The welfare of the child coincides with community and school welfare. Confidence in the institution and its personnel plus the intelligent knowledge of its purposes, problems, and difficulties should lead both to the ability and the desire to play a major part in the triangle of learning.

Public Opinion

Those who understand and who participate will serve as disseminators of information and will also watch with zealous eye the welfare of the child. There is little occasion to stimulate a well-informed and intelligently aggressive group of mothers. They seem to sense conditions quietly and prevent many selfish attacks on the child's interests.

Advisory

From mutual respect and confidence and the development both by parent and teacher of looking somewhat more objectively at their particular task, from understanding based on serious study and observation, it is entirely possible for the parent-teacher association to act in a definitely advisory relationship both to the teaching profession and to the board of education. The interested layman has a perfectly valid contribution to make, and there is no reason to object to advice, whether from individual members or from the group. Since these local associations are most frequently organized around a specific school, they should also furnish an excellent means of keeping the principal and teachers informed of trouble spots within the building's attendance area. The location of trouble spots by friendly eyes is most helpful in public administration.

Improvement

No group could achieve the preceding objectives without becoming definitely aware of the weaknesses and inadequacies of the existing schools. These deficiencies due to the weight of tradition, poorly trained personnel, and inadequate finance will be corrected only as intelligent parents see the need for improvement and create a dynamic public opinion to support desirable change. At times the desire of an active and well-directed group for improvement may be well in advance of the immediate ability or desire of the professional organization to follow. In this instance it is necessary to reverse the ordinary process and permit the lay group to educate the professional.

In this aspect of the local parent-teacher association objectives the question of fiscal support for "stimulative" activity must be considered. There is no logical excuse for a parent-teacher association to raise funds to support any activity in a tax-supported school system. If the desired activity has validity, it should be spread on the tax rolls and paid for by the community. Any other method tends to promote class discrimination. To the plea that boards of education will not appropriate money immediately for any new or experimental activity there can be only one answer. A board of education appropriates money under law and in accordance with definite expression of public opinion. If even a very new activity has some degree of popular support, it is possible to secure essential experimental appropriations, except in times of severe economic emergency. There is no need to make the local parent-teacher association a ladies' aid society. It represents to many an inert executive the easiest way of doing the job. Though there may be possible extenuating circumstances, it is better to lean over backward in this respect than to step into the dangers and abuses of extralegal support of portions of a public tax-supported activity.

In summary, the local parent-teacher organization must be considered in a dual aspect as a coöperating educational and as a secondary community interpretative agency. It may best achieve its plans and purposes by adopting a series of objectives which include social and educational phases, developing active coöperation, creating public opinion, acting in a lay advisory capacity, and ever striving for improvement.

RELATIONSHIP TO SCHOOL ORGANIZATION

The proper relationship of the parent-teacher association to public-school organization must be determined by analysis of the legal structure of public education as presented earlier.[6] If the idea of legal responsibility and power is carried to its logical conclusion, it is quite obvious that no specialized extralegal organization should possess any authority to determine, to interfere with, or to change the working of the community educational plan. As individuals the members possess the legal right to appraise the workings of the plan and to vote for changes or for enlargements and contractions. Their opinion should be expressed legally and through regular channels. More specifically, the power of these voluntary groups, whether they be called good government leagues, chambers of commerce, or parent-teacher associations, is limited to the creation and development of public opinion through which other individuals may be influenced, but they have no direct authority to interfere with the working of the legal plan or to dictate what the board of education and its professional executives shall do.

Functional Organization

The functional definition of a parent-teacher association might be expressed as follows: the parent-teacher association is an extralegal or voluntary agency composed of parents and of the teachers of children. It furnishes an orderly means for developing more easily the partnership concept in American public education. Its primary purpose is that of a clearing house for the presentation and discussion of educational problems in order that parent and teacher may, through personal contact, develop greater understanding and better coöperation and thus solve more effectively the

[6] See Chapter 1.

educational problems of the individual child. A secondary purpose is as a social nucleus for the education of the community to the purpose, worth, condition, and needs of public education. In a large sense, the parent-teacher association is distinctly a community interpretative agency made necessary by the complications of our

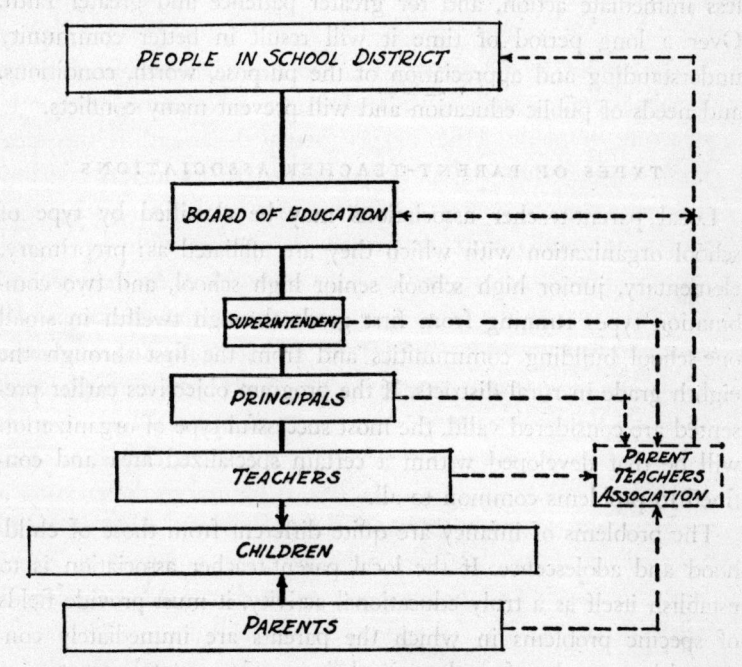

```
┌─────────────────────────────┐
│  PEOPLE IN SCHOOL DISTRICT  │◄─────┐
└──────────────┬──────────────┘      ┊
               │                     ┊
┌──────────────┴──────────────┐      ┊
│      BOARD OF EDUCATION     │┈┈┈┈┈┈┨
└──────────────┬──────────────┘      ┊
               │                     ┊
┌──────────────┴──────────────┐      ┊
│        SUPERINTENDENT       │┈┈┈┈┈┈┨
└──────────────┬──────────────┘      ┊
               │                     ┊
┌──────────────┴──────────────┐      ┊
│          PRINCIPALS         │┈┈┈┈┐ ┊
└──────────────┬──────────────┘    ┊ ┊
               │                 ┌─┴─┴──────┐
┌──────────────┴──────────────┐  │  PARENT  │
│           TEACHERS          │─►│ TEACHERS │
└──────────────┬──────────────┘  │ASSOCIATION│
               │                 └─┬────────┘
┌──────────────┴──────────────┐    ┊
│          CHILDREN           │    ┊
└──────────────┬──────────────┘    ┊
               │                   ┊
┌──────────────┴──────────────┐    ┊
│           PARENTS           │┈┈┈┈┘
└─────────────────────────────┘
```

The parent-teachers association located functionally as coöperating with teachers and adviser to the superintendent and board of education.

existing social organization. There is a very definite place for it in the functional organization.

Since it is composed of parents and teachers in their individual aspects the parent-teacher association must be considered as an advisory and coöperating group outside of the legal organization. It is distinctly an agency through which essential parental education activity may be carried on. The effect of this program of education should be the development of definite attitudes and ideals and their dissemination to the people of the district as a whole. It does not direct, threaten, or cajole the legal or professional organization but acts simply and completely as a voluntary coöperating agency.

The functional conception of a parent-teacher association calls for more intelligent and careful leadership, for harder work and less immediate action, and for greater patience and greater faith. Over a long period of time it will result in better community understanding and appreciation of the purpose, worth, conditions, and needs of public education and will prevent many conflicts.

TYPES OF PARENT-TEACHER ASSOCIATIONS

Local parent-teacher associations may be classified by type of school organization with which they are affiliated as: preprimary, elementary, junior high school, senior high school, and two combination types running from first grade through twelfth in small one-school building communities and from the first through the eighth grade in rural districts. If the program objectives earlier presented are considered valid, the most successful type of organization will be that developed within a certain specialized area and confined to problems common to all.

The problems of infancy are quite different from those of childhood and adolescence. If the local parent-teacher association is to establish itself as a truly educational activity, it must provide fields of specific problems in which the parents are immediately concerned because they face them in their current parental aspect.

City Organization

In the typical city elementary school, comprising the kindergarten and the first six grades, it might be desirable to establish at least three study divisions within the local association, including preprimary, primary, and post-primary. In like manner the problems of early and late adolescence are of burning interest when the parent is immediately confronted by them. In city schools it is possible to secure an easy division through the physical differences in the junior and senior high-school plants. In smaller communities where a six-year high school exists, it may be highly desirable to follow the suggestion for the elementary school and to organize two divisions: one including early adolescence (grades seven, eight, and nine) and the other including the upper three years.

Small-Town Organization

In the school district with a single school building the unit parent-teacher association may be subdivided into four or five smaller groups or divisions to secure the same degree of interest and provide study possibilities. It is not necessary or even desirable to form four or five separate and distinct organizations in these situations. There are certain community problems that must be brought to the consciousness of the entire group and general interest built up around them. The subdivisions suggested may be simply classified as specialized study groups.

Rural Organization

The rural association is different in many of its aspects from associations found in cities and towns. It represents much more fully a truly complete community group. Mothers, fathers, and children belong, and all three groups attend meetings. A different procedure and technique is required for the direction and education of these rural organizations. The National Congress has recognized some of these rural problems and has recently provided for the organization of rural community councils in which related areas are brought together and greater opportunity afforded for best leadership and guidance.

Activity Classification

A brief consideration of these organization types as three broad activity types is desirable. Though the concept and theory of the movement is splendid and its potentialities almost unlimited, it is also essential to be realistic to their shortcomings to make correction and prevent similar future mistakes. These may be considered as the functional, the "window-dressing," and the "proprietary."

Functional Type

In the first group are all of the associations that are bending their efforts to establish intelligent coöperative relationships between home and school through parental education and are also attempting to interpret the schools to the community. The outstanding characteristics of this group are superior professional and lay leadership, skilfully organized in terms of worthy objectives with the practical elimination of selfish personal ambition and flamboyant demagoguery.

Impotent Type

The second group includes a series of moribund associations developed primarily as "window-dressing" and impotent because of poor leadership. Certain school executives have been timid about the parent-teacher organization because they feel it to be a distinct danger to institutional complacency, traditional routine, and authority. But every one else is having parent-teacher associations, so they, too, must have them. So they are organized and purposely kept harmless and innocuous. Their potential powers are not used. State and national affiliation is too frequently completely discouraged. Within this division is another group which, because of community conflict or unwise leadership, has lost its prestige and has degenerated into merely a name. Sometimes these groups live along for many years with little or no constructive achievement. A few elect officers regularly, but have little else in their favor. Some die out after a few years.

Proprietary Type

The third or "proprietary" group also has two divisions. The first represents those aggressive groups which for one reason or another have mistaken their real function and attempt to become the dominant educational force in the community. In matters of policy they make themselves felt in no uncertain terms, dictating actions to the board of education, interfering with the hiring and discharging of personnel, determining curricular content, advising superintendents and principals respecting method, and to all intents and purposes, acting as a second board of education. There is no implication that all of these demands are unworthy or unintelligent. On the contrary, in many instances, they may represent what the board of education should actually have done long before. The question is the validity and desirability of the method employed over a long period of time, the dangerous assumptions of a minority organization, beyond the limits of the legal plan as promulgated by the will of the entire people.

The second division includes these associations sometimes used by unscrupulous professional and lay individuals to secure their own personal advancement. Lay leaders use them as excellent steps upon which to climb to elective office and political preferment. Again, faddists secure control of certain groups and proceed to push their program upon the community regardless of need. These fads may take the form of "compulsory milk for every child" regardless of whether milk agrees with all of them or not; they may include superemotional stress upon little authenticated theories regarding mild narcotics, or upon obsolete physiological concepts. Sometimes they form the battleground for the intense and bitter struggle of two women for social supremacy. These programs have also taken the form of ultra-conservatism in the maintenance of *status quo,* based upon some peculiar notion that democracy is a static social organization. The outstanding characteristics of this group are conflict, poor leadership, unbalanced programs, misconception of function, and trouble-making in general. They are not confined to the very small communities by any means, but also exist in the larger districts. Fortunately the third group is not in the majority.

PROGRAMS AND MEANS

The range of programs suggested for local parent-teacher organizations varies directly with the concept of and attitude toward function. At one end of the scale may be found the "easiest way" program which simply makes of this important agency another ladies' aid association whose interests have been transferred from the church to the school. Excessive sociability, perpetual projects for improving the building, constant effort to raise funds to supplement tax income and fill the association treasury and practically everything else non-educational in character is included. One specific illustration of the type and effect of the use of the money-raising activity may serve for illustration.

A certain board of education built libraries in new school buildings but, as is frequently the case, did not equip them with books. Since library books are essential to modern instruction, they are just as much a general school-district responsibility as the provision of the physical library. Yet many boards of education make no financial provision for them. The executive (principal or superintendent) realizes the need and desires quick action, a frequent characteristic of executives. Proceeding without much preparation, he is rebuffed by the conservative board of education. Rather than laboriously educate the board to a real understanding of the entire instructional problem, he appeals to the parent-teacher association. The organized group responds in a generous fashion, and the books begin to accumulate. The immediate problem has been solved, and many eager executives then proceed to find other weak spots that may be upholstered financially by interested parents and teachers.

This procedure is functionally wrong. True, the immediate want has been satisfied, but this attitude represents a very short view. What actually happened is that the board of education has been able to throw part of its social responsibility to a voluntary group and place the financial burden upon this group when in justice the charge should have been borne by general taxation.

The functional procedure should have been as follows. The problem of lack of library books has been noted. The existing policy of the board of education has also been noted. The executive's first task is to educate the board to a different concept of the instructional policy. Since this involves expenditure of public moneys, it is also desirable that an intelligent public or community opinion be formed upon the subject. The parent-teacher associations should likewise be educated to the necessity for library books in the teaching program. The complete problem may be presented, discussed, and a definite group opinion developed. The parent-teacher associations will then serve as nuclei to form public opinion upon the subject in the community. This expression of public opinion, plus the education of the legislative body by the executive, will result ultimately in the development of a new policy which recognizes the value and place of library books. The books will be purchased and the problem solved. The second method is a better one to pursue over a long period of time. However, it does take much more time.

This example might be multiplied by scores. Generous parent-teacher associations have been pressed for financial aid in many, many instances and have responded nobly. Their response is to be applauded. In each case the board of education has shifted part of its burden from the whole to the few, and the entire community has not been educated to the value of the agency as a part of the instructional process. Incidentally, in certain centers with more than one organized group, it has led to rivalry between schools and has given to schools that are favorably situated economically far greater benefits and appointments than the poorer districts can afford.

First Phase

The parent-teacher association operating functionally needs a program built around the specific purposes for which it is to work. Consideration of a directive policy for an entirely new organization that is totally unacquainted with its purpose or its limitations might be considered on a generalized basis somewhat as follows. The first objective is the development of mutual confidence, respect, and tolerance through the method of social contact. Programs for early meetings should therefore emphasize the acquaintance aspect rather heavily and sufficient provision for sociability should be made at every gathering. Acquaintance between teacher and parents made at these school meetings may be further supplemented by contacts outside of the school in neighborhood gatherings and in home and school visitation. It requires much time and conscientious effort to evolve any worth-while degree of confidence through social contact.

Second Phase

The second phase includes the education of the group with respect both to community and to educational problems. There are three means, used separately or in combination, through which these objectives may be attained. They are listening, discussion, and working programs. If the first step in parent-teacher education is to establish a social confidence in the school and its personnel, the second is to establish some degree of confidence of the parents and teachers in themselves.

A good means for this purpose is the discussion or modified "jury-panel" method. All shades of opinion should be represented, both lay and professional, from the ultra-conservative to the ultra-progressive. A series of problems relating immediately to the school community may be selected for discussion, and an attempt made to secure some conceptions of actual beliefs and prejudices held by the group. Under skilful leadership (the principal can act as coordinator) the panel device is most valuable for group education. After two or three of these discussion groups when sufficient interest has been aroused, it may be possible to bring specialists in anthropology, sociology, geography, economics, political science, philosophy, and education into the community to present certain problems that are difficult for local personnel to consider. These specialists may operate with a panel as a supplement for later discussion. These lectures or discussions may be supplemented by popular home reading.

These discussions may be organized also as "questioning panels" in which a group of competent professional and lay individuals meets with the parents and answers any questions that may arise. It is desirable to include the president of the local chapter, a member of the board of education, either the superintendent or principal of the school, one or two teachers, and some community leader. A prominent district leader may act as chairman. This method forms not only a good device for correcting erroneous views and impressions but also for discovering what the community is thinking and for locating incipient trouble spots.

Third Phase

With a working knowledge of the community, state, and nation as a basis on which to build, the third phase of this long-time program is a detailed study of the activity of public education itself. Numerous programs may be arranged starting with the various points of view behind the purpose and outcome. Different philosophies may be considered and discussed. Practical applications of the theoretical ideal may be studied and discussed. On a basis of understanding, constructive appraisal of the local situation may be made, the conditions noted, and means for improvement evolved. As in the second phase, the consideration of the school should be well interspersed with discussion sessions through which the degree of understanding may be determined.

Since communities may vary in their needs, it may also be desirable to reverse the process, starting with the individual child and his needs and working from this departure to a definite understanding of the democratic process and the importance of the educational activity to its continuance and development. It is undesirable to attempt standardization of programs and practices. They should remain flexible to meet varying conditions.

Direct outcomes of these programs will be the ability to interpret the schools to the community, to understand their value, and to stand firmly against selfish attempts to curtail the rights of the children.

Time Involved

It may require three, five, or even ten years, depending on the general intelligence of the group and the traditional community set, to achieve the objectives on which the success of the parent-teacher organization is based.

State Aid

There are several state movements under way that promise to overcome some of the current inadequacies of educational and community leadership in the development and functioning of the parent-teacher association. These include state programs evolved by the state branch either directly, in conjunction with the National Congress, or in coöperation with institutions of higher learning.

At several universities and in many of the state teachers' colleges work of both a formal and informal nature is being carried on to provide more intelligent use of the parent-teacher movement for school betterment. Prospective teachers may now study the nature, work, and possibilities of the parent-teacher association.

Universities are bringing the parent-teacher movement into closer institutional relationship through their extension divisions. These institute programs, supplemented throughout the year by help in making programs, furnishing speakers, and offering library service and general aid, are far removed from the typical "ladies' aid" activities of the traditional group. With the aid of these movements the parent-teacher association may more quickly become a thoroughly vital phase of adult education and correspondingly more valuable in social interpretation.

State and national education associations are also ready to furnish aid and advice in organizing programs and securing speakers. Local leadership must come from the educator, not in the form of blatant personal publicity but rather in quiet unobtrusive analysis and coöperative solution of problems.

METHOD OF ORGANIZATION

The technique of organization has been standardized to such an extent that it is now only necessary to get in touch with the state president or the state education association and ask for advice and assistance.

The position of the teacher in this coöperative association has been a moot question for some time. Many principals and teachers believe that their personal holding of office is necessary to insure success and their own credit. In most instances this attitude represents the short view. Successful tenure of public or quasi-public office is short. The average ex-officer has little influence and numerous opponents. It is far better technique for the educator to allow laymen to hold all of the titles and to remain quite discreetly in the background exercising leadership through indirect means, never attempting to secure personal publicity from the work of the association. The entire movement represents group or coöperative effort, and the credit for achievement also devolves upon the group.

The best position for professionals is continuing membership and representation on all of the committees, without holding even chairmanships. Mere membership in these small working groups permits one to be heard and to direct discussion.

CONFLICTS

Conflicts arising through the operation of parent-teacher association programs and activities are of two major types, personal and functional. Their existence is one reason why the traditional educator fears the organization.

Personal Conflicts

Personal differences occur when either professionals or laymen secure partial or complete control of the activity and use it to further personal, social, political ambitions or dislikes. Observation indicates that both the principal and the "born leader" in the community are equally responsible. The outcomes are costly for the professional, and the layman is quickly swept into oblivion. If skill and intelligence are employed, this type of personal exploitation may continue for several years. The program suffers, and the community suffers. Finally, stronger leadership replaces the "individualist" or the association gradually drifts into complete or partial inactivity. In some few instances the exploitative leader is able to form cliques and partizan group support. In this case the result is worse, and the sooner the organization is allowed to pass away quietly the better for the community. The parent-teacher association need not become the community heir of the older minister-choir conflicts.

Functional Conflicts

Functional conflicts include those group struggles that occur when the parent-teacher association through mistaken concept of function and activity gets into serious community trouble. Many of these include conflicts with the board of education, with the superintendent and teachers, with political or other interest groups. The most general cause is poor leadership and program direction that cause the association to develop tactics and measures characterizing other special interest groups employing a "pressure technique." The minute the parent-teacher association steps from its truly educational aspect into foreign fields and methods diversely different from those of creating public opinion, trouble ensues.

The elimination of many community conflicts engendered by the parent-teacher association is possible only through a careful development of the activity in all of its functional aspects and the growth of a group ethic governing individual and group procedure.

SUMMARY

The parent-teacher association is an extremely valid and vital agency in any consistent program of community interpretation. Both its possibilities and limitations must be thoroughly understood by the educator before attempting to organize and use it. The parent-teacher association has a very definite functional relationship to the public-school system growing out of the American partnership concept. Trouble generally ensues if the organization steps beyond these points of reason and safety. The purpose of the agency is to provide direct means for closer and more understanding relationships between home and school and to act as a builder of public opinion. This concept of function naturally determines the program pattern. The present tendency is away from consideration of the parent-teacher association as a ladies' aid society attached to the public-school system and also away from consideration of the school system as a semi-charitable institution subsisting partially on the "dole" of bazaars and benefits. Intelligent use of this agency to improve both school conditions and community relations requires much hard work and the best type of leadership. The total effectiveness of the parent-teacher association will be conditioned largely by the quality of professional leadership.

Chapter 17

PARENT COUNCILS AND VARIATIONS

THOUGH the parent-teacher association is an unusually excellent agency through which the partnership concept between home and school may be effectively established, community organization in the United States presents so many variations that it is doubtful whether one standardized pattern will meet all needs and fit all occasions. Many educators have felt that certain weaknesses of the parent-teacher association due to the type and location of the school, conflicts resulting from previous failures, and language difficulties where the foreign born predominate, make it desirable to develop other agencies to serve the same purpose. Recognition should also be given to the fact that variations may appear to be desirable from the professional standpoint to permit greater control in determining school-organization relationships.

As a result there is a distinct experimental tendency toward other forms of parent groups that may possess large potentialities. These types will be considered as: (1) home-room and grade councils, (2) parent or school councils, (3) mothers' and fathers' clubs, (4) community organization, (5) neighborhood groups, and (6) school-improvement leagues.

HOME-ROOM AND GRADE COUNCILS

The secondary school may require much more specialization in organization than the elementary school. There is a distinct change in parent-child relationship during adolescence representing a natural revolt against the nurturing parental attitude of early childhood. The adolescent wants independence and wants to assert himself as a personality. In most families where several children are growing up the adolescent normally finds himself with more responsibility and better able to escape minute parental surveillance.

The secondary attendance district is not so homogeneous in character as the elementary school. Drawing from a series of elementary attendance districts, the secondary school usually presents far greater social and economic diversity. Curricular differentiation also becomes more noticeable, causing further divergence of parental interest. As a result it is much more difficult to secure immediate unified parental interest in the school as a whole.

From the standpoint of the school itself, the secondary teachers have inherited the academic tradition of the subject-matter specialist and in only a few cases seem to be interested or qualified to take the larger overview of the entire problem. These and a combination of many other factors, including the secondary institutional desire to dominate and control completely, are increasing the tendency toward the gradual elimination of the school parent-teacher association and are substituting in its place some variation like those indicated under the titles of "home-room group," "mothers' councils," "parent advisory council," and "grade council."

It is still possible to provide for effective parent-teacher organization if the suggestions made in the previous chapter are followed. Small specialized study groups can be created easily as sub-groups of the larger organization.

Organization Factor

The organization of the school will determine whether small and compact parent councils will be built around the home room, the grade, or the specialized curriculum. The variation is not significant. Where the home-room organization is used for administrative, social, and guidance purposes, the parent council is its logical complementary organization. The best expression of home-room organization is that where the teacher remains with the group throughout its school life acting as educational, social, and vocational guide.

Under this plan it is possible for the home-room teacher to secure close contact with the parents and thus solve the very important problem of home contacts. It is also more easily possible to bring the father as well as the mother into closer relationship to the child and school. Successful parent councils appear to attract more men than the typical secondary parent-teacher associations. This may be due to organization or program differences.

Programs for home-room councils may be developed as parent education and built specifically around the immediate problems of the group. General problems may be more profitably discussed by the school parents' council, where membership in this group is general. If the home-room council is an independent group, program must be modified to meet these conditions.

The home-room council may have its own officers, and to these the teacher occupies the relationship of guide and counselor. Teachers should not themselves act as officers of these groups. The responsibility for the development of the program and contact of the parent with the other teachers involved belongs distinctly to the home-room teacher.

Monthly council meetings are desirable. Individual visitation of parent to the school and home visitation by the teacher are desirable program outcomes. By means of the home-room group the problem of school and home visitation is greatly reduced for the teacher over the unorganized indiscriminate and haphazard plan. The plan has great potentialities.

Difficulties

The difficulties interfering with the success of this plan are lack of recognition given by many schools to the social and educational importance of the home room and consequent lack of time provided for it. So long as the home-room period is considered as simply another expression of extraclass activity, the results will fall far short of potentiality. The already overworked teacher cannot logically give one or more hours out of a much too crowded day to plans and procedures essential to home-room success. This difficulty can only be solved as administration develops more functional concepts of teacher load and makes balanced provision for their execution.

A second difficulty grows out of teacher personality. Not every classroom teacher is socially capable of becoming a home-room teacher. This weakness sometimes arises out of the undue haste with which the plan is inaugurated and lack of administrative understanding of its importance.

Sound Theory

The underlying theory in this development is sound. It recognizes the differences of size and departmentalization and the necessity for organization of the home and school problem around some easily comprehended unit. The home or grade room is the natural base, selection varying with the specific method of internal administration. The home-room teacher, the outgrowth of the older grade "mother concept," sees the child as a whole and in more than his specific subject-matter learning aspects. On this account he is better qualified to tie home and school interests together than principal or the subject specialists. The home-room groups are small and through them much more intimate contact and knowledge is possible than in the larger more generalized parent-teacher association. The home-room plan represents a healthy tendency in the direction of a more effective working group for the secondary school.

PARENT OR SCHOOL COUNCILS

Parent councils may be classified as organizations initiated by and directly under the control of the school. They are favored in secondary schools where parent-teacher associations have failed or are moribund, where polyglot population provides language difficulties, where social distinctions in economic groups make coöperation difficult and in new centers in the process of development.

Organization

In some instances the parent or school council is a federation consisting of representatives of home-room or grade councils, each unit having one or two representatives in this central group. Since the educational programs are cared for in the smaller divisions built around an immediate grade or curricular interest, the school council concerns itself with more general problems affecting the school as a whole. Its purpose is to provide a central point of interest for the entire school and also to serve as a means of providing direct parental responsibility for and participation in certain social activities such as parties and dances. In this disputed area the school can quietly protect itself against much community conflict by securing parental agreement on type of social program and then delegating supervisory responsibility directly to the school council.

Another variation in smaller schools is the organization of the parent or school council as a general organization through which the entire program of parent education is carried on. In this form, the council is in many respects similar to the parent-teacher association although the teachers tend to occupy more of a specialized advisory than a colleague relationship.

Where the council is a central pseudo policy-making body, its program is rather narrowly confined to a discussion of problems arising out of the home-room or grade programs. In case of the generalized council the normal educational programs are generalized to meet the needs of a varied group.

The advantage of the parent or school council to the educator lies in the possibility of complete control which is not so easily possible in the parent-teacher organization. More careful direction may be offered particularly in delicate or strained community situations, and conflicts may be more easily avoided. This condition is its own greatest weakness since the desirability of complete institutional control of any parental coöperating group is questionable. If the fundamental partnership concept is to be effective, the parental organization should have sufficient independence to establish a condition of equality in relationships. The school is also forced to a somewhat different educational technique in meeting an independent community group than in merely "telling" a controlled group what it may do.

There are instances where too closely controlled parent or school councils have resented institutional domination and professional condescension, revolting to form independent parent-teacher associations.

Despite these weaknesses and dangers there can be little question of the value of the school council under conditions of community conflict, failure of another type of organization, or the need to meet the diverse and varied problems of the secondary school. It is a secondary-school movement that may be rightfully encouraged.

MOTHERS' AND FATHERS' CLUBS

Voluntary schools have been pioneers in the development of a collateral secondary-school movement in the organization of mothers' and fathers' clubs, the type depending on the appeal of the school. This movement has been receiving some recent attention in the public secondary schools, but here it is still in its infancy. The private school has developed these organizations for the twofold purpose of securing sufficient parental interest to make the procurement of new students easier and to serve directly as donors to institutional need. Buildings, special gifts, and scholarships are already direct evidence of their success.[1]

The educational purpose behind this movement in public education is to take advantage of the normal parental interests that tend to mark the adolescent period. The mother has always been a potent force in the school, but the father's interest has been much more difficult to secure. By capitalizing upon the natural desire of the normal father to establish a comradely relationship between himself and his maturing son, the school is offered a new approach

Organization

Mothers' and fathers' clubs may be organized both as a home-room and school activity. Since the mothers' club was actually a forerunner of the parent-teacher association, its program possibilities have already been rather well explored as organized and informal adult educational activities. There is more uncertainty about the father and the means of developing a continuing interest, and this problem is still in the exploratory stage. Most of the programs to date have started in an attempt to develop parallel interests in hobbies of the different types and also in the field of play. Many schools plan father-and-son tennis, golf, shooting, and other athletic contests; others are attempting to secure initial interest through having father and son work together in shop and studio developing

[1] See *The Nation's Schools*, Vol. 18, No. 4 (October, 1936), pp. 41-43.

some project in wood, metal, or other hobby fields such as photography. As a movement it undoubtedly has possibilities, but these need careful and cautious exploration.

COMMUNITY ORGANIZATION

Another type of formal organization is that most generally known as the community league. A generalized description would be as follows: Every organized activity in the community elects a representative or delegate to a central community council. A small community, with three churches, two fraternal orders, a commercial club, a farmers' Grange, a literary society, and several women's organizations would each choose a delegate to represent their interest. The resulting community league council consists of ten to fifteen delegates, including one to three representatives from the schools. This directing council chooses the regular quota of officers, who comprise the executive committee.

All questions of business and policy will be first discussed and planned by the executive committee and will then be submitted to the council for approval or disapproval. If approved, each delegate returns to his or her organization and informs the membership of the action taken by the council and the part the several contributing organizations are to play.

The movement was started about 1910 in the East in rural districts to develop a community program through organizations already in existence. During the War it came into some prominence in rural districts and sometimes in cities. It has a fair spread in the Middle West in village and rural life.

An organization of this type furnishes a good means of developing a program of community activities. However, as ordinarily developed, the league council has many interests. It is responsible for building community programs, recommending policies, and studying the needs of the community. The representation is very broad, including every type of organization and every shade of opinion.

The community league must be given a secondary position when compared with the parent-teacher association. Though the community league is a valuable adjunct to the school under certain conditions, its interests are too wide and varied.

Program

The community program includes every phase of group activity. The several contributing groups do not always concur in respect to all activities decided upon. This breadth of program range is a weakness in the public-school interpretation program. The parent-teacher association has a homogeneity of interest that is not true of the community league. Its members are first of all parents; their interests are centered around the child in his immediate environmental relationships, and their efforts are constantly centered upon a single community problem, the public school.

The use of the community league, although it tends to be less effective than the parent-teacher association, is not to be slighted. It has the possibility of adding another strong link to the chain of community agencies and might well be encouraged in larger centers as well as in rural districts.

NEIGHBORHOOD GROUPS

The neighborhood group evolving as an educational and sociological agency is much more functional in character than the community federation. The underlying theory is that within the elementary attendance districts, quite arbitrarily established in most instances, there are a number of fundamental sociological problems involved in the school's success. It may be possible to rebuild the neighborhood group of former days around common educational interests and needs. Within a typical attendance district of one square mile there may be twenty or thirty of these neighborhood groups, whereas the same area might be represented by a single parent-teacher association. The neighborhood movement is still in its infancy, but it rests on a sound theory and has much to commend it. Development of the neighborhood group does not exclude the local parent-teacher association, but may be used to supplement it and to secure additional community advantages by combining both agencies.

There is also a possibility in this organization for the secondary school that has a very mixed student population. By using the elementary neighborhood groups as a nucleus, it may be possible to secure initially better home relations in the case of the first-year student. Gradually these groups may be redirected or merged with other existing organizations.

SCHOOL-IMPROVEMENT LEAGUES

There are two types of school-improvement leagues. Those organized by states and operating in a manner somewhat familiar to the parent-teacher association have been studied and reported by Butterworth.[2] The local school-improvement league grew out of the movement in urban centers to form sectional or district associations for the attainment of better physical conditions that would stimulate business development. These improvement associations were initiated either by chambers of commerce as regional branches, by associations of the so-called neighborhood stores, or by realty speculators who saw in an organized movement better opportunity to secure without much expense to themselves physical improvements for outlying areas, including paving, lighting, sewers and water, fire and police protection, and even schools. Sometimes these improvement associations have allowed the schools to be represented. In their essential plan and method of procedure the district improvement associations and school-improvement leagues represent interest pressure groups organized and acting to meet some particular local need usually in utter disregard of the totality of community need. If their political pressure is strong enough, the program may be achieved regardless of merit. The result of many of these "pressure programs" was one of the reasons for difficulties in which large cities found themselves during the depression. Accumulated debt structure for financing of non-essential requirements and "green subdivisions" created trouble for many urban school systems.

The school should be very careful in its relations to these regional

[2] Julian E. Butterworth, *The Parent Teacher Association* (New York, The Macmillan Co., 1928), ix + 149 pp.

groups or the separate school-improvement leagues; otherwise it may find itself embarrassed by their "pressure programs."

SUMMARY

There are many interpretative possibilities in the development of collateral parental organization entirely apart from the parent-teacher organization. This conclusion does not in any way disparage the value of the state and national organization but recognizes rather the high complexity of relationships and the great diversity of interests existing particularly in our public schools. For diversity, spread, and balance it is far better that the schools have at their disposal a wide range of organization choice in home-school contacts rather than a single group. Collateral organization of the types considered here are all comparatively young, and specific technique for their use is not so well developed as in the case of the parent-teacher organization. Their place in the educational program demands much study and careful exploration of all possibilities. Each of them will probably find an ultimate place in organization of the interpretative activity.

Chapter 18

THE LAY ADVISORY COMMISSION

PUBLIC education in the United States is the concern of all the people. Though the teaching profession as members of the community participates in appraisal of activity and exercises individual civil right of franchise, the legal right to make general educational policies rests with the people and is expressed through the board of education as its legal agency.

Education is so powerful an instrument in social reproduction and in the indoctrination of the children that the American people have continued to maintain close direct control throughout its history. Public education has fortunately grown as forty-eight independent state systems, each organized so that local as well as state popular control of policy is possible. It has been developed separately from civil government and has so enabled the people within each local district to maintain close attention to this problem without interference from extraneous activities. They may decide questions of educational policy without considering its effect on the tariff, the Supreme Court, or other unrelated political factors. The decentralized organization of the educational function is one of the greatest safeguards for democracy since it can effectively prevent the use of the schools to promote the immediate interests of the major political parties.

Education and Dictatorship

The importance of the educational process as a major agency of political and social propaganda is obvious in even a casual study of the totalitarian state. The Japanese system of education has long been highly centralized and is used specifically by the government as a conditioning control. The Japanese ministry of education has even created a bureau of thought supervision, and through rigid inspection and surveillance, variations in the educational process considered as "dangerous thoughts" are carefully prevented. In both Italy and Germany the educational process has been developed as a device for the complete indoctrination of the children to Fascist and Nazi ideology. In Russia and in Mexico the same organization and control have prevailed, and the schools cease to be educational institutions in the American sense of the term, having become governmental instruments solely for the perpetuation and extension of dictatorial control. This is a natural concomitant of dictatorship since the importance of the educational process is such that unless it is completely controlled in both child and adult phases, there is too great a danger to the single scheme of government.

Education and Democracy

Only in those cultures where the educational process is relatively free and where the people have a voice in its management and direction does democracy appear possible. The Scandinavian, British, and American systems of schools are quite different both in character and in scope from those of Italy, Germany, Japan, and Russia.

Popular control of public education in the United States places the determination of program in the hands of parents and other adults within the community. It is impossible for central authority to dictate what shall or shall not be taught within the formal institution. The pressure of diverse groups with different opinions makes it difficult under normal procedure for any single opinion to prevail. The pattern of the American school is sufficiently broad to provide for the teaching of different points of view and to emphasize the need for social variation while conditioning the individual in the democratic tradition. The democratic pattern provides for emphasis on personal or civil liberties through which variation is made possible. The democratic pattern makes it possible to teach tolerance and respect for the viewpoint of others, regard for personality, friendliness, and a view of social organization as an essential operating compromise among all types of opinion. It is to-day possible within the framework of American public education to teach the dynamic process of democratic life.

If the public school to-day falls short of the idea of democratic teaching, the fault lies with the teaching profession. Recognition of the nature of the democratic process, its normal current limitations, and consideration of the nature of the school in a democratic society require the focusing of professional attention on the manner of institutional functioning. If the American public school is to remain a classless institution, it must be representative of all interests within the state. If it is a definite partnership between home and state, provision must be made for more active and real parental participation. If, as a popular institution, its efficiency of functioning is contingent on popular understanding and appreciation, it is only necessary to develop means for the creation of a sustaining public opinion. The ultimate effectiveness of the American public schools will probably be conditioned directly by the intelligence of the teaching profession in learning and accepting its responsibilities under a democratic plan of life.

Conventional teacher attitude toward what is considered "lay interference" with an assumed professional prerogative in the complete control of the public school is one of the difficulties that must be overcome. The public-school teacher is not primarily to blame since this assumption of professional infallibility and undivided power is the result of distinct conditioning by institutions of higher learning. The transfer of medieval academic concepts of higher education unfortunately still hampers the presumptively democratic tax-supported college and university to-day. Thus the teaching profession is still hypercritical of possible lay contributions. Few will dispute the fact that in methodology the professional teacher does have elements of superiority, but the same contention cannot be easily upheld with respect to the validity of lay contributions to the teaching program. On the basis of this orientation the lay advisory commission will be discussed as: (1) local advisory groups, (2) state advisory groups, and (3) technical consultants.

LOCAL ADVISORY GROUPS

Theoretically the local board of education should be well balanced with respect to extremes and central tendencies of opinion. The trend of current public opinion within any community or state is normally conservative or right of center. This fact is expressed in the personnel of the civil and school legislative bodies. The popular representatives are generally past middle age, substantial in the economic sense, and tend to be representative of a few interests, with the lawyer, doctor, and small business man predominating. Neither is it possible to insure at all times careful appraisal of the individual candidate for office. Personality has unusual influence in the popular canvass for votes. Until it is possible through more highly perfected political organization to secure better balance in educational representation, it appears desirable to develop and use supplementary devices of an extralegal nature.

The well-balanced local school organization that is seeking means whereby it may capitalize upon community talent and varied points of view will probably find it desirable to use at least four voluntary groups as advisors in the development of policy and execution of the technical plans. These include the organized teaching profession as a technical group independent from their institutional activities; the parent-teacher association, as representative of the actual operating partnership between home and institution; the community advisory commission, composed of representatives of all group interests; and highly capable outside technical specialists in education. The activities of the teaching profession and the parent-teacher association in this advisory capacity have already been considered.[1] The discussion in this chapter will be limited to the lay and technical advisory groups.

Community Advisory Commission

Each community includes numerous interests, and these are generally expressed through some form of organization. Though the officers of these groups usually represent the aggressive leadership, it must not be overlooked that the effective planning leader seldom holds office and is distinguished by other means. If continuity in commission membership is desired, selection should be made of the most influential member; though the official representative may

[1] See Chapters 4 and 16.

serve, membership is limited in time and is rotative in character.

The community educational advisory commission may include from nine to twenty lay members depending on size and diversity of interest. Labor and capital (banking), industry and commerce, agriculture, the learned professions, and parents will comprise the major interests. Although public education must remain completely non-sectarian in functioning, a community advisory group may well include representatives of institutionalized religion. However, if one religious point of view is included, all major sects should be represented. Religion is a delicate emotional field, and extreme caution should be exercised so that no single view can predominate. In selecting representatives from these groups, it is desirable to secure a spread of opinion so that the group may be balanced instead of swinging either to the left or to the right.

The authority to create continuing advisory groups is well within the implied powers of a board of education and requires no enabling legislation. The board may retain the power of selecting advisors, or may delegate it to the group itself. Selection by the board of education is preferred since this method makes it possible to secure non-conflicting personalities. It is not desirable for either board members or superintendent to be official members of this group.

Membership

Typical community advisory commissions would probably include the following in membership:

Small Community	Medium Community	Large City
1 Agriculture	1 Industry	1 to 3 Industry
1 Banker	1 Banker	1 Banker
1 Labor	1 Labor	1 to 2 Labor
1 Business	1 Business	1 Business
1 Doctor	1 Doctor	1 Doctor
1 Lawyer	1 Lawyer	1 Lawyer
2 Women	2 Women	3 to 6 Women
1 Religion	1 to 3 Religion	1 to 5 Religion

Commission Work

These commissions are and should remain strictly advisory. Educational problems arising within the community may be presented to them for study and consideration. The presentation in itself may be an education to the members of the purpose, conditions, and needs of the schools, and it will probably require considerable time for the initial orientation of the individuals both to method and to work. The commission may meet with representatives of the board of education and the superintendent of schools for the study of these problems. Initial presentation may be made by the president of the board of education with delegation of the technical presentation and preparation of data to the superintendent as general executive of the legal organization. Discussion within the commission should be unhurried and thorough. It may take months to consider a single problem such as the best manner of teaching controversial issues, the extension of a curricular activity, the teaching of venereal disease prevention, the enlargement of the physical plant, the increase of teachers' salaries, or the development of adult community education.

Thus the needs of the schools as viewed from the professional standpoint are presented to the community leaders who are members of this lay group. The initial step is their direct education to the institutional problems. This presentation may be considered as institutional interpretation. The commission members study, discuss, and argue about these problems, translating them progressively into their own background and understanding and suggesting either contractions or enlargements. Their reactions and points of view brought back to the organization through this discussion may be considered as community interpretation for the organizational group. During the process of consideration both aspects of the interpretative activity are thus brought together, and a group opinion is progressively built up.

A balanced public opinion within so diverse a commission requires time. Even after extended discussion it may not be possible to secure a balanced agreement among the members. If that happens, it simply means that the community is not yet ready to accept the practice as part of the larger community pattern. Since the purpose of the advisory commission is to learn what the community is thinking and what is acceptable by the people, the decision of the commission must carry weight with the legal organization. It does not interfere with the functioning of the legal organization but merely insures safety in functioning. Community minority points of view are entitled to the same consideration and protection that they receive in the larger social organization. When time is not a factor, action should be postponed until a relatively unanimous agreement may be secured around a central tendency compromise.

Method of Operation

It is desirable that the president of the board of education act as discussion moderator. Although the commission may choose its own officers, the creation of a neutral moderator will permit free discussion by all members and interests represented on the commission without forcing any member into silence because of position. The chairman and secretary of the commission could still be its reporting officers.

When a board of education uses three or four of these advisory devices, a certain precedence in presentation may be employed. Since it is a first essential in institutional change to secure understanding and attitudes from the professional personnel, the teaching profession may be first exposed to the problem. It can then be considered by the parent-teacher association and, third, by the educational advisory commission.

Care must be exercised by both board of education and the executive to avoid using these advisory devices as pressure groups to achieve more rapidly a program considered essential by the professional. Both the parent-teacher association and the lay advisory commission will quickly see through any scheme that attempts to exploit them and merely encourage the laymen to be more critical of the teaching profession. Objectiveness and personal disinterestedness are essential to effective functioning.

STATE ADVISORY GROUPS

Public education is a state function, and major enlargements or changes in educational policy must be approved by the state legislature.[2] The responsibility for the discovery of problems and the development of technical plans for their solution is definitely a function of the state educational authority. In a sense, however, the state authority occupies a position to the entire state similar to that of the local board of education to the local community. Though responsible for technical planning the fact should never be minimized that state plans for improvement of the educational function should also come from the people. Their approval by the legislature will depend at any time on the strength of the supporting public opinion as determined by the members of the law-making body. Legislative approval is seldom given until the representatives are certain of adequate support.

In state as in local educational planning the partnership concept of American education should be more completely recognized and provided for by voluntary advisory organization just as in the local district. It is a much more democratic procedure in determining the limits of supporting public opinion and an unusual device for the education of representative leaders to conditions and needs of public education.

The state department may use five types of advisory groups. The teachers' state professional organization and the state parent-teacher association both have specific interests in the educational process, one as the technician, and the other as parent. The state educational advisory commission, state educational councils, and the technical specialists form the other three desirable agencies.

Advisory Commission

The state educational advisory commission may be kept reasonably small by selection of only a single representative of organized interests or may be expanded into a reasonably large membership by the inclusion of several representatives. The smaller group is

[2] See also Chapter 13.

preferred, and since it is distinctly a layman's group, care should be taken to restrict the number of educational representatives. A suggested membership might include the following: 2, agriculture; 1, extractive industry; 1, finance; 1, medicine; 1, lawyer; 1, engineer; 2, labor; 1, industry; 1, commerce; 1, school-board representative; 4, women; 5, professional education; 3, clergy—a total of 24.

Agriculture requires both Grange and farm bureau representation; labor has two distinct organizations; the Catholic, Jewish, and Protestant faiths must be in balance; the several divisions of the educational process, elementary, secondary, higher education, teacher-training, and the teaching profession represent these specialized interest fields.

If the organization of local coöperative advisory boards were effective, the community discussions might be easily projected to a state-wide basis, with extent of the problem as the major difference. The state educational advisory commission would then be able to do its work on the basis of an already enlightened public opinion. Since that is unfortunately not the situation, it is generally necessary to duplicate completely in these state advisory commissions the local methodology in lay group education. If the state authority is vested in a board of education, the president of the board may act as moderator with the state superintendent of education as technical director. Where no state board exists, the state superintendent may also be obliged to act as moderator.

Device Practical

The device of the state educational advisory commission is not new. Michigan has had four years of experience covering three legislative sessions. It was first organized as the state educational planning commission, but changed in 1936 to the educational advisory commission.[3]

[3] For more detailed discussion see:
Paul F. Voelker, "Educational Reconstruction in Michigan," *The Nation's Schools*, Vol. 14, No. 2 (August, 1934), pp. 12-16.
The Improvement of Education, Fifteenth Yearbook of the Department of Superintendence, pp. 196-197.
Arthur B. Moehlman, "Michigan's Educational Problems," *Michigan Education Journal*, Vol. 13 (April, 1936), pp. 280-286.

The Michigan Educational Planning Commission was actually responsible for the formulation and acceptance of *The Goals of Public Education in Michigan*,[4] improvement in teacher-training and certification, increase in state financial aid, high-school tuition for rural districts, and the solution to many other problems. The Michigan experiment is significantly interesting because here for the first time representatives of conflicting interest groups met around a table and under skilful leadership focused their attention on the needs of the children and of the state. Competitive group interests if not forgotten were at least kept from interfering with consideration of the central theme—education. Michigan's experience in educational reconstruction through the use of this device is definite evidence of the possibilities of lay coöperation in the improvement of the educational process.

The same warning noted under the work of the local advisory groups holds true even more vitally in the state plan. The state educational authority must be willing to develop these devices in their complete interpretative possibilities and should avoid any possible implications that only the influence and active political support of strong lay groups is desired to support official state plans. Unless this danger is carefully avoided, the state advisory plan is doomed to early failure. Coöperation between professional and lay leaders should really mean working together in the best interests of society and the child and not, as a student in a moderately progressive school recently defined it for a parent, as "coöperation is doing what the teacher wants you to when she wants it."

Educational Councils

There are numerous educational interests within a state apart from those immediately affected by legal organization. These include the voluntary institutional groups such as independent schools and colleges and the large number of non-institutional adult-education groups that already form activity of wide proportions, Labor education, the Grange, women's interest groups, and a host of other developments.

[4] For statement of these goals see Chapter 5, pp. 110-111.

Though it is not the function of the state to control and direct voluntary educational effort, there is need for a general clearing house through which the different groups may consider problems of general educational importance and develop understanding and appreciation of these different efforts. Representatives of every group engaged in educational programs of one type or another are organized into a state educational council.[5] Its function is somewhat different from that of the educational advisory commission as its purpose is more specifically the development of an understanding of the entire range of educational effort within the state rather than the preparation of plans and procedures for enlargement of the legal organization. Its efforts will be restricted more to discussion and progressive development of a coöperative attitude. It is therefore more completely a device for interpretation than an organization for specific planning.

Planning Boards

As a result of depression problems and at the invitation of the Federal government forty-five states have organized state planning boards since 1933. The general purpose of these agencies is to take inventory of state resources; study state economic, social, educational, and governmental needs; and prepare long-range plans through which these problems may be solved. So far education has received comparatively little attention in the work of these state boards, but the fault probably lies with the teaching profession's slowness in recognizing the need for coöperation in a larger social plan. Though it is highly desirable to maintain the concept and practice of the school state in planning and in popular control, it is also necessary that in organization and the larger aspects of finance public education be willing to consider its relation to the total scheme of institutional activity.

[5] *Educational Policy*, Vol. 1, No. 1 (October 15, 1937), reports the current operation of nine state educational councils, although the function of these several organizations varies from that of planning to discussion and coördination.

TECHNICAL CONSULTANTS

Technical Advisors

Both state and locality are constantly faced by technical problems which require special solution. These include specialized areas in instruction, finance, plant, child accounting, and personnel management. In the broader social background many problems arise that require expert analysis by the sociologist, the psychologist, and the political scientist. The typical school system is not capable of meeting these demands for higher technical specialization within the executive organization. This fact is also true when the advisory commission is used.

It is good sense for both state department and local organization to admit frankly the limits of organization competency and to employ for the solution of specific problems those technicians and specialists who are available through institutions of higher learning. These technical advisors should be under the direction of the legal organization whether working specifically with the superintendent and teachers or with the advisory commission. Their authority should be limited to the technical study and solution of the problems presented and they should never be entrusted with executive authority. As experts they are not competent to execute a plan and generally are too far removed from social administration to function efficiently as practical administrators. Their normal limitations are those of the expert technician. The special consultant personnel has no direct relation to the problem of interpretation. Indirectly, through careful analysis of needs and assistance in developing technical means of procedure, they are capable of furnishing a plan through which costly mistakes and conflicts may be avoided.

SUMMARY

The partnership concept of American public education may be translated more completely in practice by the organization and use of lay interest groups to act as advisors to the legal organization. Four possibilities are immediately available in this area including the teaching profession, the parent-teacher association, the educational advisory commission, and the technical specialist. The educational advisory commission should include in membership representatives of all the vital community interests and be organized so that a balanced spread of opinion is secured. By means of the advisory commission it is possible to correct the normal tendency of the legal organization to centering on special group interest and toward unusual conservatism. The plan also makes possible a new device to secure information concerning community opinion and to educate commission members to an active realization of the problems confronting public education. By using these advisory groups it is possible to realize more effectively the partnership concept in American public education and to insure safer and more consistent functioning of the school as a dynamic social institution.

Chapter 19

COMMUNITY LAY GROUPS

THERE are in every community many varieties of organized lay groups apart from the several classifications already considered under parental interest. The only difference in this respect between the small and large communities is the number and influence. In the smaller community many of these groups possess proportionately greater influence than their fellow organizations in larger centers where greater diversity and competition of outside interests tend to restrict the orbit of power of a single unit. These organizations differ from the types already considered in so far as their purpose is specialized, their organization interest restricted, and their direct interest in the public school is either of a relatively minor nature or entirely non-existent. The technique of institutional use is accordingly different from those types whose affiliation and major purpose are directly with the schools. These organizations will be discussed according to their general types which include: (1) civic, (2) cultural, (3) economic, (4) hobby, (5) political, (6) professional, (7) propaganda, (8) social, (9) welfare, and (10) women. Within each category these groups may be subdivided by sex into organizations appealing directly to women, men, or to mixed groups. Each group will be discussed in terms of type, major interests, possibilities of interpretation, and of types of material.

CIVIC ORGANIZATIONS

The civic organizations include those types whose primary interest is the improvement of community life in some specialized area. They include garden clubs, municipal leagues, better government leagues, clean election groups, extralegal appraisal groups, sectional and regional improvement leagues, and organizations devoted to maintaining the separation of church and state. The administrative type of organization is predominant. They are usually the outcome of a desire by a small leader group to develop sustaining public opinion for some specialized objective they have in mind. The organization starts with a board of directors and then extends invitations to general membership by direct appeal or through mail solicitation. The directors usually secure the services of a professional secretary who is responsible for the membership promotion and the execution of the program. The control of policy and program is allocated to the board of directors.

Interest

The interests of these groups are confined to the specific objective and may be discovered by reading their letter heads or special literature prepared for an informatory purpose. Since they are attempting to improve the functioning of government either through direct education of the people or through non-partizan extralegal appraisal of the functioning of government, their program frequently carries them into the public-school field.

Possible Use

The school organization contacts with these groups are probably best confined to knowing the organization and its directing personnel, and keeping them informed through personal contacts and written material. As official personnel of a social activity under constant scrutiny by these specialized interest groups, the teachers should maintain a friendly interest without direct affiliation. Some superintendents advocate teachers becoming sustaining members and many of these groups also encourage the participation of teachers to stimulate membership and increase support. Direct affiliation is debatable since it is obvious that appraisal by these interests will be conditioned to a certain extent by source of support. If these civic organizations are to exercise their unquestioned and highly desirable right to study critically the functioning of local government, they should not be embarrassed by being forced to investigate their own members.

Materials

The civic group directors may be kept constantly supplied with written material published by the school organization. Their executive officer and president may also be invited to attend all board meetings and to feel free to discuss educational problems with either board members or the superintendent. If their program includes mass meetings of members, the president of the board and superintendent may appear before them at regular intervals to make a specific accounting of the condition of the schools and to be ready for questioning. These organizations furnish a possibility of organized appraisal of the community that should certainly not be neglected.

CULTURAL

An aspect of informal adult education that is prominent in larger communities is the large number of very small groups that meet weekly or bi-weekly just to talk about things that appeal to their interest. They range in character from the democratic box stove discussion group in the small town to the highly selective groups devoting their time to esoteric matters. The cultural group covers a large variety of fields. It may be interested in books or certain phases of literary expression, in art, landscaping, architecture, political philosophy, transportation, or communication. Membership is largely professional in type, and their specific leisure time interests arise out of something close to their professional interest. As a rule they are small enough to meet at the homes of different members or at some downtown club. In composition these groups are usually male, and their organization is extremely informal but generally highly selective. They choose members for the value of their mental rather than their financial contributions.

Interests

Their interests are usually confined to the academic aspect of a problem. They have no purpose except enlargement of point of view, stimulus through discussion, and the sheer joy of sitting around comfortably with fellow human beings and maintaining an intellectual friendliness.

Possibilities of Use

Since membership is highly selective, the possibilities of their direct use in interpretation are limited. If certain members of the school staff disclose unusual talent in some field of endeavor they will probably be invited to membership by some group. The sole effect will be secured from the projection of professional personality on a contributing basis to the lay group. The respect of the group for the schools will probably be determined by the extent to which they develop respect for the ability of the members with whom they come into direct contact. On rare occasions outsiders are invited before these meetings, and the possibility of invitation represents the second use.

Materials

The type of individual sitting with these groups is not interested in publicity broadcasts. He represents the intellectual who makes up his own mind and determines his own interests. There is little to be gained by conventional publication coverage. Personal pressure or annoyance through unsolicited material may lower instead of increase his interest.

ECONOMIC GROUPS

Economic groups include among their principal organizations the generalized chambers of commerce; manufacturers' associations; specialized organizations such as banking, accounting, transportation, realty, advertising, engineering, and architecture; general and specialized labor groups including the vertical C.I.O. and the horizontal craft unions; the so-called service clubs of Rotary, Kiwanis, Lions, Exchange, and Zonta; the Grange and farm bureau; and specialized coöperative groups such as the American Automobile Association. Some of these groups are local in character, but most of them are simply branches of national groups.

Interests

Their purpose is indicated by classification. With the exception of the luncheon clubs each one has its own specific area of interest and other factors are of minor consequence. They exist for the purpose of improving their technical efficiency and maintaining their specific interests. Manufacturing and labor have a collateral interest in the school because its graduates furnish labor for the varied economic activities. Financial and manufacturing groups are interested in public spending which brings one aspect of the schools to their attention. Manufacturing, labor, and agricultural interests believe they have a stake in vocational education and have sturdily supported Federal subvention for vocational training. Of these groups only the luncheon clubs have a generalized directed interest in civic and social problems.

Possible Use

With the exception of the luncheon clubs, the numerous economic interests must be approached in terms of their major interest which is that aspect of education most nearly approximating their major work. Diversity and specialization of staff in larger city school systems make a goodly number of the specialized teachers actually eligible for active membership. Vocational teachers as individuals may retain affiliation with labor groups; commercial teachers may become eligible for accountants' associations; home-economics teachers and lunchroom directors have strong interests with specialists in the field of public eating; whereas doctors and nurses maintain their major interest affiliation with their specific associations. The possibilities of personal interest affiliation within large city organization are many.

The major use is the building of institutional confidence through the effects of personal contact. Certain leaders within each group may be kept aware of school conditions and needs by exposure to official publications, but in general mass circulation of all of the members is inadvisable. Though teaching personnel as individuals may be encouraged to make personal affiliation with their specific field of interest, it is debatable whether principals or superintendents should become members. A cultivation of friendly relations with all groups and membership in none is probably better administrative practice. The schools must exercise extreme care to prevent their exploitation by any of these aggressive economic groups. The use of official school stationery to advertise the community's major economic activity is a dubious venture.

The luncheon clubs differ in type from the rest of these economic groups. They represent cross-sections of economic interest with the exception of labor, and their purpose and program are more generally educational than those of the highly specialized economic interest groups. It is perfectly feasible for administrator and teacher to represent education in their personal capacity by accepting active membership. The greatest current weakness with respect to educational representation is that membership appears to be limited in most instances to superintendents and principals, which tends to confirm the popular concept of the managerial organization of public education. It is desirable that effort be made to extend this membership so that at least every major type of teaching service is represented. It is the superintendent's responsibility to bring out the teachers and to suggest possible affiliation.

Material

The best type of contact with specialized economic interest groups is personal. Interchange of ideas, answering of questions, and general availability of information probably exhaust the list. Caution must be observed not to be too aggressive in pushing educational interest in an area where active interest is bound to be restricted. The luncheon and dinner clubs are different. Their programs are a form of generalized adult education comprehensive in scope and listening in character, covering wide ranges of interests. Because of the high sensitivity of individual members their program discussions unfortunately avoid controversial issues and to that extent are inclined to be innocuous. The program value could be greatly increased through the general discussion by the members of different points of view in mooted fields. To judge from the program of a luncheon club the conclusion might be reached that the people operate socially in a vacuum where all is sweetness and easy acquiescence. Strong presentations of problems are not encouraged, and realistic discussion is almost completely absent. Several meetings each year are devoted to consideration of educational problems and offer opportunity for presentation of general or special institutional problems. Since the educator is judged by the impression made in competition with many capable outside speakers, it is well to follow certain special rules in preparation. If invited to speak, the educator should take time to make careful preparation, plan to present one specific problem, speak clearly, simply, and above all, briefly. A quiet, dignified, and reasonably slow delivery is preferred for its lasting impression to the tiring rapid-fire technique of a Floyd Gibbons or the ultra-dramatic expression favored by public relations representatives of the Federal Bureau of Investigation.

Printed material used in institutional interpretation may be sent to the limited memberships of these luncheon clubs. Social eating permits also ample opportunity for general discussion with fellow-members once a week. The extent of these talking contacts is limited by the number of educators who are members of the group. Sometimes these clubs take an active interest by providing college and university scholarships for capable individuals who are handicapped economically. These ventures may well be encouraged since they create a much more active personal interest.

HOBBY ORGANIZATION

Extended leisure has also brought with it an increase in the possibilities of use. Individual hobbies that were formerly kept a dark secret from every one except the family have now been so heavily publicized and stimulated that open confession of interest is possible. The individual who formerly secreted himself in the cellar may now bring his ideas into the open without raising doubt and may meet with others similarly interested and thus increase the social value of hobby activities. The hobby has become as socially respectable as golf.

The extent of hobby organization is limited only by the bounds of the human imagination. Hobbies include music, drawing, ceramics, painting, sculpture, and drama in the fine arts, collecting interests ranging from old bottles to stamps, creative interests in wood and metal work, physical recreation, exploratory interests in camping and hiking, communication activities in the building and use of short-wave transmission and radio receiving sets, gardening, and others too numerous to mention here.

Interests

The interests of these groups are in their particular hobby, representing a satisfying means of expressing their creative urge. They do not therefore lend themselves easily to a division of interest by the introduction of an extraneous subject.

Possible Use

The use of the hobby groups in interpretative plans must be indirect. The chief institutional objective should be to make the school building the center of these informal and spontaneous group ventures and to encourage them to meet regularly in the building. It is a reasonable adult use of the public-school plant with all of its possible facilities. The dramatic and music groups may make the school theatre their working laboratory; other fine arts groups may be invited to use the studios; gymnasiums and pools furnish excellent facilities for recreational interests; the shops can materially assist wood and metal workers; science laboratories have appeal to the gardener, the chemist, and the amateur in electricity, radio, and photography. Stamp collectors should be provided with display and trading space.

If the building is to be used, competent advisory direction is necessary. Teachers may be urged to follow their hobby interests and work with whatever groups they desire. Thus through direct interest and leadership possibilities the teacher becomes one of the group. Adult interest is frequently supplemented by child interest and offers opportunity for the normal development of closer play relationships between parent and child. In fact the hobby field is so replete with natural opportunity for the development of the school as a vital agency in adult community life that its gross neglect by educational organization is difficult to explain.

Program

Hobby groups make their own program, and it is advisable not to interfere or to attempt formal institutionalization through organization. Results for interpretation are indirect. The friendliness of the institution, the growing realization of personal value, the environmental effects of a well-equipped and comfortable school plant are all silent workers in the creation of attitudes of understanding and appreciation.

POLITICAL GROUPS

Political groups include the major parties with their smoothly functioning organizations that begin with the friendly contacts of the precinct worker and terminate in the highly centralized state administrative structure. In addition there are minor political perimeter movements constantly springing up and dying down as problems arise. Sometimes these movements are significantly capitalized by the major parties, but more frequently they remain beyond the pale of organization because they represent too narrow a minority interest.

Interests

Political interests are limited to the achievement of power through election of party candidates and the accruing patronage that victory provides to keep organization alive. Their interests are narrowly confined to program and operate upon an extremely realistic basis.

Possible Use

It is extremely dangerous procedure for a state institution to become affiliated with partizan political organization. As a classless institution of a social nature where opportunity may be offered for the harmonization of all points of view and whose popular function is fundamentally in the creation of public opinion through extension of the educational process into adult life, extreme caution should be observed to remain free from political entanglements. The political machine offers nothing free since every favor must be balanced by an equal or even greater favor. Political bookkeeping is of the double entry type. Neither is it necessary to incur the danger of short-sighted policy by playing with one group as opposed to another. Educational interests must always remain the interests of both major parties, and neither should be permitted the pleasure and profit of becoming the sole defender and guardian of the process.

A good illustration of this danger may be drawn from the second Rooseveltian campaign. Both political parties tried to capitalize upon the possible "teacher vote," as they did on the "soldier vote," the "labor vote," and other organized interests, drawing their inspiration for bringing education into politics from the aggressive activities of what the practical politician calls the national teacher lobby and which the profession more euphonically refers to as "professional education of our national representatives."

Education was discussed largely in terms of what each side purported to be the candidate's beliefs and practices. Governor Landon was pictured by his opponents as the indifferent spectator at excessive curtailment of educational opportunity in Kansas. It was assumed that he might reasonably have been expected to step into the breach and attempt to reverse the Kansas state policy with respect to state subventions. His friends and supporters pointed out that he really was the champion of local control of the educational process in accord with our time-honored tradition. They pointed with pride to this policy which they claimed was responsible for the low percentage of illiteracy in Kansas. Here they neglected to state that these records were based on the results achieved in pre-depression days. Finally, Governor Landon was pictured as the very close friend and supporter of public education.

Turning to the democratic side, President Roosevelt was pictured by his campaign committee as the savior of public education during dark depression days. They pointed with considerable pride to the large appropriations made out of emergency funds for school-house reconstruction; for emergency experimental activity in pre-primary and adult-education fields; to active support through C.W.A.,

F.E.R.A., and W.P.A. of rehabilitation programs; to the employment in large numbers of surplus teachers who, desperate because of unemployment, threatened the stability of the teaching profession, and to subventions to worthy youth through N.Y.A. The popular success of C.C.C. camps and educational programs under T.V.A. were pointed to with pride. In fact, after reading all the campaign propaganda, it seemed as if the democratic candidate's entire time had been devoted to the solution of educational problems.

However, President Roosevelt's opponents carefully pointed out that he had set a bad example to local school boards by paying unemployed teachers mere relief wages, thereby weakening a profession already on the verge of disorganization. They accused him of attempting to federalize public education and of placing educational administrative responsibility in non-professional hands. They pointed out that through indirect aid the principle of undivided school support had been abrogated and that specific aids to the school plant were given only because schools represented a socially defensible expenditure for public moneys.

Objective analysis of the claims and counter claims of both candidates and their supporters indicates that the complete truth lay in neither camp. It is very doubtful whether impartial analysis of deeds and alleged misdeeds would give sufficient evidence to damn one or to enthrone the other. The emotions and distortions that naturally accompany these struggles for high political office, the progressive interpretation of uninformed laymen of only partial evidence in both cases stated in the most assured and dogmatic manner did not make for truth. No one yet knows what the exact truth is. The records are not clear or complete. Neither candidate's record with respect to education was significantly clear for final labeling. Candid analysis leads to the conclusion that both candidates, because education is not primarily a political issue, gave only the most casual and generally indifferent attention to the activity. There is nothing derogatory to either gentleman in this conclusion. It is the natural political reaction to a field of problems that has been, and should continue to be, treated as a non-political and fundamental cultural problem.

The general conclusion is that dragging the public-school problems into the presidential campaign in an effort by both sides to secure what must be euphonically called the "teacher vote" was not particularly helpful to the campaign, to the teaching profession, or, what is of most importance, to public education itself.

Materials

Political affiliation and activity may well be restricted to the fields of individual choice. Neither the public school nor the organized teaching profession should form alliances and truckle to partizan politics. The individual must be careful not to capitalize or exploit his institutional affiliation to the detriment of function and not to drag his fellow professionals into a campaign as teachers. The institution must avoid taking sides. It may be friendly to all parties and candidates by encouraging the use of school buildings for political gatherings and for polling places. Though furnishing to both sides complete information with respect to need, it must be careful not to permit the wily and crafty politicians to place it in a position where it appears to be offering partizan support and comfort. It is a dangerous sea that requires much navigating skill.

PROPAGANDA GROUPS

Interest groups with aggressive objectives generally become propaganda groups at some stage of their program. Their propaganda may be of a mild ladylike sort or may be distinctly aggressive in character. A few classifications may be considered as fairly constant but in general this category represents a shifting field and is subject to careful study at all times by the educator. They may be classified as conservator, economic, professional, political, racial, religious, social, and reformatory.[1]

Interests

The interests of an organized group devoted to advancement through use of propaganda need no elaboration. The school need not worry about establishing relations with them since it is defi-

[1] See Chapter 3, and Chapter 10, pp. 110-111.

nitely part of their plan to reverse the tables and establish relations with the schools. Some of the interests represented by propaganda agencies are sound in their nature and, if generally accepted, might be worthy of institutional consideration. Other types are selfish in character and frequently highly antisocial in type, and it is necessary that the public institution be protected from these propaganda barrages. Some of the propaganda is extremely subtle and difficult to detect, whereas other types carry their own labels.

Possible Use

It is primarily not a question of effective use but the problem of maintaining reasonable relations with these groups that the school must handle. The institution should be thoroughly familiar with each—its purpose, methods, and strength. Effort to use the schools for their own ends must be defeated without leaving a bad taste or creating ill will. The listening and explanation technique may be employed to advantage.[2]

PROFESSIONAL GROUPS

Professional groups include building and landscape architects, engineers, doctors, dentists, and lawyers. Their interests are primarily those of group association for improvement of the profession and protection of their members. They represent the *intelligentsia* in interest groups.

Interests

By nature of their work members of the professional groups have a definite community interest. The alert doctor is distinctly interested in more healthful living conditions and better education; the architect and engineer believe in good buildings. As members of a profession, they tend to possess greater initial interest and understanding of the school as a social institution.

Possible Use

Membership is limited to technically qualified individuals, so the possibility of direct contact through affiliation is more restricted

[2] See Chapter 3.

than in many other types. Occasionally members of secondary vocational faculties are also licensed engineers and architects and can maintain relations with these groups primarily through appearance on their institute programs and through educational literature. Representatives may be used as members of local educational advisory commissions.

Materials

The materials employed are normally limited to regular publications of the board of education. It may be desirable to keep all members of these professional groups on the regular mailing list.

SOCIAL GROUPS

The adult American dearly loves to play Indian and pirate, and to satisfy this craving he has evolved a tremendous diversity of social organization with high sounding ideals, welfare benefits, satisfying ritual, and gaudy uniform. There are nearly five hundred different social organizations of these types covering every conceivable mundane purpose. They include groups with a religious motive, such as the Masonic order and the Knights of Columbus; pure fun and fellowship characteristic of the animal orders such as Owls, Moose, Elk, and others; a distinctly insurance base including the Maccabees, Woodmen, and Redmen.

Interests

Whatever their official nature they are a purely democratic phenomenon for satisfying the human's desire for friendly companionship, offering also means of escape and self-expression. Their inherent democracy is fundamental. Janitor, junkman, lawyer, doctor, merchant, preacher, and teacher meet on the common ground of universal brotherhood and the protecting wings of mother lodge. Preferment within the order is determined by the worth of the individual to the order and not by name or wealth. The unskilled laborer may rise to chief potentate while the millionaire may start and remain as keeper of the outer gate. The ritualism of the lodge satisfies the individual's emotional craving for the mystical. Sonorous phrasing in the manner of the King James Version thrills. And then there is the element of sanctuary. Within the lodge all brothers protect one another; in the busy marts of life they may raise distress signals. Lodge badges are sound traveling and credit credentials in many areas. Above all they offer a chance for real fun, a yearning that the adult male never quite outgrows. If the helpmate is restive under the master's absence from home, she may join the ladies' auxiliary and become a daughter of something or other. The lodge is the male's last unconscious stand against the all-developing female influence. It is a vestige of the male community meeting place in simpler cultures.

Possible Use

Although the depression gave the larger fraternal orders a heavy setback and their interest has declined in the more sophisticated urban centers, there is little danger of fraternalism dying out in the United States. These organizations have continuing value to the socially inclined male. The nature of their interests makes little direct contact possible. They operate on a basis of friendship and value a man not so much for his inherent ability as for his friendliness. They appraise and follow a man because of confidence established through friendship. Vital contacts are limited to active membership. It is desirable that the teachers as individuals follow the line of their interest and affiliate with one or more groups. The greater the spread of membership in numbers, the better will be the results for the school.

Materials

Except for occasional speeches before these groups, materials may well be limited to informal friendly discussions and the answering of questions that arise.

WELFARE GROUPS

Welfare groups include those voluntary and official agencies through which the social-service work of the community is carried on. These groups are organized both as independent and as church agencies. The school meets them independently as family welfare agencies, child care, visiting nurses, settlement or social center groups, Red Cross, the so-called character-building groups such as the Y.M.C.A., the Y.W.C.A., Y.M.H.A., and others. They are generally organized into a federation in middle-sized and large communities under the title of the Community Chest.

Interests

The interests of these groups are centered around the relief of suffering and the improvement of submerged people. They represent the progressive institutionalization on a community-wide basis of the charitable work which was formerly the direct responsibility of the church. They are interested in children and in adults and are in frequent relationship with the schools.

Possible Use

The school's relationship to these groups should be one of hearty coöperation for the purpose of mutual assistance. Through the school these agencies may become quickly aware of individuals and areas needing attention. Economic and social difficulties confronting the schools may be helped through the ministrations of these agencies. The schools have continuing contact through their social workers and school nurses. It is possible to develop further relations through the establishment of the school as a clearing house for social information and through consultation and conference on problems of mutual interest. The social worker as a person of reasonably high educational qualifications understands the nature and the value of the school to a greater degree than is generally assumed. Constant contact furnishes an excellent means for the appraisal of the institution's social efficiency. Though current material may be of casual value, the best results are secured through the effectiveness of mutual relationships.

WOMEN'S ORGANIZATIONS

The major classifications under this division are the Federation of Women's Clubs, the American Association of University Women, and the League of Women Voters. These organizations include a wide membership and are directly concerned with adult-education programs.

Interests

Their interests are primarily those which will advance the status of women and child welfare. Though much of their work is concerned with the improvement and extension of their own organization, a fair percentage of time is devoted specifically to public educational problems. Women as a whole have always exercised great influence in American education. As the first line in safeguarding the child, the women may also be considered as having a very large stake in the improvement and enlargement of the educational function.

Possible Use

These women organizations are serious and studious in character. Informal study groups are organized each year in a variety of fields including parent education and child study. They may be self-directed on the basis of a national program or include the use of outside talent. The membership represents a high level of community intelligence and is unusually serious in the consideration of problems. The first direct contact of public education with these groups may be through teacher membership in one or more of the classifications. Participation should be voluntary and allowed to follow the line of interest. It is possible to have a teacher as member of the program committee to assist in the preparation and carrying out of plans. Through the stimulation of interest it is possible to have in each organization a series of programs or study courses in child welfare in which the institution receives indirect attention. Frequent open meetings make possible presentation of specific institutional conditions and needs.

Materials

The membership in these organizations is intellectually capable of using textual material of collegiate rank, and this fact makes a wide selection possible. Since most of their work is organized around specific study objectives, there is a greater consistency and higher level of learning than in any of the other organizations considered. In addition significant material prepared by the schools in the form of reports, descriptive bulletins, and state publications may be used as material for reading and discussion. It is also desirable that the school provide in each building a compact but comprehensive adult library, setting aside definite space for this purpose so that the material may be available during the day as well as in the evening.

SUMMARY

There are at least ten large divisions of organized lay interest groups. The number of individual organizations within each of these categories may range from a score to more than a hundred. The extent and diversity of lay organizations are determined by the size of the community. There is no difference in the technique of interpretation regardless of size. Most of these organizations are national in scope and the local pattern of organization and function is well standardized. Since the type of organization conditions both program and membership, it is necessary for the school to study each category in terms of possibilities of continuing personal contacts, possibilities for the development of specific programs and the nature of the material. The range of possibilities runs all the way from mere personal relations to highly organized adult-education classes. It is desirable that the public school offer as many as possible of these groups the advantage of a comfortable meeting place in convenient buildings. Provision for a special room that may be used as an adult and professional library where good reference material may be kept easily available is extremely helpful in the progressive development of these adult-education activities. Special care should be taken not to use a standardized procedure for all of these groups but to be flexible and adjust to specific interests and needs. The range of interests and the number of organizations make the teacher the most important agent in the maintenance of personal contact through membership.

Chapter 20

THE RADIO

THE radio and talking pictures are two relatively new agencies that are rapidly supplementing the daily newspaper as added means of communication for the dissemination of information and possibly as instruments of appraisal.[1] Their progressive development and increasingly efficient use will probably result in many sweeping changes in the character of the daily press. They have already challenged the press as co-agencies in the formation of public opinion to an extent unforeseen at the time of their introduction. The radio will be considered as an agency in institutional interpretation of the public schools from the standpoint of: (1) radio possibilities, (2) educational programs, (3) agencies, and (4) difficulties.

RADIO POSSIBILITIES

Radio may be viewed as a mechanical interpretative device whereby audience relations between the institution and the community have been made possible through extension of the carrying power of the human voice. An institution or an individual desiring to make direct vocal contact with large numbers of people at times most convenient to the listeners need no longer depend completely upon successive small audiences gathered in central meeting places or through the medium of the daily press. The radio furnishes opportunities for supplementing the older agencies and methods.

Direct contact between audience and speaker through the medium of the voice means that dilution and coloring typical of the newspaper may be avoided. In the daily press an original statement is subject to dilution and coloring successively by the reporter, the editor, and the publisher's news policy. Prior to the advent of the radio the newspaper was all powerful as an extralegal appraisal

[1] For discussion of motion pictures see Chapter 22.

agency. It could easily make or break men and institutions. To-day, since it is possible to overcome this monopoly through direct vocal appeal, the power of the press as an agency in the forming of public opinion is waning.

The radio furnishes an additional agency whereby public education may go directly to the people to checkmate possible unfairness and bias on the part of a newspaper or propaganda by a special interest group. The potential strength of the radio may result in an enormous improvement in the newspaper itself. Proprietor controlled and dominated policy may be replaced by a return to the fundamental purpose of the newspaper as an impartial reporting and appraisal agency.

Magic power lies not within the radio itself but in its possible use. Its effectiveness depends upon the ideas projected, the method of expression, and the personality behind them. During the 1936 campaign President Franklin D. Roosevelt, Father Coughlin, Doctor Francis E. Townsend, the Reverend Gerald Smith, Governor Alfred M. Landon and their miscellaneous followers all used this agency extensively. The audience, divorced from the influence of the personal presence, was apparently able to listen more objectively to the ideas presented and to form its own judgments. The ultimate possibilities of the radio as an agency in the interpretation of public education have just begun to be sensed. Its limitations have been obvious for a longer time.

The American policy of permitting this new communication agency to be developed by private initiative under governmental supervision is in accord with American tradition. However, private ownership may well be supplemented by stations owned and operated by either educational institutions or the state governments. Though certain weaknesses are obvious under private management, they are by no means so fraught with dangers of control as might be possible under complete governmental ownership and operation. The dedication and use of the state-owned radio in the totalitarian state as a completely controlled propaganda agency in maintaining and extending dictatorship are too well known to require extensive discussion. In the American plan, survival of a private radio broadcasting system is contingent upon listener appeal. The demands of the audience determine the level of functioning. In the state-controlled radio the reverse is more likely to be true. The policy of the national commission in frowning upon newspaper ownership of the air makes the radio a practical competitor of the newspaper and prevents its use to maintain and extend individual newspaper influence. The insistent demands of large and vocal groups for spread of time on the air between commercial and educational programs are slowly resulting in a progressive extension of educational programs. Under the American plan it should be possible for public education to secure sufficient time to maintain continuous popular contact by this means.

However, the time given to educational programs will not be an important factor as long as the privately owned station is the sole judge of what is "educational" and has complete choice of time assignment. Though the total time devoted to educational programs has been extensively increased within the past five years, the programs are moved to ineffective "open" hours, are subject to sponsor whim, and may include some peculiar choices.

There is definite need for an official definition of an educational program and the assignment of some effective hours. The United States Office of Education might well consider this problem as one of its responsibilities.

If the radio is to remain completely under private control and still be used as an effective democratic means for the education of the adult population to its problems and needs, it must provide for the presentation of all points of view. The radio should be available to the national government, the state educational authority, the local school district, and to the organized teaching profession for presentation of information concerning the value, conditions, and needs of the schools. If other interest groups disagree with either state or teaching profession, they should also be allowed opportunity to express their point of view. Restriction of use to one specific viewpoint or permitting either official or private censorship will mean the negation of the democratic principle of freedom of discussion by individuals and groups. Thus the effective social use of this new instrument depends upon the freedom of use. The United States can profit greatly by studying the educational use of the radio made by England.

EDUCATIONAL PROGRAMS

Although there is no finality as to the best technique of use, it is possible to present certain general principles that may be valuable as guides in improving interpretative programs.

Educational presentations may be more effective if confined to the presentation of a single idea. The radio listener probably finds it somewhat more difficult to maintain attention over a wide spread of ideas than if he were seated in an auditorium in direct contact with the personality of the speaker. There are more laughs and quicker reactions in the small broadcasting audience studios than from the home listener.

Presentation of educational information should be brief, probably not more than five to ten minutes in length. It is possible to produce information in a terse and condensed style instead of following the conventional extended verbal pattern of the professional teacher.

Educational information must be organized to attract and hold the listener through some fundamental personal interest. The teaching profession as a whole is quite remote, and the people are only casually interested in the teacher as a generalized person, even though they may be keenly interested in a very small number of teachers with whom they maintain personal relations. The child and his interests form a basis for appeal that has universal interest with every adult, and particularly to parents. Thus Angelo Patri as an interpretating agent through his writings on child problems in a large number of daily newspapers has created an unusual parental interest in public education and its problems. The same newspapers that pay well for his daily feature are frequently cold to the presentation of conventional educational news.

The recital of educational "facts" and involved statistics should be carefully avoided. They are not only difficult for the listener to grasp, but uninteresting unless they can be dramatized to make them significant.

Educational broadcasts must be reduced to very simple language. There is no place for professional patter, high emotionalization of the work, or conventional flights into fields oratorical. The presentation of an idea in simple, concise and restrained language will probably reach more people. Speeches should be presented slowly and distinctly. The development of an effective radio style is a task requiring much concentration and rehearsal. School radio programs may therefore use profitably an expert radio voice. Since teachers are not competent in this field they need not be adverse to having experts advise on the preparation and presentation of material.

Interpretative broadcasts should not attempt to imitate the conventionalized professional pattern. The comparative appeal of capable professionals as opposed to amateur mediocrity will turn the dial in favor of the professional. However, the schools might profitably imitate the commercial broadcaster's zeal to discover more effective means of presentation. Every studio production is constantly submitted to rigid and cold appraisal. Little is taken for granted and every effort is made to discover actually the effect of broadcasts. Too often, educational programs are too prosaic in thought or pattern. Exceptions too frequently go to the other extreme of trying superficially to "jazz" programs in the worst commercial manner. Neither extreme is desirable.

The ultimate value of the radio appears to lie in the continuing program, organized for a definite group interest around a definite purpose and supplemented by printed bulletins, materials, bibliographies, and direct contacts. These ventures point toward the more formal organization around problems of specific adult interest.

The distinctive and worth-while qualities of the educational programs will attract the serious listener without the appeal of amateur "trimmings." Through the process of continued experimentation it should be possible to produce a technique so distinctive and intrinsically appealing that its value will be quickly recognized and continuing interest established. This is in itself a most direct challenge to the teaching profession.

Audience

The audience range and appeal will be determined by the specific nature of the program. There are potentially as many radio audiences as there are topics and modes of presentation. Since the organization of radio programs on a nation-wide, state, and local basis is suggested as a possible means of effective use, it seems desirable that these different types of broadcasting do not duplicate each other in too many respects.

It is also possible to develop specific audiences for continuing programs and then point these offerings to the interest concerned. Thus educational broadcasts may be directed on a continuing basis to the parent-teacher association, women's organizations, economic and other specialized groups. Specific publicity may be given these programs through notice in the daily press, by means of descriptive outline programs mailed to organization officers, and by direct mail postcard "tickler" notes. Selection of a specific audience simplifies program preparation by concentrating on specific types of presentation and selection of subject-matter.

Program Range

The national or great mass appeal indicates a fairly generalized program that emphasizes educational problems of national interest and scope. State programs may be generally limited to those problems that are of immediate interest to the people within the legal organization area, whereas local programs may consider much more intimately the problems peculiar to the community. There is no conflict between these three programs; they represent rather a progressive enlargement of interest from local to state and national problems. It would seem that the start of developing radio as an interpretative instrument should proceed logically from the small to the larger audience. Since local programs are limited to larger communities, the state may probably be chosen as the more significant program field. Public education is a state function and is better understood by the people in terms of its legal organization.

Program range may be considered under five major divisions

including the objectives of public education, the social importance of public education within a democratic order, the nature and value of organization, the conditions and needs of the schools. Each of these divisions may be further subdivided into a series of specific problems. Conditions and needs divide themselves normally into the areas of instruction personnel, plant, and finance, each of which has distinct possibilities of appeal in terms of child conditions and needs. Frequent presentation and elaboration of the major goals of education might form an excellent base for a series of nation-wide programs. The American educational philosophy is national in scope although for the sake of safety from civil governmental dominance and to protect the partnership concept actual control has been retained by the people within the individual state. The social importance of the complete educational function may also be stressed by national programs.

Organization, conditions, and needs may be effectively presented through state programs where they are closer to the people and more capable of improvement. Educational conditions vary greatly by states and seem to offer the greatest possibilities at a point where interest and social action for improvement are naturally lodged. This recommended allocation does not preclude the consideration of educational problems nationally in terms of a possible integrated and complementary program, but merely means that they may be more effectively accomplished by the state.

Type of Program

Educational interpretative programs may be considered as direct and indirect with reference both to type and to material. The direct type is the presentation of an idea through a single speaker, a group of speakers, a discussion panel, the interview technique, or a dramatization. The indirect type depends upon interest and the development of attitudes through the presentation of a child product. The direct type may well be confined to the professional or lay adult, whereas the indirect type is most effective when organized and presented completely as a child product, including musical and dramatic presentation.

A third type of program includes direct broadcasting into the schoolroom. Though this activity is primarily designed as a curricular aid, many adults tune in and are thus indirectly informed on many things. Curricular broadcasting must be aware of this casual audience. Material may deal directly with educational information or with events, news, and biography which indirectly give educational information.

A word of caution is desirable concerning child programs. In an attempt to secure attractive but cheap programs some commercial sponsors are turning their attention to the exploitation of the children. School authorities should be chary of permitting the commercial use of children in programs over which they have no direction or control.

Adult Education

The radio has many unexplored possibilities as an agency for continuing adult education either formally or informally. Since the adult program represents attempts at direct instruction in various areas of interest, it may be desirable to assign responsibility to the institutions of higher learning. These programs have only an indirect interpretative value and should be considered primarily as continuing the training of adults. Universities and state colleges have already made significant progress in adult education through radio. As experimentation and experience result in the development of more effective radio techniques, these extramural efforts will become of increasing importance. The institutional programs may be either state-wide or national in scope.

One particularly bright adult possibility lies in the field of parent education. It is possible through the radio, in coöperation with the parent-teacher association, to build consistent programs around the problems of the child in the home, the school, and community, and to provide educational stimulation of the parent in all of the aspects of child care and home-making. These adult ventures may be pointed so that a specific collateral interest is developed by the parent in child-school relationships and so promote the partnership concept. It is possible through these adult programs to touch a range of subjects in which the small isolated community may find difficulty in initial approach either because of conventional community thinking or inadequacy of a restricted personnel.

AGENCIES

The agencies through which educational use of the radio for interpretative purposes may be carried vary with the type and appeal of program.

National Agencies

The United States Office of Education has a definite leadership responsibility for the stimulation and development of national programs. It is primarily the function of this office to gather pertinent information within and without the country of educational conditions and needs, to pioneer in the development and popular translation of general problems, and to keep the people as a whole informed of high and low spots in our educational plan. Since a governmental agency of such character may be limited at any time by the specific administrative policies under which it is operating, it is desirable to supplement its work through at least two voluntary interest groups representing the various major professional groups and the parent-teacher association both concerned primarily with the child. The National Education Association, the Progressive Education Association, the American Council on Education, and similar groups have coördinate responsibility with the National Congress of Parents and Teachers for keeping the people informed. Independent of governmental supervision these interest groups have a wider practical opportunity for more complete presentation of conditions and problems. They may in turn be supplemented by individual leaders working independently or coöperatively.

State Agencies

The major responsibility for generalized interpretation on a state-wide basis rests directly with the state educational authority. As an appraisal and planning agency it is responsible for reporting not only to the legislature and the state executive but also directly to the people. Too many state educational authorities are still heavily handicapped by their political organization and partizan affiliations. Here again aid from the professional and parent-teacher state organizations is highly desirable. Where the lay educational advisory commission is used, this agency may also participate effectively in the program of interpretation by coöperating with state and professional programs or operating independently. Regularity and reasonable frequency are requirements of these programs.

Local Agencies

Except in the case of large population centers the local district is dependent on state and national programs for use of the radio. The small local school system can do much, however, in directing community attention to worthy educational programs having interpretative implications for that locality. One device is the organization of "listening" groups; another may direct the attention of community lay groups to special programs. State and national programs might be used as a basis for parent-teacher discussion groups. The small community that neglects to develop local interest in educational broadcasting is missing a distinct opportunity. The large city programs have opportunities for the development of presentations that are particularly pertinent to the specific area of functioning, thus supplementing rather than duplicating state and national broadcasts. Though the legal organization should accept major responsibility, the local organized teaching profession and the city parent-teacher council may again coöperate in these institutional efforts or provide specific programs of their own. The local program has larger possibilities in indirect interpretation possibly than either state or nation.

DIFFICULTIES

The major difficulties conditioning the use of the radio in institutional interpretation are primarily those involved in the use of a new agency for which no perfected technique has yet been developed. All current efforts in this field may therefore be considered as experimental and subject to constant change as spot appraisal indicates strength and weakness. It is inadvisable to do more than suggest possibilities at the present time.

In addition to the major problems there are a number of other difficulties confronting educational broadcasting. Educational programs involve the use of many amateurs of various types so far as personnel is concerned. Amateur effort always offers many problems that the professional has already solved. The educational program will do well to avoid poor imitation of professional effort and devote itself instead to the serious development of its own technique in capturing and holding adult interest.

One of the weaknesses of the professional educator is his almost constitutional inability to say things simply, easily, and without excessive words. Educational broadcasting demands a new non-academic method of presentation, void of rolling phrases and florid figures of speech.

The educator also is prone to the great platform fault—inability to provide terminal facilities. Like many orators he hates to stop. Despite the absence of direct audience stimulation many educational presentations are much too long to maintain the interest of unseen listeners.

There is also the difficulty in securing good broadcasting time. Placement is immediately more of a problem than amount of time. It is also annoying to adjust to commercial studio rehearsal demands, but this difficulty might be overcome by the development of special school studios. Lack of genuine interest in vital educational programs produces a dearth of expert advice and assistance and insecurity in the carrying out of carefully planned programs at times originally specified. Programs may be suddenly and unexpectedly shifted to the great interference with institutional plans.

SUMMARY

The radio may be considered as an independent supplementary agency in facilitating communication between school and community. Because it is a new medium, the radio involves many delicate problems in use that will be solved only as experimentation and experience provide better controls. As an agency for institutional interpretation the radio should be considered as parallel and complementary to the free press. It is doubtful whether it can ever achieve a position of importance so that it overshadows direct personal contacts between school and home. Its use will probably be limited in value to the same extent that other mechanical communication and agencies are. The radio lends itself much more effectively to national and state broadcasts than to extensive general use in local communities. The national and state official agencies are responsible for leadership in radio use, but their efforts should be distinctly supplemented by the professional organization and the parent-teacher association either as direct collaborators or as independent efforts.

Chapter 21

THE NEWSPAPER

THE function of the free press in a democratic pattern is to provide means for the dissemination of current happenings or news and to act as an extralegal appraising agency for social and voluntary institutional efficiency. The foundation of the American newspaper is the constitutional guarantee of freedom of publication which, in theory, should permit an independent voluntary organization to be sufficiently strong to tell the truth without fear or favor. In practice, however, the extensive investment in plant, franchises, and good will, together with its corporate interests and the nature of its organization, tends to subordinate its major function in favor of satisfying the stockholder's desire for dividends and the owner's desire for political or social power.

The expensively produced daily newspaper is one product that sells below cost and still shows a profit. This paradox is due to the fact that the major financial support of a publishing venture is derived from advertising. The heavy advertiser will normally watch his own interests carefully and probably influence editorial policy and news presentation to some extent. Since advertising revenue depends on breadth and type of circulation, the reader's desires enter as a third element. In practice the independence of the typical newspaper is conditioned by the triangle of publisher, advertiser, and reader interest, representing so much of a compromise that it generally falls far below the concept of function. It is frequently possible for a clever publisher to color the news columns to satisfy his own prejudices and ambitions for some time before the readers discover what is going on. He may also offer a particular brand of political doctrine adjusted to his peculiar news presentation, attracting a group of subscribers who feel the same way and like to have their views confirmed. Publisher bias undoubtedly affects news presentation as much as advertising or reader influence.

The publisher's policy is limited by the extent to which the large advertising interests believe his news presentation stimulates readers to study their products. Advertisers are definitely conscious of type. The Hearst papers are an illustration of this fact. Though their lurid headlines and jangled superlatives attract a certain type of circulation, these papers do not possess the same substantial reader appeal and have always been outdistanced in advertising by more conventional publications. The highest publishing dividends are paid by the more conservative, better written, and politically independent newspapers. Advertisers undoubtedly attempt to influence editorial and news policy. Every good newspaper office presents a constant struggle between the editorial and business divisions. The editorial branch, conscious of its functional responsibilities, tries in vain to maintain its complete independence. Sometimes these struggles become so bitter that the publisher himself becomes the referee, and the best the editorial end can receive is a compromise. In general, advertising influence is extended more to having the paper refrain from critical comments concerning commercial personnel and sales practices and to censoring news of accidents or other embarrassments that may arise, than to dictating general news coverage. Frequently this hush policy is extended to the owner of stores and factories and his relatives. As a totality the advertising influence on basic policy is less than is popularly assumed.

Since advertising depends on circulation and circulation is conditioned by reader interest, it is of vital importance that the publisher meet his readers' wishes to a reasonable extent. The subscriber has a most potent weapon by which he also determines newspaper policy in a large measure. If the reader does not agree with editorial policy or feels that he is being exploited, his personal remedy lies in rejecting the paper. If circulation falls significantly, advertising rates also decline and their volume shrinks. Circulation is so important that it is considered the barometer by which the daily newspaper judges its progress. Though it is possible to point out significant instances where publisher bias or advertising interest has actually determined the basic policy of the news organ, the final level of newspaper honesty is usually the result of a compromise between the trilogy of publishing, advertising, and reader interest. Thus the general level of the newspaper is determined by the intelligence of the readers and their degree of taste. Mere literacy is not sufficient. The ultimate level of the public press will be determined by the demands of the people for better papers.

The daily newspaper is an important agency in social interpretation, and these relationships will be considered in the following aspects: (1) position in social interpretation, (2) institutional information needs, (3) types of newspapers, (4) press relations, (5) news, and (6) operating difficulties.

POSITION IN SOCIAL INTERPRETATION

The daily newspaper has an important but certainly not the first place in social interpretation. As a reflector of community opinion it furnishes an opportunity for the public institution to secure an understanding of community feeling and thought; as an agency for the dissemination of news it offers daily opportunity for institutional news to reach the mass of the people. As an extralegal appraising agency the newspaper has the responsibility for passing personal judgment upon the operation of the educational function. Public education is concerned with all three aspects of the free press.

Press Not Supreme

Certain tendencies and developments now condition the effectiveness of the newspaper. Though they may possibly be temporary in nature, they must be given adequate consideration by institutions. Of these the waning power of the newspaper as the chief voluntary instrument in the formation of public opinion should be of much significance to the teaching profession in its programs of institutional interpretation. Many authorities believe that the importance of the proprietary press as the principal interpretative agency has been overrated. The results of the 1936 presidential election may be cited as support for this contention. Although 80 per cent of the privately owned newspapers of the country were vigorously opposed to the administration and presented their news, editorials, and cartoons colored in terms of this policy, the sweeping results of the popular vote indicated that the power of these presentations was distinctly inferior. Even the editors themselves appear to realize this fact for Captain Joseph Medill Patterson of the New York *News* said, in part, in an editorial after the election that "this election demonstrated that the power of the press to sway public opinion is dying, if not dead...that people read newspapers these days to get facts...but that they don't read or rely on editorials."

There are a number of reasons for this condition. Besides the traditional personal contact there are now new outlets of increasing importance for the dissemination of information that are beyond the control of the newspaper. These include the talking picture and the radio. Both of these agencies permit a direct personal appeal that is unclouded by transmission through news columns. They offer to the people a new basis for appraisal. The policy-controlled newspaper suffers as a result. The coloring and dilution that a newspaper normally provides before stories can be presented to the public have certainly assisted in the weakening process.

The immediate application of this decreasing newspaper influence to the field of institutional interpretation does not mean that the teaching profession can ignore the newspaper but simply reorients it with respect to proportional value. The most important agency in the process of continuing interpretation lies in the field of adult education where through direct and radio contact with individuals and groups the educational institution and the organized teaching profession can reach the interested audience directly and, without a series of interpretations and dilutions, analyze problems and suggest solutions. The audience is sufficiently mature and capable of forming its own decisions. All education needs is the opportunity to make the presentation. If a dynamic public opinion can be formed among the people, the proprietary press will be one of the first agencies to sense this fact and adjust its editorial policies accordingly since circulation is co-king with advertising in the publishing field.

It is patently no longer necessary to prostitute the schools to a newspaper publisher's whim or fancy, nor to permit the exploitation of the schools for the selfish interests of newspapers. It is only essential to maintain natural and professionally possible relations with the press.

A Good Press

The institution normally expects a good press. There is no rational reason for this expectation except that it has become habitual thinking. Every individual and voluntary interest group likewise desires a good press. If all agencies achieved their desire, there would be a complete eclipse of the newspapers' initial function. The best means of securing a good press is to do a good teaching job and help the press discover it. There is little sense in wasting time and energy worrying about what the paper will say the next day. A good press is deserved only as institutional efficiency is worthy of it.

INSTITUTIONAL INFORMATION NEEDS

Before considering the actual use of the newspaper in social interpretation, it is essential that the schools know their local newspapers. From the standpoint of community interpretation all of the publications within a community should be read continuously and conclusions comparatively developed. It is also desirable to use all of the local newspapers in institutional interpretation.

Newspaper Appraisal

Appraisal of the current press is not difficult. The institution may first determine ownership and basic policy. The newspaper owner quite generally remains effectively in the background and becomes a shadowy figure to the readers. However, corporate statements of ownership are definitely available in official reports, and investigation of the owners in terms of their interests and prejudices is not difficult.

The specific policy of the newspaper may be gained from its editorial pages. The degree of political partizanship, fairness in considering all sides of a question, and the quality of social-mindedness may be judged over a brief period of time.

The type and quality of advertising may shed some light on publishing attitudes and upon the fairness of news presentation. News coverage and news coloring lend themselves to comparative study by examination of significant stories in all local newspapers against such yardsticks as *The Christian Science Monitor, The New York Times, The New York Sun, The St. Louis Globe Democrat,* and *The Kansas City Star.* Bias in local news must be determined by comparison of known facts with all points of view expressed by the different papers.

The degree to which the local paper serves its major obligation as an appraising agency is possible of objective determination by the institution that has all of the facts and the newspaper's interpretation of these facts. In this area the institutional set of perfect righteousness usually interferes with the objectivity of its attitude. Only through a complete detachment regarding institutional effort and attempting to view problems through the eyes of the layman is it possible to make adequate appraisal of the newspaper's fairness and editorial intelligence.

TYPES OF NEWSPAPERS

Local newspapers may be classified according to circulation appeal as general and special-group; with respect to contents as news-advertising, advertising-news, news, and advertising; in terms of publication as daily, weekly, morning, and evening; and with respect to policy as conservative, middle-of-the-road, and progressive.

The news-advertising type may be considered as the typical daily newspaper published either in the morning or afternoon in which news and advertising are in fair balance with emphasis on the news aspect. The advertising-news group includes the "throw away" or free circulation type generally issued for sectional consumption and covering only a part of the community. There is sufficient news to make the advertising attractive, but the general policy, since its entire revenue is secured from merchants, is so distinctly colored that it may be classified as advertising propaganda. These types of publication are peculiar to sections of the larger population centers where neighborhood merchants feel that their interests are better served than through general circulation.

The strictly news sheet represents those occasional publications prepared and maintained by some interest group to serve its peculiar purposes. Although theoretically independent of advertising, these sheets are definitely dependent on a very limited circulation and for financing upon a specific interest. Their news value is conditioned by these facts, and they are distinctly limited in both coverage and appeal.

The advertising sheet has little interest to the institution as an interpretative agency. Its appeal is completely merchandising and may be operated on either a proprietary basis or directly by a large commercial establishment.

Rural Press

The small-town and rural press differs considerably from its large city brother. It is the last stronghold of personal journalism, and its influence is probably still fairly strong as a molder of public opinion. Issued three times a week, as a weekly, or a bi-weekly, it is much more dependent on circulation for revenue than the larger papers. Its advertising appeal is distinctly limited, and as a result it carries a relatively larger amount of news in relation to advertising. It caters heavily to the human desire for news about one's fellow-men and hence features personal items as local news, which in the city newspaper is relegated to a select group on the so-called "society page." In recent years the small-town paper has been characterized by the increasing amount of "boiler plate" news it buys from national news syndicates. These stories are received in the form of mats or plates ready for use in printing. The small-town newspaper is distinctly a personal affair and operates to a large measure in terms of personality reactions.

PRESS RELATIONS

Recognition of the nature and function of the press should form the basis for determining a policy with respect to relations between the press and institutions. As an extralegal appraisal agency the free press is entitled to make its own independent study of institutional functioning without direction, qualification, or censorship. The school as a social institution must stand perpetually in the strong light of public scrutiny, and the newspaper is one of the agencies that performs this investigation activity for the great mass of people. Since the newspaper is a very human institution, its fundamental attitude toward the institution will be conditioned to a large extent by the degree of confidence it has in the capacity and honesty of institutional personnel. The extent to which the newspaper is convinced that nothing is hidden and that all phases of functioning are open to public scrutiny will play a large part in determining newspaper policy toward the school. The public institution needs to realize that the true function of the press is not to act as a propaganda and booster agency for the official personnel but rather as a true reflector of actual conditions.

The first institutional requirement in press relations is to maintain an open-door policy, inviting press representatives to all official meetings and assisting them in running down news leads. The second is to be able to take bad news without becoming emotional. The effect of a single news story is forgotten before many editions since the variety and spread of constantly accruing events makes retention difficult.

On the current level of functioning with a spread of newspapers and editorial policy it is difficult if not impossible to secure unanimity of viewpoint on all questions and practices. Certain sections of a diversified daily press are bound to run critical stories and to make pointed editorial suggestions. So long as these publications are honest in their presentation there can be no objection from institutional personnel. Some authorities even incline to the belief that a heavy opposition from a single paper will result in healthy support by others and may serve as an institutional stimulus.

The institution must also be honest in its news policies and fair to all of the papers. The mere reason that a board member or executive dislikes the policy or personnel of a particular paper is no excuse for holding back news. Regardless of a newspaper's attitude it is entitled to information. Any censorious or restrictive policy is dangerous and cannot be defended from the institutional standpoint.

Personal Contact

The third requirement in press relations is the development and maintenance of personal relations with publisher, editors, and reporters. The superintendent and principals should become acquainted with newspaper personnel and attempt to understand its points of view, the current limitations on accuracy, and the conditioning effect of publisher policy. If the publisher, editors, and reporters are impressed with the fundamental honesty of purpose and technical capacity of the educator, this attitude will affect its news stories and to some extent its editorial policy. In general a newspaper does not find it too profitable to criticize local institutional effort without cause. Such practice is out of line with pride in local achievement and the American "booster" theory. Newspapers are not inclined to be overly critical editorially of educational practice without good reason. If a board of education persists in internal struggle or if institutional personnel is fighting an embittered internal battle, it is the paper's job to report it just as it does other news. The results of institutional weaknesses cannot be held against the press.

Exceptions

There are numerous exceptions to this general statement. Sometimes proprietary social, religious, or economic bias finds expression in peculiar ways. A few years ago in one of the larger cities a newspaper was distinctly critical of the building efforts of the board of education. The board was daily charged with extravagance and wastefulness. These attacks became so serious that the board ordered a quiet investigation of its own efforts. Outside specialists were called in, and extremely detailed comparative studies were made of local and other large city practice. When these investigations had been completed, the city under fire discovered that in terms of quality it was paying less per child for buildings than neighboring centers. A committee of board members took this information to the publisher and suggested that he might be interested in the real facts. No attempt was made to influence policy besides presenting these facts. The publisher after careful reading candidly admitted the truth of the statement, but stated that he did not believe in free secondary education at all. Since a direct attack upon the free secondary school was not good editorial policy, he felt that the undermining of popular confidence in the board of education by accusations of extravagance would result in decreased appropriations for buildings and thus achieve his program. Assuring the members of his personal confidence and friendliness, he told the committee that nothing could be done about changing policy. The attacks continued until his death a few years later. Since this represented only one newspaper, and a consistent program of interpretation in the form of direct adult education was in progress, these attacks had little effect. In the meantime, without reference to these attacks, the other newspapers ran the report of the survey and probably created a good counter effect.

Prepared News

The typical newspaper is swamped with prepared news more commonly known as "hand outs." Hundreds of interest groups flood the editor with their propaganda. Most of this finds its way into the large waste-baskets that form an essential part of newspaper office equipment. Editors are very suspicious of "canned" material. It is therefore better practice to eliminate entirely the use of prepared news except for small-town and rural papers. Neither is it desirable to hire a professional newspaper man to maintain press relations. The professional publicity man is the bane of a good newspaper office, and press agents are viewed in the same light as "hand outs." If advice on preparation of material is desired, it is much better for the institution to invite local reporters and editors to give such technical information. They are generally glad to do so. The infrequent practice of directly subsidizing a reporter for "special work" cannot be condemned too strongly. In its highest form it is unwise, and in its poorest expression it amounts to outright bribery.

Decentralized News

Better and greater news coverage may be attained if the institution will decentralize its news gathering, permitting principals and teachers to discuss and present material in accordance with the policy of the board. Under this plan the superintendent's office furnishes general information and news concerning the board of education, suggesting to the reporters points of special interest in the individual school.

Reporter Relations

Where several papers are in competition, it is desirable to establish fixed hours for joint press conferences at which reporters may ask the superintendent or board members any questions. Monday morning is an excellent time since there is usually a dearth of news on this day. Incidentally, all school news of the previous week should have been reported to the central office late Friday or Saturday. General news information may be given out at this time and thus insure fair treatment for all papers. If regular reporters fail through sickness or some other accident to be present, it is well to protect them by seeing that their paper receives the regular information.

When questions are asked, it is always good policy to tell the truth and to tell it so simply that there is no opportunity for misunderstanding. If certain news cannot be released at the time, a good reporter may be depended upon to keep a confidence. If news is damaging to individual reputation, it is also possible under most conditions to prevent publication. As a policy, however, it is highly desirable that few such requests be made or the newspaper may conceive the idea of censorship. Newspapers are almost as sensitive as teachers.

If a plan or problem is brought before the board of education, and it is apparent that the reporter does not understand it, it is always good practice to spend some time explaining it regardless of the pressing nature of other engagements. By attitude and practice it is possible to build in a reporter the consciousness of sound reporting of all public affairs. However, it is entirely gratuitous to make extensive preachment on the need for high ethical conduct. The intelligent reporter understands the limitations of his newspaper as well as any public official.

If a reporter calls for information at times other than the regular press conferences, it is good practice to see or talk to him immediately. Daily papers do have publishing deadlines which the reporter must meet, and he appreciates any effort that is made to help him. One of the most successful large city superintendents will interrupt any conference whether with board members, staff, or parents, to meet a reporter's request for some specific information. These and a multiplicity of other little human acts have probably helped considerably to get the schools of that city a good press over two decades.

Reporters may also dig up stories from leads of their own. If this is the case it is the school man's duty to respect all confidences and never "tip the story" to a rival reporter. In general good reporters will protect their news sources even to the extent of going to jail for them. They expect a similar loyalty from those with whom they work.

WHAT IS NEWS?

News may be considered as the direct reporting of any occurrence of popular interest filtered through reporter ability, editorial skill, and publishing policy. A newspaper may treat some news with complete fairness and may color other information to fit its own purpose. It may write news objectively or introduce editorial opinion in presentation. The most dangerous practice is the complete suppression of news. News that is published may be easily checked for accuracy, but news that is omitted creates blind spots. Even in its highest expression the collection and publication of news has certain limitations. The pressure of time seldom makes it possible for the reporter, unless he is unusually capable and well informed, to discover all of the truth. His training and experience lead him to seek for certain emotional values in presentation. On the large paper the man who gathers the news generally telephones it to an office writer who develops the story from the telephoned facts without direct personal contact with the field conditions. The editorial desk makes the copy conform to the paper's style and policy and determines emphasis. It then goes to the headline writer who determines the point of appeal. After this successive filtration through at least four people, it is remarkable that the news story still bears much semblance to the original material.

The small-town publication differs in news gathering and preparation. Generally the man who gathers the information also writes, edits, and headlines it, thus producing a product more nearly integrated with the original facts than is possible by specialized production.

News Policy

The news policies of different papers vary greatly. Some papers are characterized by straightforward factual presentation without high emotional coloring, whereas others specialize on the morbid and esoteric in the belief that sin is news. Whatever the specific policy, it is obvious that conflict is currently the fundamental basis for most news stories. It may be conflict between nations, between major interest groups, athletic teams, institutional or personal differences, but the net result is the same. Stories that have inherent conflict value make the front page, and purely factual presentation goes nearer to the advertising. Since it is emotional value that determines reader interest the school is offered a definite clue in the developing of news value.

Straight News

The public schools have many possibilities for straight news. Meetings of the board of education and official action taken by that body are information that the public requires, and newspapers are glad to print it. To the extent that other school activities have interest and appeal they may be placed in this category. Names make reader appeal; so events such as dramatic programs, debates, athletics, and commencements have straight news value. There is a reader appeal in seeing one's own name in print.

Feature Stories

Feature stories may include those presentations where the emotional value is of sufficient reader appeal despite a low direct news value. They include the unusual, the bizarre, and the "human interest" type such as the "Man Bites Dog," the Dionne quintuplets, and the crippled child achieving against heavy odds. Though the people enjoy conflict, they also like to read about animals and children. Children and their work have high feature if little direct news value. The schools are replete with possibilities of child interest stories that a good reporter can easily discover. If a new curricular practice is adopted, it may be worth a few inches as news. The effects of change in curricular content or methodology upon the children have far greater presentation values. Feature stories also lend themselves to pictures which will enhance the reading appeal of any story. Effective pictures of normal child activity require an expert in photography. The chief criticism of most of the pictures currently used is their woodenness and lack of photographic imagination and artistry.

News Placement

The concentration of local school news on a single school page is considered good editorial practice in many large city newspapers. From the newspaper standpoint the school page serves as special home-reader appeal for its weakest editions. The school page specializes on diversity of information, names, activity pictures, and news of the parent-teacher association. It is an excellent means for a concentration of items that might otherwise escape attention if treated for their intrinsic news value. The support of a school page, however, is no reason for neglecting any other aspect of possible news placement. It may be considered as an excellent supplement to a general publicity policy.

DIFFICULTIES

There are a number of difficulties that the institution encounters in its press relations. One of the most important arises from the apparent inability of the educator to get the news man's point of view. Consequently there are frequent conflicts and a "bad press" results owing to purely personal reasons. The reporter receives the impression that he is being talked down and that the educator is a "stuffed shirt." The educator on his part tends to consider the reporter as something rather low that should be despised and scorned. These unfortunate interreactions resulting primarily from initial inability to understand each other may be easily overcome if each is willing to move half way. Possibly the best means of removing personal friction is through the development of social relations between school man and reporter. A luncheon or dinner table is an excellent place for relaxation and the development of understanding. Official relationships may for the time merge into purely mutual consideration of each other as human beings. If mutual respect and confidence can be established, one of the real difficulties in press relations may be easily surmounted.

Tell the Truth

Since the essence of successful institutional-press relationships is mutual confidence, the educator must realize that a newspaper wants the truth or all of the available facts and wishes to make its own judgment as to value. Both institution and press need never forget their respective functions, the one to do and the other to publicize and appraise. Any attempt by the institution to control news or direct editorial opinion is bound to end disastrously for the institution.

If the press is suspicious of the politics or activities of board of education members, that is both its right and privilege. There is so frequently good and sufficient reason for this attitude that institutional personnel need not be disturbed by the normal suspicion the newspaper man holds of local public officers. If the board of education or the schools get a "bad press," it is generally the fault of the board of education. If board members persist in carrying adolescent activities into adult public life, their personal differences and conflicts make good news. Operation of the board of education on the technique earlier presented will furnish few occasions for this type of reporting and consequently eliminate one possible difficulty.[1]

Avoid Boycott

Frequently a news story is neither appreciated nor understood. Teachers and board members react as if such criticism is almost in the category of sin. In their annoyance they sometimes urge a boycott of the offending paper or threaten to withhold news. Both methods are impractical and inadvisable. Circulation boycott will not be helpful in promoting friendliness since it is a direct threat at newspaper prosperity, and the withholding of news merely places the reporter in a position where he must defend himself. Both practices stimulate rather than harmonize conflict and may accordingly be placed among a number of other undesirable practices.

Misquoting

Another frequent difficulty arises out of what is frequently referred to as the misquoting of a speaker by a reporter. It may be used consciously as a device to secure public reaction, or it may be applied merely as a result of an emotional set toward the reporter. The fault probably lies midway between the two parties. The typical informal speaker seldom says exactly what he thinks he does. There is an audience stimulus about public speaking that carries away even seasoned speakers. After a man has talked for twenty minutes or longer without notes, he is not capable of determining the exact shade of coloring and meaning concerning what he did say. The reporter, even though only reasonably accurate, is probably just as certain of his hearing as the speaker is of his speech. Unless the speech has been transcribed directly, it is a question of the veracity of the two individuals. If the reported speech receives considerable critical comment, it is probably better for the speaker to let the incident pass. Raising the issue of being misquoted simply places the reporter on the defensive and questions his technical skill in understanding and transcribing, which

[1] See Chapter 8.

does not normally produce a friendly after-effect. If the speaker takes the story with a grin or possibly as a joke he runs fewer chances of being "misquoted" in the future than if he had created a conflict through repudiation. It is impossible to convince a professional news man of the sincerity of the speaker who cries "misquote" on the slightest provocation, and he receives little future consideration.

Avoid Exploitation

An ever present danger from the institutional side is the increasing demand for institutional coöperation with some press project. Circulation is so vital that few editors can escape the circulation department's demand for help in its expansion programs. Of recent years many of these plans have included the schools. Spelling bees, the stimulation of athletic events, debating contests, music contests, hobby shows, pet shows, and numerous other activities fall within this category. While these events may have some intrinsic value, it is a dubious procedure for the schools to ally themselves with private enterprise for the exploitation of children.[2] The real work of the school is inevitably affected by preparation for these events; in fact, in some instances, regular work practically stops while the activity is under way. If already involved in these "coöperative" ventures which are in actuality circulation drives, the institution finds it difficult to escape except through the slow but possible method of playing down child interest and allowing the teacher to use personal judgment with respect to time involved. The school that has been able to escape these newspaper importunities up to date is fortunate and by simulating willingness to participate, if time and program permit, may through gradual education turn away outside demands. There is no more reason why a newspaper should be permitted favors by a public institution any more than any other private enterprise. By maintaining a rigid neutrality policy applicable to all outside demands it should be possible to remain free.

[2] See, also, Chapter 15.

Personal Publicity

The personal publicity seeker more commonly known in newspaper parlance as a "publicity hound" is another bane of the free press. The public official who carries pictures of himself and family in his bill-fold so that they may be easily available to a willing reporter falls into this category. The superintendent or principal who leans heavily on the first person singular and seeks the spotlight of publicity may do well for a time, but sooner or later his trials will begin. The American news interest span is short. It is difficult for even the highest official to hold the front page continuously. Personal publicity is a most gossamer thing and emphasis upon it frequently creates a deep-seated suspicion of the institution and the remainder of its personnel. A publicity-seeking superintendent may easily nullify the efforts of many earnest teachers and principals who are seriously attempting to educate the public to the needs of the schools. There is an easy and simple way of avoiding this danger. Superintendent and principals may request that they be kept in the background and the institution given more prominence. Turning the newspaper's attention to child and parent activities is also a good method. This discussion is not an invitation for superintendents to go on camera-breaking sprees and to hide from public view, but merely to minimize their own personalities for the sake of institutional advancement.

SUMMARY

The newspaper is an extremely important extralegal agency through which institutional activity may be reported to the people. It also serves as a popular appraisal agency. An understanding of the function of the press makes it possible for the institution to recognize the right of the newspaper to criticize institutional practice. Admitting the importance of the newspaper as a molder of public opinion, public education should realize that it is only one of many agencies and, though important, not finally vital to the exclusion of everything else. The public school has at its disposal sufficient means and avenues for popular education of the adult so that even an adverse press need not be considered as a total handicap. The American psychology of protecting the underdog through a sense of fair play will generally come to the support of the schools if their confidence in its program and personnel can be maintained. There is nothing so fleeting as the effect of a critical news story or two and nothing quite so devastating and one-sided as a conflict between a newspaper and a public institution. The institution has little chance in this type of battle because its defense does not include this type of weapon. The strength of the school is in the minds of the people and not in the front page of the newspaper. It is good strategy never to fight a newspaper. Though a favorable press serves to extend the interpretative process, it is totally unnecessary for the schools to prostitute themselves to secure it. The best possible press relations result from institutional friendliness, honesty, and willingness to tell the truth. Over a long span of time these methods will prove superior to those of subservience. The public official needs a thick skin and a low sensitivity to criticism if he is to survive in a democratic order.

Chapter 22

SCHOOL PUBLICATIONS

WRITTEN devices form a large part of the contacts between school and community. In many instances the original purpose of these publications as interpretative agencies has been lost sight of because of their mechanical standardization. As a result many educational publications are completely useless for their primary purpose. This chapter will attempt to discuss the purpose, types, editorial methods, and circulation in terms of the following types: (1) annual reports, (2) diplomas and certificates, (3) financial reports, (4) house organs, (5) home contacts, (6) proceedings of the board of education, (7) school programs, (8) research bulletins, (9) school papers, (10) survey reports, and (11) pictorial material.

ANNUAL REPORTS

The oldest method of written reporting to the people is that form classified as the annual report. It is still required by law in many states and localities, and in some cases failure to present such report has been the technical reason for the dismissal of the superintendent. The annual report normally has two purposes, including the current reporting of conditions and needs and the laying up in condensed form an archival record of achievement. A generation ago much more space was devoted to a discussion of school needs. To-day the primary emphasis is on current conditions and achievements.

Types

Annual reports center around two principal types that may be considered as primarily archival and popular. The archival type usually includes the heavier reports in which attempt is made to carry out the statutory requirements for a complete report of happenings during the year, written for the record rather than for popular consumption. Each department or division makes an individual report to the executive and these are edited into a single volume preceded by a generalized statement prepared by the superintendent. They range in size from two hundred to nearly one thousand pages. St. Louis school reports fall in this general classification.

The second type is the completely popular report in which the story of the schools is told in pictures, with relatively little written material. They may "high spot" the entire range of school program or may present one section or major activity annually. Designed for popular consumption their archival value except for pictorial interest is distinctly limited. They represent a complete break with the conventional report and may thus be considered as heavy emphasis on the interpretative purpose. Cleveland and Milwaukee reports fall in this division.

A third type attempts to maintain balance between archival and interpretative interests by preparing a complete report in light journalistic style with tersely written narrative and 25 to 50 per cent of illustration. A recent second variation of this type presents the annual report in two sections, the first a popular pictorial survey of all school activities and the second part devoted to a satisfactory description of the year's events. Detroit reports for the past two decades are examples of both tendencies.

Editorial Methods

The conventional report is edited as a combination of individual reports, whereas the modern expression represents an impersonal product that is purely an organization achievement. The essential editorial need is timeliness. Reports that appear a year or more after the close of the school year have only archival value, but those that can be published within ninety days have direct news as well as current interpretative value.

It is entirely possible to produce the annual report within a short time after the end of a school year provided adequate provision is made within the organization for editing and preparing copy. Instead of making July 1 the deadline for the close of everything but statistical data, May 1 or June 1 may be chosen as the terminal point and all of the material prepared for final editing before the close of the year. If the report is developed sectionally, the final statistical interpretations may be added when completed. Pictures may be gathered throughout the year as they record the significant events or activities.

Circulation

The annual report has a significant but limited use in institutional interpretation. It is a relatively expensive production, and because of this fact and its general appeal the circulation is generally limited to schools, libraries, office holders, newspapers, and a limited key group of leaders including the clergy. Even the annual report as a pictorial presentation costs too much for general distribution. The best means of attracting mass attention to the annual report is through accompanying newspaper stories. Each section of the report may be developed into a good news or feature story at the time of writing. By careful organization of a publishing schedule it is possible to release these stories at regular intervals prior to publication of the total report. The report as a whole is worth only one news story upon publication, but by use of journalistic sectional previews it is possible to secure from six to a dozen good stories for each publication. Where possible, pictures may accompany the news stories.

Report Variations

There are numerous variations in printed information for adult use that may best be considered as aspects closely related to the annual report. These include the various types of bulletins and other material that are used to publicize phases of curricular activity or organization practice. One of the best recent illustrations of this type is the series of popular bulletins issued by the Baltimore public schools to describe the purpose, extent, and actual operation of various phases of the instructional program. They are issued periodically, confined to one group of activities, and form a means for developing adult interest in the work of the schools.

DIPLOMAS AND CERTIFICATES

The purpose of a certificate or diploma is to furnish each individual a record of his achievement in the schools. The certificate is either a semester or annual report of accomplishment, whereas the diploma represents evidence of graduation from either elementary, early, or later secondary school. The conventional certificate records a statement of promotion from one grade to another with or without information of relative achievement in subject marks, whereas the diploma conveniently classifies all holders as satisfactory in scholarship and of high moral character. Secondary-school diplomas are sometimes differentiated with respect to scholarship as *cum laude* and *magnum cum laude*.

In recent years there has been a distinct tendency away from the older eight by eleven, twelve by eighteen, and eighteen by twenty-four inch "sheepskin" that, in substantial frames, graced the walls of the American home of the nineties and early decades of the twentieth century to a small folder with protective art leather cover possible of easy filing and also of use as a credential. This tendency is a happy trend toward practicality.

Diploma Weaknesses

The school diploma has a generalized achievement meaning to the average adult. Children frequently make use of this record as a credential in seeking employment. The adult is inclined to take it at face value and is unable to make clear differentiation of low, medium, or high capacity. Since the diplomas are all standardized into one form, the employer has difficulty in ascertaining exactly what the graduate is prepared to do or his possible level of achievement. If high-school graduation is taken as the basis for employment in terms of what the adult conceives secondary-school attainments to be and the graduate fails in his job, the normal emotional reaction of the employer is to consider the school liable. So long as the school offers only a vague and generalized credential, it is difficult to avoid rise of these opinions. Explanations after the fact are really of little avail, regardless of possible facts, and it is far better practice to avoid misunderstandings through correction of existing weaknesses.

Diploma Possibilities

The secondary-school population is no longer a selected cross-section of high intelligence but rather a popular school that ministers to a wide range of ability. This change in the nature of the American secondary school is not yet clear to the business man. It is therefore desirable to differentiate on the diploma as to capacity and achievement of the individual. A possible institutional answer that supplementary material is readily available to the employer does not meet the condition. The individual normally presents that credential which has the greatest potential value to him and which receives the most respectful attention.

It is possible to improve upon the European diploma or continuing certificate, which indicates the specific courses completed, by providing on the reverse of the American document a statement of the curriculum pursued and the achievement in that curriculum, together with a general statement of the probable level of competency in the field of preparation. It is merely a question of telling the truth about the graduate's record and recording it as part of the final graduation certificate. Such a procedure would prevent many a professional and business man's reaction as to the general efficiency of the public secondary school.

In a few large cities where the guidance and placement activity is highly developed these precautions may be unnecessary, but for the large majority of local school systems specific statements concerning capacity and skills are quite desirable.

FINANCIAL REPORTS

Financial reports include technical accounting and budget statements to the board of education and popular expressions of these statements for the people in general. The typical financial statements presented to the people through the medium of the annual report are difficult to understand and, as an observing layman recently expressed it, are "designed to retard rather than promote understanding." Financial reports to the board of education must continue to be technical although even these may be considerably improved and their effectiveness increased. Summary reports for popular consumption either by direct circulation or through the medium of newspaper stories should be complete, simple, and capable of meaningful translation.

Types

There are three general types of financial reports including current statements of expenditures and balances, balance sheets, and budget reports. Each of these may be considered as designed for either board of education or popular consumption. In general both phases should be organized and presented in terms of objectives and service rather than presented purely as statistical compilations.

Finance is a delicate field in public administration and requires great skill to make it intelligible both to the board member and to the layman. Though the board member is interested and must receive much detailed financial information, the general public is not technically interested and has little capacity for interpretation.

The board of education should be continuously informed with respect to the financial condition in order that it may be constantly aware of actual conditions. The first contact is through the budget. Educational budgets usually encounter some difficulty because of their method of presentation. A budget is merely the translation of current educational policies into money and cannot be presented except as such translation. The superintendent is only the executive agent through whom the translation is accomplished. The budget is by no stretch of the imagination the superintendent's personal report any more than legally adopted educational policies can be so considered. The initial task is to build the budget so that the board members are constantly confronted with the fact that required expenditures result from some action of their own instead of arising from the active imagination of the superintendent. The superintendent, even in his official presentation of the budget, must be extremely careful to subordinate the personal element and orient himself purely as an executive agent in "preparing the budget of the public schools in accord with board of education policy." This technique of presentation makes it difficult for individual board members to shift responsibility for cost increases to the executive.

All financial information necessary for complete consideration should appear in the technical budget which may be effectively prepared in three divisions, the first containing a generalized statement of required expenditures and anticipated income, the second a detailed analysis by activities and subactivities, and the third section providing all detailed information upon which the first and second parts have been built.[1]

This form permits the board member who gives only casual attention to finance to secure an overview. For those desirous of more detailed information the activity analysis is available, and finally the minority leader or the "watchdog-of-the-treasury" type has all supporting detail available through which he can carefully and minutely check each computation.

The theory behind this presentation is to keep board attention on finance as an extension of policy rather than stimulating the typical woodpecker method of pecking at and isolating minor items apart from educational policy. The smart executive can protect himself from board of education or community criticism by keeping the issue of financial need strictly on a policy basis. The professional staff need not be presented to the board as individuals but rather as positions, and thus prevent personality sniping.

Either during or after adoption a popular budget may be prepared in non-technical form which tells the teachers and the people in simple language the purposes for which the money will be expended. If the popular budget is prepared after official adoption,

---

[1] For detailed study of functional technical budget, see Arthur B. Moehlman and Philip C. Lovejoy, *The Budget Procedure of the Hamtramck, Michigan, Public Schools*, Research Studies No. IV (Hamtramck, Published by the Board of Education, 1931).

See also Arthur B. Moehlman, *Public School Finance* (Rand, McNally and Co., 1927), Chs. XI, XVI, XVII, and XVIII.

provision for public budget hearings should be made by the board of education during which any interested persons may appear and express their views or merely listen to the discussion. Those individuals or groups who have capacity and show interest may be invited to study the complete technical budget. An excellent example of a popular budget issued prior to official adoption but, by its contents limited in appeal to the leader group, is that used in recent years in Rochester, New York. However, even simpler and shorter budgets are necessary if complete community coverage is desired.

Balance Sheets

Simple interpretative balance sheets may well follow the recent practice of banks in popularizing a statement of financial condition to the people through newspaper publication. The major items may be rendered in non-technical terminology. In addition to publication in the press, it is desirable to print both condensed budget and balance sheet as a popular leaflet as information readily available on request.

Monthly Statements

Monthly statements of appropriations, expenditures, and balances are desirable for the board of education. These reports permit a board to keep close account of progressive expenditure in routine manner and act as possible checks against overdrafts or the incurrence of deficits.

HOUSE ORGANS

The purpose of the house organ is to maintain contacts between central office and the field as a supplement to desirable personal contact, to develop group morale and solidarity, to stimulate growth and to serve as a means of conveying definite information to the executive agents. It is primarily a device for internal organization use in personnel management and should thus be considered as a secondary means in institutional interpretation. The publication must be representative of the entire organization, playing no favorites and permitting the maintenance of continual departmental balance. The interests of the clerical and custodial personnel are relatively just as important as are those of the teachers.

Types

The house organ may be either mimeographed or printed. In smaller systems there is a tendency toward the former because of cost. The two dominant types are the newspaper and magazine, of which the latter is also frequently classified as a bulletin. In frequency of publication it varies from weekly to monthly. If it is combined with a news bulletin, weekly publication may be desirable, but general preference appears to be for two issues a month.

The house organ as a distinctly local publication may present national and state educational high spots in digest form, but it is probably better policy to leave this field to the numerous specialized publications covering teaching and administrative interest.

The house organ has diverse purposes that should be expressed in the publication. It should serve as a means of bringing official news to the field, but these announcements may be wisely limited to things of general interest which cannot easily be covered by the principals. Many teachers desire a medium through which questions may be asked and problems discussed, and the house organ serves excellently for that purpose. It is also important as a morale builder.

Since it is desirable to keep the house organ bright and sprightly so that high interest may be maintained, it is doubtful whether highly technical material can be effectively presented. Results of research and experimentation may best be developed in separate monograph form where condensation is unnecessary and single interest may be attained. Teacher suggestions form a distinctly valuable part of the publication and should be encouraged.

Methods of Editing

As an official administrative organ editorial control will probably rest in administration. Careful observation of practice throughout the country leads to the belief that more effective results are possible if the activity is made representative and coöperative in character. A good means of developing interest and providing excellent training for different individuals is to supplement the editor with an editorial committee or board representative of all the major interests in the school system. If the term of office of editorial board members is staggered and made rotative, it is possible to provide training for many persons for a period of years.

Some executives still incline to the belief that all contributions, except the official news, should be anonymous. If the personnel objective is given consideration, it is difficult to maintain this point of view. One of the fundamental objectives for the house organ in personnel management should be the stimulation of individual effort and the provision of means through which all possible credit and recognition be given the teachers. It should be a fundamental tenet of educational journalism that every one is entitled to express a rational opinion or point of view provided he is willing to assume personal responsibility. On all counts, the impersonal policy in the editing of house organs belongs to the past.

In a study of teachers' reactions to house organs, Stevenson found that the following five items of publication ranked highest: educational news and teaching information, official calendar and news, articles by teachers, editorials and financial information. The following rated lowest: reports of other systems, pictures, "clipped" humor, and cartoons.[2]

Circulation

The primary circulation of the house organ is to all professional and non-professional employees of the school and to members of the board of education. Secondary circulation as a direct interpretative agency may include the press, members of lay advisory groups such as the educational advisory commission, the parent-teacher association, and leaders of other interest groups within the community.

[2] Fred G. Stevenson, *The House Organ in City School Administration*. Unpublished doctoral dissertation, University of Michigan, 1932.

HOME-CONTACTS REPORTS

The purpose of the home-contacts report is to promote greater understanding between home and school through keeping the parents intelligently informed of the child's progress. It may be considered as mechanical means which have for its basic purpose the stimulation of increased personal relations between parent and teacher. In practice, purpose has unfortunately become confused with protection, to the detriment of home relations.

Though the periodic home report was originally designed as a means of maintaining liaison between home and school and keeping the parents continuously informed of the progress of the child, it was standardized at an early date both for convenience and economy. Used at first only in the elementary schools it later became a definite part of secondary-school home contacts. The pointing was different in the secondary school, and in too many cases the original purpose was submerged in its consideration as an institutional defense mechanism. Children could not be failed in their work unless the parents had been previously notified. Many conflicts between teachers and irate parents informed the secondary institution of this fact. As a result the home report became largely a series of negative contacts informing the parents only that the student was remiss in certain phases of the curricular offering. Even these negative contacts were formalized to such an extent that only the name of the child, the subject involved, and the teacher's name were required to complete the home report. The school expected poor work and built a printed report around its expectations!

The fact that students intercepted these reports apparently mattered little. The school had a record of notification, and it was safe from attack. Neither did it appear important whether the individuals springing from diverse cultural groups within a school district could actually read the report. As a result of institutional attitude the home report has degenerated considerably from its fundamental purpose and to-day forms one of the weakest links in the home contacts chain.

Types

The most frequently used type of home-contacts report is that employed in the elementary schools and tells on a standardized form what the teacher's opinion of the child's standing in a series of subjects has been during a period of four to eight weeks. Many secondary schools still report only failures, using the mails instead of the child as messenger service.

In recent years a number of efforts have been made to improve the conventional report by expansion. These tendencies may be generalized as increasing the size from one to four pages and reporting separately in greater detail achievement in subject-matter, activities, and citizenship. Achievement is still expressed in grades and some study of "citizenship" indicates that it is chiefly old man "deportment" in a new dress. Though highly indicative of desirable tendencies in weaning many from mechanized practice, these new reports still fall short of possibilities.

Voluntary schools widely separated from their patrons have been experimenting for some time with personal letters to parents at regular intervals. A few experimental and public schools have also done exploratory work in this field. These letters attempt in a very friendly way to give a generalized statement of the child's progress and relative achievement. In most cases progress is still measured in terms of the class achievement, though they also attempt to present progress based on individual capacity. Generalization is followed by specific comment on weakness and strength so that the parent receives a fairly complete impression. Superior achievement is emphasized as well as shortcomings. In this manner standardization has been replaced by individualized reports, and the old defense mechanism has practically disappeared.

Method

Since the schools should consider home contacts as a means of increasing understanding and stimulating greater coöperation in the interests of improvement of institution-home relationships and the instructional process, it is doubtful whether the standardized home-contacts form of whatever description has much value. The personal letter written not more than twice a semester has greater potentiality, provided that it is intelligently prepared. There is no need for these materials to be "gushy," saccharine, or "Pollyanna" in type. They may be written so that the parent understands the progress of the child and will be stimulated to coöperate through personal visitation and discussion of problems. They need not be longer than three hundred words and may be considered as containing four distinct parts: generalization, diagnostic reference to weakness, description of strength, and suggestions for improvement. If their institutional preparation is staggered, it should be possible for the home-room teacher to prepare them without large increase in school clerical service.

Unfortunately even the substitution of the personal letter for the conventional home-contacts report is not sufficient in many areas. City schools are handicapped by parents who use only some foreign language. Even a letter, unless it can be translated into the home language, is of little value here. Contact with the immigrant parent may be better made by the visiting teacher, provided that persons selected for this purpose are familiar with foreign customs and the home language. This adjustment of the school to adult language problems appears to be a sensible procedure. There is little merit in the contention of some educators that the American language is English; evening schools teach English and therefore the foreign-born parents must first learn English before satisfactory home relations may be established.

General Letters

Prior to the depression there were certain tendencies toward a generalized type of home contacts through so-called letters to parents prepared by the superintendent.[3] They were generally four-page leaflets five by seven inches in size, explaining to the parents the nature and function of the public school. Their value as personal contacts was limited by the fact that any printed material is necessarily mechanical and lacks the warmth of a personal letter. City

[3] For good examples see Detroit and Hamtramck, Michigan.

superintendents who used them felt that they were of considerable help.

These written contacts are unnecessary in the small community, and might be made much more personal in the large community if the general pattern were set by the central office, but the actual signing and delivery of this information decentralized within the elementary attendance districts. Some of the modern processes for producing personal letters by mass reproduction are superior to printing. Since the superintendent is a very shadowy figure in the large city, the principal in his direct relationship to the children and the family is much more favorably situated to make a personal appeal of this type. In general, however, less stress should be placed upon the value of written or printed material and much more upon personal contacts. The printed or written word is a mighty poor substitute for the warmth of human personality.

PROCEEDINGS OF THE BOARD OF EDUCATION

The proceedings of the board of education are an official record or journal in which are recorded the legal actions of the local educational legislative body as a basis for executive authority. Every board of education keeps a legal journal although many of them are quite rudimentary in form and never see the light of day.

Types

The official proceedings of the board of education may vary in type from handwritten entries in a journal ledger to highly organized cross-referenced printed proceedings which contain very full and accurate accounts of group action at regular and special meetings. These proceedings are much more condensed than the journals of state legislatures and the national congress and are not verbatim reports of the entire meeting.

Methods

Rural and very small communities usually enter the minutes of meetings in a journal ledger by long hand. These entries are so sketchy that they occasionally give rise to legal difficulties. Many school districts in medium-sized cities keep typewritten proceedings and also publish the condensed minutes in some local paper within a week after the meeting. Large cities print their official journal in loose-leaf form, binding them together in annual volumes, and some also publish the proceedings in the official community newspaper.

Possibilities of Use

The journal of the board of education is the only official legal record available to the people. It has considerable value in the interpretative activity as a means of informing the people constantly of official action taken by their popular representatives. It is highly desirable that these proceedings be given the widest publicity. A board of education should keep sufficient copies of its own records in either mimeographed or printed form so that copies are readily available for inspection in the superintendent's office, the individual school buildings, and in the public library. If the school district is sufficiently large to justify the printing of the official journal, its circulation may be extended to a selected list of community leaders and made available as reference to the people through banks, drugstores, and other outlets to which people go for specific information. It is exceedingly good practice to provide also for official publication in one of the local papers that has been contractually accepted as the official reporting medium. In addition to the publication of the proceedings it is desirable, even where the law does not require, also to publish printed notice of requests for bids for the purchase of materials and supplies.

SCHOOL PROGRAMS

Printed, duplicated, or mimeographed programs are features of nearly every school system regardless of size. They are prepared as guides to such events as athletic contests, dramatics, musical programs, commencements, exhibits, fairs, and a number of miscellaneous happenings.

Types

The most general type is a clear-cut presentation of program with possibly some art work or a picture of the school or an activity. They usually contain both information and names. The residual appeal is in the names of the participants which parents usually delight in collecting even if kept only until the next general housecleaning.

Possibilities

Every program may be considered as having several interpretative possibilities. The first is the appeal of the program itself, and the second is the possibility of presenting in a few brief paragraphs something about the work of the school, an invitation to parents to visit the building or to join the parent-teacher association. Buffalo schools used this method extensively over a period of years to stimulate school visitation with unusually effective results. Other schools have availed themselves of this opportunity to give briefly either the generalized objectives of the school or a popular analysis of purposes for which tax money was spent. Greater popular appeal may be secured through preparing these programs as classroom projects in fine arts and in language classes, reducing expense and creating greater parental interest.

Circulation

The circulation is limited to the audience although some school systems use unusually attractive programs as special mailing pieces.

RESEARCH PUBLICATIONS

Research and experimentation may produce interesting results. If these activities are to be of value to the entire system, they must be publicized. One method frequently employed is to prepare special monographs devoted to the reporting of a specific project. The purpose of such publication is primarily to present information to the teaching personnel for information and stimulation.

Possible Use

The use of the technical publication is limited rather narrowly to the teaching profession and possibly a small group of technically capable laymen. The production of results of conditions or experimental exploration is also desirable as institutional responsibility in making this fresh information available to teacher-training centers. Popular appeal and interest may be secured through the translation of results into straight news stories and also through speaking.

SCHOOL PUBLICATIONS

School publications include the newspaper, the magazine, the yearbook, and handbook. In some cases the newspaper, magazine, and handbook are combined effectively into a single quarterly publication.[4] They exist in profusion in all sizes of school districts, varying only in scope and quality. The primary purpose of the newspaper is to serve as a terminal and integrative activity for certain curricular activity and as experience in the art of written communication. The school magazine attempts in similar manner through publication of the children's creative efforts to provide an outlet for literary expression in the same manner that the better professional publications do, whereas the yearbook is merely a means of recording for individual and institutional use all of the interesting information concerning a specific class. The secondary-school handbook is a means for bringing purpose, regulations, and other essential school information before the student.

Possible Use

The use of school publications in the field of adult interpretation is distinctly limited if these publications remain true to their fundamental purposes. There is a possible indirect value in so far as the adult develops an interest through stimulation by the child. It is desirable also as a definite interpretative policy to maintain these publications within their normal educational niche and to eliminate

[4] See DeVilbiss High School *Digest*, Toledo.

undesirable exploitation through worship of the championship cult or use as a direct organ for institutional or professional promotion.[5]

SCHOOL SURVEYS

Periodically many school systems engage in survey activity of the internal or external type. The internal survey arises as a result of the board of education's policy to provide for specific information concerning aspects of current functioning or a continuing research into the entire program as a basis for long-time planning. The internal survey may be carried on by the professional organization itself or with the assistance of specialized consulting service. The outside specialist in this case acts as advisor to the board of education and the executive and not as judge and jury. The outside survey generally arises from a feeling of uncertainty by either community or board of education as to the effectiveness of organization plans, procedures, and outcomes. It represents an appraisal by a presumably judicial personnel that has no connection with the school system.

Methods

The method of the internal survey is through quiet examination and study to determine the effectiveness of program and to make plans for its improvement. There is no pressure or flaring publicity. The internal survey is presumably a democratic procedure whereby operating personnel through its own leadership assisted by capable special technicians may become aware of its needs and voluntarily accept the implications of change. The outside survey frequently degenerates into a witch hunt. Too many surveyors favoring and participating in this form of investigation feel that justification for their employment is the location and high publicizing of low spots. They step out of their true function of advisor to become judge. The typical outside survey is accompanied by a current stream of front-page publicity. It is impossible to produce a finality of judgment from the type of activity that most frequently characterizes the outside surveys. Financial limitations make thorough study

[5] See, also, Chapter 15.

impossible, and the artificial attempts to secure a constant stream of front-page news mean that the "expert" must find something wrong. Too frequently the outside survey operates on the theory that "sin is news." Although there is a specific place for the outside survey, its typical procedure pattern may produce unfortunate negative results in institutional interpretation, although in an apparently accidental way much personal publicity accrues to the surveyor. Some of these professional surveyors even carry their publicity specialists with them.

Possible Use

Properly conducted, both the inside and the outside surveys have high potential interpretative value. The possible psychological effect on the community is that its institutional activities are constantly under scrutiny to provide betterment. They provide objective information with which lay criticism may either be controverted or proved to be right. The inside survey through progressive attack on various problems furnishes the means for dignified publication not only of results but also of plans for improvement. The outside survey may confirm the doubts of the board of education or community or may disprove them. Either result is worth while. To be really helpful and to secure organization coöperation the outside survey needs to revise its typical high-pressure type of investigation and publicity.

Circulation

The circulation of technical survey reports is naturally limited. These technical studies must be translated to invite popular appeal.

PICTORIAL MATERIAL

Pictorial material includes motion pictures and "stills" for the purpose of presenting varied institutional activities for both teacher and adult layman. Their primary purpose is to increase the effectiveness of speaking. The use of pictures eliminates the necessity for actual child demonstration in unusual places, before strange groups and in the evening when the pre-adolescent particularly is better off in bed. As demonstration material the pictures attempt to eliminate possible adult criticism of breaking child routine for adult pleasure. They also represent a convenient means for describing to a group in one section of the community activities taking place in other sections or in neighboring communities.

Types

There are two types of pictures including the motion film and the progressive projection of "stills" in a sequence that may be easier for comprehension. Both rapid and slow motion pictures are employed, and the "still" may also present an actual activity or pictorial summarization of research findings.

Possible Use

The first use of pictures is as a means of interpreting differentiation of program to teachers and represents a type of in-service training material. It is surprising how little the typical teacher in a large city system knows about what is taking place in different sections of the community. Both types of pictures may be used effectively as demonstration material. Methods employed in other school systems and experimental centers may be brought before the local teachers by use of this agency. A second possibility is to bring examples of good procedure to the teacher-training institution so that the personnel in training may secure visual contact with programs as they are carried out under actual field conditions.[5]

A secondary and very important use is supplementing discussion by board of education, parents, and other adult groups with actual demonstration. The layman may listen attentively to the best prepared professional presentation, but misses much unless he can also observe at the same time evidence of the activity in actual functioning. Contact with the outside educational world through pictures is an excellent educational device.

Unless a very general presentation is desired, these films should be normally confined to the illustration of a single activity in sev-

---

[5] See George A. Stracke, "Around the Clock in a 2A Classroom," *The Nation's Schools,* Vol. 20, No. 4 (October, 1937), pp. 18-21.

eral different aspects of functioning. Concentration around a single activity or even a phase of activity is much more fruitful in both illustrative and retentive possibilities than more diversified material.

SUMMARY

Every school system presents a large variety of possibilities in printed material which may have an immediate or secondary value in the interpretative program. The extent to which a particular system uses these media of communication will be conditioned by the size of district and the specific types of problems present. No hard and fast rules for specific use are desirable. Certain general interpretative principles may be followed in any type of publication but sufficient freedom must be permitted to adjust to current need. Mechanical standardization is a handicap rather than a help in school publications. Care should be taken to maintain every type within its desirable functional area and to refrain from any plan which may tend to reduce their interpretative effectiveness. Publications are expensive and should be employed only when sufficiently reasonable assurance of their general effectiveness is possible. They are distinctly supplementary to personal contacts and may be considered as stimulants to the increase of understanding not only through the printed or pictured word but in increasing the possible range of personal contacts. Both motion and "still" pictures have interpretative possibilities that may be extensively explored.

Chapter 23

THE SCHOOL PLANT

UNLIKE other phases of interpretation, the school buildings in any community are tangible and concrete. They represent the use of land and building materials formed into permanent structures, and most of them are too large to be easily hidden. They are part of the total community social effort and not at all isolated or separate. They stand day and night as physical evidence of an activity and of an ideal. Since school buildings are merely a physical agency through which public education of children and adults is carried on, they are finally important only as they serve this purpose. Their character, extent, and type will be determined at any time directly by the educational policies in operation and the number of children and adults to be instructed or cared for in other ways.

The interpretation of an institution is dependent to a large degree upon visual symbols. The physical plant has always been and always will be the symbol of public education. In fact the "little red schoolhouse" has become so sentimental a symbol of an earlier phase of education that it acts to-day as an emotional brake on the rapidity of change. The school plant is one of the most essential and most valuable agencies in any program of interpretation, and it is also one of the most neglected. In too many cases it is definitely a center of actual conflict.

The school plant will be considered as an interpretative agency from the standpoint of: (1) function, (2) changing school-plant concepts, (3) conflicts, (4) elimination of conflicts, and (5) use as an interpretative agency.

SCHOOL-PLANT FUNCTION

The school building is a translation of curricular needs into permanent form. It expresses through brick, stone, and mortar the work and the ideals of a democratic system of education. To the extent that it reflects them effectively it is a mute but eloquent agency. School buildings should be both useful and beautiful. Use without beauty is a degeneration of function. Usefulness is determined by the skill in educational designing; beauty is a function of architecture and landscaping.

Evolved from our meaning of education and in conformity with the best thought in architectural achievement, the school building should represent more than stark utility. It must first of all be useful or serve truly its fundamental purpose in the facilitation of instruction; it must be built primarily around the needs of the child as expressed through the curriculum. The ideals of education demand, second, that the school-house be inspirational in form and in general impression. To inspire, the school building should be beautiful, and since the highest expression of pure beauty is simplicity, this fourth characteristic will also reflect the spirit of democracy. Harmony with itself and its surroundings is the fifth essential. Usefulness, inspiration, beauty, simplicity, and harmony are the determining factors in school-house construction if the American school is to fulfil its basic functions of educating children and adults and leaving the imprint of its idealism upon the community.

If the aims of public education are translated into Ruskin, the school building must meet these tests: "The high and ennobling art of architecture is that of giving to buildings, whose parts are determined by necessity, such forms and colors as shall delight the mind.... The nobility of each building depends on its special fitness for its own purposes." Or further, "We require from buildings, as from men, two kinds of goodness: first, the doing their practical duty well; then, that they be graceful and pleasing in doing it."

CHANGING SCHOOL-PLANT CONCEPTS

The field of public educational activity within a community is complicated just to the extent that life has become complicated. Education is the means by which each generation should be adjusted to the environmental conditions under which we must live. So long as we desire to maintain the democratic way of life, on which all of our growth and development since the birth of the nation has taken place, it is fundamentally necessary to provide for public education in accord with the needs of each generation. So long as social change continues, public education needs will also change, for they are at all times only a reflection of community life about us.

Educational Change

The educational requirements are changing so rapidly that the typical existing school plant is no longer representative or adequate for the present, let alone the future. Since the purpose of education is to prepare the child for effective social living, all of these major economic and social changes will result in corresponding social change in our schools. The next few years will see many new developments in the curriculum, in methodology, in administration, and in the physical plant. Provision must be made for intelligent use of leisure and for the continued education of adults both for vocational and recreational ends. It will be necessary to provide means whereby the local neighborhood groups can meet regularly in their schools for the study of governmental and local problems, for play and recreation, and for creative expression in the shops and the fine-arts studios.

Larger Sites

The future school plant must have larger sites. Fifteen to twenty acres will be necessary for elementary schools and twenty to forty acres for secondary buildings. The community school will be obliged to provide recreation space for both children and adults. The new site must also have space so that the building may be adequately landscaped and screened from the street and the neighbors. Many of the school's troubles have grown out of difficulties that playing children provided for the neighbors. Noise and other annoyance of the school site may be almost completely eliminated by the proper use of planting for screening purposes. A school site that looks like a park will increase rather than diminish surrounding property values.

Nature aids in softening architectural lines, and planting also has acoustical value.

The corridor educational exhibit has teaching value for the students and interpretative value for the adult.

School Gardens

The school site will also have a garden and conservatory where flowers and other desirable plantings may be propagated by the community as an incentive to home gardening. A botanist or school gardener will provide leadership for the development of home gardening for the sheer pleasure of watching things grow and reveling in the gorgeousness of nature. On summer evenings the children and adults of the neighborhood may bring their instruments for good music in that part of the site set apart as a grove. An outdoor theatre will also provide means for neighborhood pageants and theatrical presentation. Each school site will offer abundant means for individual and group expression and for the constructive use of leisure in favorable weather.

More fundamental changes will take place in the building itself. As stated earlier, a building is merely a concrete expression of teaching needs and teaching practices. The minute divisions of subject-matter will probably disappear in the very near future to be more generally succeeded by larger divisions, each of which provides for continuity from the pre-primary years through the junior college or higher secondary education. These curricular changes will greatly affect the current typical school building. Most of them may even now be found in progressive centers.

Health Education

To provide for health education there must be gymnasiums, swimming pools, sun rooms to secure the benefit of the ultra-violet rays, rest rooms, cafeterias, dental and medical clinics. Specialized units will have apparatus designed to assist those unfortunates who have been crippled by disease or accident. Every means to enable a child to develop a healthy physical body will logically become a part of the school plant.

On the instructional side many changes will take place. There will be more specialized classrooms and more small centers where children may work individually or in small groups. Instead of segregating the hard-of-hearing, the partially blind, and those of low mentality, provided they are stable emotionally, these atypical children will be given their training with specialized physical facilities within the community school. Since these youngsters must learn to live with people who are free from physical and mental defects, they must learn in school to adjust to each other, instead of growing up as social misfits because of segregation. There are many social activities in which the entire group may participate, and special classrooms and apparatus may be supplied to meet their peculiar individual needs.

School Clinics

Since much of the success of the new school will depend on how much the teaching staff knows of the individual child in his many and diverse aspects, provision must be made for many clinics for dental, medical, and neurological investigation and care, and for psychological, sociological, and instructional investigations. Children will not compete against each other in terms of the old mass instruction, but individual achievement will be measured on the rate of growth possible to his own inborn capacities and potentialities. Children who do not learn easily or who show great variations in learning will not be dismissed as in the past because they annoy the teacher, but will be studied by medical, psychological, endocrinological, educational, and sociological specialists to determine cause and to provide remedies.

For the social sciences in the typical community, provisions must be made for small but effective anthropological or cultural museums where material showing the economic, social, and ethical evolution of man may be displayed and constantly used as visual accessories. In the exact sciences, there will also be provision for many visual exhibits, including the fields of physics and chemistry and that of biology. In the natural sciences particularly there will be provision for small but carefully chosen zoos through which the children may study the life cycles of various animal forms and types.

Fine Arts

The fine arts, that curricular division whose object will be to provide means for individual appreciation, esthetics, and self-expression, will demand a large extension of facilities. Laboratories for drawing, ceramics, metal work, and modeling will form a necessary part of the adult's work as well as that of the child. There will be an art gallery in which copies of the treasures of the ages may be shown. Whether these exhibits will be placed in the corridors and rooms or in special rooms will depend largely on local policy.

Auditoriums or little theatres are essential for adult as well as child activity. These rooms will also be used for community meetings, for social and political forums, for the school of the future must provide means whereby the political education of the entire community can be carried on continuously. No longer will it be considered desirable to exclude political discussion from the schools because of its "bad influences upon the children." Instead, each school building will become a laboratory in practical democracy and will serve as the primary unit in political activity.

Though the emphasis will probably be shifted from directly vocational to pre-vocational and exploratory courses in the shops, there will be an increase in these mechanical laboratories. They will serve as means of expression both for adults and children. Here child and adult will be enabled to express themselves in wood and metal and to carry on their manual hobby activities. Opportunities will be offered for small groups to work together on individual and group ideas.

School Library

Last of all, but decidedly not least, is the need for an adequate library in every school. The library should be one of the finest and most attractive rooms in a building with plenty of quiet corners (and an open wood fire, if possible) in which one may read for sheer enjoyment. The shelves will be filled not only with reference books but also with the finest printed expressions of that which marks the best creative efforts of men in all countries and in all times. These libraries can be specifically provided with one section of books bearing on parenthood and intelligent living within the family.

SCHOOL-PLANT CONFLICTS

Despite the unusual importance of the school plant, it is to-day one of the low spots in the general scheme of interpretation. Little or no preparation has yet been made to adjust popular concepts to the needs of the changing plant; even the present structures are centers of very serious conflicts. These conflicts may be considered as: (*a*) economic; (*b*) physical; (*c*) social; and (*d*) nuisance.

Economic Conflicts

Community differences of opinion concerning buildings have their inception around the methods employed in securing them. Too many structures are still planned on the basis of political expediency or monumental urge. Planning of this character is bound to result in wide differences of opinion and much emotion. Even when carefully conceived with respect to need, the conventional method of securing approval results in difficulties. Most buildings are paid for through borrowing. Authority to borrow is generally derived from a high-pressure campaign that rises to a climax in a carefully timed election. These campaigns make for much division of community opinion. In the heat of the campaign many statements are made by those who favor the project and by those who are opposed. It is very difficult to keep their discussions objective. They soon begin to revolve around personalities and tend to center on a few individuals. The exposed leader easily becomes the sacrifice as many a superintendent has discovered to his sorrow.

There is usually little emphasis on ultimate costs in these campaigns. They develop the general impression that borrowing is not expensive. The second conflict, when the full realization of cost is finally brought home to the taxpayer, is one that may require years to eliminate. The American citizen may forgive much but seldom forgets what he considers unwarranted attempts upon his pocket-book. In many states the program of administrative reorganization has practically come to a standstill because the conventional methods of borrowing for large central schools have made the farmer and suburbanite cold to change. The campaign for a new building may win easy initial approval, but the long continued disgruntled and critical attitude engendered toward the school may handicap its program for many years to come.

The typical board of education and superintendent are not highly skilled in problems concerned with school buildings. They frequently pay too much for poorly designed and cheaply constructed buildings. The amateur does not understand educational designing or building specifications. As a result much is left out of a building either by accident or design. Making the building usable requires additional expenditures which list as "extras." Even though explained as intelligently as possible, the layman does not understand these "extras" and criticism quickly starts. Local newspapers can make much of these incidents. The board of education is easily placed in an unenviable position. In addition to ignorance, there is frequently considerable dishonesty in the erection of buildings. Architecture, like every other profession, has its share of members whose ethical principles are low. The construction trades have more than their share. Board of education members are also sometimes involved for direct financial or political benefit, but contrary to general impressions, graft in public building does not always involve money for all participating individuals. In general, too much public construction is still secured at prices far in advance of what the people should pay.

Physical Conflicts

School buildings cannot be successfully hidden. If mistakes have been made, they stand out glaringly. The people can always refresh their memories by looking at them. Conflicts resulting from size and location are frequent. In a certain community, a new building was planned some years ago on an imposing site high above the surrounding territory. Plans were made to flood light it at night so that the school would stand constantly as a symbol of public education. Extra care was taken to make the architectural design worthy. In an extra effort to secure the best results, the architect unwisely designed each of the portico columns as a solid piece of stone instead of laying them up in blocks. This item was missed in checking the plans, and the extra cost was rather high. It was soon discovered and community feeling ran high. Up to a year ago, the board of education had not lighted the building at night, possibly still fearful that there might be a community reaction.

School buildings, with few exceptions, dwarf surrounding buildings. Since too little care is exercised in securing sufficiently large sites, many structures are poorly placed and do not improve the neighborhood. Peculiar architecture, much applied ornament, or monumental expressions quickly transfer themselves into severe criticism and sometimes into serious conflict. If stone is used when the community thinks of brick; if large units, such as auditorium and gymnasium, tend to dwarf the conventional classrooms; if extravagance seems indicated by the internal design, then the way is open to long continued community conflict that may even develop into bitter feuds.

Conflicts frequently develop over location and may be long continued. Owing to neglect in the past, many school buildings have actually resulted in the depression of adjacent property values. Large, ugly, poorly designed and poorly placed buildings do not improve the neighborhood. Residents who find the selling prices of their homes diminished as a result cannot be expected to remain friendly to the cause of depreciation. From the building to the instructional program and teaching personnel is a short span for this conflict.

Social Conflicts

Internal arrangements of school buildings lend themselves to gossip which in turn may affect the entire educational activity adversely. Many highly conventional administrators insist on solid doors for both classrooms and offices. Frequently these are also locked when in use. The teaching profession is so highly feminized that the typical male teacher or principal must, so far as the public and children are concerned, exercise extreme care over his relationships with colleagues of the opposite sex. Any physical conditions which produce secrecy or seclusion tend to accentuate gossip possibilities. Closed and locked doors, poor placement of office furniture, and indiscretion in personal conferences have ruined the career of many an innocent principal and superintendent.

Nuisance Conflicts

Difficulties under the nuisance classification result from noise, traffic, trespass, and vandalism. Changing school programs have brought with them problems of noise. The playground and gymnasium are ordinarily very noisy. The extensive development of instrumental and vocal music provides problems within and outside of the building. Budding violinists and saxophone players have spoiled many a beautiful friendship. During part of the year shop windows are open, and machines and tools create much noise. In many places the cafeteria is so placed that the neighborhood is annoyed both by noise and the odor of burning refuse. Noise is a most potent source of conflict especially since school buildings are frequently in use during the evening as well as during the day. Any neighbor, whose normal right to quiet is violated, becomes a potential and frequently an active critic of the school program.

With the automobile in general use to-day small as well as large school districts face a traffic problem that is frequently annoying to the neighbors. When a householder finds it impossible to use his own right of way to the street because child or faculty cars are parked there for the entire day, considerable annoyance develops. Heavy concentrations of children within a small area frequently bring other traffic annoyance before and after school hours.

Too frequently small playgrounds are unfenced. Conventional economy classifies a fence as an extravagance. However, children must play, and baseballs have a frequent habit of being batted or thrown into neighboring yards. Sometimes they go through windows; more frequently they land in flower borders. In retrieving them, the children are guilty of trespass and the age-old conflict of the adult and the small child over playing material is easily renewed. Though sympathy readily inclines to the child, the normal rights of the adult and the too frequent destruction of property, without compensation, must not be overlooked. Unless these conflicts are harmonized, they may have serious results in community life, particularly in the small town. Constant irritation and annoyance quickly generate into active dislike which may and does find frequent expressions in many other channels.

An unfortunate termination of conflicts arising out of trespass is retaliation by adults in retaining the children's balls or demanding police protection. The children normally revolt and likewise make retaliation. Ripe vegetables, decayed animals, "tick-tack-toos," water cans on the sidewalk connected with strings, and other "accidents" develop. In a short time a merry feud blossoms forth and is harmful to both school and neighbor.

POSSIBILITY OF ELIMINATING CONFLICTS

Although conflicts arising from the school plant are among the most serious encountered in the relation of school to community, it is possible to eliminate most of them and harmonize the rest if the entire problem is given serious study, and intelligent plans are made to overcome these difficulties.

Economic Conflicts

Most economic conflicts arise from a lack of comprehensive longtime planning that results in emergencies. A practical definition of an emergency is a situation that arises as a result of lack of foresight. The teaching profession possesses to-day sufficient knowledge so that the typical "emergency" is unnecessary. It is possible to plan sufficiently far ahead so that the community can be progressively brought to an appreciation of building need without the use of pressure. Time is the most potent factor in change. If a building on which the community sets a sentimental value must be replaced, it is possible to determine that fact at least a decade before the crucial date arrives. A continuing program of education as to this future need will gradually result in the creation of a supporting public opinion. If the program is intelligently carried out, the pressure for change will finally come from the community itself rather than from the board of education or the professional personnel. Democratic functioning requires long-range planning and sufficient time to secure voluntary acceptance of the plan. Time is just as important as the plan.

The conflict arising out of methods of financing the building is also susceptible to harmonization by working on different methods of achievement. The typical future school districts will not be very large. School districts will be built around the typical community, and the average unit is small. To avoid burdensome debt it will be necessary to consider the state as the unit in financing future building. With the local borrowing difficulty eliminated, there will be little opportunity for conflicts over cost of financing.

Difficulties with "extras" for items omitted or forgotten require only serious attention to educational designing and to checking of plans and specifications. If the school district is too small to maintain specialized building services, it may easily employ for the specific jobs specialists in designing and in the construction analysis field. The use of educational specialists is not expensive. Superior architectural service costs less eventually than mediocre or poor service. The cost of these services will be repaid manyfold in a better building, the inclusion of every desirable item in the original bid, and the elimination of "extras." There is no financial conflict, except those growing out of direct dishonesty, that cannot be solved through careful planning.

Physical Conflicts

The harmonization of conflicts arising out of location, size, and architecture is primarily dependent on skill in planning. Large sites, rationally spaced, will be of foundation value. If the site is sufficiently large, it is relatively simple to provide a proper setting for the building itself. Employment of the most capable architectural service is assurance that the design and height of structure will be in harmony with the surrounding residential area. In mild climates it is possible to make school and community harmonize perfectly through the use of low buildings. In northern areas, the most glaring current inconsistencies may easily be eliminated.

The architecture of a school should be honest. It need not depend for its effect upon extraneous ornament or upon a rococo effect. The best design is that which secures its effect from proportion, balance, and massing. Plainness and beauty are not incompatible. Careful attention to design in relation to the community tradition should result in harmonization of the building and surroundings.

Sites and buildings should be as free as possible from hazards. Children can be protected against traffic by mechanical means or the police. Dangers on the playground or in the building itself are inherent in the educational and physical plans. Sensible application of all that has been learned about school hazards in new plans will provide against major hazards. In the last analysis, the elimination of school accidents is an administrative problem. Buildings and playgrounds cannot be made automatically safe. Constant instruction of the children in principles of safe living is still essential. Unusual care must be exercised in supervision of all child activity.

Conflicts arising out of the use of material require careful education of the adult community. School buildings receive unusually hard treatment. Materials in corridors and certain special facilities should be chosen in terms of their durability. Marble and tile are relatively cheap materials when the total building life is considered. Initially, these and other similar materials may be more expensive. In popular thought they are normally classed as luxuries. The school building critic speaks glibly of "marble halls" and "marble palaces" when making sweeping comments on "undue extravagance." It is possible to show that plaster, cement and paint are the most expensive materials to use in corridors and toilets because of their susceptibility to damage. School systems with good accounting systems have sufficient factual evidence to demonstrate the cost of "cheap buildings." Operation and upkeep are excellent reflectors of initial price building.

Social Conflicts

There is nothing in a school building that requires secrecy. Public business should at all times be conducted in such a manner that nothing is hidden. If these suggestions are followed in the designing of school buildings, most of the conflicts arising out of secrecy may be completely avoided. The best building plan is one in which the citizen may visit and see, without difficulty or annoyance, everything that is taking place. Democracy believes in the "goldfish bowl" for its public servants. Classroom doors should have at least one-third of their surface in clear glass to permit easy inspection from the corridors. Shades on doors are unnecessary and may well be omitted. Their presence is always a temptation to use.

School building inner offices should have clear glass partitions and doors without locks. The best designed offices are those which insure quiet and privacy without destroying vision from the corridor or waiting room. For the protection of the principal it is desirable that the secretary or stenographer should be able to see him constantly. Comfortably designed reception or waiting rooms for parental visitors are highly desirable for initial contact with the physical plant.

Within the offices, careful attention should be given to the furniture and its arrangement. For interviews, dictation, and other business, the desk is an excellent intervening medium between chairs. There is never an occasion in child, parent, or professional interviewing that requires close placement of chairs on the same side of the desk. Office design is very important in the prevention of damaging gossip.

Nuisance Conflicts

The entire range of nuisance conflicts arises out of site and building inadequacies. Correction of these shortcomings will be most helpful in solving these difficulties. If neighboring property is to be saved from depreciation, if the school plant is to perform its dual function of use and beauty, then much more serious attention must be given to planning to meet these problems.

The first requirement is a site sufficiently large to provide for adequate placement of the building, playground facilities in proportion to the size of building and method of administration, parking area, and sufficient land for landscaping approaches and boundaries.

Next to site size, the best investment a school district can make is to provide adequate fencing, six to eight feet high, around the playground. If the site is sufficiently large it will be possible to design playing fields to prevent annoyance to neighboring houses. If not feasible, then high and strong wire screens to a height of eighteen feet can be placed so that it will be impossible for balls to be batted or thrown into neighboring yards and gardens. Baseball fields and tennis courts can be easily screened.

Future site plans must include provision for the parking of the automobiles which a school building attracts. One of the major means in preventing traffic accidents is the elimination of all automobiles from the highways, thus maintaining these arteries for their primary purpose of facilitating traffic. Neither is it feasible for automobiles to encroach permanently on neighboring frontage. Both safety and the right of the people to maintain free access to their property require a more sensible attitude toward parking provisions.

Acoustical treatment within the building and landscaping of the site will reduce the noise factor to a minimum. Though the primary purpose of planting the school site is to improve its appearance, the acoustical value of this planting must not be minimized. Vines of different types and roses can be trained along the fence. For acoustical value the long-stemmed, multi-leaved ivies have especial value. Virginia creeper or woodbine, in addition to furnishing gorgeous fall coloring, makes a particularly good screen and has much acoustical value.

If the school building is located in an area free from smoke and soot, it is possible to use evergreens between the fence and the sidewalk. Red and white cedars, Austrian pine, and hemlock are particularly effective because of their dense foliage. Junipers of various varieties may be planted in the foreground and serve as excellent base planting. If the district is affected by smoke, it may be more desirable to use deciduous trees, especially those with heavy leaf surface. The locusts, plane trees, certain maples, and chestnuts are most effective. There are available to-day so many varieties of plants, vines, shrubs, and trees at reasonable price that local peculiarities

An attractive entrance corridor welcomes both students and parents. A dedication tablet such as the one below is also used as an interpretative device.

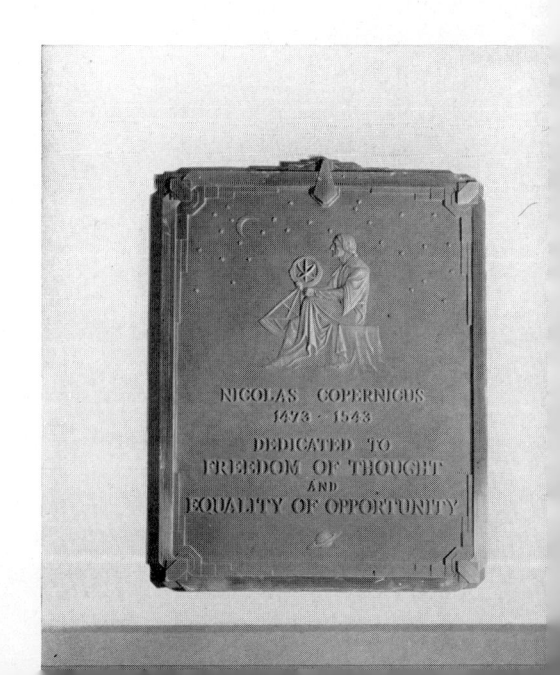

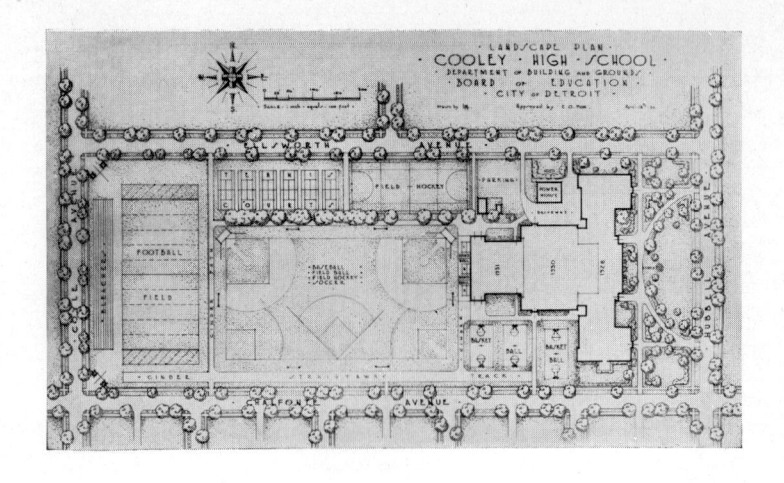

School sites well screened through the use of shrubs and trees reduce neighborhood conflicts.

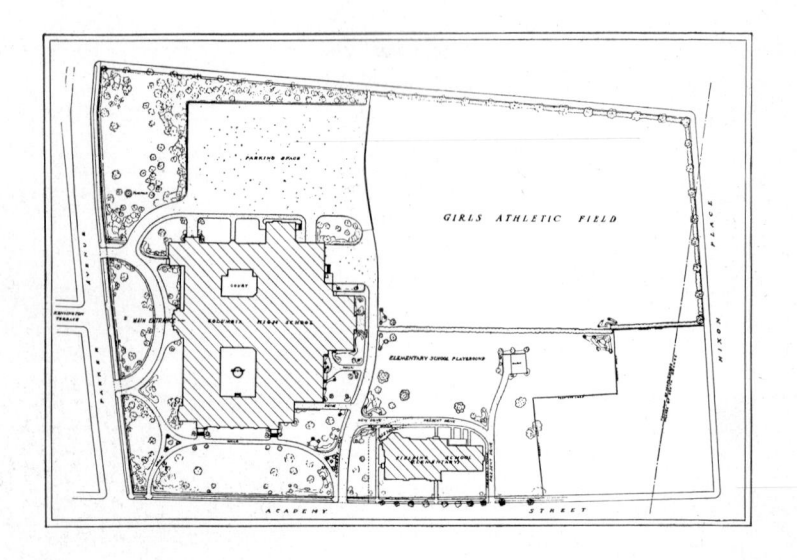

may be easily provided for. Within the playground itself the specialized areas can be so designed that inner secondary screening by planting is possible. These internal screens are of great help in reducing noise and add considerably to the beauty of the grounds.

Much of the playground noise is also reflected from the hard building surface. Dense foliage vines, especially ivy and woodbine, some of nature's best sound absorbents, may be trained on all outside walls. In addition to improving the appearance of the building, they will absorb rather than reflect the noise. If these landscaping suggestions are followed, the playground will become a place of beauty and a neighborhood feature instead of a conflict center.

Within the building itself, the acoustical problem is not difficult. Those units which produce noise beyond the normal amount must be studied and treated mechanically. Music units require not only a soft floor (cork carpet or linoleum) but acoustical material on both walls and ceiling. If the building uses the duct system for heating and ventilating, it is also necessary to provide special treatment in this area to avoid vibrations being carried through the entire building. It is mechanically possible so to insulate music rooms that there is no outside disturbance even when the windows are open.

Shops are noisy because of their activity and the manner in which they are designed. The desire for realism on the part of some educators and architects has led to the introduction of factory construction in shops. Unusually hard wall material simply accentuates the normal noise. The use of wood or composition floors, instead of concrete, and the treatment of walls and ceilings acoustically will quickly subdue the shop so that its nuisance factor is low.

Gymnasiums may be treated by covering the usually open ceiling with acoustical material and treating the walls above six or eight feet with acoustical plaster, canvas, or felt. There is no need for the use of glazed brick or tile above a maximum of eight feet in the gymnasium. As a matter of safety all swimming pools should be acoustically treated. Ceiling treatment is usually sufficient.

Cafeterias are generally much too noisy. Softer floor covering, soft table tops, window drapes, acoustical ceiling treatment in both the kitchen and eating room are desirable.

Corridors can be made quiet by acoustical ceiling treatment and linoleum floors. For other units ceiling treatment is usually sufficient.

The use of mechanical stokers and the introduction of units for reducing the smoke nuisance will prevent conflicts arising out of the periodic shower of soft-coal soot and minute cinders on and in neighboring houses. Garbage-disposal units can be designed to eliminate annoying odors.

USE AS AN INTERPRETATIVE AGENCY

The school plant is one of the most important interpretative agencies. As a symbol of public education its effect is constant. Physical possibilities of making this symbolic use more effective through better planning and through intelligent reduction of conflicts has been already considered. The secondary value is in its direct use as a rallying ground.

The building provides means for generalized or mass contacts through attendance at school programs of various types. Since initial interest centers in the child, the first generalized contact will be at those programs which the children themselves prepare and present, including music, dramatics, athletics, and exhibitions. The second group of generalized contacts are those arising out of parent-education programs. If the interest engendered through home contacts and these generalized school contacts is successful, the outcome should be a constant increase in individual meetings between parent and school through which increased understanding of and coöperation with the institution is possible.

Care should be exercised in designing the building to provide adequate and comfortable space for individual or small group meetings. Facilities that are capable of dual child and community use, such as auditoriums, gymnasiums, shops, cafeterias, libraries and clinics must be planned to meet adult as well as child requirements. Each building should provide for at least one parents' reception room where conferences may be held under pleasant surroundings. Rooms of this type should be non-institutional in design and fitted with comfortable furniture. The preferable location is close to the offices so that records and other material may be easily available.

Each building should be easy of access to visitors. Directive signs in a corridor are helpful in orienting visitors with the least possible annoyance. Visitors should normally make initial contact with the central office rather than with individual teachers. These signs may indicate the nearest way to the office. Neat building directories are also desirable in the vestibules of all main corridors. It is sufficient if these wall directories list the location of the principal rooms with sufficient space for the announcement and location of any special child or adult gatherings.

Specialized rooms, such as auditorium, cafeteria, gymnasiums and libraries, lend themselves to the organization of adult programs suggested in earlier chapters.

Offices may be so designed that it is possible for the school secretary to realize quickly the presence of visitors. Nothing is so disconcerting and annoying as apparent neglect of visitors by members of the school staff. An information center is suggested as one means of bringing visitors to the general offices or reception room.

Attractive buildings and well-landscaped playgrounds lend themselves beautifully to evening exhibition through the use of effective flood lighting. The lighting costs little and has unusual value in maintaining visual continuity so far as the building is concerned.

Exhibit cases make corridors interesting and are of real educational value in demonstrating for children and adults alike the work of the school or curricular exhibits of interest. There is plenty of opportunity for their inclusion in building plans.

Special Groups

The school plant holds much of interest and value for special interest groups. The coöperation of local chapters of the Garden Club of America will provide a supporting public opinion for well-landscaped grounds and building. Florists can be shown the community value of school gardens and herbariums. It is also possible to interest architects and engineers in good building design and to secure their active support in stimulating better building.

SUMMARY

The school plant is a very vital agency in the social interpretation program. Its effectiveness is determined by the degree of skill with which the building serves its symbolic value. Current low adequacy of the school plant as an interpretative agency is due in large measure to the number of economic, physical, social, and nuisance conflicts that school buildings engender. Analysis of these conflicts indicates that they are possible of harmonization if sufficient care is exercised in the planning and development of grounds and building. If these additional sums will make the school plant a community asset instead of a liability and result in the reduction if not the total elimination of trouble spots and neighborhood conflict, then no possible investment could be more justified in terms of institutional values. The building should be ultimately considered as an agency for stimulating and improving both mass and individual contacts with the school as a social institution. Physical provision for the reception and comfort of the visitors will do much to attract them. In general, much more attention must be given to the building as an interpretation agency in the future if it is to meet its possibilities as a constructive agency.

Chapter 24

THE SCHOOL IN ACTION

EVERYTHING the public school does has direct and indirect social interpretative value. The school in action should represent a totality of instructional activities based on the larger needs of society and the individual and social needs of the child. The perfect functioning educational organization may be considered as one that understands the purpose and place of the school in the social order; understands realistically the processes of democracy; operates through broad policies and efficient procedures; has a thorough understanding of the community in which it exists; provides a continuing program of complete information to the people concerning the problems of education, to secure a strong backlog of supporting public opinion; instructs through a curriculum that has been determined by current social need instead of the dead hand of tradition; employs democratic organizational and instructional methods to develop efficient democratic citizenship; remains open-minded and flexible to changing need; and acquits itself as a classless social institution in a classless state.

Though the American public school falls far short of this ideal to-day, it has made unusual progress in the past century and, despite its obvious shortcomings, gives hope for future possibilities. Its potentialities as a means of assisting in the development and improvement of the democratic process are limited only by the professional ability and vision of its operating personnel. The school in action will be considered in this chapter as a totality in terms of: (1) general qualities, (2) practices to avoid, (3) the adult program, (4) the child program, and (5) functional interpretation.

GENERAL QUALITIES

Since all that a school actually does or omits doing, from inception of program through the effect of the physical plant upon the community, has both direct and indirect interpretative value, there are certain general qualities essential to smooth and efficient functioning.

Institutional Democracy

The American public school must strive first of all to be truly democratic. It is time that definite steps were taken to eliminate the paradox of training for participation in the democratic life through autocratic administrative and classroom practices. As the professional personnel rises in technical and social competency, it is both possible and desirable to reappraise institutional organization and practice in the light of democratic possibilities and to provide for progressive change from the autocratic to the democratic pattern. Fragmentary experimentation in different school systems indicates that such reorganization is practical to the extent that the teachers and administrators are ready to accept their responsibility for operating upon a high professional level. The democratic thread must run through the entire cloth of institutional operation. It must show respect for the personality of every child and develop means whereby highly diverse inborn capacities may attain their highest possible expression. Extended to the adult the democratic point of view indicates that here also there can be no class distinction and no expressions of the too frequent "better than" and "superior to" professional concept. Recognition of individual mental, economic, social, and cultural variation is possible without labeling.

Institutional Teaching

The preservation and improvement of the democratic way of life require constant striving toward the great ideal of equality of educational opportunity in accordance with inborn capacity. Progressive achievement of this ideal means the inculcation both in children and adults of a deep regard for those qualities essential to a society of free self-governing men and women. These qualities include an understanding and appreciation of democracy and democratic institutions; the development of characteristics that have democratic significance such as individual capability and intelligent acceptance of social responsibility, open-mindedness, understanding, and coöperation in the promotion of the common good; and the use of teaching methods through which the democratic goals may be attained.[1]

Institutional Reasonableness

The public school must be reasonable in its demands upon both the community and the child and flexible in organization and method. Dogmatism and determinism have little place in democracy. Current limits of human knowledge are so narrow that the truly intellectual attitude may be optimistic about the future. As the intellectual frontiers are advanced it may be possible that even the hopeless moron of to-day will have possibilities of growth in the future far beyond that imagined to-day. Research in the field of endocrinology already holds great hopes for startling discoveries. Medical science is merely starting an attack on the field of human improvement. New findings that will result in more productive teaching methods based on greater understanding of the human psyche are anticipated products of the psychological laboratories. Sociology may have large possible contributions in more scientific analysis of the individual in his group relationships and means for the improvement of social technique. Evolutionary changes in the economic structure and the alleviation of the age-old poverty problem with its devastating terminal physiological, psychological, social, and spiritual effects are entirely within the range of possible achievement. Regardless of current possibilities the attitude of the democratic school must be one of understanding and sympathy to the children it serves.

Institutional Tact

The social institution can operate tactfully in the midst of high individual and social sensitivity. Complete honesty of purpose and operation are possible through the use of delicate and sympathetic perception of what is fitting, graceful, and considerate. Harshness, intolerance, and quantitative negativism have no place in the democratic educational process. Flexibility, sensitivity, sympathy, and tact

[1] See also Chapter 2.

do not imply sentimentality or "softness" in the teaching process. They merely represent attitudes through which more intelligent institutional operation is possible. It is, however, the direct antithesis of the doctrine of institutional infallibility.

Institutional Fairness

The democratic school must promote fairness. In the development of this quality the institution itself furnishes the best example. Complete fairness on the part of the teacher in her relationships with children and parents, regardless of conventional academic set and bias, is the first essential. An attitude of fair play in the mutual relationships of all professional and non-professional personnel will reflect and project itself into the totality of functioning.

Institutional standards and attitudes are created out of the interplay of personal qualities. Codes may be written in the most beautiful expressions possible, ideals may be sonorously expressed and mouthily phrased, but unless the breath of life is placed into them through actual practice by the individuals involved in the total process they are of little value. The case of the midwestern principal, noted for his long and earnest prayers each week in an open Baptist prayer meeting in behalf of the "tender lambs entrusted to our nurturing paternal care," but who actually spent the greater portion of his daily administrative life devising and using new and unusual methods of physical punishment as a means of applying this "nurturing paternal care" to these same "tender lambs," may be poignantly illustrative. To the degree that the public-school personnel finds it possible to accept these same qualities as guides in personal and professional life will their projection into institutional operation be possible. All of these institutional qualities must become part of the individual's equipment.

Institutional Tolerance

In addition, a broad tolerance and respect for the personality and opinions of others as a fundamental democratic characteristic is essential. Tolerance is not a cloak that may be thrown over the shoulders merely in time of inclement social weather. It is an attitude growing out of internal convictions that the other man's point of view, his practices and beliefs, may be just as valuable as one's own. An outstanding mark of a truly educated person is the degree of tolerance he possesses toward the beliefs and opinions of others. Again, by a strange paradox the current level of educational institutional functioning is such that there is frequently a strong tendency toward intolerance. College students who throw speakers into the river because they express opinions not agreeable with student conditioning, teachers who develop almost homicidal attitudes toward their colleagues who fail to "yes" all conventional patterns of thought, teachers who use punitive marking to express personal or intellectual dislike are good examples of the tendency toward intolerance.

Institutional Humor

An outstanding characteristic of all institutions of learning is the absence of a sense of humor on the part of its agents in their institutional work. It is probably asking much to expect its inclusion within the organized pattern, although it is theoretically desirable. Yet a broad sense of humor is an absolute essential to democratic functioning, a safety valve through which by absurd contrast it is possible to relieve tenseness and strain by bringing into play the muscles of laughter and relaxation. The superintendent who, after the first "open house" in an experimental social center had ended in a racial riot, was able to reply to a reportorial question that a certain individual had been hit "in his social center" turned a possible serious incident into a humorous news feature. This lack of humor in institutional life is one of the many reasons for stiffness, pomposity, and is frequently the underlying cause of stupidity. It arises out of lack of understanding of function, a low appreciation of realities, absence of a sense of balance, and an exaggerated emphasis on the individual's institutional importance. Since an institution cannot be humorous, the element of humor must be supplied by the individual operating agent and used constantly as a device for maintaining balance in choice and relieving tension. A teacher with a well-developed sense of humor is a sparkling jewel in the institutional setting. Everything operates more effectively where laughter is ever present serving as a distortion mirror to reduce bumptiousness and conceit.

Institutional Taste

Above all the public school must show taste or discrimination in emphasis of the finer possibilities for the good life, so essential in a mechanistic culture that tends too much in the direction of utilitarianism as opposed to intellectual and spiritual values. Into the retort of public education are poured many diverse individuals with different cultural backgrounds. The educational process should not attempt to standardize, conventionalize and condition the individuals to a common form but should, through the development of personal taste, provide means for a possible social integration around generally desirable social purposes while encouraging individual freedom and choice in perimeter areas. The formation of standards of taste, which may also be translated to include vision and ideals, and voluntarily recognized as essential to improvement in living are definitely a responsibility of the school.

PRACTICES TO AVOID

The democratic school has the responsibility for teaching children and adults methods of thinking. Intelligent and effective participation in the democratic plan requires understanding and appreciation instead of blind obedience. Open-mindedness and ability to investigate and to consider all points of view before arriving at a reasoned decision grow out of knowing how to think. Teaching what to think may be relegated to propaganda. The foundation of this objective rests in the civil liberties guaranteed each individual under the written covenant by which the people delegated some of their power to the state. Teaching how to think requires a catholic attitude toward life and the ability to study objectively the various elements that contribute to a problem. Thus it is necessary to provide training whereby there always remains in the individual mind the element of reasonable doubt which means willingness to maintain an open mind and to be ready always to change upon the admission of additional evidence. Learning the processes of reflective thought entails also the development of a critical attitude toward available evidence. In meeting its responsibility the public school must teach the nature of propaganda and the methods by which it may be judged. In so doing the school in action must above all things avoid being propagandistic whether for institutional or individual advantage. The possible exception is in those areas where the public schools are expected to indoctrinate for living in a democratic pattern.

Avoiding Conflicts

Progress through conflict is difficult and represents an inefficient means of accommodation to change. The school is expected to project its psychological knowledge of human relations into realistic practice and so operate that it may avoid possible conflict and harmonize those areas in which conflict already exists. The institutional agent must be constantly on guard to avoid the weakening of social institutional confidence through the unwarranted projection of stiff and inflexible individual or institutional actions into a pattern whose fundamental requirement is flexibility and reasonableness.

Being Practical

The typical school man believes in being practical and with good reason. In the classroom he has probably listened attentively for book credit to advanced theories and programs. His sense of reality tells him that many of these suggestions are impossible of functioning in the current world in which the public-school teacher works. Unfortunate emphasis on technical education to the detriment of a broad general training has probably reduced his own perspective to sense the difference between the value of higher education in advancing frontiers of knowledge and the immediately current functioning of elementary and secondary public education. The combination of all these elements results in creating an unfavorable attitude toward theory as mere academic vaporings and stimulating his belief in the practice of opportunism.

In his inability to harmonize theory as a directive navigating chart with practice as an expression of daily achievement, the school man goes to the other extreme of opportunism. This weakness has been particularly evident in social interpretation. The theory of institutional function in a democratic pattern definitely indicates that the progress of the school is dependent upon the development of community appreciation and acceptance of need, making the first step in institutional change, as indicated earlier, the education of the adult. Lack of appreciation of this fact together with administrative impatience with the restrictions imposed by the time element has resulted instead in many instances in programs of opportunism in which the attempt is made to impress the institutional will upon the people through a high-pressure technique. Opportunism in social interpretation disregards completely the implications of democratic functioning.

Sound practice rests on the firm base of sound theory, and institutional plans must have their foundation well grounded in tenable theory. The apparent conflict between the two is probably due to the lack of a discriminating background for interpretation and harmonization. As a social institution the public school should make every effort to avoid a policy of opportunism in favor of long-term functional planning.

Controversial Issues

It is generally considered safe to teach the truth in schools about what is long dead and buried. However, when "Big Bill" Thompson, Chicago's demagogic mayor, decided that William McAndrew wasn't politically pliable enough as a superintendent of schools, the Mayor's appointed board of education found what it considered to be sufficient evidence in the careful extraction of single sentences from their textual context in certain elementary- and secondary-school American histories to result in his dismissal. The conclusions reached by more impartial investigating committees unhampered by political pressure actually found no reason for William McAndrew's retirement. The generalization may be that politics knows devious ways to attain its objectives.

Current issues that arouse warmth of opinion are even more dangerous to institutional safety. These reactions may be due to super-emotionalism and also to the feeling that the classroom teacher may not be completely judicial in presentation. There is sufficient evidence of propagandistic teaching to give this popular feeling some validity. As an impartial democratic institution the school should not take sides in these emotionalized issues. There are always many solutions for every social problem. To deny this fact is a declaration of intellectual poverty that certainly need not characterize the teaching profession. If the public has sufficient confidence in the judicial attitude of the teaching profession and if the adult community has been educated to the need for free and objective discussion of principles and problems as essential to the democratic way of life, the school need not avoid any controversial issues.

The school should also avoid giving the impression to the community that the teaching profession has a completely proprietary interest in a coöperative social enterprise except as citizens.

Danger of Rapid Change.

Swift change in minor objectives or actual program must be avoided. This is a fundamental principle of good organization. Success in planning is conditioned not only by the intrinsic value of the plan but also by the skill with which organization prepares for it. All change requires time to educate the personnel involved in its execution and to educate the adults who have a partnership interest in its functioning and a personal interest in its outcomes. Change without preparation is not only unintelligent, but institutionally disastrous.

THE ADULT PROGRAM

The attainment and improvement of the democratic way of life make necessary the extension of the educational function deep into adult life. One of the purposes of the time devoted to the training of the child is to produce competency in social functioning and intelligent acceptance of individual responsibility in civic duties. The adult must be constantly exposed to means through which he may progressively improve his individual and social competence. Some of these means may be institutionalized, but most of them will probably operate more effectively on an informal and voluntary basis. The responsibility of the school for the adult is to provide means whereby he may improve both his individual and social efficiency.

A specialized aspect of adult education is providing means whereby the individual may be kept informed of the purpose, value, conditions, and needs of public education as a vital activity in the maintenance and improvement of the democratic process. This aspect may be further subdivided into the area of general civic education and special parental education. Through the first, improvement in civic intelligence and understanding of institutional problems is possible; through the second, the partnership concept between home and school may be more fully and effectively realized to the improvement of home and school. The institution that is capable of recognizing this peculiar relationship has unlimited possibilities. The active adult program involved in the interpretative process is threefold in its nature including the creation of actual classroom learning conditions, learning through mutual coöperation with the teacher in improving home and school relationships, and by both active and passive audience participation in the activities of the school.

The direct education of the adult for his partnership responsibilities may be carried out through the diversity of methods and activity considered earlier in this presentation. Personal contacts, written material, visual presentation, and specially organized classroom instruction may also be employed. Indirect learning may be conducted through the influence of the school as a totality, through the reactions of the individual parent to its worth and value in terms of his child, and through listening programs in which the immediate accomplishment of the children whether in classroom, studio, or auditorium is presented for adult appraisal.

It is also possible for the school to furnish parents other services of a more personal nature. If a sufficient degree of confidence can be established between home and school, the parent will seek institutional advice on specific child problems. The modern school has the potential means for individual diagnosis and for rendering valuable advice. The ultimate possibilities of this service envision the school as the laboratory center from which the community may draw significant service and receive personal educational benefits. Other possibilities are the development of parental libraries and informational service to which adults will normally come for help in areas where they plan self-exploratory programs.

The terminal purpose of adult education in which the school is interested from the interpretative standpoint is to secure rational interest and institutional support through a conviction of the worth of the institution as a service agency to community and state. Since the normal condition of a democratic institution should always be considered as one of transition, the process of adult education must likewise be looked upon as one that terminates only with the life of the institution. Institutional acceptance of this point of view is merely recognition of the nature of the democratic process. The operation of the adult interpretative program should be so smoothly integrated with the actual functioning of the institution that it is accepted as an essentially normal activity instead of something that requires occasional attention through pressure methods.

THE CHILD PROGRAM

The child program in its formalized and informal expression in direct instructional, recreational, creative, and social aspects should operate in accord with the highest level of efficiency under current conditions of community understanding and support. Recognition of the fact that the greatest interpretative possibility of the school rests upon the base of the totality of its effectiveness in performing its task means that the internal program must be adjusted to child and social needs at all times. There is no occasion at any time for the disruption of a balanced program to meet the special demands of selfish minority groups whether these arise within or outside of the institution. Although there must be realistic recognition of the current limits of program effectiveness at any specific time, there is no occasion to accept these current limitations as permanent but rather to recognize them as new frontiers to be attacked in the adult field.

Everything the school does has interpretative value and the development of this fact as a criterion for the appraisal of institutional functioning may be considered as a guiding principle in the normal program of the school.

The second effect of the functioning school is the direct reaction of the adult to its formalized achievement. Since participation of the adult as audience and judge is highly desirable, the child program of socialized and audience activity such as dramatic presentation, musical programs, and athletic contests should be pointed with this objective clearly in view. This attitude necessitates the subordination of the unfortunate trend toward the profit motive to one of general participation made possible through the absence of admission charges or their reduction to a very small sum to make large participation possible. Though adult audience appeal is a desirable factor to consider in program organization, care must be taken to maintain the primary purpose of activities and demonstrations as child events and avoid any possible attempts toward exploitation of child or institution for the entertainment of the adult. A change from the conventional to the functional attitude with respect to purpose and pointing may be difficult for a time but in the long run will receive more firm adult approval than any other less desirable practice.

The cultivation and improvement of the partnership concept between home and school will result progressively in more effective institutional functioning. It will also permit the spread of partial responsibility back to the home, particularly in the field of social activity, thus making easier the path of institutional operation. This progressive adaptation of the public school to actual community needs will increase the ease and smoothness of social interpretation.

FUNCTIONAL INTERPRETATION

The operation, interpretation, and improvement of the school as a social institution should proceed as a smoothly integrated process in which to all outward appearances there are no divisions. Functional interpretation means that plans, programs, and appraisals of the means used in social interpretation will not be painfully obvious or awkwardly periodic. It avoids high and low spots by eliminating emergencies through exact knowledge and careful long-range planning. The professional's ability to keep ahead of the social procession is directed into purposeful channels and into recognition of current limitations, the whole a smooth running process in which the operator always remains superior to and in control of the machine.

Current interpretative practices are far from this ideal but represent no major difficulty in moving to greater effectiveness if the participating agents become thoroughly conscious of institutional methods of operation and the techniques required to keep them ever alert and flexible to social need, thus avoiding the disintegrating effects of revolution which usually confront the inefficient and static institution. The school must recognize its responsibility for improvement, a process that starts with the teacher and ends with the institutional product.

RECOMMENDED READINGS RELATED TO SOCIAL INTERPRETATION

General Texts

FARLEY, Belmont, *School Publicity*. School Economy Series (Stanford University, Calif., Stanford University Press, 1934).

GRINNELL, John E., *Interpreting The Public Schools* (New York, McGraw-Hill Book Co., 1937).

HINES, Harlan C., and JONES, Robinson G., *Public School Publicity* (New York, The Macmillan Co., 1923).

MILLER, Clyde R., and CHARLES, Fred, *Publicity and the Public School* (Boston, Houghton Mifflin Co., 1924).

MOEHLMAN, Arthur B., *Public School Relations* (Chicago, Rand, McNally and Co., 1927).

REEDER, W. G., *An Introduction to Public-School Relations* (New York, The Macmillan Co., 1937).

WALLER, J. Flint, *Public Relations for the Public Schools* (Trenton, N. J., MacCrellish and Quigley Co., 1933).

Chapter I

ARNOLD, Thurman W., *The Symbols of Government* (New Haven, Yale University Press, 1935).

BEARD, Charles A., *The Unique Function of Education in American Democracy*. Prepared for the Educational Policies Commission of the National Education Association, 1937.

COUNTS, George S., *Dare the School Build a New Social Order?* (New York, The John Day Co., 1932), No. 11.

DE MADARIAGA, S., *Anarchy or Hierarchy* (New York, The Macmillan Co., 1937).

GOODSELL, Willystine, *The Family as a Social and Educational Institution* (New York, The Macmillan Co., 1924).

HOCKING, William E., *Man and the State* (New Haven, Yale University Press, 1926).

———, *The Lasting Elements of Individualism* (New Haven, Yale University Press, 1937).

LANGFORD, Howard D., *Education and the Social Conflict* (New York, The Macmillan Co., 1936).

LASKI, Harold J., *The Dangers of Obedience* (New York, Harper and Bros., 1930).
——, *The State in Theory and Practice* (New York, The Viking Press, 1935).
LEPPERT, Julius, *The Evolution of Culture* (New York, The Macmillan Co., 1931).
LIPPMANN, Walter, *The Good Society* (Boston, Little, Brown and Co., 1937).
LOWIE, Robert H., *The Origin of the State* (New York, Harcourt, Brace and Co., 1927).
KALLEN, Horace M., Ed., *Freedom in The Modern World* (New York, Coward-McCann, Inc., 1928).
MEAD, Margaret, *Coming of Age in Samoa* (New York, William Morrow and Co., 1928).
——, *Growing Up in New Guinea* (New York, Blue Ribbon Books, 1930).
NOCK, Albert Jay, *Our Enemy the State* (New York, William Morrow and Co., 1935).
PARMELEE, Maurice, *Bolshevism, Fascism and the Liberal Democratic State* (New York, John Wiley and Sons, 1934).
RUSSELL, Bertrand, *Freedom Versus Organization: 1814–1914* (New York, W. W. Norton and Co., 1934).

CHAPTER 2

ARNOLD, Thurman W., *The Folklore of Capitalism* (New Haven, Yale University Press, 1937).
BABBITT, Irving, *Democracy and Leadership* (Boston, Houghton Mifflin Co., 1924).
BURGESS, Ernest W., *Personality and the Social Group* (Chicago, University of Chicago Press, 1929).
CHILDS, Harwood L., *A Reference Guide to the Study of Public Opinion* (Princeton, N. J., Princeton University Press, 1934).
COOLEY, Charles H., *Human Nature and the Social Order* (New York, Charles Scribner's Sons, 1902).
LASKI, Harold J., *Politics* (Philadelphia, J. B. Lippincott Co., 1931).
LE FEVRE, Louis, *Liberty and Restraint* (New York, Alfred A. Knopf, 1931).
LIPPMANN, Walter, *The Method of Freedom* (New York, The Macmillan Co., 1934).
——, *The Phantom Public* (New York, Harcourt, Brace and Co., 1935).

MOEHLMAN, Conrad Henry, *The Catholic-Protestant Mind* (New York, Harper and Bros., 1929).
——, *The Christian-Jewish Tragedy* (Rochester, N. Y., Leo Hart, 1933).
ODEGARD, Peter, *Pressure Politics* (New York, Columbia University Press, 1928).
ROBINSON, James Harvey, *The Mind in the Making* (New York, Harper and Bros., 1921).
SCHRIEKE, B., *Alien Americans* (New York, The Viking Press, 1936).
SOULE, George, *The Future of Liberty* (New York, The Macmillan Co., 1936).
SUMNER, William G., *Folkways* (Boston, Ginn and Co., 1906).
THOMPSON, Carl D., *Confessions of the Power Trust* (New York, E. P. Dutton and Co., 1932).
WALSH, James J., *A Catholic Looks at Life* (Boston, The Stratford Co., 1929).

CHAPTER 3

BERNAYS, Edward L., *Propaganda* (New York, Horace Liveright, 1928).
BIDDLE, William W., *Propaganda and Education,* Contributions to Education, No. 531 (New York, Bureau of Publications, Teachers College, Columbia University, 1932).
BOWDEN, A. O., and MELBO, Irving R., *Social Psychology of Education* (New York, McGraw-Hill Book Co., 1937), Chs. VI, VII, VIII.
BROOME, Edwin C., Ch., *Report of the Committee on Propaganda in the Schools* (Washington, D. C., National Education Association, July, 1929).
DUFFIELD, Marcus, *King Legion* (New York, Jonathan Cape and Harrison Smith, 1931).
Institute for Propaganda Analysis, *Propaganda Analysis* (Published Monthly, 132 Morningside Drive, New York City).
LUMLEY, Frederick E., *The Propaganda Menace* (New York, D. Appleton-Century Co., 1933).
PIERCE, Bessie L., *Citizen's Organizations and the Civic Training of Youth,* Part III of the Report of the Commission on the Social Studies, American Historical Association (New York, Charles Scribner's Sons, 1933).
——, *Civic Attitudes in American School Textbooks* (Chicago, University of Chicago Press, 1930).
RAUP, Bruce, *Education and Organized Interests in America* (New York, G. P. Putnam's Sons, 1936).
WALLER, J. Flint, *Demands on the Schools,* Contributions to Education,

No. 542 (New York, Bureau of Publications, Teachers College, Columbia University, 1932).

WILLIAMS, Michael, *The Shadow of the Pope* (New York, McGraw-Hill Book Co., 1932).

CHAPTER 4

BEALE, Howard K., *Are American Teachers Free?* (New York, Charles Scribner's Sons, 1936).

KANDEL, I. L., Ed., *Education Yearbook of the International Institute* (New York, Bureau of Publications, Teachers College, Columbia University, 1935).

KILPATRICK, William H., Ed., *The Teacher and Society, First Yearbook* of the John Dewey Society (New York, D. Appleton-Century Co., 1937).

MARSH, J. Frank, *The Teacher Outside the School* (Yonkers, N. Y., World Book Co., 1928).

OVERN, Alfred V., *The Teacher in Modern Education* (New York, D. Appleton-Century Co., 1935).

PATTERSON, William H., *Letters From a Hard-Boiled Teacher to His Half-Baked Son* (Washington, D. C., The Daylion Co., 1935).

PORTER, Martha Peck, *The Teacher in the New School* (Yonkers, N. Y., World Book Co., 1930).

SELLE, Erwin S., *The Organization and Activities of the National Education Association,* Contributions to Education, No. 513 (New York, Bureau of Publications, Teachers College, Columbia University, 1932).

WATTENBERG, William W., *On the Educational Front* (New York, Columbia University Press, 1936).

CHAPTER 5

BOGOSLOVSKY, Boris B., *The Technique of Controversy* (New York, Harcourt, Brace and Co., 1928).

CHAFEE, Zechariah, Jr., *Freedom of Speech* (New York, Harcourt, Brace and Co., 1920).

The Improvement of Education, Fifteenth Yearbook of the Department of Superintendence of the National Education Association (Washington, D. C., National Education Association, 1937).

EVERETT, Samuel, *Democracy Faces the Future* (New York, Columbia University Press, 1935).

HOLLINGWORTH, H. L., *The Psychology of the Audience* (New York, American Book Co., 1935).

RECOMMENDED READINGS

LONG, John C., *Public Relations* (New York, McGraw-Hill Book Co., 1924).

Low, A. Maurice, *The American People, A Study in National Psychology* (Boston, Houghton Mifflin Co., 1909), 2 Vols.

ODEGARD, Peter, *The American Public Mind* (New York, Columbia University Press, 1930).

OVERSTREET, H. A., *Influencing Human Behavior* (New York, W. W. Norton and Co., 1925).

RUSSELL, Bertrand, *Education and the Modern World* (New York, W. W. Norton and Co., 1932).

STEINER, Jesse F., *The American Community in Action* (New York, Henry Holt and Co., 1928).

STUDEBAKER, J. W., *The American Way* (New York, McGraw-Hill Book Co., 1935).

WILDER, R. H., and BUELL, K. L., *Publicity* (New York, The Ronald Press, 1923).

CHAPTER 6

GARTH, Thomas R., *Race Psychology* (New York, McGraw-Hill Book Co., 1931).

MOEHLMAN, Arthur B., and KEYWORTH, M. R., *The Public School Code of the Hamtramck, Michigan, Public Schools,* Research Series No. 2 (Hamtramck, Mich., Published by the Board of Education, 1928).

NEWLON, Jesse H., *Educational Administration as Social Policy* (New York, Charles Scribner's Sons, 1934).

REEDER, Ward G., *The Fundamentals of Public School Administration* (New York, The Macmillan Co., 1930).

WILSON, Lester M., and KANDEL, I. L., *Introduction to the Study of American Education* (New York, Thomas Nelson and Sons, 1934).

CHAPTER 7

BEACH, Walter G., and WALKER, Edward E., *American Social Problems* (Stanford University, Calif., Stanford University Press, 1934).

BOGARDUS, Emory S., *The New Social Research* (Los Angeles, Jesse Ray Miller, 1926).

BRUNNER, Edmund de S., and LORGE, Irving, *Rural Trends in Depression Years* (New York, Columbia University Press, 1937).

Community Conflict, copyrighted by E. C. Carter (New York, The Inquiry, 1929).

COLE, William E., and CROWE, Hugh, *Recent Trends in Rural Planning* (New York, Prentice-Hall, 1937).

EVERETT, Samuel, and others, *The Community School,* a publication of the Society for Curriculum Study (New York, D. Appleton-Century Co., 1938).

GARRISON, Winfred Ernest, *Intolerance* (New York, Round Table Press, 1934).

LA PIERE, Richard T., and FARNSWORTH, Paul R., *Social Psychology* (New York, McGraw-Hill Book Co., 1936).

LYND, Robert S., and Helen Merrell, *Middletown* (New York, Harcourt, Brace and Co., 1929).

———, *Middletown in Transition* (New York, Harcourt, Brace and Co., 1937).

MOEHLMAN, Arthur B., *Public School Plant Program* (Chicago, Rand, McNally and Co., 1929).

———, and KEYWORTH, M. R., *Housing the Children,* Research Series No. 1 (Hamtramck, Mich., Published by the Board of Education, 1926).

Recent Social Trends in the United States, Report of the President's Research Committee on Social Trends (New York, McGraw-Hill Book Co., 1933), One Volume Edition.

SCHRIEKE, B., *Alien Americans* (New York, The Viking Press, 1936).

STRUNSKY, Simeon, *The Rediscovery of Jones* (Boston, Little, Brown and Co., 1931).

WOOD, Arthur E., *Community Problems* (New York, D. Appleton-Century Co., 1928).

CHAPTER 8

Administrative Code of the Board of Education, City of Cleveland (Cleveland, Published by the Board of Education, 1925).

ALMACK, John C., *The School Board Member* (New York, The Macmillan Co., 1927).

ARNETT, Claude E., *The Social Beliefs and Attitudes of American School Board Members* (Emporia, Kan., Emporia Gazette Press, 1932).

COUNTS, George S., *The Social Composition of Boards of Education* (Chicago, University of Chicago Press, 1927).

GRILL, George W., *The Minutes of a Board of Education* (Milwaukee, The Bruce Publishing Co., 1932).

KEYWORTH, M. R., *Legal Aspects for Records of Proceedings of Boards of Education* (Milwaukee, The Bruce Publishing Co., 1931).

MENDENHALL, Edgar, *The City School Board Member and His Task* (Published by the author in 1929 and distributed by the College Inn Book Store, Pittsburg, Kansas).

MOEHLMAN, Arthur B., and KEYWORTH, M. R., *The Public School Code of the Hamtramck, Michigan, Public Schools,* Research Series No.

2 (Hamtramck, Mich., Published by the Board of Education, 1928).

MOREHART, Grover C., *The Legal Status of City School Boards,* Contributions to Education, No. 270 (New York, Bureau of Publications, Teachers College, Columbia University, 1927).

"The School Board Member," *Research Bulletin* of the National Education Association, Vol. 10, No. 1 (January, 1933).

OLSEN, Hans C., *The Work of Boards of Education,* Contributions to Education, No. 213 (New York, Bureau of Publications, Teachers College, Columbia University, 1926).

SHULL, Frank L., *The School Board and Efficient Administration* (Portland, Ore., Published by the Board of Education, 1929).

WEST, John C., and others, *A Handbook for Boards of Education* (Grand Forks, N. D., August, 1932).

CHAPTER 9

BOLTON, Frederick E., COLE, Thomas R., and JESSUP, John H., *The Beginning Superintendent* (New York, The Macmillan Co., 1937).

HILL, Clyde M., Ed., *Educational Progress and School Administration* (New Haven, Yale University Press, 1936).

HART, Joseph K., *Educational Resources of Village and Rural Communities* (New York, The Macmillan Co., 1914).

Educational Leadership, Eleventh Yearbook of the Department of Superintendence of the National Education Association (Washington, D. C., National Education Association, 1933).

Critical Problems in School Administration, Twelfth Yearbook of the Department of Superintendence of the National Education Association (Washington, D. C., National Education Association, 1934).

MOEHLMAN, Arthur B., and KEYWORTH, M. R., *The Public School Code of the Hamtramck, Michigan, Public Schools,* Research Series No. 2 (Hamtramck, Mich., Published by the Board of Education, 1928).

PIGORS, Paul, *Leadership or Domination* (Boston, Houghton Mifflin Co., 1935).

CHAPTER 10

BRYSON, Lyman, *Adult Education* (New York, American Book Co., 1936).

The Principal and His Community, Eleventh Yearbook of the Department of Elementary School Principals of the National Education Association (Washington, D. C., National Education Association, 1932).

ELLIOTT, Harrison Sackett, *The Process of Group Thinking* (New York, Association Press, 1928).

FARLEY, Belmont, *Interpreting the Secondary School to the Public,* National Survey of Secondary Education, United States Department of the Interior, Office of Education, *Bulletin,* 1932, No. 17, Monograph No. 16 (Washington, D. C., Government Printing Office, 1933).

HARRIS, Pickens E., *The Curriculum and Cultural Change* (New York, D. Appleton-Century Co., 1937).

HERRING, John W., *Social Planning and Adult Education* (New York, The Macmillan Co., 1933).

KENT, Frank R., *The Great Game of Politics* (New York, Doubleday, Page and Co., 1924).

MAXWELL, C. R., and KILZER, L. R., *High School Administration* (New York, Doubleday, Doran and Co., 1936).

MEAD, Cyrus D., and ORTH, Fred W., *The Transitional Public School* (New York, The Macmillan Co., 1934).

OTTO, Henry J., *Elementary School Organization and Administration* (New York, D. Appleton-Century Co., 1934).

THORNDIKE, Edward L., *Adult Interests* (New York, The Macmillan Co., 1935).

CHAPTER 11

ADAMS, Henry F., *Advertising and Its Mental Laws* (New York, The Macmillan Co., 1922).

BAIN, Winifred E., *Parents Look at Modern Education* (New York, D. Appleton-Century Co., 1935).

BEACH, Walter G., and WALKER, Edward E., *American Social Problems* (Stanford University, Calif., Stanford University Press, 1934).

CALDWELL, Otis W., and COURTIS, Stuart A., *Then and Now in Education* (1845-1923) (Yonkers, N. Y., World Book Co., 1924).

CARNEGIE, Dale, *How to Win Friends and Influence People* (New York, Simon and Schuster, 1937).

CARPENTER, W. W., and RUFI, John, *The Teacher and Secondary School Administration* (Boston, Ginn and Co., 1931).

Teacher and Public, Eighth Yearbook of the Department of Classroom Teachers of the National Education Association (Washington, D. C., National Education Association, 1934).

HART, Hornell, *The Science of Social Relations* (New York, Henry Holt and Co., 1927).

HEATH, Esther, *The Approach to the Parent* (New York, The Commonwealth Fund, 1933).

LAIRD, Donald, *Why We Don't Like People* (New York, A. L. Glaser and Co., 1935).

McCready, Agnes, *A Day at School* (New York, E. P. Dutton and Co., 1936).

Odencrantz, Louise C., *The Social Worker* (New York, Harper and Bros., 1929).

Pulliam, Roscoe, *Extra-Instructional Activities of the Teacher* (New York, Doubleday, Doran and Co., 1930).

Rice, George A., Conrad, Clinton C., and Fleming, Paul, *The Administration of Public High Schools Through Their Personnel* (New York, The Macmillan Co., 1933).

Chapter 12

Farley, Belmont, *School Publicity* (Stanford University, Calif., Stanford University Press, 1934), Ch. III.

Reeder, Ward G., *An Introduction to Public-School Relations* (New York, The Macmillan Co., 1937), Ch. IX.

Waller, J. Flint, *Public Relations for the Public Schools* (Trenton, N. J., MacCrellish and Quigley, 1933), Ch. IV.

Chapter 13

Ade, Lester K., *Recent Educational Trends,* Proceedings, Education Congress, 1935 (Pennsylvania State Department of Public Instruction, 1935).

———, *Educational Planning,* Proceedings, Education Congress, 1936 (Pennsylvania State Department of Public Instruction, 1936).

———, *The Program* (Pennsylvania State Department of Public Instruction, October, 1936).

Cubberley, Ellwood P., *State School Administration* (Boston, Houghton Mifflin Co., 1927).

Elliott, Eugene B., *Michigan's Future Citizens* (Michigan State Department of Public Instruction, Lansing, Mich., 1937).

Engelhardt, Fred, *Public School Organization and Administration* (Boston, Ginn and Co., 1931).

Graves, Frank P., *Administration of American Education* (New York, The Macmillan Co., 1932).

Henry, David D., "State Department as an Agent in Educational Public Relations," *Education,* Vol. 55, No. 5 (February, 1935), p. 330.

Chapter 14

Selle, Erwin S., *The Organization and Activities of the National Education Association,* Contributions to Education, No. 513 (New York,

Bureau of Publications, Teachers College, Columbia University, 1932).

WATTENBURG, William W., *On the Educational Front* (New York, Columbia University Press, 1936).

CHAPTER 15

BRUNSTETTER, M. R., *How to Use the Educational Sound Film* (Chicago, University of Chicago Press, 1937).

FOSTER, Charles R., *Extra Curricular Activities in the High School* (Richmond, Va., Johnson Publishing Co., 1925).

FOX, Lillian M., and HOPKINS, L. Thomas, *Creative School Music* (New York, Silver, Burdett and Co., 1936).

GEHRKENS, Karl Wilson, *Music in the Junior High School* (Boston, C. C. Birchard and Co., 1936).

HANNA, Paul R., *Youth Serves the Community* (New York, D. Appleton-Century Co., 1936).

HUME, Samuel J., and FOSTER, Lois M., *Theater and School* (New York, Samuel French, 1932).

LASKER, Bruno, *Race Attitudes in Children* (New York, Henry Holt and Co., 1929).

McKOWN, Harry C., *Commencement Activities* (New York, The Macmillan Co., 1931).

———, *Home Room Guidance* (New York, McGraw-Hill Book Co., 1934).

MATHER, Charles C., SPAULDING, Alice H., and SKILLEN, Melita H., *Behind the Footlights* (New York, Silver, Burdett and Co., 1935).

OTTO, Henry J., and HAMRIN, Shirley A., *Co-Curricular Activities in Elementary Schools* (New York, D. Appleton-Century Co., 1937).

ROEMER, Joseph, and ALLEN, Charles F., *Extra-Curricular Activities* (Boston, D. C. Heath and Co., 1926).

CHAPTER 16

BUTTERWORTH, Julian E., *The Parent-Teacher Association and Its Work* (New York, The Macmillan Co., 1928).

EDMONDSON, Edna H., "Parent-Teacher Associations," Indiana University Extension *Bulletins*, Vol. 5, No. 11 and Vol. 6, No. 11.

ENSIGN, Forest C., *Parent and Teacher,* University of Iowa Extension *Bulletin,* 1921, No. 76.

HOLBECK, Elmer S., *Achievement of the Parent-Teacher Association,* Contributions to Education, No. 601 (New York, Bureau of Publications, Teachers College, Columbia University, 1934).

RECOMMENDED READINGS

HOYT, Edith E., *Parent-Teacher Associations,* University of Wisconsin *Bulletin,* 1918, No. 1122.

LOMBARD, Ellen C., *Parent-Teacher Associations at Work,* Office of Education, United States Department of the Interior *Bulletin,* 1925, No. 30.

———, "Significant Programs of High-School Parent-Teacher Associations," Office of Education, United States Department of the Interior *Pamphlet,* No. 64.

MASON, Martha Sprague, Ed., *Parents and Teachers* (Boston, Ginn and Co., 1928).

MEYER, Harold D., Ed., *Parent-Teacher Handbook for North Carolina,* University of North Carolina Extension Division, Vol. 7, No. 8 (December, 1927).

MOORE, M. E., *Parent, Teacher and School* (New York, The Macmillan Co., 1925).

REEVE, Margaretta W., "First Steps in Parent-Teacher Coöperation," *Proceedings of the National Education Association, 1926.*

ROBINSON, William McKinley, "The Functioning Rural Parent-Teacher Association," *Parent Education,* A symposium published by the Extension Division and the School of Education, University of Michigan, 1932.

Bulletins of the South Carolina School Improvement Association, published by the State Department of Education, Columbia, S. C.

WEEKS, Ila D. "Parent-Teacher Associations," University of Iowa Extension *Bulletin,* 1926, No. 142.

Current publications of the National Congress of Parents and Teachers, available through state branches or national headquarters in Washington, form worth-while current material for local associations and for educators.

CHAPTER 17

DRURY, S. S., *School, Home and Company* (New York, Farrar and Rinehart, Inc., 1933).

GUY, George W., *The Coöperative Education Association of Virginia,* Office of Education, United States Department of the Interior, *Bulletin,* 1923, No. 5.

HEATH, Esther, *The Approach to the Parent* (New York, The Commonwealth Fund, 1933).

LATHROP, Edith A., "State School Improvement Associations," Office of Education, Rural School Leaflet No. 42, 1937.

LOMBARD, Ellen C., *Essentials in Home and School Coöperation,* Office of Education, United States Department of the Interior, 1937.

A Coöperative Study of Community Relations, Michigan Federation of Teachers Clubs, Michigan Education Association *Bulletin,* No. 24 (Lansing, Michigan Education Association, 1932).

Chapter 18

Critical Problems in School Administration, Twelfth Yearbook of the Department of Superintendence of the National Education Association (Washington, D. C., National Education Association, 1934).

The Improvement of Education, Fifteenth Yearbook of the Department of Superintendence of the National Education Association (Washington, D. C., National Education Association, 1937).

Chapter 19

Brock, H. I., *Meddlers* (New York, Ives Washburn, 1930).
Burns, C. Delisle, *Leisure in the Modern World* (New York, D. Appleton-Century Co., 1932).
Coe, George A., *The Motives of Men* (New York, Charles Scribner's Sons, 1928).
Courtis, Stuart A., *Some Social Aspects of Coöperation,* Reprints from Volume 9, *Michigan Education Journal,* 1933.
MacIver, R. M., *Society, Its Structure and Changes* (New York, Ray Long and Richard R. Smith, 1932).
Merz, Charles, *The Great American Band Wagon* (New York, Garden City Publishing Co., 1928).

Chapter 20

Education by Radio, A Bulletin To Promote the Use of Radio for Educational, Cultural, and Civic Purposes. S. Howard Evans, Secretary. Published Monthly. National Committee on Education by Radio, 1 Madison Avenue, New York City.
Lumley, F. H., *Measurement in Radio* (Columbus, Ohio, Ohio State University Press, 1934).
MacLatchy, Josephine, Ed., *Education on the Air,* Yearbooks of the Institute for Education by Radio, 1930, 1931, 1932, 1933, 1934 (Columbus, Ohio, Ohio State University, 1934).
———, *Education on the Air, Seventh Yearbook* of the Institute for Education by Radio (Columbus, Ohio, Ohio State University, 1936).
———, and Tyson, Levering, Eds., *Education on the Air and Radio and Education,* Proceedings of the Sixth Annual Institute for Education by Radio, combined with the Fifth Annual Assembly of the National

Advisory Council on Radio in Education (Chicago, University of Chicago Press, 1935).

TYSON, Levering, Ed., *Radio and Education,* Proceedings of the Annual Assembly of National Advisory Council on Radio in Education, 1932, 1933, 1934 (Chicago, University of Chicago Press).

CHAPTER 21

ANGELL, Norman, *The Press and the Organization of Society* (Cambridge, England, The Minority Press, 1933).

BENT, Silas, *Ballyhoo* (New York, Horace Liveright, 1927).

CORBIN, Charles R., *Why News Is News* (New York, The Ronald Press, 1928).

FARLEY, Belmont, *What to Tell the People About the Schools,* Contributions to Education, No. 355 (New York, Bureau of Publications, Teachers College, Columbia University, 1929).

FLINT, Leon N., *The Conscience of the Newspaper* (New York, D. Appleton-Century Co., 1925).

HARRIS, Emerson P., and HOOKE, Florence H., *The Community Newspaper* (New York, D. Appleton-Century Co., 1923).

HARWOOD, Dix, *Getting and Writing News* (New York, Doubleday, Doran and Co., 1927).

KINGSBURY, Susan M., HART, Hornell, and associates, *Newspapers and the News* (New York, G. P. Putnam's Sons, 1937).

MICHAEL, George, *Handout* (New York, G. P. Putnam's Sons, 1935).

SELDES, George, *Freedom of the Press* (Indianapolis, Bobbs-Merrill Co., 1935).

———, *You Can't Print That* (New York, Garden City Publishing Co., 1929).

SINCLAIR, Upton, *The Brass Check* (Pasadena, Calif., Published by the Author, 1920).

CHAPTER 22

CLARK, Zenas R., *The Recognition of Merit in Superintendents' Reports to the Public,* Contributions to Education, No. 471 (New York, Bureau of Publications, Teachers College, Columbia University, 1931).

GREENAWALT, Lambert, *School Press Management and Style* (New York, McGraw-Hill Book Co., 1930).

HARDING, T. Swan, *T.N.T.* (New York, Ray Long and Richard R. Smith, 1934).

HUFF, Bessie M., *How to Publish a School Paper* (New York, Mentzer, Bush and Co., 1924).

Ramsay, Robert E., *Effective House Organs* (New York, D. Appleton-Century Co., 1932).

Wells, George C., and McCalister, Wayde H., *Student Publications* (New York, A. S. Barnes and Co., 1930).

Chapter 23

Engelhardt, N. L. and Fred, *Planning School Building Programs* (New York, Bureau of Publications, Teachers College, Columbia University, 1930).

Engelhardt, N. L., and others, *The Planning and Construction of School Buildings,* Part I of the *Thirty-Third Yearbook* of the National Society for the Study of Education (Bloomington, Ill., Public School Publishing Co., 1934).

Moehlman, Arthur B., *Public School Plant Program* (Chicago, Rand, McNally and Co., 1929).

Spain, Charles L., Moehlman, Arthur B., and Frostic, Fred W., *Public Elementary School Plant* (Chicago, Rand, McNally and Co., 1930).

Chapter 24

Bagley, William C., *Education and Emergent Man* (New York, Thomas Nelson and Sons, 1934).

Groves, Ernest R., *Social Problems and Education* (New York, Longmans, Green and Co., 1925).

Jacks, L. P., *The Education of the Whole Man* (New York, Harper and Bros., 1931).

Kilpatrick, William H., and others, *The Educational Frontier* (New York, D. Appleton-Century Co., 1933).

Russell, Bertrand, *Education and the Good Life* (New York, Boni and Liveright, 1926).

Schermann, Rita, *A Mother's Letters to a Schoolmaster* (New York, Alfred A. Knopf, 1928).

UNPUBLISHED RESEARCH ON SOCIAL INTERPRETATION

1. ADAMS, J. Harry, *A Study of the Relationships of the Schools and the Press in Michigan During 1933-34,* Unpublished Master's Thesis, University of Michigan, July, 1934. Michigan editors give their views on the effectiveness of "press hand outs."
2. ALBAUGH, Dana M., *Public School Relations and the Protestant Churches,* Unpublished Master's Thesis, University of Michigan, June, 1934. A questionnaire and interview study of the conflicts and coöperation existing between public schools and the Northern Baptist denomination.
3. BRISCOE, A. O., *A Newspaper Publicity Policy for City School Systems,* Unpublished Master's Thesis, University of Missouri, 1923. A study of the news stories from the leading papers in nineteen cities of 4,000 to 8,000 population in Missouri and the literature pertinent to the subject. A score card rating news stories. Statistically computed relations between the publicity practices and the accomplishments of the school systems. The author found that there is only slightly more school news in spring than in autumn and that athletics lead, with faculty and parent-teacher associations following. Greater amounts of school news go with greater school accomplishments and a better quality of teachers.
4. CROSSWHITE, C. C., *The City School House Organ,* Unpublished Master's Thesis, University of Missouri, 1926. The official publications of boards of education in twenty-one cities in sixteen states were studied with a score card developed by the author. He found that the editorials were most often on tax levies and on the aim of education, while feature stories were often of long addresses, poorly written and with no human interest. The quality was unusually low and the material uninteresting.
5. GARLIN, R. E., *A Study of Educational Publicity in Texas Newspapers,* Unpublished Doctor's Dissertation, University of Texas, 1926. School news and advertising in all Texas newspapers for seventeen months are tabulated under topical, monthly, seasonal, and departmental headings. Special treatment is given newspaper publicity on the Texas School Survey. The need for better organized news efforts on the part of the schools is pointed out.

6. GORDON, Caius A., *Social Composition of Boards of Education in Oakland County, Michigan,* Unpublished Master's Thesis, University of Michigan, January, 1934. A study of 603 school-board members of Oakland County in terms of birth, race, educational background, economic affiliations, religious beliefs, political affiliation, and service records.
7. GRANGER, O., *School Publicity in Newspapers,* Unpublished Master's Thesis, University of Chicago, 1924. Fifty newspapers of midwestern cities are analyzed periodically throughout a school year. Space given school news is topically classified and listed in order of space given. Very similar to other studies of this nature, although periodic stressing of certain types of news items may be studied somewhat casually.
8. GRINNELL, J. E., *Newspaper Publicity for Public Schools of Minnesota,* Unpublished Master's Thesis, University of Minnesota, 1925. Public-school publicity in newspapers was studied from the point of view of the reporter. Accurate school news is difficult to secure and is obtained through the efforts of the newspaper reporters. Student reporters are the greatest contributors. The attitude of the school authorities toward newspapers is clearly portrayed and soundly criticized.
9. KINDRED, Leslie W., Jr., *A Sociological Survey of Two Wards in the Ann Arbor School District,* Unpublished Master's Thesis, University of Michigan, 1934. A detailed study and analysis of certain types of community conflicts in one of the Ann Arbor attendance districts.
10. LEWIS, G. H., *The Public High School in the Public Press,* Unpublished Master's Thesis, University of Southern California, 1926. Four newspapers, *The Ontario Daily Report, Los Angeles Times, San Francisco Chronicle,* and *Humboldt Standard,* were studied consecutively for a period of six months each. School news was listed in order of frequency. This study is especially valuable in that it permits a study of the effect of seasons of the year upon school topics. Dr. R. G. Reynolds' study of newspapers gives a more extensive and accurate picture of the general publicity given schools.
11. MCRUER, J. T., *Effective Reporting of the Public Schools,* Unpublished Master's Thesis, Stanford University, 1922. An attempt is made to determine the form or content and material necessary to a valid and effective program for the annual reporting of public schools. Reports are analyzed, and opinions of university professors and graduate students are used in the formation of criteria for judging the value of the materials and methods of good annual reporting programs. The topic does not lend itself readily to scientific treatment.

12. Manier, D. L., *Status of Publicity in Tennessee High Schools,* Unpublished Master's Thesis, George Peabody College for Teachers, 1926. Results of a questionnaire to Tennessee high-school principals and a survey of Tennessee newspaper files show that all school publicity media are being used by the high schools of that state, but that this is not due to any special effort by the schools.
13. Misner, Paul J., *A Study of Popular Attitudes Toward Public Education,* Unpublished Doctor's Dissertation, University of Michigan Graduate School, April, 1935. Determination of public opinion with respect to public education in Washtenaw County, Michigan, through a survey conducted by means of the interview technique.
14. Parkinson, B. L., *School Reports in Southern Cities of from 5,000 to 25,000 Inhabitants,* Unpublished Master's Thesis, George Peabody College for Teachers, 1920. This study is based upon results of 103 questionnaires giving the opinions of superintendents and a comparison of twelve particular reports with forty others from other sections. The author recommends that the present practice of publishing reports be abandoned or that scientific methods be applied to their preparation.
15. Peters, A. J., *What the Parents Want to Know About the Schools,* Unpublished Master's Thesis, George Peabody College for Teachers, 1920. The author confined his study to one city of 5,500 population in Missouri and attempted to discover the exact inquiries made by parents by telephone or otherwise. He suggests that parents do not concern themselves to any great extent with problems not pertaining to the welfare of their own children unless the question is suggested to them.
16. Phelps, S., *School Surveys by High School Pupils,* Unpublished Master's Thesis, George Peabody College for Teachers, 1916. A study of a survey of the schools of Gallatin, Tennessee, made by the high-school pupils in that city. High-school students did do valuable and accurate work under the close surveillance of the superintendent of schools and the author, who acted as directors. The possibilities in this field are not fully developed, but the author points the way for very valuable work by other superintendents.
17. Stevenson, Fred G., *The House Organ in City School Administration,* Unpublished Doctor's Dissertation, University of Michigan Graduate School, April, 1932. Development of a plan of appraisal for the city school-house organ. Results for Cleveland, Detroit, Cincinnati, and Hamtramck are given in full.
18. Thurston, Lee M., *An Analysis, Interpretation and Appraisal of the Codes of Ethics of Thirty-Eight State Teachers Associations in*

the United States, Unpublished Doctor's Dissertation, University of Michigan Graduate School, January, 1935. A thesis to determine the ethical principles involved and the professional philosophies expressed.

19. VER BEEK, John J., *A Comparative Study of Report Cards to Parents in Michigan,* Unpublished Master's Thesis, University of Michigan, April, 1933. Deals with current opinions, studies, and experiments on report cards to parents; administrative procedure in the use of report cards in Michigan; and an analysis of contents of report cards in current use in Michigan Schools (1931-32).

INDEX

Activities, curricular, formal, 298-300; informal, 300-307; extracurricular, 300-307; teacher, 230
Addams, Jane, 300
Administration, professional, 11
Adult, education, 383-384; programs, 283, 455-457
Advisors, technical, 356
Advisory groups, local, 347-352; state, 352-355; technical, 356
Alumni, 307-308
American Association of University Women, 113, 373
American Automobile Association, 361
American Council on Education, 19, 384
American Federation of Labor, 34, 87-88
"American Gothic," *frontispiece*
American Legion, 31, 60-61
American Medical Association, 249
American Teacher, 88
Angell, James B., 300
Ann Arbor School District, 141
Annual reports, 275-277, 407-410; circulation, 409; methods, 408-409; types, 407-408; variations, 409-410
Anti-Cigarette League, 68
Anti-Saloon League, 31, 68
Appraisal, state, 262
Association for Repeal of Eighteenth Amendment, 31
Attendance officers, 251

Barnard, Henry, 300
Berger, Victor L., 8
Bible, King James Version, 67, 372
Birney, Mrs. Alice McLellan, 314
Boards, planning, 355; school, 161-186
Board of education, 161-186; audit, 177; community contacts, 177-179; community education, 164-165; community needs, 163-164; conflicts and remedies, 179-186; discussion techniques, 170; education of, 123-124; executive member, 181-182; executive session, 174; experimentation, 164; finance orientation, 197; individual contacts, 178-179; legal plan, 162-163; meetings, 170, 172-175; nature of, 161-165; new members, 168-169; plans and procedures, 167-177; policies, 169-170; reports and records, 175-176; responsibility, 165-166; secrets of success, 166-167; tax statements, 176-177
British schools, 346
Bryan, William Jennings, 28
Bus drivers, 239, 255-256
Butterworth, Julian E., 343

Census enumerators, 251-252
Chambers of commerce, 144
Change, danger of, 455; educational, 430; method of, 44-46
Chicago Teachers' Federation, 88
Child accounting, 195
Child Labor Amendment, 314
Child training, 46
Children, 295-312; championship problems, 308-311; curricular activities, formal, 298-300; informal, 300-307; institutional limitations, 296-298; institutional responsibilities, 295-296; post-school relationships, 307-308
China, 103
Christian Science Monitor, The, 393
Civic organizations, interests, 359; use, 359; materials, 360
Civil Liberties Union, 9
Civilian Conservation Corps, 368
Clerk, 193-194; 239-241
Cleveland, 408
Clinics, 432
Commencements, 305-306
Committee for Industrial Organization, 88, 361

479

Community, demands, 173-174; economic life, 143; education, 164-165; ethical life, 144; interpretation of needs, 163-164; leisure, 146; political organization, 145-146; problems, 197-198; welfare bureau, 143
Community Advisory Commission, 348-352; membership, 349; operation, 351; work of, 350-351
Community-chest clearing houses, 143, 373
Community lay groups, 358-376; civic, 358-360; cultural, 360-361; economic, 361-364; hobby, 364-366; political, 366-369; professional, 370-371; propaganda, 369-370; social, 371-372; welfare, 372-373; women, 373-375
Community organization, centralized, 150; decentralized, 150-151; history of, 149, 341; program, 342; size, 152; social conflict, 149-150
Community survey, 138-158, 209; essential information, 139-149; history of, 149; methodology, 152-156; organization, 149-152; pitfalls, 156-158; racial and cultural composition of, 142; social conflicts, 149; types of, 140-149
Conflicts, 238, 453; cultural, 222; economic, 221-222; elimination of, 438-444; intentional, 48; irrational, 49; political, 222; professional, 219-220; rational, 50; religious, 222; types of, 434-438
Contacts, community, 224-225; custodial, 255; home, 235; individual, 226; legal, 243-244; press, 225; publicity, 277-278; social, 149-150, 235, 242; technical, 244-245
Contests, 304-305
Controversial issues, 79-80, 454-455
Constitution League, 60
Coöperation, organization, 268-269; parent-teacher, 269-270; parent-teacher association, 320; professional, 269
Coughlin, Father Charles E., 377
Councils, educational, 354-355; subsidiary, 316
County Works Administration, 367
Craft unions, 361
Cultural groups, interests, 360; materials, 361; use, 361
Cultural organization, 4-6

Curricular, formal activities, 298-300; informal activities, 300-307
Custom and tradition, 20

Daughters of the American Revolution, 60
Democratic, elements, 10; organization, 26-36; personal liberty, 28-29; process, 26-52; structure, 36; variation, 27-28
Dentists (school), 247-248
Department of Superintendent, 353; *Proceedings,* 89; Committee on Longer Planned Programs, 89
Detroit, 408, 419
Dionne quintuplets, 401
Diplomas and certificates, possibilities, 411; weaknesses, 410
Discipline, 233
Doctors (school), 247-248
Dumond, Dwight L., 9, 34
Duties, of principal, 208-209; of superintendent, 188-189; of teacher, 229

East Lynne, 301
Economic groups, interests, 362; materials, 363; use, 362
Edison, Thomas A., 28
Education, adult, 47, 383-384; community, 164-165; experimentation, 164; function, 14; health, 431; legal structure, 15; local organization, 17; of new board members, 168-169; primitive, 6; rôle of, 46-51; state organization, 16
Educational, change, 430; concepts, 229; councils, 354-355; interpretation, 22-23; programs (radio), 379-380
"Educational Policies Commission," 89; recommendations, 89-91
Eliot, Charles H., 300
Elks (B.P.O.E.), 371
Exchange Club, 361
Exhibitions, 304
Extracurricular activities, 300-307
Extralegal organization, 18

Family conditions, 142-143
Farm bureau, 284, 361

INDEX

Farmers' Grange, 284, 353-354, 361
Fascist ideology, 346
Federal, Bureau of Investigation, 364; Emergency Relief Administration, 368; government, 265-266; Trade Commission, 31
Federation of Women's Clubs, 280, 373
Federations, teachers', 88, 94
Financial reports, balance sheets, 414; monthly statements, 414; types of, 412
Fine arts, 303-304, 433
Ford, Henry, 28, 56, 63
Foundation influence, 19
Franklin, Benjamin, 300
Froebel, F. W. A., 58
Functioning, difficulties in, 47-51
Fundamental policies, 117-137; difficulties, 131-137; method of development, 121-124; nature, 119-121; suggested social-interpretation policy, 120-121; types of, 124-131

Garden Club of America, 30, 445
Gardens (school), 431
General Electric, 63
General Motors, 63
German schools, 103
Germany, 54, 346
Gibbons, Floyd, 364
"Goals of Public Education in Michigan," 110-112, 354
Great Britain schools, 54
Greenfield Village, 56
Gregory, Attorney-General Thomas W., 8
Group, leader, 146-147
Groups, hobby, 365-366; lay, 358-376
Guardians of Liberty, 9

Hamtramck, Michigan, 419
Hancock School, Detroit, 314
Harper, William Rainey, 300
Harris, William T., 300
Harrison-Black-Fletcher Bill, 315
Health education, 431
Hearst papers, 389
Hearst, Mrs. Phoebe A., 314
Hobby groups, interests, 365; programs, 366; use, 365

Home, reports, 236; visitation, 226-237
Home-contact reports, letters, 419-420; method, 418-419; types, 418
Home-room and grade councils, difficulties, 337-338; organization, 336-337; theory of, 338
House organs, circulation, 416; editing of, 415; types, 415

Improvement of existing schools, 321-322
Individual diversity, 32
Information, continuous, 126; maintaining, 156; periodic, 125-126; sources of, 153-154
Institutional, democracy, 448; fairness, 450; humor, 451-452; lag, 42-44; limitations, 12-13, 107, 120, 296-298; reasonableness, 449; requirements, 243; responsibilities, 295-296; support, 37; tact, 449; taste, 452; teaching, 448; techniques, 76-79; tolerance, 450-451
Institutions, social, 4
Interest-group organization, 29-30
Interests, educational, 269
International Harvester Company, 63
Interpretation, definition and goals, 104-107; definitive differences, 105-106; difficulties in, 114-115; objectives, 106-107; principles of, 103-116, 107-108; programs and program methods, 108-114; state, 262-263
Italy, schools of, 54, 346

Janitor, 239, 240-241
Japanese schools, 54, 103, 345-346
Jefferson, Thomas, 300
Johnson, Hugh S., 43
Jones-Miller Anti-Narcotic Bill, 315

Kansas, 367
Kansas City *Star*, 393
Kiwanis Club, 361
Knights of Columbus, 371
Ku Klux Klan, 9, 33

La Follette, Robert M., 75
Land use, 140

Landon, Alfred M., 33, 367, 377
Laski, Harold J., 7
Lay Advisory Commission, 345-357; education and dictatorship, 345-346; education and democracy, 346-347
Lay groups, 280; Educational Advisory Commission, 270; relationships, 290
Leadership, local, 290; state, 262
League of Women Voters, 280, 374
Limitations, institutional, 296-298
Limits to popular expression, 40
Lincoln, Abraham, 300
Lions' Club, 361
Lobbying, 292
Lovejoy, Philip C., 413
Lumley, Frederick E., 54
Lunchroom, adult use, 256-267; operators, 256

McAndrew, William, 454
McGuffey, William Holmes, 242

Maccabees, 371
Madison, James, 300
Mann, Horace, 45, 300
Marsh, Harriett, 314
Mason, Marion Sprague, 314
Masonic Order, 371
Meetings, board of education, 170
Mexico, 54, 346
Michigan, 274; Educational Planning Commission, 354; "General School Laws (1927)," 162; "Goals of Public Education," 110-112
Milwaukee, 408
Misconceptions of teaching function, 232-233
Moehlman, Arthur B., 314, 353, 413
Monroe, James, 300
Moose Lodge, 371
Mothers' and Fathers' Clubs, organization, 340

National Congress of Mothers and Parent-Teacher Associations, 314-315
National Congress of Parents and Teachers, 314-315, 325, 384; membership, 313; organization, 313, 324

National Education Association, 315, 384; *Proceedings,* 88
National Kindergarten Union, 58
National Relief Administration, 44
National Youth Administration, 368
Nation's Schools, 340
Nazi ideology, 346
Neighborhood groups, theory of, 342-343
New Deal, 61
New Jersey, 274
New York *News,* 391; state, 271; *Sun,* 393; *Times,* 393; University of the State of, 274
News, definition, 399-401; letters, 277; types of: 397-398, 400-401; placement, 401
Newspaper, appraisal, 392-393; difficulties, 401-405; function, 388; institutional information needs, 392-393; policies, 389, 400; position in social interpretation, 390-392; press relations, 394-399; tendencies, 390; types of, 393-394
Non-teaching personnel, 247-258
North Carolina, 265
Nurse (school), 239-244, 249-250

Owls, 371

Palmer, Attorney-General A. Mitchell, 8
Parent councils and variation, 335-344; advantages, 339; community organization, 341-342; home-room and grade, 335-338; mothers' and fathers' clubs, 340-341; neighborhood groups, 342-343; parent and school, 338-340; school improvement league, 343-344
Parent-teacher association, 280, 313-334; character of, 315-316; conflicts (personal and functional), 333-334; history, 313-315; membership, 19; methods of organization, 332-333; programs and means, 327-332; purpose, 317-322; relationship to school, 322-324; types of organizations, 324-327
Parents and Teachers, 314
Patri, Angelo, 379
Patterson, Captain Joseph Medill, 391
Peabody, Elizabeth, 300

INDEX

Pennsylvania, 274
Personnel, contact, 193; training of, 215-216
Personnel (non-teaching), 247-258; book store, 257; informational, 193-194; non-professional, 252-258; professional, 247; recognition, 254; recompense, 254; training of, 257-258
Pictorial material, types of, 426; use, 426-427
Planning, progressive, 264-265; state, 263-264
Planning Board, 286, 355
Plant, 224, 428-446; use of, 195-196
Policies, 117-138, 280; desirable, 130-131; development of, 121-124; difficulties, 131; examples, 132-137; interpretation, 122-123; legal approval, 124; method, 127-128; nature of, 119-121; need of, 122; organized-fact, 129-130; partial-fact, 128; types of, 120-121, 124-131; unorganized-fact, 129
Political groups, interests, 366; materials, 369; use, 366
Pressure, 284; groups, 30-31
Principal, 207-227; function, 208-219; harmonizing conflicts, 219-223; methods and devices, 223-227
Proceedings, board of education, methods, 420-421; types, 420; use, 421
Professional, groups, 370-371; membership standards, 285; publications, 282, 288-289
Programs, execution of, 216-217; school, 422; state, 266; types of, 381
Progressive Education Association, 384
Propaganda, 283; definition, 53-54; good and bad, 55; groups, 369-370; methods, 68-76; casual, 68; direct, 69; examples of, 71-75; indirect, 69
Propaganda, types of, 60-68; conservator, 60-62; economic, 62-63; political, 65; professional, 63-64; racial, 66; religious, 66-67; social, 67-68; value of, 56
Propaganda Analysis, 54
Propaganda and the schools, 53-81
Protestant faith, 353
Public opinion, 37; development of, 39-40; differences in, 34; formation, 41; rôle of, 36-42; value of extreme, 35-36

Publications, annual report, 275-277, 407-410; professional, 282, 288-289; research, 423; school, 423; school paper, 301-303
Publicity, direct, 291; personal, 405

Radio, 376-387; agencies, 384-385; audience, 371; control, 376-379; difficulties, 385; educational programs, 379-384; possibilities, 376-379
Red Cross, 143, 373
Redmen, 371
Relationships, advisory, 320; colleague, 239-241; community, 241-245; post-school, 307-308; reporter, 398; teacher-child, 232-235; teacher-parent, 235-239; other, 240
Religious beliefs, Buddhist, 235; Catholic, 353; Jewish, 234-235, 353; Mohammedan, 234-235; Protestant, 353
Reports, 236; annual, 275-277, 407-410; financial, 411-414
Research, 287; publications, 423
Reserve Officers' Training Corps, 64
Responsibilities, institutional, 295-296
Rochester, New York, 414
Roosevelt, Franklin D., 34, 43, 367, 368, 377
Roosevelt, Theodore, 28, 33
Rotary Club, 361
Russia, 54, 346

St. Louis, 408; *Globe Democrat,* 393
San Antonio public-school teachers association, 88
Scandinavian countries, 54, 346
School, activities, 224; clinics, 432; improvement leagues, 343-344; library, 433-444; programs, 422; surveys, 424-425
School in action, 447-459; adult program, 455-457; child program, 457-458; functional interpretation, 458-459; practices to avoid, 452-455; qualities, 447-452
School in society, 3-25
School Laws of Michigan, 162
School plant, 428-446; changing concepts, 429-434; conflicts, 434-438; function, 428-429; interpretative

School plant (*continued*)
  agency, 444-445; possibility of eliminating conflicts, 438-444
School publications, 407-427; annual reports, 407-410; board proceedings, 420-421; diplomas and certificates, 410-411; financial reports, 411-414; home contacts, 417-420; house organs, 414-416; pictorial material, 425-427; research bulletins, 422-423; school papers, 423-424; school programs, 421-422; survey reports, 424-425; use, 423
School state, 17
Settlement centers, 143
Sheppard-Towner Maternity and Infancy Bill, 314
Sites, 430
Smith, Alfred Emanuel, 33, 271
Smith, Reverend Gerald L. K., 377
Smith-Hughes Act, 265-266
Social change, 42; events, 306-307; groups, 371-372; workers, 249-250
Sociological centers, 143
Sons of American Revolution, 60
Staff duties, 190-191
Standards, membership, 285
State, achievement, 264-265; appraisal, 262; concepts of, 7-8; democratic, 10; extralegal organization, 18; function, 261-262; interpretation, 262-263; leadership, 262; legal structure, 15; limitations, 18; local organization, 17; organization, 16; planning, 263-264; problems, 266-271; programs, 266-271; regulatory activities, 265
State advisory commission, 352-355; device, 353-354; membership, 352-353
State educational authority, 261-278; activities, 271-273; difficulties, 273-278; function, 261-266; programs and problems, 266-271
State education departments; coöperation, 268-269; improvement, 268; weaknesses, 267-268
Stevenson, Fred G., 416
Stracke, George A., 426
Sunday, Billy, 33
Superintendent, 187-207; appraisal of program, 204; methods of organization, 189-194; relationship to board of education, 194-199; relationship to colleagues, 199-202; relationship to people, 202-204; totality of function, 188-189
Supplies, service of, 196-197
Supreme Court, 345
Surveys, community, 138-158; methodology, 152-156; pitfalls, 156-157; records, 155-156; school, 424; sources of information, 153-154; types of 140-149

Taft, William, Howard, 28
Teachers unions, 88; objects, 88-89; types of, 92-95
Teaching, fine arts, 299; language, 300; mathematics, 299; socio-civic, 298-299
Teaching personnel, 228-246; colleague relationships, 239-241; community relationships, 241-245; function, 228-230; qualities, 231; teacher-child relationships, 232-235; teacher-parent relationships, 235-239; training, 231
Teaching profession, 82-99; difficulties in functioning, 97-98; current views and practices, 87-91; function of, 82; functional organization of, 84; improvement of, 83-84; needs, 91-95; responsibilities, 95-97; teacher aspects, 84
Teaching profession program, 279-294; activities, 287-293; methods, 285-287; program policy, 279-285
Technique, description, 250
Tendencies, state, 265
Tennessee Valley Authority, 368
Thompson, "Big Bill," 454
Toledo, 423
Townsend, Francis E., 377
Trouble spots, 217-218

Unions, objects of, 88-89; teacher, 88
United Daughters of the Confederacy, 60
United States, Department of Commerce, 144; Department of Labor, 144; Office of Education, 378, 384; War Department, 64

Visitations, home, 237; school, 238
Visiting nurses, 143

Voelker, Paul F, 353
Washington, George, 300
Welch, James W., 88
Welfare groups, interests, 373; use, 373
Wilson, Woodrow, 33, 75
Wives, meddling, 240
Women's Christian Temperance Union, 31, 68
Women's organizations, interest, 374; materials, 374-375; use, 374
Woodmen, 371

Works Progress Administration, 368
World War, 8, 9, 32, 43, 53, 65, 75, 91

Young Men's Christian Association, 373
Young Men's Hebrew Association, 373
Young Women's Christian Association, 373

Zonta, 361

(1)